Realizing the Profound View

THE LIBRARY OF WISDOM AND COMPASSION

The Library of Wisdom and Compassion is a special multivolume series in which His Holiness the Dalai Lama shares the Buddha's teachings on the complete path to full awakening that he himself has practiced his entire life. The topics are arranged especially for people not born in Buddhist cultures and are peppered with the Dalai Lama's unique outlook. Assisted by his long-term disciple, the American nun Thubten Chodron, the Dalai Lama sets the context for practicing the Buddha's teachings in modern times and then unveils the path of wisdom and compassion that leads to a meaningful life, a sense of personal fulfillment, and full awakening. This series is an important bridge from introductory to profound topics for those seeking an in-depth explanation from a contemporary perspective.

Volumes:

1. *Approaching the Buddhist Path*
2. *The Foundation of Buddhist Practice*
3. *Saṃsāra, Nirvāṇa, and Buddha Nature*
4. *Following in the Buddha's Footsteps*
5. *In Praise of Great Compassion*
6. *Courageous Compassion*
7. *Searching for the Self*
8. *Realizing the Profound View*

More volumes to come!

THE LIBRARY OF WISDOM AND COMPASSION • VOLUME 8

REALIZING THE PROFOUND VIEW

Bhikṣu Tenzin Gyatso,
the Fourteenth Dalai Lama

and

Bhikṣuṇī Thubten Chodron

Wisdom

Wisdom Publications
199 Elm Street
Somerville, MA 02144 USA
wisdomexperience.org

Library of Congress Cataloging-in-Publication Data
Names: Bstan-'dzin-rgya-mtsho, Dalai Lama XIV, 1935- author. |
Thubten Chodron, 1950– author.
Title: Realizing the profound view / Bhikṣu Tenzin Gyatso,
the Fourteenth Dalai Lama and Bhikṣunī Thubten Chodron.
Description: Somerville, MA, USA: Wisdom Publications, [2022] |
Series: The library of wisdom and compassion; volume 8 |
Includes bibliographical references and index.
Identifiers: LCCN 2022020662 (print) | LCCN 2022020663 (ebook) |
ISBN 9781614298403 | ISBN 9781614298618 (ebook)
Subjects: LCSH: Sunyata. | Mādhyamika (Buddhism) | Buddhism—Doctrines.
Classification: LCC BQ4275 .B778 2022 (print) | LCC BQ4275 (ebook) |
DDC 294.3/42—dc23/eng/20220709
LC record available at https://lccn.loc.gov/2022020662
LC ebook record available at https://lccn.loc.gov/2022020663

ISBN 978-1-61429-840-3 ebook ISBN 978-1-61429-861-8

26 25 24 23 22
5 4 3 2 1

Photo credits: cover, courtesy of the office of His Holiness the Dalai Lama; p. vi, Jillian Yuen; p. xii, Paul Arps; pp. xx, 58, Sravasti Abbey; p. 6, Tibetan Nuns Project | tnp.org; p. 144, Mike Nowak; p. 174, © Daniel - stock.adobe.com; p. 260, Ānandajoti Bhikkhu (www.photodharma.net); p. 364, Mikaku
Cover and interior design by Gopa & Ted 2. Interior typeset by PerfecType, Nashville, TN.

Printed on acid-free paper that meets the guidelines for permanence and durability of the Production Guidelines for Book Longevity of the Council on Library Resources.

Printed in Canada.

Publisher's Acknowledgment

The publisher gratefully acknowledges the generous help of the Hershey Foundation in sponsoring the production of this book.

Contents

Preface

Searching for the Self, the previous volume of the *Library of Wisdom and Compassion*, delved into the topic of the ultimate nature of reality that has been sprinkled throughout the books in this series. In our Dharma study and practice, it is important not only to understand cause and effect and how things function to produce happiness or suffering, but also to know their ultimate mode of existence, for it is such awareness that cuts self-grasping ignorance, the root of saṃsāra.

In the previous volume we discussed the different levels of misconception and distorted grasping sentient beings hold regarding persons and other phenomena, as explained by the four tenet systems—Vaibhāṣika, Sautrāntika, Yogācāra, and Madhyamaka. Each system has its own way of asserting the Middle Way, in which it claims to fall neither to the extreme of absolutism that superimposes a mode of existence that phenomena lack nor to the extreme of nihilism that negates what exists. We also began to investigate the nature of the person, the I or self, that lies at the center of our being by examining the Buddha's famous refutation in the Pāli sūtras, "This is not I, not mine, not my self."

In the present volume, we will continue the search for the self and expand it to see the relationship between grasping an inherently existent I and mine, on the one hand, and grasping inherently existent phenomena, especially the aggregates that are the basis of designation of the I, on the other. We will also focus on the subtlest object of negation—inherent existence—as rejected by the most sophisticated tenet system, the Prāsaṅgika Madhyamaka. To do this, we will investigate employing reasoning and logic, tools that His Holiness and the other great masters have emphasized to clarify the nature of reality. Emptiness is not realized by blind faith, foggy belief, or incorrect arguments, but only by being open-minded, using our intelligence, and having an earnest aspiration to attain liberation and full awakening.

As in the previous volume, you will encounter new vocabulary and concepts. We are not expected to understand everything at the first reading, or even at the tenth. Deepening our understanding depends also on purifying our mind, accumulating merit, listening to teachings, self-reflection, and study that is guided by qualified spiritual mentors. So don't feel despondent if everything isn't crystal clear at the beginning. Continue your daily practice and continue to study, listen to, and contemplate teachings. Slowly, gradually, your understanding will grow and you'll come to realize the nature of reality and eliminate the scourge of duḥkha and its cause, ignorance, that have been plaguing us since beginningless time. Equally important is to cultivate compassion and bodhicitta, so that as our wisdom increases so does our appreciation of the kindness of all sentient beings and our heartfelt aspiration to benefit them and show them the path to full awakening.

How This Book Came About

We shared the story of the origins of the *Library of Wisdom and Compassion* in volume 1, *Approaching the Buddhist Path*, and elaborated on it in the seventh volume, *Searching for the Self*. The origins and the completion of this project span decades, and given the reality of impermanence and dependent arising, the old vanishes and its continuum carries on with the creation of something new.

My initial request to His Holiness was to write a short text that Tibetan lamas could use when teaching non-Tibetans, especially people from the West who come to the Dharma with very different preconceptions and assumptions than those who grew up as Tibetan Buddhists. At His Holiness's wish, this transformed into my editing some of his Dharma talks to make a longer book. That in turn became a long manuscript that would consist of a few books. When His Holiness said that he wanted the project to also include teachings from the Pāli tradition and from Buddhism in China, it again expanded. To my objections, he also insisted that I be a coauthor, not an editor.

When His Holiness said he wanted me to include teachings from the

Pāli tradition in the *Library of Wisdom and Compassion*, his office gave me a letter requesting Theravāda monks to teach me and allow me to stay in their temple. Thus I spent two weeks studying and practicing with Ajahn Anan at Wat Marp Jan in Thailand. This was followed by studying Bhikkhu Bodhi's lengthy series of teachings on Majjhima Nikāya and meeting with him, and later corresponding with him to ask questions. This led to reading about the Pāli Abhidharma, participating in a vipassana retreat, and discussing the Dharma with Western monastics whom I met at our annual Western Buddhist Monastic Gatherings. Having taught the Dharma in Singapore for almost two years, I also got to know some monks from the Theravāda tradition, participated in panel discussions with them, and was invited to speak at their temples. This study and engagement with the Pāli tradition has helped my own Dharma practice considerably.

My knowledge of Buddhism in China also expanded, but that will be described in the next volume, *Appearing and Empty*, where we further our study of Madhyamaka philosophy in Tibet and look at Madhyamaka in China as well.

Overview of Realizing the Profound View

His Holiness begins with setting the stage for this text by explaining how to practice and generate the proper motivation to practice. *Searching for the Self* introduced us to emptiness, whereas this volume primarily explains the analytical investigations and meditations necessary to realize emptiness by forcefully and completely negating inherent existence.

We begin in chapter 1 with an overview of the main arguments used to establish the emptiness of inherent existence of persons and phenomena, and then proceed to Candrakīrti's seven-point examination using the example of a chariot—we updated the example to a car, which you are undoubtedly more familiar with. Candrakīrti's argument can be traced back to the Pāli sūtras and to the *Questions of King Menander* (*Milindapañha*), a text written about 100 BCE, in which King Menander questions Bhikṣu Nāgasena, asking, "Who or what is the person?" The monk presents the seven-point examination in which he leads the king to see that something that is truly the chariot cannot be found either among its parts or separate from them. The chariot exists conventionally but cannot be found when analyzing its ultimate mode of existence. Chapter 2 follows up on this, explaining Nāgārjuna's five-point analysis of the Tathāgata found in his *Treatise on the Middle Way* and similar versions in his *Letter to a Friend* (*Suhṛllekha*) and *Precious Garland* (*Ratnāvalī*). This analysis is also found in the Pāli sūtras. Chapter 3 then applies the seven-point analysis to the person and concludes that although the person is unfindable when searched for in the individual aggregates, the collection of the aggregates, or elsewhere, it still exists on the conventional level.

Chapter 4 presents an argument from a different angle, investigating whether an inherently existent I is findable in the six elements that form what we call "person"—earth, water, fire, air, space, and consciousness. We then follow the similar analysis in the Pāli sūtras examining whether any of these six elements are the self. Chapter 5 explains the meaning of ultimate analysis and probing awareness and clarifies two diverse meanings of "self"—the person and inherent existence. When studying these refutations, we must be able to discern these two to avoid getting confused. But not finding the person under ultimate analysis does not mean there is no person or that the person is only a name, sound, or word. The mere I that exists by being merely designated in dependence on the aggregates exists, and this dependently existing person carries the karmic seeds from one lifetime to the next.

Chapter 6 discusses the argument entitled "diamond slivers" in which we investigate how a cause gives rise to an effect. Is something produced from itself, from something other than itself, from both, or causelessly? This well-known refutation is found in the first stanza of *Treatise on the Middle Way* and has been taught and debated for centuries ever since.

In chapter 7 we continue to examine whether the world exists objectively, using the refutation of the arising of existents and nonexistents to negate inherent existence and dependent arising to establish the conventional existence of the world. Up until this point, our analysis has focused on impermanent phenomena, so this chapter concludes with demonstrating the emptiness of permanent phenomena as well.

Dependent arising is called the "monarch of all reasonings" because it not only refutes inherent existence but also establishes conventional existence and in this way establishes the Middle Way, free from the extremes of absolutism and nihilism. In chapter 8 we learn the three levels of dependent arising as noted by Tsongkhapa as well as His Holiness's way of delineating them. This chapter also speaks of the three criteria for conventional existence and how the various types of dependence are related. Chapter 9 follows up on this by explaining how other reasonings meet back to dependent arising and how Mādhyamikas differ from essentialists, who assert true existence.

Chapter 10 continues the discussion of emptiness and dependent arising, showing how the two come to the same point. Here His Holiness fleshes out the argument Tsongkhapa presented succinctly in his "Three Principal Aspects of the Path" with a spectacular explanation of how, for a person who has realized emptiness, emptiness dawns as the meaning of dependent arising and dependent arising dawns as the meaning of emptiness. This is the culmination of the correct view.

The perfection of wisdom consists of space-like meditation and illusion-like meditation, the former focused on disproving inherent existence and the latter showing that after emerging from meditation on emptiness, practitioners see people and phenomena as like illusions—they exist, but they do not exist inherently as they appear to. Just as it is important to establish what does not exist—inherent existence—it is equally important to establish what does exist—illusion-like dependent arisings. This is the topic of chapter 11.

Chapters 12 and 13 explore how selflessness is presented in the Pāli tradition, relying on arguments the Buddha presented in the sūtras. The Buddha made clear various types of wrong views to be abandoned and asks us to examine if there is a self that controls the aggregates. We often feel that there is an I that governs and directs our body and mind. But just because we feel there is and assume there is, does such a self exist? These chapters also discuss the three characteristics and insight meditation in the Pāli tradition.

Through the interweaving of the Pāli and Sanskrit traditions' analyses throughout the previous chapters of this volume, we see that Nāgārjuna's and Candrakīrti's analyses rest on refutations found in the Pāli sūtras. Chapter 14 explores other passages that show the common themes regarding selflessness and emptiness in these two traditions. Indeed the Buddhadharma has one teacher but many traditions.

Please Note

Although this series is coauthored, the vast majority of the material is His Holiness's teachings. I researched and wrote the parts about the Pāli tradition, wrote a few other passages, and composed the reflections. For ease of reading, most honorifics have been omitted, but that does not diminish the great respect His Holiness and I have for the excellent sages, learned adepts, and practitioners throughout Buddhist history. Foreign terms are given in italics parenthetically at their first usage. Unless otherwise noted with "P" or "T," indicating Pāli or Tibetan, respectively, italicized terms are Sanskrit, or the term is the same in Sanskrit and Pāli. When two italicized terms are listed, the first is Sanskrit, the second Pāli. For consistency, Sanskrit spelling is used for Sanskrit and Pāli terms in common usage (nirvāṇa, Dharma, arhat, Abhidharma, sūtra, and so forth), except in citations from Pāli scriptures. Tibetan terms and general definitions of terms can be found in the glossary. A list of recommended readings will direct you to reliable resources to learn more.

The term *śrāvaka* encompasses solitary realizers, unless there is reason to specifically differentiate them. To maintain the flow of a passage, it is not always possible to gloss all new terms on their first usage, so a glossary is provided at the end of the book. "Sūtra" often refers to Sūtrayāna and "Tantra" to Tantrayāna—the Sūtra Vehicle and Tantra Vehicle, respectively. When these two words are not capitalized, they refer to two types of scriptures: sūtras and tantras. Mahāyāna here refers principally to the bodhisattva path as explained in the Sanskrit tradition. In general, the meaning of all philosophical terms accords with the presentation of the Prāsaṅgika Madhyamaka tenet system. Unless otherwise noted, the personal pronoun "I" refers to His Holiness.

Appreciation

My deepest respect goes to Śākyamuni Buddha and all the buddhas, bodhisattvas, and arhats who embody the Dharma and with compassion teach and guide us confused beings who seek happiness but are ignorant of the means to create the causes for it. I also bow to all the realized lineage masters of all Buddhist traditions through whose kindness the Buddhadharma still exists in our world. I appreciate His Holiness the Dalai Lama's kindness in giving me the opportunity of working on the *Library of Wisdom and Compassion* with him. May these volumes bring peace and awakening in the minds of sentient beings and instill compassion in society for time without end.

This series appears in many volumes. For their aid in this eighth volume I want to express my gratitude to His Holiness's translators—Geshe Lhakdor, Geshe Dorji Damdul, and Mr. Tenzin Tsepak. I am grateful to Geshe Dorji Damdul, Geshe Dadul Namgyal, and Bhikṣuṇī Sangye Khadro for checking the manuscript, and to Samdhong Rinpoche, Geshe Yeshe Thabkhe, and Geshe Sonam Rinchen for clarifying important points. Geshe Thupten Jinpa clarified some of the most difficult points, which I greatly appreciate, and I am grateful for Bhikkhu Bodhi's clear teachings on the Pāli tradition and thank him for generously answering my many questions. He also kindly reviewed the sections of the book on the Pāli tradition before publication.

The staff at the Private Office of His Holiness kindly facilitated the interviews with His Holiness, Sravasti Abbey supported me while I worked on this volume, and Mary Petrusewicz skillfully edited this book. I thank everyone at Wisdom Publications who has contributed and continues to contribute to the successful production of the *Library of Wisdom and Compassion*. The kindness and compassion of my fellow monastics at Sravasti Abbey sustained me through the writing and rewriting of the manuscript. All errors are my own.

Bhikṣuṇī Thubten Chodron
Sravasti Abbey

Abbreviations

BV *Commentary on Bodhicitta* (*Bodhicittavivaraṇa*) by Nāgārjuna. Translated by Geshe Thupten Jinpa.

CŚ *The Four Hundred* (*Catuḥśataka*) by Āryadeva. Translated by Ruth Sonam in *Yogic Deeds of Bodhisattvas* (Ithaca, NY: Snow Lion Publications, 1994).

CTB *Compassion in Tibetan Buddhism* by Tsong-ka-pa. Translated and edited by Jeffrey Hopkins (Ithaca, NY: Snow Lion Publications, 1980).

Dhp Dhammapada.

DN Dīgha Nikāya. Translated by Maurice Walshe in *The Long Discourses of the Buddha* (Boston: Wisdom Publications, 1995).

EMW *Emptiness in the Middle Way School of Buddhism: Mutual Reinforcement of Understanding Dependent-Arising and Emptiness: Dynamic Responses to Tsong-kha-pa's "The Essence of Eloquence: IV,"* by Jeffrey Hopkins (Dyke, VA: UMA Institute for Tibetan Studies, 2019). https://uma-tibet.org/pdf/greatbooks/EMPTINESS%20IN%20THE%20MWS%20GEN%20EXPO.pdf.

EY *Emptiness Yoga: The Tibetan Middle Way*, by Jeffrey Hopkins. Edited by Joe B. Wilson (Ithaca, NY: Snow Lion Publications, 1995).

FEW *Tsong-kha-pa's Final Exposition of Wisdom,* by Jeffrey Hopkins. Edited by Kevin Vose (Ithaca, NY: Snow Lion Publications, 2008).

GP *The Guru Puja* by Panchen Losang Chogyen (Ottawa: Sumeru Press, 2012).

GR *Illuminating the Intent: An Exposition of Candrakīrti's "Entering the Middle Way"* (T. *Dgons pa rab gsal*) by Tsongkhapa. Translated by Thupten Jinpa (Somerville, MA: Wisdom Publications, 2021).

HSY *How to See Yourself as You Really Are*, by His Holiness the Dalai Lama. Translated by Jeffrey Hopkins (New York: Atria Books, 2006).

Iti *Itivuttaka.* In *The Udāna and the Itivuttaka.* Translated by John D. Ireland (Kandy: Buddhist Publication Society, 1997).

LC *The Great Treatise on the Stages of the Path to Enlightenment* (T. *Lam rim chen mo*) by Tsongkhapa, 3 vols. Translated by Joshua Cutler et al. (Ithaca: Snow Lion Publications, 2000–2004).

LS *Praise to the World Transcendent* (*Lokatistava*) by Nāgārjuna. Translated by Thupten Jinpa. http://www.tibetanclassics.org/wp-content/uploads/2020/09/WorldTranscendentHym.pdf.

MMA *Supplement to "Treatise on the Middle Way"* (*Madhyamakāvatāra*) by Candrakīrti.

MMK *Treatise on the Middle Way* (*Mūlamadhyamakakārikā*) by Nāgārjuna.

MN Majjhima Nikāya. Translated by Bhikkhu Ñāṇamoli and Bhikkhu Bodhi in *The Middle-Length Discourses of the Buddha* (Boston: Wisdom Publications, 1995).

OR *Ocean of Reasoning by rJe Tsong Khapa.* Translated by Geshe Ngawang Samten and Jay L. Garfield (New York: Oxford University Press, 2006).

P. Pāli.

PDA *Praise to Dependent Arising* (T. *rten 'brel bstod pa*) by Tsongkhapa. Translated by Thupten Jinpa. http://media.dalailama.com/English/texts/in-praise-of-dependent-origination-ENG.pdf.

PSP *Clear Words* (*Prasannapadā*) by Candrakīrti.

RA *Precious Garland* (*Ratnāvalī*) by Nāgārjuna. Translated by John Dunne and Sara McClintock in *The Precious Garland: An Epistle to a King* (Boston: Wisdom Publications, 1997).

RGV *Sublime Continuum* (*Ratnagotravibhāga*, *Uttaratantra*) by Maitreya.

RM *Recognizing My Mother: An Experiential Song on the View* by Changkya Rolpai Dorje. Translated by Thupten Jinpa (Portland, OR: FPMT, 2021). http://media.dalailama.com/English/texts/recognizing-my-mother-ENG.pdf.

RSS *The Rice Seedling Sūtra: Buddha's Teaching on Dependent Arising*, by Geshe Yeshe Thabkhe. Translated by Joshua and Diana Cutler (Somerville, MA: Wisdom Publications, 2020).

SN Saṃyutta Nikāya. Translated by Bhikkhu Bodhi in *The Connected Discourses of the Buddha* (Boston: Wisdom Publications, 2000).

Sn Suttanipāta. Translated by Bhikkhu Bodhi in *The Suttanipāta* (Somerville, MA: Wisdom Publications, 2017).

SRR *Self, Reality, and Reason in Tibetan Philosophy: Tsongkhapa's Quest for the Middle Way*, by Thupten Jinpa (New York: RoutledgeCurzon, 2002).

T. Tibetan.

Ud *Udāna*.

V *Refutation of Objections* (*Vigrahavyāvartanī*) by Nāgārjuna.

Vism *Visuddhimagga* by Buddhaghosa. Translated by Bhikkhu

Ñāṇamoli in *The Path of Purification* (Kandy: Buddhist Publication Society, 1991).

YS *Sixty Stanzas of Reasoning* (*Yuktiṣaṣṭikākārikā*) by Nāgārjuna. Translated by Geshe Thupten Jinpa. https://www.tibetanclassics.org/html-assets/SixtyStanzas.pdf.

Introduction

REALIZING THE PROFOUND VIEW, the eighth volume of the *Library of Wisdom and Compassion*, is the second of three volumes that center on the correct view of both the ultimate and conventional natures of reality. In his commentary to Dharmakīrti's *Commentary on the "Compendium of Reliable Cognition"* (*Pramāṇavārttika*), Gyaltsab explains the best way for us to approach this important and subtle topic. He recommends that we begin with deep contemplation of how we enter saṃsāra and the path to free ourselves from it, focusing on saṃsāra's general and particular disadvantages so that we generate a mind that aspires to be free from its constraints, especially its causes—afflictions and polluted karma. Although these topics have been covered extensively in volume 3, *Saṃsāra, Nirvāṇa, and Buddha Nature*, a short explanation will refresh them in your mind.

If we begin with our own experience, we discover that we have a strong thought of a real, independent I to which we are very attached. Seeking the happiness of that I, we crave a good reputation, praise and approval, wonderful sensual pleasures, and possessions. We also seek to avoid their opposites: disrepute, criticism and disapproval, unpleasant sensual experiences, and lack of possessions. These are known as the eight worldly concerns, and they lead us to engage in actions such as hiding our faults, pretending to have excellent qualities we don't have, conniving, lying, taking things that aren't ours, cheating, and so on. In extreme cases, they lead to physical violence, sexual predation, oppression of an entire group of people, denial of equal opportunity, and so on. In short, grasping an I that seems to exist from its own side, independent of all other factors, stimulates clinging to what we believe will bring us well-being, craving to destroy whatever we think interferes with our happiness, and attachment to the status quo when we are okay. These in turn lead to actions (karma) that bring duḥkha—all the unsatisfactory experiences we must contend with in saṃsāra, the cycle of rebirth under the control of mental afflictions and karma. In short, by examining our own experience we can see that craving acts as the cause of suffering.

This leads us to conclude that the root of this dilemma is grasping the I and other phenomena as having a self. Here "self" refers to an inherently existent essence, something that exists under its own power and has the ability to set itself up. This can be verified through our experience; it is not an intellectual theory that someone made up.

Every sentient being, no matter what life form they take—human beings, animals, insects, and so on—wants only happiness and the absence of suffering. Despite this fervent wish, due to our ignorance of the causes of happiness and the causes of suffering, we are trapped in a self-sabotaging mechanism in which we harm both ourselves and others by means of our destructive actions. That others suffer because of our self-centered actions is evident, but our harmful actions also destroy our own happiness by laying the seeds of these negative actions on our mindstream, only to have them ripen as misery either later in this life or in future lives.

For example, although none of us want illness, let alone a pandemic, we are responsible for creating the karmic causes for it. Earlier in this life and in previous lives we created destructive actions motivated by our mental afflictions. These afflictions are rooted in self-grasping ignorance, especially ignorance grasping the inherent existence of the I. This ignorance is erroneous because such an inherently existent I does not exist at all. Similarly, the inherently existent internal and external phenomena that we believe will bring us pleasure do not exist. But that doesn't mean nothing at all exists. We, other sentient beings, and our environments exist as dependently arisen phenomena that are merely designated by term and concept. Understanding this with profound wisdom conjoined with deep concentration brings liberation from saṃsāra.

To return to Gyaltsab's advice, on the basis of understanding how we enter and are liberated from saṃsāra, he counsels us to practice the three higher trainings, beginning with the higher trainings in ethical conduct and concentration. These two topics were explained in volume 4, *Following in the Buddha's Footsteps*. We then progress to the higher training in wisdom, the topic of the previous volume and of this and the next volumes. Gyaltsab advises us how to approach the higher training in wisdom:

> If [practitioners] act thusly, their study of and reflection on the treatises will be very meaningful, and they will seize well the essence of the [human existence] that is the basis of freedom and fortune. If they think otherwise—that they [should] obtain possessions, respect, and fame—then their mindstreams will be considerably impaired by their vices and the transgressions [of their precepts]. [In that case,] when they memorize, they will not retain the words; when they reflect [on the teachings], they will not understand the meaning; and when they meditate, [the meditation object] will not arise in their mindstreams. Therefore, even if they claim to have spent their whole lives striving to study and understand [the Dharma], the way their minds ordinarily operate will be no different in the degree of their desire and the degree of their renunciation of saṃsāra than the way [the mind of] a farmer ordinarily operates. Not simply making the path an [intellectual] object of their minds, they should strive earnestly to generate it as the nature of their minds.[1]

Since our mind is easily distracted and captivated by the eight worldly concerns, we cannot hear such advice enough. Especially today, when some people who have not studied and practiced extensively proclaim themselves to be great spiritual mentors, and when students may be gullible and easily impressed with titles, charisma, and colorful Tibetan hats, it is important that both spiritual mentors and disciples check their motivation and continuously reaffirm an attitude of compassion and bodhicitta, underlain by an aspiration to be free from saṃsāra. If this is done, the Dharma will spread and thrive; if it is not done, the Buddha's teachings will become just another fleeting interest to discuss with our friends.

In learning the Dharma, see all scriptures as personal instructions for your practice. If you neglect to do this, you may listen to many teachings but will feel that something is missing. To remedy that, relate whatever you learn to your life and to what you see occurring around you. The topics of your meditation should be the teachings that you have heard and contemplated. We can't consider ourselves to be practitioners without learning the Buddha's teachings in the three baskets of scriptures—the Vinaya, Sūtra, and Abhidharma—and practicing the three higher trainings in ethical conduct, concentration, and wisdom. If you do this well, with a sincere motivation, you will be able to pass on to others what you have understood.

If a particular teaching is too advanced for you now, don't criticize yourself or think that you lack the capacity to understand. Every sentient being has the buddha nature, and when the causes and conditions come together, they will be able to understand and practice every Dharma instruction. So focus on creating the causes and conditions to understand the more complex teachings in the future by engaging in purification practice, accumulating merit, making requests to the Three Jewels for their inspiration, and making strong aspirations to master those teachings in the future.

Seeking our own liberation from saṃsāra is a virtuous aspiration, but it is limited to benefiting ourselves. All sentient beings have been kind to us in previous lives, are kind to us now, and will continue to be kind to us in the future. For example, to heal certain physical conditions I have had surgery a few times in my life. My health depends on the efforts of the doctors, nurses, lab technicians, janitors, clerks, and so many other people at hospitals and clinics. Any knowledge or abilities I have came about through the kindness of all those who taught me, from my parents to my tutors to my advisors. Our buddhahood too depends on other sentient beings because bodhicitta—the aspiration to attain full awakening in order to benefit all beings most effectively—depends on having compassion for all sentient beings, omitting none, not even the mosquitoes that bite you.

Our self-centered thought limits us so much. It not only creates problems for ourselves and others here and now but also impedes our attainment of full awakening. As Panchen Lobsang Chogyen (1570–1662) says in *Guru Pūjā* (GP 91–92):

> This chronic disease of self-centeredness
> is the cause of all unwanted suffering. . . .
> Caring for my mother sentient beings and seeking to secure them in bliss
> is the gateway to infinite virtue.

Some of the scientists I have spoken with assert that our basic human nature is compassionate. Young children care little for differences among themselves and others; they are simply happy to play together. And young children are delighted to help their parents with certain tasks. It's only as they grow older and begin their education that they learn to observe distinctions. Modern education would do well to pay more attention to inner values, encouraging children to cultivate and enhance their natural sense of warm-heartedness. We are social animals, and our future and our happiness depend on those around us. Over-emphasizing secondary differences only leads to trouble. It is much better to remember that we are all the same in being living beings and to work together to fulfill the common good. So let's open our hearts and be aware of our common predicament as sentient beings in saṃsāra, and seek the highest awakening in order to liberate all beings.

Every day I dedicate my body, speech, and mind to the welfare of others, so I am happy to be of benefit by sharing with you my thoughts and those of the lineage of great Buddhist practitioners regarding dismantling false views and realizing the profound view.

Bhikṣu Tenzin Gyatso, the Fourteenth Dalai Lama
Thekchen Choling, McLeod Ganj, India

1 The Seven-Point Analysis: How Does a Car Exist?

FAILING TO APPREHEND OURSELVES and other phenomena as they actually are, sentient beings suffer cycling in saṃsāra, taking one rebirth after another in fortunate and unfortunate realms. The source of this cycle is self-grasping ignorance that superimposes a type of existence on phenomena that they do not have. The mind that knows the absence of this superimposed, reified existence is the wisdom of the emptiness of inherent existence. This wisdom apprehends the exact opposite of the object grasped by ignorance: ignorance grasps all persons and phenomena as inherently existent, whereas wisdom apprehends their emptiness of inherent existence. However, emptiness doesn't appear spontaneously to our mind by banishing all thoughts. We must first refute the existence of the conceived object of ignorance—inherent existence. A conceived object is the main object with which a conceptual consciousness is concerned and is the same as the apprehended object of that conceptual consciousness.[2]

Analysis is needed to negate the existence of the conceived object of ignorance. This analysis isn't a mere intellectual exercise, nor is it a game of words and long-winded arguments; it is an essential factor leading to the direct perception of reality, which brings liberation and full awakening. Probing awareness investigates: How do I really exist? What are phenomena really? The *King of Concentration Sūtra* decisively states (LC 3:107–8):

> Although worldly persons cultivate concentration,
> they do not destroy the notion of [an inherently existent] self.
> Afflictions return and disturb them,
> as they did to Udraka who cultivated concentration in this way.

> If you analytically discern the lack of self in phenomena
> and if you cultivate that analysis in meditation,
> this will cause the result, the attainment of nirvāṇa.
> There is no peace through any other means.

Udraka Rāmaputra was one of Siddhārtha's teachers after he left the palace but before he attained awakening. Udraka taught a mode of meditation that led to the meditative absorption of the peak of saṃsāra, a profound state of samādhi that is still under the influence of ignorance and karma and thus within saṃsāra. For this reason, it is essential not only to develop powerful concentration but also to cultivate the sharp analytical wisdom that sees that the self of phenomena—the conceived object of ignorance—does not exist at all. (Here "self" refers to inherent existence, although in other contexts it refers to the person.) There is no other path to nirvāṇa aside from this.

Analysis Relates Back to Experience

Although Madhyamaka texts say true existence, ultimate existence, and inherent existence are the object of negation, we can't understand from merely reading these words what they refer to. However, by investigating our own mind, examining how objects appear to us, and questioning if they exist in the way they appear, we will gradually understand that how things appear to us does not accord with how they actually exist. An awareness of this dissonance leads us to identify the object of negation.

What is the object of negation? The people and things around us do not appear to exist dependent on their causes and conditions, their parts, or being designated by name and concept, even though that is how they conventionally exist. Instead they appear to exist in their own right, objectively, unrelated to the mind, and independent of all other factors. Existence without depending on being designated by conceptuality is inherent existence, the object of negation.

If we leave the inherent existence that objects appear to have as it is and instead refute something else, we miss understanding emptiness. It is precisely the inherent existence that objects appear to have that is the object of negation. Our investigation involves probing to discern if things actually exist in this way. If they do, we should be able to find them.

In many of the refutations of inherent existence that follow, it is said that if phenomena existed inherently they would be permanent, they would arise without causes, or they would exist independent of their parts. While this is true, the opposite of those three qualities—being impermanent, arising due to causes, and depending on parts—are not the meaning of emptiness. Believing things to be permanent, unproduced, and independent of parts—qualities of a soul or of partless particles—are coarse misconceptions that are acquired afflictions.[3] They are not the root of saṃsāra. Nevertheless, if phenomena existed in the way they appeared to us—as truly existent—they would have these qualities. The understanding that they don't exist in this way leads us to realize their emptiness.

A person who has studied emptiness may *assert* phenomena lack true existence, but their mind still *grasps* true existence. Knowing the words of the teachings isn't sufficient, we must seek experiential realizations. This comes about through first understanding the teaching conceptually, then gaining a conceptual inference of emptiness, and finally perceiving emptiness directly.

In this and upcoming chapters, we will examine several analytical methods to explore if the person truly exists. For example, we question if the person is one and the same as the aggregates or totally separate from them. The person is the I or self. The aggregates are five in number, and dependent on them we know a person is present:[4]

1. Form (*rūpa*) in general refers to objects apprehended by our sense consciousnesses, and when speaking of the person, it refers to the body.
2. Feeling (*vedanā*) is the mental factor of the experience of pleasure, pain, or neutrality.
3. Discrimination (*saṃjñā*) is the mental factor that apprehends the distinctive characteristics of an object and can distinguish one thing from another.
4. Miscellaneous factors (*saṃskāra*) are mental factors other than feeling and discrimination, such as emotions, attitudes, and views, as well as abstract composites such as karmic seeds and latencies of afflictions.
5. Primary consciousnesses (*vijñāna*) consist of the visual, auditory, olfactory, gustatory, tactile, and mental primary consciousnesses that

apprehend the general type of object—sights, sounds, smells, tastes, tangibles, and mental phenomena respectively.

Aside from being either identical to or completely distinct from the aggregates, there are no other possibilities where a truly existent person could be found. Then we investigate: Is there any fault with saying the self is inherently one with the aggregates? Is there a problem saying it is inherently different from the aggregates? We search for faults such as these that can be known by a person's reliable cognizers. We cannot prove that all phenomena lack true existence by saying "The person does not truly exist because the Buddha said nothing exists in that way." This won't prove our thesis that all phenomena are empty of true existence to others, and we may not believe it ourselves! However, if we say, "The person is not inherently different from the body and mind because it cannot be found separate from the psychophysical aggregates," intelligent people who are receptive will understand this.

Although nondeceptive consciousnesses apprehending veilings (conventionalities) do not have the capability to directly apprehend the ultimate truth—the emptiness of inherent existence—they can contradict certain premises that arise when analyzing the ultimate nature. In other words, we must use the conventional reliable cognizers that we have to help us investigate the deeper mode of existence. Although these cognizers themselves cannot directly apprehend emptiness, they can steer us in the right direction by eliminating many of the wrong views that are detours on the path.

Scriptural quotations direct our analysis and affirm the conclusions of our analysis, but reasoning and logic are the reliable avenues to approach the ultimate nature. Words and concepts, syllogisms and refutations, are all helpful and necessary aids to cultivating wisdom. Employing them, we must develop understanding in our own mind. At first this understanding is conceptual, but when it is combined with firm concentration, it can penetrate reality to the core, directly perceiving emptiness without reliance on words and concepts.

Two styles of presentation help us to investigate a matter, and both are used when seeking the ultimate nature of reality. One is a clear and direct presentation given through reasoning that proves a tenet. We follow the reasoning and understand its conclusion. For example, our spiritual mentor explains the syllogism "Consider the I, it is empty of inherent existence because it arises dependent on causes and conditions." Using reasoning and examples, we contemplate this and understand that the thesis is true. Another style of presentation is the continual refutation of things that are not tenable, such that we end up with only one conclusion that is possible. After all other possibilities are refuted, we have no alternative but to accept the reality of that position. For example, if the I existed inherently, it would have to be either inherently one with the aggregates, separate from the aggregates, possess the aggregates, be the base of the aggregates, or be what is based on the aggregates. We investigate all these possibilities and see that the I can't inherently exist in any of these ways. The conclusion that remains is that the I doesn't inherently exist.

Because reasoning is so essential in this process, I often recommend to the monastics who engage in debate as part of their studies in Tibetan monasteries to endeavor to establish rebirth without resorting to scriptural quotations. If they can do this, they will be able to explain Buddhist concepts in a more coherent and acceptable manner to scientists. In addition, they will gain firm conviction themselves in the existence of rebirth. The same applies to understanding emptiness.

The great Madhyamaka scholar-adepts refuted others' positions with a compassionate motivation to release them from wrong views. Their compassion was especially strong for non-Buddhists who lacked a perfect teacher such as the Buddha to prevent them from falling to the extremes of absolutism or nihilism and who did not know correct meditation methods to cultivate the wisdom realizing the ultimate nature. Although Madhyamaka debaters' refutations may be unrelenting, the purpose of their arguments is not to win a debate but to gain clear realization themselves and to lead others to also gain clear realization of the path.

When reflecting and meditating on emptiness, a genuine spirit of inquiry is important. In fact, having doubt and a certain type of skepticism without cynicism spurs us on. We have to have an insatiable curiosity that wants to know: Who am I? How do my body and mind exist? What is reality? Are what my senses perceive true? Such heartfelt questioning opens the door to deeper understanding. This is what Chan (Zen) calls "the Great Doubt."

REFLECTION

This book contains extensive reasonings to refute inherent existence, but some shorter meditations can also give you a taste of emptiness.

1. When you are hungry, ask yourself: Who is this hungry person?
2. Then reflect: How is hunger quelled? Can you identify one mouthful of food that alone will stop the hunger?
3. When you are angry, pause and ask: Who is angry? Try to find the I that is angry.
4. When you are very attached to something, reflect: What is this object that means so much to me? Where is the attractiveness in it? Try to find its attractiveness.

The Main Arguments to Establish Emptiness

In the Sanskrit tradition as practiced by Tibetan Buddhists, we negate inherent existence by means of five principal arguments:

- Diamond slivers (*vajrakaṇahetu*, T. *rdo rje gzegs ma'i gtan tshigs*), which analyzes causes, has its roots in the early sūtras and was expanded and emphasized by Nāgārjuna.
- Reasoning refuting the arising of existents and nonexistents (*sadasadutpādapratiṣedhahetu*) analyzes effects.
- Reasoning refuting the four alternatives of arising (*catuṣkoṭyutpādapratiṣedhahetu*) analyzes whether one cause produces one effect or many effects, or many causes produce one effect or many effects.
- Reasoning of dependent arising (*pratītyasamutpādahetu*) eliminates both the extremes of absolutism and nihilism and is my preferred argument.
- Reasoning of neither one nor different (*ekānekaviyogahetu*) analyzes the nature of phenomena. It is the preferred argument of Śāntarakṣita, the eighth-century scholar-adept from the Yogācāra-Svātantrika Madhyamaka system, who brought Buddhadharma and the monastic

ordination to Tibet. It is also the main reasoning used in the stages of the path literature.[5]

Tsongkhapa presents the mental process of analyzing the ultimate as having four stages: (1) examining if the object—for example, the person or the body—exists inherently, (2) by doing this, proving the absence of its inherent existence, (3) examining if emptiness is inherently existent, and (4) establishing that emptiness too does not exist inherently. The conceptual or nonconceptual probing awareness that does these analyses then confirms the absence of inherent existence that is a nonaffirming negation.

Nāgārjuna speaks of two objects of negation. The first is the ignorance grasping inherent existence; the second is inherent existence. The former exists—it is the root of saṃsāra. Although it cannot be refuted, it can be counteracted. The latter is the object apprehended by that grasping; it does not exist at all and is the object negated by probing awareness. Destroying self-grasping is not one sudden event like smashing a porcelain plate with a wrench. Rather it is a gradual process that occurs through first applying reasoning to prove to ourselves that inherent existence cannot possibly exist. Done with conceptual probing awareness, this leads to the correct inferential understanding of emptiness. Then with the unity of serenity and insight, practitioners familiarize themselves with that realization over time. As the mind becomes more and more accustomed to the emptiness of inherent existence by continuous intense meditation, the conceptual appearance of the inferential realization of emptiness fades and a direct, nonconceptual realization of a yogic direct perceiver that cognizes emptiness now emerges. As inherent existence, the apprehended object of self-grasping, is disproved repeatedly, the self-grasping mind naturally is damaged until it finally ceases.

The Selflessness of Persons and of Phenomena

The correct view consists of realizing the selflessness (emptiness) of persons and the selflessness of phenomena. What is the relationship between these two kinds of self and two kinds of selflessness?

To answer this, first we must know the perspective of the tenet system from which the questioner seeks an answer. Some tenet systems—for example the Vaibhāṣika and Sautrāntika—speak only of a self and selflessness of persons, not of phenomena. There are also divergent notions regarding the object of negation in the selflessness of person and of phenomena. The Svātantrikas and below refute self-sufficient substantial existence to realize the selflessness of persons, whereas Prāsaṅgikas refute the inherent existence of the person. The assertions regarding the object of negation to realize the selflessness of phenomena differ for the Yogācāra, Svātantrika Madhyamaka, and Prāsaṅgika Madhyamaka systems. Also some tenet systems refute a certain type of self on persons, but that selflessness is considered a selflessness of phenomena. For example, when Svātantrikas refute true existence on the person, they realize a selflessness of phenomena.

In general, practitioners meditate first on the selflessness of persons because it is considered easier to realize than the selflessness of phenomena, such as the aggregates. From the Prāsaṅgika viewpoint, there is no difference in the subtlety of the two selflessnesses; the difference lies in the person being the base of selflessness. This is so because the person depends on the aggregates. Absent the physical and mental aggregates, there is no person; the person is designated in dependence on the collection of the aggregates, which is its basis of designation. In addition, to apprehend a person, we must first apprehend one of the aggregates; to know that Joan is there, we must either see part of her body or hear her voice. Similarly, based on grasping her aggregates as inherently existent, we grasp Joan to exist inherently.

For that reason, the selflessness of persons is usually taught first. However, to understand the method of examining how a person exists, the example of a commonly known external object is explained first. In ancient India, a chariot was used as the example; we will update it to a car. In both time periods a vehicle was a useful object that could be an object of attachment.

Someone may say, "Wait a minute. You just said that realizing the selflessness of the person is easier to realize than the selflessness of phenomena. Why then are you giving the example of a car—a phenomenon? Isn't the emptiness of this external phenomena more difficult to understand than the emptiness of a person?"

A car is used as an example only to show how the sevenfold reasoning works; just as a car is dependent on its parts, so too is a person dependent on its parts—the five aggregates. Just as a car cannot be found among its parts, in the arrangement of its parts, or separate from its parts, so too a person cannot be found in any of the aggregates individually, in the arrangement or the collection of the aggregates, or apart from the aggregates.

When discussing philosophical topics, examples are often used, especially in syllogisms, to help us understand the meaning. For example, someone will say, "Consider the I, it is empty of inherent existence because it is a dependent arising, like the reflection of a face in a mirror." It is difficult to understand what inherent existence would be like if it existed and why the appearance of inherent existence is false. However, as adults we know that there isn't a real face in the mirror and that the appearance of a face is false. The reflection exists; it arises from its causes and conditions, but the face that appears in it is false. Similarly, a person exists; it arises from its causes and conditions, but the inherently existent person that appears is false. Just as thinking the face in the mirror is a real face will bring problems—people have been known to throw something at their reflection in the mirror when they are mad at themselves—thinking we exist inherently as we appear to brings problems such as attachment, anger, and arrogance.

The Chariot Travels through Time

The first time the chariot was used to illustrate selflessness was during the Buddha's life. One afternoon, the Buddha's disciple Bhikṣuṇī Vajirā was meditating in a grove. Māra, the personification of self-grasping, sought to disturb her meditation by asking a question about an external creator. Recognizing the speaker as the troublemaker Māra, Bhikṣuṇī Vajirā replied (SN 5.10.553–4):

> Why now do you assume a being?
> Māra, is that your speculative view?
> This is a heap of sheer formations:
> here no being is found.
>
> Just as, with an assemblage of parts,
> the word "chariot" is used,
> so, when the aggregates exist,
> there is the convention "a being."[6]

The Sanskrit version of this verse is similar, but with some notable differences. It reads:

> "Self" is a demonic mind;
> you have a wrong view.
> These conditioned aggregates are empty;
> there is no living being in them.
>
> Just as the word "chariot" is used
> in dependence on a collection of parts,
> so when the aggregates exist,
> there is the convention "a living being" in dependence upon the aggregates.

The first difference between the two versions is that in the Pāli, Māra is seen as a being who disrupts and impedes sincere practitioners' practice. In the Sanskrit, the "demonic" mind—the self-grasping ignorance that is the root of saṃsāra—is the great impediment to liberation. Self-grasping ignorance is demonic in that it gives rise to the four māras, or negative forces. These are (1) the mental and physical aggregates under the control of afflictions and karma, (2) the afflictions, which are the causes of a person taking these aggregates, (3) death under the control of afflictions and karma, and (4) external hindrances such as Māra that cause difficulties.

The second difference is the phrase "in dependence on" in the Sanskrit verses. This emphasizes that the word "chariot" is conventionally designated in dependence on the aggregates, but the chariot is neither the aggregates nor the collection of the aggregates. Similarly, the self, person, or I is not the aggregates, nor is it independent of the aggregates. Rather the I is designated in dependence on the collection of the aggregates.

Bhikṣuṇī Vajirā used the example of a chariot to illustrate that the person is neither the aggregates individually nor the collection of the aggregates. Just as a chariot is not found in its parts and exists by being designated in dependence on the assembly of its parts, so too is the person a mere convention, without any findable essence.

The example of the chariot is found a few centuries later in the *Questions of King Menander*, a text written around 100 BCE. This text is included in the Khuddaka Nikāya of the Sixth Council Burmese version of the Pāli canon, although in other Theravāda traditions it is not a canonical text. King Menander asked the Buddhist monk-arhat Nāgasena about the nature of the self. The book relates a witty yet pointed discussion between the two.[7]

After greeting each other, the king asks the monk for his name. He replies "Nāgasena," and goes on to explain that that is only a designation, that there is no self or soul there. Puzzled, the king asks who lives an ethical life, who meditates, who attains nirvāṇa? Who kills, steals, lies, and creates other nonvirtues? If there is no person, then there cannot be virtue or nonvirtue; there would be no one who creates virtue and nonvirtue and no one who experiences the results of karma. If that is the case, there are no Buddhist teachers and Nāgasena's ordination is void.

Nāgasena didn't flinch, but simply replied, "I don't say that, great king."

The king continued, asking Nāgasena if he were any part of his body or if he were one of the four mental aggregates. Again Nāgasena responded no. In frustration, the king cried out, "Ask as I may, I can discover no Nāgasena. Nāgasena is a mere empty sound! Who then is the Nāgasena that we see before us? It is a falsehood that your reverence has spoken, an untruth!"

Seeming to change the subject, Nāgasena asked how the king traveled to their meeting. The king responded that he had come by chariot. Nāgasena proceeded to ask if the pole, axle, wheel, spokes, framework, ropes, yoke, or goad were the chariot. "None of these," the king responded. "Is the chariot the assembly of its parts?" "No." "Is it something separate from the parts?" "No."

Nāgasena called out, "I can discover no chariot. Chariot is a mere empty sound. What, then, is the chariot you say you came in? It is a falsehood that Your Majesty has spoken, an untruth! There is no such thing as a chariot!" The king then understood that in dependence on the collection of parts, the designation "chariot" was imputed. It was in such a merely imputed chariot that he traveled, and the king that rode in it was likewise merely designated due to the presence of the five aggregates.

Many centuries later, in the *Supplement to "Treatise on the Middle Way"* (*Madhyamakāvatāra*), Candrakīrti investigated how the I exists. To do this, he began his inquiry with the example of a chariot and its relationship with its parts. After understanding that a chariot does not exist inherently yet exists by being merely imputed in dependence on its parts, he applied this to the relationship between the person and the aggregates to show that a person does not inherently exist, yet exists by being merely designated in dependence on his or her aggregates.

REFLECTION

1. Go through the above dialogue, using a car as the example. Examine the relationship between a car and its parts.
2. Is the car the same thing as one of its parts? If it is one part, then there is no need for many parts to be assembled for a car to exist.
3. Is it exactly identical to the collection of its parts? Since each car part is not a car, a collection of car parts is an assembly of non-cars. That is not a car.
4. Is it found apart from its parts? If the car can be found separate from the car parts, you can ride an elephant and call it a car.

If you have a nice car that you are attached to or proud of, this analysis will be especially effective!

By using this example, we approach the reasoning refuting inherent existence gradually. Although you may have strong attachment to your car, grasping the inherent existence of the I and attachment to the I are even stronger because the I stands at the very center of our lives. Our lives revolve around pleasing and defending this I. This distorted conceptualization exaggerates everything pertaining to the self; when someone asks us an innocuous question about what we are doing, our ignorant mind explodes in anger, "You're questioning my competence? You're criticizing me when I know perfectly well what I'm doing? Stop it!" However, if that person asks the same question to the person sitting beside us, we would be nonplussed. Grasping our car can be problematic, but grasping the self is much more intense and harmful.

King Menander and Nāgasena mainly investigated if the chariot could be found in its parts or if it was totally separate from them. Candrakīrti expanded these two points, making them into seven (MMA 6.151):

A chariot cannot be said to be different from its parts;
it is not identical with its parts, nor does it possess the parts;
it is not [based on] the parts, nor are the parts [based on] it;
it is not the mere collection [of its parts], nor is it [their] shape.
[The self and the aggregates are similar.]

If a car existed inherently, probing awareness that examines the ultimate should be able to establish it in one of seven ways. Probing awareness is of two kinds: conceptual probing awareness analyzes how an object exists and realizes its emptiness inferentially, and nonconceptual probing awareness is a yogic direct perceiver of emptiness. These two are cause and effect. An inferential probing awareness is generated through study, thinking about, or meditating on emptiness; it is the cause of a probing awareness that is a yogic direct perceiver. Together, these two awarenesses encompass the process of realizing the Middle Way view, beginning with refuting wrong views, progressing to gaining the correct conceptual understanding of the Middle Way view that refutes inherent existence, and deepening to gaining and maintaining an ārya's yogic direct perceiver of emptiness. This wisdom is then used to gradually cleanse the mind of all afflictive obscurations and, when conjoined with bodhicitta, to eradicate all cognitive obscurations as well.

Using the sevenfold analysis, a probing awareness examines the relationship of the designated object to the basis of designation. The basis of designation is the parts and the collection of the parts and the designated object is what is imputed in dependence on that basis. The object exists by being imputed or designated on a basis of designation and fulfilling the three criteria for an existent: (1) it is known to a conventional consciousness, (2) it is not discredited by another conventional reliable cognizer, and (3) it is not discredited by a reasoning consciousness analyzing the ultimate. These three are described in depth in the next volume, *Appearing and Empty*. In this case, the car parts as well as the collection of these parts are the basis of designation and the car is the designated object. Usually we confound the two, thinking that the basis of designation is the designated object, and on that basis we think the car has its own intrinsic essence—it exists inherently. If that were so, the car would have to exist in one of seven ways:

1. The car is totally separate from its parts: that is, the designated object—the car—and its basis of designation—its parts—are unrelated and different.
2. The car is identically one with its parts: the designated object and its basis of designation are inherently the same or identical.
3. The car possesses its parts: the designated object possesses the basis of designation either as a different entity, in the way a person possesses a dog, or as one entity, in the way a tree possesses its core.
4. The car is [based] on its parts: the designated object is inherently based on the basis of designation.
5. The car is what its parts are based on: the designated object is what the basis of designation is inherently based on.
6. The car is the collection of its parts: the designated object is the basis of designation.
7. The car is the shape or arrangement of its parts: the designated object is the shape or arrangement of the parts of the basis of designation.

One and Different, One Nature and Different Natures

Before exploring these seven points, it is useful to understand some terminology. According to Buddhist philosophy, there are two ways in which two objects can be related: (1) They can be cause and effect; for example, the seed and the sprout that arises from it. To be in a cause-and-effect relationship, two things cannot exist at the same time and one must have the potential to produce the other; the cause must exist prior to the effect and must cease for the effect to arise—for the sprout to grow, the unsprouted seed must cease. (2) They can be one nature (one entity). Two things that are one nature exist at the same time, and at the time they both exist, one cannot exist without the other.[8] Within being one nature, the two objects can be associated in various ways:

- Two things are mutually one nature if they are mutually inclusive—that is, everything that is the first is also the second; the two are equivalent. An example is impermanent things and products.
- Two things are unidirectional one nature when one is part of the other or an attribute of the other but not vice versa. For example, the yellow

color of the table is *one nature with* the table, but the table is not one nature with its yellow color. The yellow of the table is just one part or attribute of the table. The attribute is one nature with the object, but the object is not one nature with the attribute.

- The extremely subtle mind and wind are one nature; they are mutually exclusive but exist inseparably from each other.
- The two truths are one nature: the table and its emptiness exist together. There cannot be one without the other.

Candrakīrti's reasoning examines the relationship between the car and its parts. Are they one or are they different? In this context, "one" and "different" have slightly different meanings than in ordinary language. *One, one and the same,* and *identical* are synonymous. *Different, separate,* and *distinct* are synonymous. It is impossible for two things to be one because no two things are identical in all respects. A cup is one with itself. It is different from the cup next to it. Even if the two cups look alike, they are not the same object. They do not occupy the same place at the same time.

Things that are distinct differ in their name, their meaning, or both name and meaning. For example, the words "flower" and "fleur," the French word for flower, may refer to the same object in the vase, but flower and fleur are different because they have different names. A porcupine and a giraffe are different in both name and meaning even though both are animals.

When we compare the two sets—one or different, and one nature or different nature—there are two options. Something cannot be one and one nature because to be considered one nature there must be two different objects. There is nothing that is one and different natures, because only two objects can be different natures. An example of things that are different and one nature is a person and his emptiness of inherent existence, and an example of things that are both different and different natures is two cups that look alike.

CHART: RELATIONSHIPS IN TERMS OF NATURE

	ONE NATURE	DIFFERENT NATURES
One	N/A	N/A
Different	Two truths, impermanent thing and product, a wheel and the car it is part of, a hand and the body it is part of	Table and chair, baby and the adult it becomes

Just as conventionally two objects must be either one (the same) or different, when examining two objects in terms of their ultimate existence, they must be either inherently one or inherently different. If two things are inherently one, they must be completely identical in all respects, and if they are inherently different, they must be totally unrelated. This is because inherently existent phenomena exist from their own side, under their own power. They are insular, independent, and completely unrelated to all other factors. Two things that are inherently different can't be one nature; nor can they be cause and effect.

How Does a Car Exist?

With this background, Candrakīrti takes us on the adventure of searching for precisely what an object is in relation to its parts and its basis of designation. How does the car exist? If it exists inherently, it should be findable among its parts or it should be totally separate and unrelated to its parts. We'll begin with the example of a car and its parts, and in chapters 2 and 3 we'll investigate the person and the aggregates.

Is the car inherently different from its parts?

If two things were inherently different, they would be totally unrelated. Two faults would result if the car and its parts were completely unrelated:

1. We would be able to see the car and its parts separately just as we see a table and a chair separately. The axle, tires, and so forth could exist in one place and the car in another. However, whenever we see the car, we also see its parts.
2. We could not designate "car" on those parts because there would be no relationship between the car and the hood, engine, and so forth. They

would be totally unrelated. The car wouldn't be the designated object and the parts wouldn't be its basis of designation.

Is the car inherently the same as (one with) its parts?

If the car were inherently one with its parts, the car and its parts would be exactly the same and inseparable. A quality that applies to one would automatically apply to the other. For example, if the car were green, the engine should also be green. Three fallacies would occur if the car were inherently one with its parts:

1. Since there are many parts, there would be many cars. Each part would be a car. The steering wheel would be a car, so would the engine, the axle, and so on.
2. Alternatively, since there is one car, there would be only one part.
3. Agent and object would be one. Normally we say the car is the possessor of parts (the agent) and the parts are what are possessed (the object). We differentiate between the agent (the part-possessor) and the object (the parts); the car is one thing; its parts are separate. However, if the part-possessor (car) and its parts were inherently one, they would be exactly the same, and this differentiation could not be made. We could not talk about the tire of the car, because the tire and the car would be identical. We couldn't change the tire, because the tire would be the car if they were inherently one and the same. In fact, even using the word "car" would be unnecessary, because we could simply say "tire" and people would understand "car," since the two would be inherently the same.

If we omit the word "inherently" and speak at the conventional level, we can say that the parts are the same nature as the car, but they are not one with the car. The parts and the car are one nature because they exist at the same time and can't exist without each other. However, they are not one, because they aren't the same in every respect. The tires are made of rubber, but the car isn't.

Conventionally, the parts and the car are different, but they are not different natures. They are different because the car isn't the parts. They are not different natures, because they can't exist without each other. In short, conventionally the car and its parts are not one, but they are one nature. They are different, but they are not different natures. But if the car existed inherently, it should be either inherently one with its parts or inherently different from its parts, and it is neither. From this analysis we conclude that the car does not inherently exist.

This may sound confusing at first, but comprehending it leads us to understand the relationship between the car and its parts. Later we use this to examine the relationship of the person and the aggregates if they existed inherently. As we will see in the next chapter, this leads us to conclude that they are empty of inherent existence.

Does the car inherently possess its parts?

There are two ways the car could possess its parts, as seen by two analogies:

1. Lobsang possesses his dog. Just as Lobsang and his pet dog are different entities and can be seen apart from each other, if the car inherently possessed its parts we should be able to see the car and its parts separately. The car could be in Los Angeles and its parts could be in New York, and you would have a hard time driving anywhere! If the car inherently possessed its parts in the way Lobsang possesses his dog, they would be inherently different, and the faults mentioned above would apply.
2. Lobsang possesses his ear. If the car inherently possessed its parts like Lobsang possesses his ear, they would be inherently one, and the faults of them being identical, as noted above, would occur.

Of course, Lobsang conventionally possesses his ear, and a car conventionally possesses its parts. This is not being refuted. What is refuted is inherent possession, which would entail their being inherently one or inherently different. Although Lobsang's ear is one nature with Lobsang, Lobsang and his ear are not inherently one; if they were, they would have to be exactly the same in all aspects.

We need to think deeply about these points. Currently it is difficult for us to differentiate the meaning of two things being inherently related from their being dependently related. In fact, we may never have looked at things in this way before!

Are the parts inherently supported by the car?

This and the next point examine the relationship of "the base and the based" or "the support and the supported" (T. *rten brten pa*). Such a relationship of two things may exist in two ways: for example, the car is the support of its parts, which is the supported, or the parts are the support for the car, which is the supported.

In the first, the car is seen as the support and the parts as the supported. The example is a bowl holding fruit: the car is like the bowl that supports its parts, which are like the fruit. If such a relationship existed inherently, the car and its parts would be totally distinct and unrelated, and the faults of being inherently different as explained above would apply.

Another example is trees on a snow mountain. Here the person, like a snow mountain, is the base and the aggregates, like the trees, are what is based on it. But if the imputed phenomenon (the snow mountain/person) were inherently the base or support on which the basis of designation (the trees/aggregates) depended, they would be inherently different and unrelated and the above faults would again accrue.

Conventionally, the car and its parts are related to each other as the support and the supported; the car is posited in dependence on the car parts. The car becomes a car based on the car parts; the car parts are car parts based on the car. The point here is that they do not inherently support, and are not inherently supported by, each other.

Is the car inherently supported by its parts?

In this case, the roles are reversed; the car is the supported and the parts are the support in that conventionally the car is based on its parts, which are its basis of designation or its support. Without the car parts, there would not be a car. Sometimes when we think about a car, the parts seem prominent—as if they exist first and are more noticeable—and the car appears afterward.

If this relationship of support and supported existed inherently, then the car and its parts would be like a lion in a jungle. Here, the car is analogous to the lion, and its parts to the jungle. The jungle is the environment in which the lion lives, and thus it supports the lion. Similarly, the car parts are the support of the car. The parts—the base or support—are more extensive than the supported, the car, which appears to exist inside of them. If the car and its parts existed in this way, they would be inherently different, and the same faults mentioned above would accrue.

Conventionally, the car is based on its parts; without them the car could not exist. But if the car and its parts were inherently support and supported, they would be totally unrelated and the car could exist separate from its parts, just as the lion and the jungle are distinct and the lion could exist apart from the jungle.

Is the car the collection of its parts?

In case we think that the collection or shape of the parts is the chariot, Candrakīrti says (MMA 6.152):

> For if the mere collection constitutes the chariot,
> the chariot would exist even when the parts are not assembled.
> Since there can be no parts without the possessor of the parts,
> that shape [or collection of parts] alone is the chariot is illogical as well.

If the car were inherently the collection of all its parts, several faults would ensue:

1. If the collection of the parts were inherently the car, then even if the parts were piled up in disarray, we would be able to see a car because the collection of parts is there. But if we see a pile of tires, an engine, seats, a hood, and so forth, we don't necessarily see a car. In fact, we may even say it's a pile of junk!
2. Since the car, which is the part-possessor, does not exist when it is dismantled, the car parts would also not exist. We can't talk about the engine of the car if there is no car. We may question: There are stores that sell car parts, but there are no cars in the store, so car parts can still exist without the presence of a car. Conventionally this is true; the term "car parts" is designated because cars in general exist and the wheels, engine, and so forth can form a car when conjoined with other parts.
3. The designated object and the basis of designation would be the same. The car is the object designated in dependence on the collection of its

parts, which are its basis of designation. That is, the collection of its parts is not the car. If the collection of parts were the car, we could not distinguish the designated object from its basis of designation. We couldn't even speak of them as two things. The word "car" would refer equally to a vehicle that could take us places and to a pile of metal, rubber, and cloth. The faults of two things being inherently one would apply.

Is the car the shape or arrangement of its parts?

If an inherently existent car were the shape of its parts, there would be two alternatives: either the shapes of the individual parts before they are assembled would be the car or the arrangement of the collection of parts after they are assembled would be the car. In either case, the car and its parts would be inherently one and the same. Conventionally the car parts and the car are one nature, but if they were inherently existent, they would have to be inherently one.

If the car were the shapes of the individual parts, then the car would be the shape of the steering wheel, the shape of the hood, the shape of the engine, and so forth. But none of those are the car; the shape of the dashboard can't take us from one place to another.

As for the second alternative, since the shape of each part isn't a car, how could a collection of shapes—all of which are not cars—be a car? If none of the shapes of the individual parts before they were assembled is the car, then just as we don't see a car before the parts are assembled, we won't see a car after they are assembled because the shapes of the individual parts have not changed. They remain the same both before and after the parts are assembled.

If each part had a new shape after all the parts were assembled, we should see these new shapes. But we don't. The wheels are still round, and the axle is still long. Conventionally we can say that when the parts are put together a new shape can be seen. But if the shapes of the parts existed inherently, a new shape could not arise when the parts are assembled because inherently existent things cannot change; they are not influenced by causes and conditions.

Although conventionally we can point to a car and its parts, ultimately we cannot find them. This indicates the difference between things existing by being merely designated and things having their own inherent, findable essence.

For a whole (part-possessor) to exist, there must be parts and vice versa. If the wheels, axle, engine, and so forth are piled up in a disorderly manner, we can't say they are the parts of the car, because at that moment there is no car. Although we may look at a wheel and say, "This is part of a car," we do that only because in the past we have seen fully assembled cars with wheels. In fact, saying the wheel alone is a car part is designating it in dependence on what it will become when a car is assembled or what it was before a car was disassembled. This is feasible conventionally but not ultimately.

Conclusion from Examining the Seven Points

The seven-point refutation—as do other refutations explained in this book—exhausts all the possible ways that a person or phenomenon could inherently exist. After examining each possibility and finding that it is not tenable for the I or the object being investigated to exist in any of those ways, we can safely conclude that without any doubt, the I or the object does not exist inherently.

Essentialists are those who assert true or inherent existence. They claim that an inherently existent car exists. What do they point to as being an inherently existent car? The thing in front of them. It is made of metal and so on and functions to efficiently move people and objects from one place to another. It is as if the car were already inherently there before anyone designated the collection of parts as "car." But for the car to come into being, didn't it necessitate people imagining such a vehicle and constructing it? The car is dependent on us as a society conceiving of that particular collection of miscellaneous things arranged in a particular manner as a vehicle that has the ability to move people and things. But that alone isn't sufficient for a car to exist. We must also agree to designate that collection of parts as a "car"—a shorthand term so that we can easily communicate with one another about it.

Essentialists claim that a car exists there, without it being conceived or designated. If that were the case, it could be found in one of the seven ways above. However, the car cannot be found as inherently existent either ultimately or conventionally through the sevenfold analysis. But when we don't analyze, by mere worldly convention, "car" is designated in dependence on the collection of parts.

Prāsaṅgikas assert that everything exists imputedly in dependence on its basis of designation. But the designated object and the basis of designation are not the same. In this case the car is the designated object and the arrangement of the collection of car parts is the basis of designation. The individual parts are not the car, the collection of parts is not the car, and the collection of parts arranged in a particular way is not the car. The car exists by being merely imputed by term and concept in dependence on its basis of designation.

If something exists inherently, we must be able to find it either in its basis of designation or apart from it. Why are we limited to these two options? The option of the car being dependent on its parts isn't feasible because we're examining if the car exists inherently, and an inherently existent car would exist independent of all other factors and things. The option of an inherently existent car being independent of its parts is also not feasible because nowhere do we find a car in one place and its parts in a different place. The option of an inherently existent car being the collection of its parts is not feasible and was refuted above.

If we accept that all phenomena exist imputedly, there is no need to find them under ultimate analysis. We simply accept that they conventionally exist. In dependence on a collection of certain parts that functions to transport a few people or things, we impute the name "car." That merely designated car exists and can take us places. Because things exist dependently, they can function. They arise, cease, and change without having a findable essence that is their unique identity. Candrakīrti says (MMA 6.158):

> Although the [chariot] is not established in these seven ways,
> both in terms of ultimate reality and the world,
> we here impute the chariot in dependence on its parts
> without analysis and through everyday convention alone.

If we search for an inherently existent referent of the word "chariot," using the sevenfold analysis, we cannot find it either conventionally or ultimately. Does that mean the chariot does not exist at all? If that were the case, how did King Menander go to meet Bhikṣu Nāgasena?

Candrakīrti explains that the chariot—and all other phenomena as well—are not established through analysis searching for the true referents of their names. Rather, they are posited by worldly convention. We agree to use the term "chariot" to refer to a vehicle with two wheels that was pulled by horses and used to transport people in ancient times. In this way, "chariot" is imputed in dependence on its parts, and we make sense of the expression "he is riding in a chariot."

Benefits of Contemplating the Seven Points

All seven points can be subsumed into the first two—the car is not inherently one with or inherently separate from its parts. Why, then, should we meditate on all seven points? When putting out a fire, using a lot of water is better than using a little, even if the initial water is sufficient to extinguish the flames. With the seven points, we explore the relationship between the car and its parts in multiple ways, each point reinforcing the conclusion that the car is empty of inherent existence. Meditation on the seven points enables us to dismiss our doubts and counteract the extreme of absolutism.

Furthermore, by qualifying that we are searching for inherent existence, not mere existence, the seven-point presentation refutes just inherent existence, not conventional existence. This mode of analysis does not impinge on the conventional existence of objects, and in this way it counteracts the extreme of nihilism. In short, proper contemplation on the seven points frees us from the two extremes.

Through familiarization with this type of analysis, yogis in meditative equipoise come to realize that nothing exists inherently. Meditative equipoise on emptiness first occurs on the path of preparation, with the union of serenity and insight on emptiness. Seeing that objects still appear inherently existent when they arise from meditative equipoise on emptiness, yogis recognize that these appearances are false and that phenomena exist like illusions in that they appear inherently existent although they are not. Yogis know that although these phenomena cannot be found in any of the seven ways, they still exist by being merely designated in dependence on their basis of designation and that they can be conventionally established by a nondeceptive worldly consciousness. Thus yogis can establish both ultimate truths and veiled truths without one contradicting the other.

Essentialists believe that if an object cannot be found when searched for with ultimate analysis, it doesn't exist at all. They also believe that if an object exists, it must inherently exist. However, such assertions contradict our experience, for in daily life we say, "I drive the car," and the car functions as a vehicle to take us places despite the fact that it cannot be found under ultimate analysis and that it does not ultimately exist. Because the car is empty of inherent existence yet arises dependently, it exists and functions.

Prāsaṅgikas assert that everything that exists must be empty of inherent existence and merely designated in dependence on its basis of designation. When we search for the car in any of the seven ways, we cannot find it. It does not ultimately exist, but this does not mean it is totally nonexistent. It exists dependently and conventionally and is established by a nondeceptive conventional consciousness.

Not only does the car not exist ultimately, its parts do not either. Candrakīrti says (MMA 6.161):

> When the chariot itself does not exist,
> neither the whole [chariot] nor its parts exist.
> When a chariot is burned, its parts do not exist;
> as in this example, [when] the fire of the [analytical] mind burns
> wholes, the parts [are also burned].

If the whole—the car—is completely burned, its parts—the engine, hood, and so forth—are also destroyed. Similarly, when the fire of analytical reason burns grasping the whole—the car—as inherently existent, it also burns grasping its parts as inherently existent.

Broadening the scope of the previous analysis, if we analyze one of the parts individually, it becomes a whole in relation to its own parts. When we analyze the engine to see if it inherently exists, we look to see if it is inherently one with or separate from its parts. Since it cannot be found in either of these ways, it is empty of inherent existence. Similarly, the analytical wisdom also sees that the parts of the engine—the spark plugs, cylinders, and so forth—lack inherent existence.

What Is Emptiness?

Before we continue, it is helpful to learn the meaning of a few words that indicate how a consciousness relates to its object.

- *Appear* (T. *snang*). The object merely appears to the mind. For example, the flower appears to the visual consciousness. Some of the qualities that are one nature with a conditioned phenomenon such as a flower—such as its shape, color, and impermanence—appear when the flower appears. However, something that appears is not necessarily apprehended or realized. An ordinary direct perceiver is unable to see all of these, but a yogic direct perceiver can see and ascertain them.
- *Apprehend, grasp* (T. *'dzin*). "Apprehend" or "grasp" means to hold. The consciousness engages the object. The consciousness may apprehend the object correctly—for example, knowing a chair is a chair—or incorrectly—for example, grasping the chair to exist inherently.
- *Ascertain* (T. *nges*). An ascertaining consciousness is able to induce a recollection of the object appearing to it, so it involves more than an object merely appearing or being apprehended. The object has been registered on the consciousness. In general, ascertaining an object applies to conceptual consciousnesses that correctly know their object. Such minds are reliable cognizers. For example, an inferential consciousness ascertains emptiness. Sometimes "ascertain" can apply to direct perceivers as well, as a visual consciousness ascertaining that the object in the field is a person, not a scarecrow.
- *Realize* (T. *rtogs*). A consciousness that realizes its object has ascertained that object and is able to (1) lead to another consciousness that has certainty—for example, an ascertaining memory of the object—and (2) eliminate misconceptions about it. The auditory consciousness realizes that sound is a dog's bark. However, the noun, realization (T. *rtogs pa* or *mngon rtogs*), usually indicates a quality or knowledge that has been cultivated over time and has now been attained—for example, the realization of bodhicitta, the realization of subtle impermanence, the realization of emptiness, and the realization of the path of accumulation.

Now, to discuss the emptiness of inherent existence. Although the experience of emptiness cannot be expressed in words, when we employ ultimate analysis to discover how persons and phenomena actually exist, we find they are empty of inherent existence. Emptiness is a nonaffirming negation. To understand the meaning and significance of this, we must understand the difference between affirmatives and negations, and within the latter, the various types of negations.[9]

Any phenomenon is either an affirmative or a negation. An *affirmative* or *positive* (*vidhi*) is a phenomenon that is comprehended by an awareness without eliminating an object of negation. An example is a chair; we can know the chair without negating anything. A *negation* (*pratiṣedha*) is an object comprehended by an awareness upon the explicit elimination of an object of negation. "The fridge is empty" simply tells us there is nothing in the fridge. Within negations there are two types, depending on how the negation is made:

1. A *nonaffirming negation* (*prasajyapratiṣedha*) is a negation in which the words expressing it do not suggest or imply an affirmative phenomenon or an affirming negation in place of the object of negation. It is a simple negation, known by explicitly eliminating an object of negation while not suggesting anything else. For example, "there are no bananas" explicitly negates bananas but doesn't suggest anything else like oranges or peaches. Another example is "the selflessness of persons," which explicitly negates self (inherent existence) but doesn't suggest anything else. We may wonder, Doesn't that phrase affirm persons? No, it does not. Persons are the *base* on which an attribute—in this case self (inherent existence)—is negated. Persons are not projected or affirmed after negating inherent existence. When we realize emptiness, a mere vacuity that is the negation of inherent existence appears to the mind. There are two types of nonaffirming negations:
    - One that negates something that exists—for example, saying "There is no flower."
    - One that negates something that does not exist—for example, saying "There is no turtle with a moustache." "The non-true existence of phenomena" likewise merely negates true existence without affirming anything in its place. "Phenomena" is the basis on

which true existence is being negated, but it is not being suggested when true existence is negated.

Nonaffirming negations may, however, suggest other nonaffirming negations of the same type. Negating the existence of a rabbit's horn suggests that the pointedness of a rabbit's horn does not exist. Nāgārjuna's *Treatise on the Middle Way* begins with a verse containing four nonaffirming negations (MMK 1.1):

Neither from itself nor from another
nor from both,
nor without a cause
does anything anywhere ever arise.

Here the four—arising from itself, from another, from both, and without cause—are negated. All four are nonaffirming negations, and together they refute inherently existent arising. The lack of inherently existent arising suggests the lack of inherent existence, which is also a nonaffirming negation, because if things don't arise inherently, they can't exist inherently.

2. An *affirming negation* (*paryudāsapratiṣedha*) is a negation where the words expressing it suggest either an affirmative phenomenon or an affirming negation in place of what it negated. The explicit negation of one thing affirms another thing. An example is impermanent sound. It negates permanent sound and projects impermanent sound. Within affirming negations, there are four types:
    - *An explicitly affirming negation* explicitly negates one phenomenon and explicitly affirms another—an affirming negation or an affirmative phenomenon. In the expression "a mountainless plateau," the words negate mountains and explicitly affirm a plateau. Similarly, "the existence of selflessness of persons" explicitly negates self and explicitly affirms the existence of the selflessness of persons.
    - *An implicitly affirming negation* explicitly negates one phenomenon and implicitly affirms another—an affirming negation or an affirmative phenomenon. The classic example is "Fat Sam doesn't eat during the day." These words explicitly negate his eating during

the day and, since he is fat, implicitly suggests he eats at night. (This example was made in the days before they knew about thyroid malfunction and other disorders.) Another example is "The vase is not permanent," in which its being impermanent is implied.

- *A negation that both explicitly and implicitly suggests another phenomenon* explicitly negates one thing and both explicitly and implicitly suggests another—either an affirming negation or a positive phenomenon. An example is "Fat Sam, who doesn't eat during the day, has a non-emaciated body." As above, his not eating in the day implicitly suggests he eats at night, and in addition, his body not being emaciated is explicitly stated.
- *A contextual negation* explicitly negates one phenomenon and, due to the context, suggests another—either an affirming negation or a positive phenomenon. We know our keys are either in the drawer or in our pocket. They are not in our pocket, so within the context of the keys being in one of two places, we know that they are in the drawer.

While all these divisions may initially seem complicated, knowing them serves a good purpose when we study and contemplate selflessness. Emptiness is a nonaffirming negation. Inherent existence is negated and nothing else whatsoever is affirmed or implied. The negation of inherent existence is complete—there are no remaining qualms, no "ifs, ands, or buts."

A mind that directly realizes the emptiness of the person, for example, does not perceive the person that is the base of emptiness or any other phenomenon. The base of emptiness is the object whose mode of existence is being examined—in this case, the person. Emptiness is an attribute of the person. Only emptiness appears to this directly perceiving mind and only emptiness is known by that mind.

An inferential realization of emptiness ascertains a nonaffirming negation. The object, emptiness, is a nonaffirming negation because nothing else is implied when inherent existence is negated. An inferential realization of emptiness knows emptiness by means of a conceptual appearance. It does not know emptiness directly because a conceptual mind cannot differentiate between emptiness and the conceptual appearance of emptiness. This is the limitation of conceptual consciousnesses.

However, according to Prāsaṅgikas, the second moment onward of an inferential consciousness is considered a direct perceiver because it doesn't rely on a reason to cognize its object. This is very different from the lower systems that assert a direct perceiver cognizes its object directly, not through a conceptual appearance. For them, direct reliable cognizers are always nonconceptual. Prāsaṅgikas have a different view. They assert that direct perceivers are consciousnesses that do not rely on a reason to know their object. Thus there are conceptual direct reliable cognizers. An example is the second moment onward of an inferential consciousness knowing emptiness: although the first moment cognized emptiness by depending on a reason such as dependent arising, the second moment onward remembers the object inferred (emptiness) directly, without renewed reliance on a reason.

In general, the base of emptiness for an inferential realization of emptiness—in this case the person—does not appear to this conceptual consciousness. Every consciousness except the wisdom directly and nonconceptually perceiving emptiness in meditative equipoise is infected with the appearance of inherent existence. When the conceptual appearance of emptiness *appears* to this inferential cognition, it appears inherently existent. However, the conceptual appearance of emptiness is not ascertained by this mind; this mind *ascertains* emptiness.

According to the Sūtrayāna, the base of emptiness does not appear to the inferential cognizer of emptiness. However, in the context of the unique tantric practice of deity yoga, the mind realizing emptiness itself is generated as the deity. The meditator then contemplates that the deity appears but is empty, the deity is empty but appears. Here, the base of emptiness—the deity—appears to the mind realizing its emptiness. This enables the practitioner to meditate on the two truths—in this case the deity and its emptiness—simultaneously.

Although emptiness is a negation phenomenon, it has meaning. It is not absolutism, nihilism, or agnosticism. It is our ultimate nature, and that fact has many important implications for both the path and the result. Emptiness is not the negation of all existence whatsoever. Only inherent existence (and its equivalents such as true existence, existence from its own side, existence under its own power, and so forth) is negated. Emptiness is the ultimate nature of all phenomena. It exists, and our perceiving it will, over time, liberate us from all defilements.

Even though a nonaffirming negation only negates an object of negation without affirming anything in its stead, it can still prove a point. Many of the reasonings used to prove emptiness—such as diamond slivers and Candrakīrti's sevenfold reasoning—are nonaffirming negations that prove the lack of inherent existence of persons and phenomena. Their proving emptiness does not make them affirming negations. As mentioned above, a nonaffirming negation can implicitly establish another nonaffirming negation of the same type; this is the case in diamond slivers. Each of the four statements is itself a nonaffirming negation, and together they negate inherently existent arising. The lack of inherently existent arising, which is a nonaffirming negation, in turn implicitly establishes the emptiness of inherent existence, which is also a nonaffirming negation.

This point is important because in meditative equipoise directly realizing emptiness, only emptiness is perceived. Veiled truths, such as a seed, sprout, or the sprout's arising, do not appear to that meditative mind, and that mind does not establish veiled truths. If the four negations in diamond slivers suggested an affirmative phenomenon in their place—for example, conventional arising—then the meditative equipoise on emptiness would realize and perceive conventional arising. That would mean meditative equipoise on reality also perceived veiled truths, which are falsities. In that way the wisdom directly realizing the ultimate nature would become a conventional cognizer that knows veiled truths. That would be absurd!

Some Tibetan Buddhist traditions assert that ultimate truth is an affirming negation, but when we deeply understand their assertions, we realize the two systems—one saying that ultimate truth is a nonaffirming negation and the other saying it is an affirming negation—though seemingly contradictory, agree on the important points despite the language they use. Even in Tantra, the actual clear-light mind, which is an affirmative phenomenon, is considered to be the ultimate truth.

When we apply ultimate analysis to meditate on emptiness, it is helpful to evaluate our experience after the meditation session. Was the nonaffirming negation that is the lack of inherent existence appearing to our mind? I heard of one person who thought he was meditating on emptiness and concluded that God exists. This is not meditation on emptiness. Similarly, the thought or feeling "I am one with everything" is not meditation on emptiness; it is meditation on a positive phenomenon—the I—and there's also a good chance that the I is being seen as inherently existent. While in meditation, if there is the sense "I am perceiving emptiness" or "I am meditating," an affirmative phenomenon—the I—appears to that mind. And if we're not careful, we may even be grasping that I as inherently existent: "*I* am perceiving emptiness. Wait until I tell my friends about this!" To gain the correct realization of emptiness of inherent existence, it is important that the object we realize is a nonaffirming negation.

In conclusion, understanding the difference between affirmatives and negations as well as the difference between nonaffirming negations and affirming negations sets the stage for a correct understanding of emptiness. First, the emptiness of inherent existence is an existent, a phenomenon. All phenomena are either affirmatives or negations. The fact that emptiness is a negation refutes those who say emptiness is not a knowable object that is capable of being perceived by mind. Although emptiness is subtle and cannot be known exactly as it is by a conceptual consciousness, it exists and can be directly and nonconceptually perceived by āryas' pristine wisdom of meditative equipoise. As an existent, emptiness can be directly known by a reliable cognizer.

Second, when a yogi is in meditative equipoise that realizes emptiness directly and nonconceptually, only emptiness appears to that mind. Conventional phenomena do not appear to that mind. This establishes this nonconceptual wisdom as a special mind, one that directly perceives things as they actually are. The false appearances of veiled truths do not appear to that mind; it perceives only reality.

Third, nonaffirming negations can establish an assertion. They don't just negate something; they can also establish other nonaffirming negations of the same type. In the case of the four statements of diamond slivers—phenomena do not arise from self, phenomena do not arise from [inherently existent] other, phenomena do not arise from both self and other, and phenomena do not arise causelessly—they together establish that arising does not exist inherently. And the fact that phenomena don't arise inherently means that they don't exist inherently. They are empty of inherent existence.

2 | Refutations Similar to Candrakīrti's Seven Points

Nāgārjuna's Four-Point and Five-Point Refutations

Candrakīrti lived several centuries after Nāgārjuna and was his indirect student. His seven-point refutation is based on Nāgārjuna's five-point analysis of how the Tathāgata exists. Although Nāgārjuna specifies the Tathāgata as the subject of our investigation to prevent us from grasping the Buddha as inherently existent, the five points can also apply to our self. He too investigates the relationship between the aggregates and the self in order to refute the inherent existence of the self. In his *Treatise on the Middle Way*, Nāgārjuna says (MMK 22.1):

> (1) Neither [one with] the aggregates, nor (2) different from the aggregates;
> (3) the aggregates are not [based on] him, (4) nor is he [based on] the aggregates.
> (5) The Tathāgata does not possess the aggregates.
> What is the Tathāgata?

Nāgārjuna uses a similar pattern in *Letter to a Friend* (*Suhṛllekha*, 49):

> It has been said that (1) the body is not the self,
> (2) the self is not the possessor of the body,
> (3) the self is not based on the body, and (4) the body is not based on a self.
> Like that, understand that the remaining four aggregates are empty too.

And in *Precious Garland*, he says (RA 82):

> The aggregates (1) are not the self, (2) nor are they based on the [self];
> (3) nor is the [self based on] the [aggregates]; (4) but without them, the [self] cannot exist.
> (5) The self and aggregates are not mixed like fire and fuel; therefore, how could the self exist?

The order of the points in these three verses is not the same. In addition, the verse in the *Treatise on the Middle Way* includes the point of the self being different from the aggregates, which is not explicitly found in the other two verses, and the verse in *Precious Garland* adds another point—that the self and the aggregates aren't mixed—that isn't present in the other verses. But the point being made in all three verses—that the person does not exist inherently—is the same.

Recall that we are analyzing how the person exists. Unlike a conventionally existent, dependent person, an inherently existent person would be self-instituting; it would exist in its own right without depending on any other factors whatsoever. But in these three verses, Nāgārjuna refutes every possible way an inherently existent person could be found. These options are also contained in Candrakīrti's sevenfold analysis discussed in the previous chapter.

- *The aggregates are not the self.* If the aggregates were the person, they would be identical in every way. In that case, the words "body" and "self" would refer to the same thing. Instead of saying the person is thinking, we could say the leg is thinking, and instead of saying the person is walking, we could say the mental factor of integrity is walking. We may say "I'm sick" when the body is sick and "I'm happy" when the aggregate of feeling is a happy feeling, but that is because the I is dependent on the aggregates, not because the I is the aggregates.
- *The self is not totally separate from the aggregates.* If the person and the aggregates were inherently separate, they would be unrelated and the person would not depend on the aggregates. In that case, the body could be in France and the person could be in India. When the body

aged, we couldn't say "I'm getting old," and when the mind is sleepy the person could be wide awake. In short, the self and the aggregates are related. The collection of the aggregates is the basis of designation of the person, and without the aggregates, a person could not exist.

- *The self doesn't possess any of the aggregates.* The person doesn't possess the aggregates the way we own a house, which is a case of the person and aggregates being different entities. The person also doesn't possess the aggregates in the way Joe possesses his head, which is a case of their being one nature. The two options of possession have the faults of the first two points—the person and an aggregate being either identical or totally unrelated.
- *The person is not the base of the aggregates.* That is, the aggregates aren't supported by or based on the self. If they were inherently based on the person, it would be like a bowl (the person) with fruit (the aggregates) inside. The person would be a distinct and independent container that the aggregates fill up. But the person and the aggregates do not exist independent of each other; one cannot be present without the other.
- *The aggregates are not the base of the person.* That is, the self is not inherently based on or supported by the aggregates. The analogy here is a lion in the jungle, which was discussed in the previous chapter. If the aggregates were the base of the self, the person and the aggregates would be distinct and unrelated, like a lion and the forest. However, conventionally the aggregates are the base of the person in that they are the basis of designation of the person. We recognize a person by perceiving one of their aggregates. When we see Tashi's form or hear his voice, we know he's nearby.

  For either of these two ways of support and supported to exist inherently, the person and the aggregates would have to be inherently unrelated and different. They would be totally distinct, like a table and an airplane. Since these two ways of dependence are untenable, the person and the aggregates are not inherently existent.
- *The self and the aggregates are not mixed.* Some people believe that the person and the aggregates are neither one nor different but have an inexpressible relationship like wood and the fire burning it. It seems that wood and fire are inseparable when the wood is burning. But if the person and the aggregates were inseparable like that, they would

> be inherently one, identical in all respects, and that has already been refuted. Alternatively, the wood would become the fire and they would have a cause-and-effect relationship. But if the person and aggregates existed in that way, they would be inherently different, just as a cause and its effect are different. Therefore the relationship of the aggregates and the person is not either of these.

Before contemplating the points in this refutation, first try to get a sense of what inherent existence would be if it existed. Things appear to us as inherently existent and we usually grasp them to exist that way. But it is difficult to identify what the inherent existence that is negated would be like—we are so used to apprehending things as inherently existent that we equate it with existence itself and do not regard it as a mistaken appearance. It's as if we were born wearing sunglasses: we're so used to our environment appearing dark that we don't even realize that the darkness is a false appearance. It is indeed challenging to identify the conceived or apprehended object of self-grasping ignorance and the view of a personal identity.

By frequently observing how things appear to your mind and how you grasp them to exist, you will gradually have a clearer and clearer idea of what inherent existence would be like. This is not an intellectual idea where we simply say the words "Oh, they appear independent and unrelated to all other factors," but a recognition of how much we believe that we are a solid, independent, truly existent entity. The innate grasping at such a person and at everything around us arises unbeknown to us every day. This view underlies all our other distorted conceptions and disturbing emotions. If we could abolish this root cause of our duḥkha by realizing that the object ignorance grasps as real doesn't exist at all, we could free ourselves from saṃsāra.

REFLECTION

How does the I exist? Contemplate:

1. If the I existed inherently, it would be a self-enclosed entity, independent of all other factors.

2. In that case, its relationship with the aggregates must be such that either

it is identically one and the same as the aggregates or completely unrelated to them. There is no room for dependent existence in an inherently existent world.

3. Then contemplate the points above to determine if it's possible for the I to exist inherently.
4. Reflect on the inconsistencies of saying the aggregates are the self.
5. Reflect why the I cannot be totally unrelated to the aggregates.
6. Reflect whether the I possesses the aggregates either in the way you possess a book or in the way you possess your hand.
7. See if the aggregates are the base of the self or if the self is the base of the aggregates.
8. Can the self and the aggregates be mixed like fuel and fire?
9. Because the above ways exhaust all possible options for inherent existence, conclude that the I cannot exist inherently.
10. When through deep and careful analysis and probing you conclude that inherent existence doesn't exist at all, let the mind rest in that emptiness of inherent existence.

In *A Debate between the Wisdom Realizing Selflessness and Self-Grasping*, Lobsang Chogyen expresses this understanding:[10]

> When, from observing the aggregates, you have a sense of I
> and, through a reliable cognizer, you ascertain
> this I not to be truly established as it seems,
> though it appears so to you,
> you have undermined [the grasping of inherent existence] that you
> otherwise could not.
>
> When you observe the aggregates and think "I am,"
> and a nonaffirming negation—
> the mere negation of a truly established [I]—

> is the apprehended object [of the cognition of selflessness],
> without losing the force of [this awareness], maintained with intense clarity
> and free of mental laxity and restlessness, you destroy the [grasping of] the objective existence of that I.
>
> When you have observed the aggregates
> and experienced "I don't exist!"
> and are skilled in sustaining a perception of the view,
> it counters the sense of a [fixated concrete] I,
> and you can evict [grasping] an I.
> But those [who have accomplished this] are as rare as a star in the daytime.

It is necessary to negate inherent existence on the aggregates as well as on the person because the I is designated in dependence on the aggregates. After negating inherent existence on the aggregates, instead of perceiving the I as inherently existent, practitioners apprehend its emptiness. This inferential understanding must be conjoined with serenity. Then when emptiness is perceived with the union of serenity and insight, this concentrated mind with intense clarity and free from laxity and restlessness can dismantle and overcome grasping the objective existence (*viṣaya siddhi*) of the I.

A person with this realization is as rare as a star in the daytime, so we must practice with joyous effort and fortitude, motivated by bodhicitta.

Similar Refutations in the Pāli Tradition

What kind of self does the Buddha negate in the early sūtras? The *Sutta of the Characteristics of Not-Self* (SN 22.59) says:

> The body is not-self. For if, bhikkhus, the body were self, this body would not lead to affliction, and it would be possible to have it of form: "Let my body be thus; let my body not be thus." But because the body is not-self, the body leads to affliction, and it is not possible to have it of the body: "Let my body be thus; let my body not be thus."

The Buddha went on to say the same of the aggregates of feeling, discrimination, miscellaneous factors, and consciousness. This statement indicates that if any of the aggregates were the self, the self would be able to control that aggregate. However, try as we may, we cannot make any of the aggregates conform to our wishes; they are under the influence of causes and conditions, not our will, and are subject to dysfunction. As such, the aggregates cannot be a self-sufficient substantially existent self that is the controller of the aggregates, nor can the aggregates be possessions of such a self.

In other passages, the Buddha negates the aggregates being a permanent, eternal, and blissful self. This is the common Indian view of the self as the innermost essence or soul of a person. The self or ātman is the transcendental Brahmān, eternal, conscious, irreducible, infinite, and blissful nature of all. Grasping such a permanent, eternal, continuously blissful self to exist is a wrong view as well as a source of suffering in that Brahmān is said to be truly existent, and like all grasping at a truly existent self or soul, it gives rise to afflictions.

The Buddha's disciple Bhikṣuṇī Dhammadinnā refutes the I as existing in any of the following ways in relation to the aggregates. When a layman asks her how the view of a personal identity comes to be, she replies (MN 44.7):

> An untaught ordinary person . . . regards (1) material form (the body) as self, or (2) self as possessed of material form, or (3) material form as in self, or (4) self as in material form.

Bhikṣuṇī Dhammadinnā then says the same about feeling, discriminations, miscellaneous factors, and consciousness. She does not explicitly say that the aggregates are not completely distinct from the self because she is speaking to a lay follower of the Buddha who already knows that a self distinct from the aggregates cannot exist. She goes on to say that the view of a personal identity does not come to be when an ārya does not regard any of the five aggregates in any of these ways. The Pāli tradition explains the four points in the quotation above:

1. Regarding the body as self is like regarding the flame of an oil-lamp as being identical to the color of that flame.

2. Regarding the self as possessing the body is like regarding a tree as possessing its shadow.
3. Regarding the body as being in the self (or dependent on the self) is like regarding the scent as being in the flower.
4. Regarding the self as being in the body (or dependent on the body) is like regarding a jewel in a box.

Regarding the first three, we may agree that a flame is not identical to its color, a tree does not possess its shadow, and the scent is not inside the flower. But regarding the fourth point, a jewel can be in a box. Since this last analogy is accurate, could the self be in the body? To understand the analogy, ask yourself if the relationship between the self and the body is like the relationship of a jewel in a box. A jewel is a phenomenon distinct from the box and can be removed from the box and looked at alone, without seeing the box. However, it is not possible to remove the self as an entity totally distinct from the body and look at it in its own right, divorced from the body, because the self is dependent upon the body. It is designated in dependence on the aggregates.

Grasping at these four views is where non-Buddhist wanderers go wrong. The wanderer Vacchagotta asks the Buddha (SN 44.8):

> What is the cause and reason why, when wanderers of other sects are asked such questions, they give such answers as: "The world is eternal" or "The world is not eternal"; or "The world is finite" or "The world is infinite"; or "The soul and body are the same" or "The soul is one thing, the body is another"; or "The Tathāgata exists after death" or "The Tathāgata does not exist after death"; or "The Tathāgata both exists and does not exist after death" or "The Tathāgata neither exists nor does not exist after death"? And what is the cause and reason why, when Master Gotama is asked such questions, he does not give such answers?

Here we see the range of wrong views propounded by spiritual seekers at the Buddha's time, all of whom were under the influence of grasping a view of self. The Buddha explains to Vacchagotta that the wanderers of other sects express those distorted and contradictory views because they regard (SN 44.8):

> . . . (1) form (the body) as the self, or (2) the self as possessing form, or (3) form as in the self, or (4) the self as in form. They regard feeling as the self . . . discrimination as the self . . . miscellaneous factors as the self . . . consciousness as the self, or the self as possessing consciousness, or consciousness as in the self, or the self as in consciousness.

Here the Buddha points out the wrong views of self that lead to expounding other wrong views about the world, the self, the aggregates, and even the Tathāgata. These twenty wrong views of self—four for each of the five aggregates—must be dismantled to see things as they are. The Buddha challenges us to investigate our own physical and mental aggregates to see if any of them can be the self or the object of possession of the self. Can any of the aggregates be found in the self or can the self be found in any of them?

Worldly people hold one or another view of self—that the self is either one of the aggregates or totally separate from the aggregates. But those who have eradicated the view of a personal identity no longer hold any erroneous view of self. They have abandoned the view of a self that exists in an impossible relationship with the five aggregates—a self that is identical with one of the aggregates, a self that possesses the aggregates, a self located within the aggregates, or a self that is the container in which the aggregates are located. Furthermore, they have abandoned the non-Buddhist assertion of an ātman, a self that is different from and unrelated to the aggregates.

These four positions, together with the self being different from the aggregates, are five positions that Nāgārjuna also asks us to investigate when refuting an inherently existent self.

Many people questioned the Buddha, asking whether, after the breakup of the aggregates, the Tathāgata exists, does not exist, both exists and does not exist, or neither exists nor does not exist. Each time the Buddha does not answer; he explains to people who are able to understand that the question is based on the view clinging to a real self. Because it is based on an incorrect understanding, such a question is impossible to answer. Meanwhile, he brings the questioner back to an essential point of the Dharma (SN 44.9):

> I declare, Vaccha, rebirth for one with fuel, not for one without fuel. Just as a fire burns with fuel, but not without fuel, so, Vaccha, I declare rebirth for one with fuel, not for one without fuel.

The fuel[11] causing rebirth is ignorance, which gives rise to the afflictions and the polluted karma they create. In another sūtra, the Buddha explains to Vacchagotta that when a fire ceases because its fuel is exhausted, the fire cannot be said to have gone in any particular direction. Similarly, when the fuel of ignorance and craving are exhausted, the aggregates do not reappear after an arhat or the Tathāgata passes away.

Does that mean that the Tathāgata no longer exists? Bhikṣu Yamaka holds a wrong view in which he claims that "a monastic whose pollutants are destroyed is annihilated and perishes with the breakup of the body and does not exist after death" (SN 22.85). He thinks the reason an arhat does not exist after death is because the five polluted aggregates have been discontinued due to the ceasing of the fuel of ignorance and craving.

Although at first glance that reason seems to make sense, the issue is deeper than this, as is seen by Śāriputra's response to Yamaka. Śāriputra does not talk about whether or not an arhat has aggregates. Rather he returns to the common theme of the aggregates being impermanent and selfless. Then he questions Yamaka if any of the aggregates is the Tathāgata, if the Tathāgata is in any of the aggregates, if the Tathāgata is apart from the aggregates, if the collection of the aggregates is the Tathāgata, or if the Tathāgata is without aggregates. Each time Yamaka replies no.

The same argument pertains to an ordinary being who takes rebirth. That is, whether discussing an ordinary being or an arhat, a living being or one who has passed away, the point is the same: Is there a real self? The confusion is not simply who or what is the Tathāgata after the breakup of the aggregates, it is also who or what is the Tathāgata while he is alive. Thinking that the Tathāgata is a real self while alive and that he becomes totally nonexistent after death is the view of nihilism. Let's examine Śāriputra's response in more depth.

First Śāriputra asks Yamaka whether each of the aggregates is permanent or impermanent, to which he replies "impermanent." Śāriputra then leads Yamaka to see that the aggregates are unsatisfactory and are not a real self. The commentary says that at this point Yamaka makes the breakthrough, sees nirvāṇa, and becomes a stream-enterer. Nevertheless Śāriputra continues questioning him so that Yamaka will show that he has relinquished his wrong view.

Śāriputra then asks: "Is the body the Tathāgata? Is feeling the Tathāgata? Is discrimination the Tathāgata? Are miscellaneous factors the Tathāgata? Is consciousness the Tathāgata?" Yamaka replies no to each question. None of the aggregates is the Tathāgata. Each aggregate is simply that aggregate, nothing more. There is nothing that constitutes a real self that is one and the same with any of the aggregates individually or with the collection of aggregates.

Śāriputra continues: "Is the Tathāgata in form? In feeling? In discrimination? In miscellaneous factors? In consciousness?" If we examine each aggregate individually, we will not find a real Tathāgata in it.

He carries on: "Is the Tathāgata separate or apart from the body, feelings, discriminations, miscellaneous factors, or consciousness?" Again Yamaka answers, "No, he is not." If the Tathāgata were separate from the aggregates, we would be able to identify him without any of his aggregates being present. In that case, the Tathāgata would be self-existent and independent.

Śāriputra persists: "Are all the aggregates taken together the Tathāgata?" Again the answer is no. If none of the aggregates individually is the Tathāgata, how could a collection of them be the Tathāgata? If an apple is not a pear, how could a collection of apples be a pear?

Lastly, Śāriputra questions: "Is the Tathāgata without form, feeling, discriminations, miscellaneous factors, and consciousness? Is the Tathāgata an absolute entity who exists in a way totally unlike every other being in that he does not depend on his aggregates?" No, the Tathāgata does not exist in this way.

This discussion about the Tathāgata in the Pāli canon foreshadows Nāgārjuna's refutation of an inherently existent Tathāgata, which we will examine in the following chapter. The point of Śāriputra's guiding Yamaka through this series of questions is this: If the Tathāgata cannot be found as either one with the aggregates or separate from them while he is alive, there is no real Tathāgata to begin with. In that case, there is no real Tathāgata who ceases to exist at the time of death. Śāriputra says (SN 22.85):

> . . . the instructed ariya disciple . . . does not regard form [and the other aggregates] as self, or self as possessing form, or form as in self, or self as in form.

He continues, saying that an instructed ārya disciple also does not regard feeling, discrimination, miscellaneous factors, or consciousness as self, or self as possessing the aggregates, or the aggregates as in self, or self as in the aggregates. Instead, this thoughtful disciple understands each aggregate as impermanent, as the nature of duḥkha, as not being a self. In this way, he does not become involved with the aggregates, bringing misery to himself. He does not cling to the aggregates, creating the cause of future duḥkha. He does not take a stand on the aggregates, saying they are my self. Thus he abides peacefully, without clinging and free from fear.

REFLECTION

The material in these chapters is rich for meditation. Take some time to investigate how you view your self. Then investigate if any of the aggregates are you.

1. Is it possible for your body or any other aggregate to be who you are?
2. Do you possess your body, your feelings, and so forth? If so, do you possess them like a person possesses a suitcase—as a separate thing? Is this an accurate description of how you and your body are related?
3. Or perhaps the aggregates are located inside of you. Is the self like a big bowl, with marbles (the aggregates) in it? Is that possible? Is the self like the frame of a jigsaw puzzle and the aggregates are like puzzle pieces that fill it in?
4. Are you inside the aggregates, like a deer wandering in a grove of trees?
5. Investigate these four possibilities and see if there is a findable, substantial self. If there isn't, who or what is the person you think you are?

Nāgārjuna based several of his reasonings on what the Buddha had taught in the Nikāyas/Āgamas. In addition to the Pāli sūtras mentioned above, there is the *Anurādha Sutta* (SN 22.86) that describes an encounter between some non-Buddhist mendicants and the Buddhist monk Anurādha. They asked him if he held the view that a tathāgata "exists after death, does not exist after death, both exists and does not exist after death, or neither exists nor does not exist after death." Anurādha replied that a tathāgata is described apart from these four options. Dissatisfied with this response, the wanderers left.

In general, the Tathāgata did not respond to questions such as these because they are based on the wrong premise that there is a findable self. They are metaphysical questions that have nothing to do with the practical task of cultivating wisdom and uprooting the causes of duḥkha. However, in this instance when Anurādha asked the Tathāgata how he should respond to such statements in the future, the Tathāgata asked Anurādha (SN 22.86):

> What do you think, Anurādha, do you regard form (the body) as the Tathāgata?—No, venerable sir.—Do you regard feeling . . . discrimination . . . miscellaneous factors . . . consciousness as the Tathāgata?—No, venerable sir.
>
> What do you think, Anurādha, do you regard the Tathāgata as form?—No, venerable sir.—Do you regard the Tathāgata as apart from form?—No, venerable sir.—Do you regard the Tathāgata as feeling? As apart from feeling? As discrimination? As apart from discrimination? As miscellaneous factors? As apart from miscellaneous factors? As consciousness? As apart from consciousness?—No, venerable sir.
>
> What do you think, Anurādha, do you regard form, feeling, discrimination, miscellaneous factors, and consciousness [taken together as a collection] as the Tathāgata?—No, venerable sir.
>
> What do you think, Anurādha, do you regard the Tathāgata as one who is without form, without feeling, without discrimination, without miscellaneous factors, without consciousness?—No, venerable sir.
>
> But, Anurādha, when the Tathāgata is not apprehended by you as real and actual here in this very life, is it fitting for you to declare . . . [that the Tathāgata] is described apart from these four options: The Tathāgata exists after death, the Tathāgata does not exist after death, the Tathāgata both exists and does not exist after death, or the Tathāgata neither exists nor does not exist after death?—No, venerable sir.

> Formerly, Anurādha, and also now, I make known just duḥkha and the cessation of dukkha.

At first glance, it appears that the Buddha replies in a practical way, as he often does to metaphysical questions. But something more is happening here because the Buddha first commented that Anurādha does not apprehend the Tathāgata as real and actual here in this life. That is, "the Tathāgata" is a mere conventional name that refers to (is designated in dependence on) a collection of impermanent aggregates that are considered unsatisfactory because they lack a permanent essence. This collection of aggregates exists while the Tathāgata is alive, and it ceases with his passing away. The Tathāgata is not real and actual while he is alive and certainly not after he passes away.

Other ancient sources for this effective analysis appear frequently in passages in the Pāli, Chinese, and Tibetan canons: In the Middle-Length Suttas, the Connected Suttas, and the Numerical Suttas (especially chapter 84) in the Pāli canon; in the Sarvāstivāda Connected Agamas, the *Mahāsāṃghika Ekottarāgama*, Mūlasarvāstivāda Vinaya, *Mahāvibhāṣā*, and *Jñānaprasthāna* (Vaibhāṣika Abhidharma) in the Chinese canon. It also appears after Nāgārjuna, when the twenty forms of the view of a personal identity are discussed in the Yogācāra treatises, the *Yogācārabhūmi* and *Compendium of Knowledge* (*Abhidharmasamuccaya*), as well as in Candrakīrti's *Clear Words* (*Prasannapadā*).

Although Bhikṣuṇī Vajirā and Bhikṣu Nāgasena applied this argument to other phenomena in addition to persons, the Pāli sūtras in general use it only to analyze the person. Nāgārjuna, however, extends the import of this reasoning to all phenomena so that it would lead to the realization of both the selflessness of persons and the selflessness of phenomena (MMK 22.16):

> Of what nature is the Tathāgata,
> of that nature is this world.
> The Tathāgata is without [inherent] nature,
> this world is without [inherent] nature.

Analysis of One and Many

The great Indian sage and abbot of Nālandā Monastery, Śāntarakṣita, synthesized the systems of Yogācāra, Madhyamaka, and Pramāṇa (logic and reasoning) in his text *The Ornament of the Middle Way* (*Madhyamakālaṃkāra*). He recommended that people adopt the Madhyamaka view of ultimate truth and the Yogācāra view of veiled truth, with an emphasis on reasoning. The analysis of one and many is the refutation that he emphasized to realize emptiness.

Another way of translating "one or different" is "one or many." Here "one" means a single thing, whereas "many" indicates plurality or many things. In *The Four Hundred*, Āryadeva examines a pot to see if it exists inherently by asking if it is one or many (CŚ 332):

> Because the pot is not separate
> from its characteristics, it is not one.
> If there is not a pot for each,
> plurality is not feasible.

Since a pot depends on its many characteristics—attributes such as hardness, color, smell, taste, shape, and so on—it is not inherently one thing. The pot's characteristics are its basis of designation, and the designated object and basis of designation are two things; they are not one and the same. Furthermore, the pot is not inherently one of those characteristics, because if it were, it would not have the other characteristics. If the pot were its color, it would not have a smell because its color isn't an odor. Nor can the pot abide in one of its characteristics, because if it did, none of the other characteristics would be related to the pot.

If a pot and the particles that compose it were a truly single entity, the pot itself couldn't be a single entity because it has parts that are different from each other. The pot can't be one thing and at the same time inherently possess many diverse components. The components are not the composite.

The pot also is not inherently many things, because each characteristic would then be a pot: the color would be a pot, the shape would be another pot, and so forth. If the pot existed in its many characteristics, there would be many pots. In that case, which pot would you make soup in? In addition, the pot would be in many places at once: the pot would simultaneously be on its surface, in its interior, in its color, and so forth. This would make cooking in a pot very difficult!

This argument concerns universals or generalities—a general category—and particulars—the specific things that make up that category. There is the generality "tree" that consists of all the various types of trees—oak trees, fruit trees, evergreen trees, and so on. Is that generality "tree" one thing? Is it many? If it existed inherently it would have to be one or the other in all circumstances.

And what about one of its particulars, evergreen trees? That is a generality in its own right. In that case, is it one or many? As a generality—a category—"evergreen trees" seems to be one thing. But it is composed of many different types of evergreen trees—fir, pine, big, small, and so forth—so how can it be inherently one thing? But if it were inherently many things, we couldn't speak of all the evergreen trees as a whole.

In addition, if the pot existed inherently, numerically it would have to be either one single object or a plurality made of many things. When we examine this, we find that the pot is neither inherently one nor inherently many. Āryadeva says (CŚ 344):

> When different things are examined,
> none of them have singleness.
> Because there is no singleness
> there is no plurality either.

A pot is not an inherently single thing because it has parts such as the top, the bottom, the handle, the lid, and so on. It also isn't inherently a plurality (many things), because if it isn't inherently one thing it can't be inherently many things, since "many" is a collection of single units. If there are no inherently existent single units, there can't be a collection of inherently existent single units to form a plurality.

Is a person's mindstream inherently one or many? Each person has only one mindstream, so isn't it a single entity? On the other hand, it is a continuum of individual moments of mind. Does that make it many? Without its individual moments, a mindstream cannot be found. But the moments are not the same—the mindstream today isn't the same as the mindstream tomorrow—so how can many different moments form something that is inherently one thing? The mindstream is not any of the individual moments, nor is it their collection, because a collection of non-mindstreams cannot become one inherently existent mindstream.

Some scientists seek to find the smallest particles that are the building blocks of the universe; they do so within the context of assuming such particles would be independently existent—that they would not depend on parts or on other factors, because if they did they could be further subdivided and would not be the smallest particles.

If such independent particles existed, each particle would have to be either inherently one thing or inherently many. Applying the argument above, it becomes clear that independently existing subatomic particles that are the building blocks of the universe cannot exist because they are neither inherently one nor many. They are not one thing because they have various attributes and they also have parts. A particle that lacks attributes and parts cannot be identified. They are not many because they are not a collection of inherently existent single units.

The refutation of one and many is also called the refutation of identity and difference (one and different). This centers on examining the relationship of an object and its parts, for example the relationship between the person and the aggregates. In Nāgārjuna's fourfold and fivefold refutations and Candrakīrti's sevenfold refutation, the four, five, or seven points are subsumed in two points: are the person and the aggregates inherently one or inherently different? If they are inherently one, they must be identical in every aspect; if they are inherently different, they are totally unrelated. When both of these possibilities are shown to be impossible, the conclusion is that the person does not inherently exist.

Bringing Analysis into Our Practice

In this chapter we touched on two of the arguments commonly used in the Sanskrit tradition to prove the emptiness of inherent existence. Using the example of the relationship of a car and its parts, we examined the relationship of the person and the aggregates according to Nāgārjuna's verses in *Treatise on the Middle Way*, *Letter to a Friend*, and *Precious Garland*. Then we employed Āryadeva's analysis of one and many from his *Four Hundred*, an analysis that Śāntarakṣita emphasized in his *Ornament of the Middle Way*. If you contemplate these arguments well and employ their reasonings in your meditation, they will impact your self-grasping.

The masters say that the most difficult part of this analysis is correctly identifying the object of negation. What does an inherently existent I created by ignorance look like? Although Buddhist texts say that the person exists by being merely designated in dependence on its basis of designation—the collection of the aggregates—the ignorant mind is not satisfied with that. Ignorance elaborates on this mere I, superimposing on it a kind of existence it doesn't have. In the case of the lower tenet systems, this superimposition is self-sufficient substantial existence; for the Prāsaṅgikas it is inherent existence. The appearance of inherent existence is so familiar to us that we easily believe it and grasp phenomena to exist that way. Our familiarity with both the appearance of inherent existence and the grasping of inherent existence interferes with recognizing the object of negation, the conceived object of the self-grasping of I. The danger when we attempt to meditate on emptiness is that if we don't properly identify what an inherently existent would be like, we may miss the target and negate either too little or too much.

To dismantle the false view of an inherently existent I, we must first correctly identify our notion of such an I—the I we are so sure exists. Being able to reject any objectified basis for such an I and remain in that mere negation with single-pointed concentration free from the impediments of laxity and restlessness will seriously undermine the power of self-grasping ignorance. To gain such realization, Buddhist masters recommend that after gaining the correct view, we go to a secluded place without a lot of hubbub and meditate, spending day and night observing our mind with its dependent yet empty nature.

As a result of many years of contemplation on emptiness, when you are able to integrate this analysis and relate it to your perception of the world and your own experience, it begins to loosen the tight grip of grasping at all persons and phenomena. When that happens, your understanding will begin to undermine any kind of gross emotional reactivity such as attachment, clinging, depression, and bitterness. Once you even temporarily experience freedom from afflictions' hold, you will be able to intuit that there is a real possibility to actualize true cessation, the enduring freedom from afflictions. In this way you will gradually develop genuine conviction that liberation and full awakening are possible. Then you will feel like Tsongkhapa did when he dedicated the merit of writing *Essence of Eloquence*:[12]

> One minute one swells with the joy of faith in the Victor;
> the next, one remembers the kindness of the champions [Nāgārjuna and Asaṅga].
> Other times one deeply reveres the expert spiritual mentors,
> one feels heartfelt love for suffering living beings,
> and one wishes for the long endurance of the precious doctrine—
> these feelings all increase as if in mutual competition.

3 | The Selflessness of Persons: Seven Points

TWO OF MY WESTERN FRIENDS were in retreat for several years, and during that time they made great effort to understand emptiness. I would suggest books for them to read, but in those years there were not as many books on emptiness as there are now. Most of the books they had access to were written by scholars for scholars, so it was often challenging for them to understand the teachings on emptiness. During a break in their long retreat, they came to see me. One of them told me she was disgruntled with having so much difficult material to read and said she would like to meditate more and study less. I told her the story of Asaṅga, who was already a bodhisattva on the third ground when his guru Maitreya told him to keep studying. She listened attentively, and at the end of our conversation I held up three fingers and said firmly, "third ground," to make sure she understood the importance of study. Nevertheless, she seemed relieved when I later told her that she didn't need to read all the books, but should continue to study the works of Nāgārjuna, Candrakīrti, and Tsongkhapa.

Over the years, by studying and reflecting on the meaning of emptiness, I have come to have a feeling for it. As a result, grasping, attachment, and so forth are not as strong as before, which makes a difference in my life. Having practiced the Dharma my whole life, I'm now hopeful to attain true cessation. I have the sense that I'm approaching the path of seeing; perhaps I am near, at the path of preparation. Progress on the path did not come about through lying on my bed, but through study and practice. But whatever stage I'm at, I still must practice. This is not a time to become complacent.

The more you progress through the stages of the path, the more you'll be able to benefit sentient beings. Try to dedicate yourself to benefit others through bodhicitta even when you dream. When people focus so much on themselves and are selfishly motivated, they become narrow-minded. Turning your mind to think of others' well-being will help overcome depression.

I (Chodron) would like to share a story here. At one of the early Mind and Life conferences I attended, the topic of low self-esteem came up and His Holiness was shocked at how many of the scientists and others who had excelled in their fields thought poorly about themselves. He thought this may be a Western phenomenon, since Tibetans didn't seem to have such negative opinions about themselves. The conference participants brainstormed several reasons ranging from culture to religion to family, but the reasons were external factors; we didn't mention incorrect or self-centered ways of thinking.

In His Holiness's teachings for months and years after that, he continually mentioned compassion as a way to overcome low self-esteem and by extension the depression that arises from it. I was perplexed because usually in the West people say that we have to love ourselves before we can have compassion for others. So why was His Holiness emphasizing compassion for others instead of love for ourselves?

I contemplated this for a long time, and then I understood: Compassion turns our mind outward, toward others, eliminating the self-focus that is often so detrimental. Compassion opens our heart and we connect with others in a beautiful, caring way. That attitude itself makes our mind happy and lightens depression. Cultivating a compassionate attitude, we connect with others, and this makes us feel good about ourselves. We realize that we can have a positive effect on others' lives, that we have goodness inside ourselves that can make a positive difference when we share it with others. Without effort, we then feel worthwhile, self-criticism fades away, and our self-esteem rises.

Daily meditation on compassion and analytical meditation on emptiness make a very strong imprint in our mind, and this familiarity in the form of imprints builds up, leading to realizations. As a result of continuous practice, if you have deeper experiences in daily meditation, these may continue in the dream state by the force of imprints on the mind.

Candrakīrti's seven-point reasoning that negates the self of persons is the topic of this chapter. Learning it well and meditating on it frequently will establish imprints in your mind, and as time goes on this will reduce your attachment, anger, and confusion.

Introduction to the Seven-Point Reasoning

Authors of treatises and commentaries base their teachings and writings on the texts and teachings of the sages that came before them. As we saw in the previous chapter, Candrakīrti's sevenfold analysis is based on Bhikṣuṇī Vajirā's retort to Māra's interference, the dialogue of King Menander and the arhat Nāgasena, and Nāgārjuna's fivefold analysis in *Treatise on the Middle Way.*

Having become familiar with the seven-point analysis by examining the relationship between the car and its parts, we'll now use that method to investigate whether the person exists inherently by examining the relationship between a person and his or her "parts," the aggregates. This meditation is of crucial importance because grasping the I to exist inherently is the first of the twelve links of dependent origination that perpetuates rebirth in saṃsāra. Furthermore, on a daily basis grasping a real Me continuously raises its ugly head, overwhelming our discerning awareness of how things actually are, bringing us duḥkha here and now, and propelling us to act in ways that cause suffering to others. Our life is founded on the presumption of a concrete, truly existent self, whose happiness and suffering become all-consuming. Everyone and everything around us is seen in terms of how it affects Me. Seeing life through the tiny periscope of I and mine, we judge everyone and everything in terms of whether they further or interfere with My happiness. This view of life is extremely limiting and causes us to feel alienated from others and alone in the universe. Realizing that such grasping is erroneous and dismantling it opens the door to understanding people and things as they actually are—empty of inherent existence and utterly dependent—and leads us to freedom.

The seven points examine how the person exists. If a person existed inherently, it would have to be in one of the seven ways. We then check if the person exists in any of these ways. When finding that this is not possible, we can safely conclude that the person does not exist inherently and release our grasping at the false appearance that it does.

Two points are important to remember in this examination: First, if a person existed inherently, there are limiting conditions to how it must exist. For example, whereas a conventionally existent person is dependent on the aggregates, an inherently existent person cannot be. This is because an inherently existent person is independent of all other factors. Second, when our examination turns up no evidence that the person exists inherently, this disproves the inherent existence of the person; it does not negate a conventionally existent person, who does exist.

Before examining the seven points individually, let's recall Candrakīrti's pivotal verse that lists them (MMA 6.151):

> A chariot cannot be said to be different from its parts;
> it is not identical with its parts, nor does it possess the parts;
> it is not [based on] the parts, nor are the parts [based on] it;
> it is not the mere collection [of its parts], nor is it [their] shape.
> [The self and the aggregates are similar.]

Is the Person One and the Same as the Aggregates?

Nāgārjuna and Candrakīrti identify four drawbacks that arise if the I is one and the same as the aggregates: (1) asserting a self would be redundant, (2) either the person would be many or the aggregates would be one, (3) agent and object would be the same, and (4) the person would inherently arise and disintegrate. Let's examine these one by one.

1. Asserting a self would be redundant

Nāgārjuna says (MMK 27.5):

> If, apart from the appropriated [aggregates],
> it is held that there is no self,
> [and if] the appropriated [aggregates] themselves are the self,
> your [purported] self does not exist.

If the self were one with the aggregates, it would be exactly the same in name and meaning. In that case, positing a person would not be necessary. In fact, it would be superfluous because the words "mind," "body," or "aggregates" could be used instead of the word "I," since they would be one and the same.

If the I were inherently one with the mind, instead of saying "I'm walking," we would say "Mind is walking" when the person is walking. If the I were inherently the same as the body, we would say "Body is thinking" when the person is thinking.

Conventionally, the aggregates and the I are one nature. But if things existed inherently, their mode of appearance and mode of existence would be the same. If this were the case, since the I and the aggregates appear to be one nature, they would be inherently one nature. In that case, they would be completely identical in all respects. To whatever mind they appeared, the aggregates and the I would appear totally the same, without being different in any way. Our body would appear to be thinking when the person is thinking, and the mind would appear to be skipping when the person skips. Seeing the absurd consequences that would follow if the I and the aggregates were inherently one, we dismiss that possibility. Instead, we understand that the mode of appearance (how things appear to exist) and their mode of existence (how they actually exist) do not agree. The person and the aggregates appear to exist inherently, independent of all other factors, when in fact they exist dependently.

2. The person would be many or the aggregates would be one

Candrakīrti remarks (MMA 6.127ab):

> If the aggregates were the self, then since
> there are many aggregates, the self would also be many.

If the self and the aggregates were the same, since there are five aggregates, there would also be five selves. Conversely, since there is only one self, there would be only one aggregate. In this case, all of our mental aggregates and our body would be one. Clearly none of these alternatives is viable.

3. Agent and object would be the same

It is said that at the time of death, the person grasps for another set of aggregates and is reborn. This indicates there is an agent or appropriator—the person—and an object or the appropriated—the aggregates. In English it sounds strange to say "He took this body," because we imagine a person sitting in space trying to decide which body to be born in. This is not what happens. Rather, the expression "He took this body" is simply a conventional way of speaking that indicates a constantly changing mindstream continuing on to the next life. If the person were one with the aggregates, they would be identical and no difference would exist between agent and object—between the person who is appropriating another set of aggregates and the aggregates that are being taken. Nāgārjuna tells us (MMK 10.1ab, 10.15abc):

> If fuel were fire,
> then agent and object would be one. . . .
> The entire process is explained
> for the self and the appropriated aggregates
> using fire and wood as analogies.

If wood were fire, agent and object would be the same, in which case how could the fire burn the wood? Similarly, we regard the person as the part-possessor and the aggregates as the parts that are possessed. We say "I have a body" and think of the person as the owner of the body, which is owned. But if the person and any of the aggregates were one and the same, this distinction could not be made, and saying "my body" would be the same as saying "I."

4. The person would inherently arise and disintegrate

Nāgārjuna comments (MMK 18.1ab):

> If the aggregates were the self,
> the self would [inherently] arise and cease.

The conventional self arises and ceases; we are born and we die. Here the word "inherently" is inferred. In that case, the consequence of the aggregates and the I being one is that the I would inherently arise and disintegrate. Is that possible?

Anything that inherently exists would be independent of causes and conditions. Whatever is independent of causes and conditions is permanent and does not change moment by moment. A person who did not change moment by moment would be fixed and static. Once one moment of that person ceased, the person would be permanently gone, and the next moment of the person would arise without cause. There would be no continuity between one moment of the person and the next; this new moment of self would be totally unrelated to the previous moment. In short, there would be no connection between the various moments of the continuum of a person if the self were to arise and disintegrate inherently.

To explain this in more depth, the consecutive moments of the body would be unrelated because each moment of the body would exist independent of the other moments and independent of any other factors such as causes. Thus Dechen's one-month-old body, two-year-old body, sixteen-year-old body, forty-five-year-old body, and seventy-year-old body would not be parts of the same continuum of her body; they would be unrelated to each other. In that case, the self associated with each body would be disconnected from the self associated with all the other moments of the body in her continuum. The self associated with her seventy-year-old body could not think, "When I was sixteen years old . . . ," because just as there would be no continuity between the sixteen-year-old body and the seventy-year-old body, there would be no continuity between the sixteen-year-old person and the seventy-year-old person.

In the same way, each consecutive moment of consciousness would be unrelated to its previous and subsequent moments. This would make learning impossible because when each moment of consciousness ceased, its knowledge would also cease, and a new moment that had none of the previous knowledge would arise. Similarly, the self associated with each moment would also be unrelated, so there would be no accumulation of knowledge, wisdom, or compassion as we aged.

However, our innate or natural sense of self perceives ourselves as a continuum, even though we sometimes have difficulties imagining ourselves as an infant or a hundred-year-old. When we are old we remember events that happened in our youth. We think, "When I was young, I did this and that." Although we may be elderly when we remember the event, we feel there is a continuity of self so that it is us who experienced that event. In other words, there is a natural sense of self that connects the various moments of the continuum. This sense of self connects the I that was young and the I that is older. But if each moment of the self were completely unrelated to other moments, we wouldn't have this sense of a self that spans time. Instead there would be totally different selves at different times in our life because there are very different bodies and mental states at different times in our life.

Many centuries before Candrakīrti, King Menander and Bhikṣu Nāgasena conversed on this topic. The king asked if the person who is born remains the same or becomes another person. Nāgasena replied neither and then asked the king if he is the same person now as the newborn he once was. When the king replied that he was a different person, Nāgasena challenged him, "If you are not that child, it would follow that you had neither mother nor father, nor teacher. You could not have been taught either learning, or behavior, or wisdom. . . . Is the mother of the baby a different person from the mother of the grown-up man? Is the person who goes to school one, and when he has finished his schooling another?"

Puzzled, the king asked Nāgasena for his idea. Bhikṣu Nāgasena said he is not the same person now as when he was a baby and gave the example of a lamp burning through the entire night. Is the flame burning at the beginning of the night the same flame as at the end? No. Is there one lamp early in the night and another in the middle of the night, and yet another at end of the night? No.

Nāgasena continues, "Just so, O king, is the continuity of a person or a thing maintained. One comes into being, another passes away; and the rebirth is, as it were, simultaneous. Thus neither as the same nor as another does a person go on to the last phase of his self-awareness. . . . It is like milk, which when taken from the cow, after some time turns first into curds, and then from curds into butter, and then from butter into ghee. Now, would it be right to say that the milk was the same thing as the curds, or the butter, or the ghee?" No, replied the king.

Nāgasena explains, "Just so, O king, is the continuity of a person or thing maintained. One comes into being, another passes away; and the rebirth is, as it were, simultaneous. Thus neither as the same nor as another does a person go on to the last phase of his self-awareness."

In other words, if the I were inherently one with the aggregates, just as the aggregates arise and cease, so would the I. In that case, what would be the relationship between one moment of I and other moments of that same person? In the context of inherent existence, if the I of this life, the I of the previous life, and the I of the future life were inherently one, then those three selves would be one and the same, indivisible. That can't be because we clearly see that people change and that the three I's occur at different times. But if those three selves were inherently distinct, they would be totally unrelated and disconnected.

What would be the consequences if each moment of the I were unrelated to and independent of the preceding and subsequent moments of I? (a) Recalling events from previous lives would be impossible, (b) actions that we did would not bring results, and (c) we could experience the results of actions we did not do.

However, upon investigation we discover that their opposites are true: Recalling events from previous lives is possible, our actions bear results, and we experience the results of our own actions, not the actions of others. This can occur only if each moment of the continuum of a person is connected to its previous and later moments. Let's examine these three more closely.

a. *Recalling events from previous lives is possible: the general I and specific I's*

If each moment of the I were unrelated to the preceding and subsequent instances of I in the same continuum, recalling events from previous lives would be impossible. Why? One moment of the self would not be the cause of the next moment, so each moment of the self would arise without a cause and would cease without producing an effect, such as a subsequent moment of the self. There would be no connection between one moment of the person and the next, or between one life and the next. In that case, you would be unable to remember what happened to you yesterday and making plans for what you will do tomorrow would be useless, because the selves of yesterday, today, and tomorrow would be totally unrelated.

In the *Descent into Lanka Sūtra*, the Buddha stated, "In that life, I was King Māndhātṛ." If the Buddha and King Māndhātṛ were totally distinct and unrelated persons, there would be no connection between them, and the Buddha could not remember events from that previous birth.

If the Buddha and King Māndhātṛ were inherently the same, then a buddha and a sentient being would be the same; but one person cannot be both an ordinary being and an ārya buddha at the same time. This brings up some questions: Are the Buddha and King Māndhātṛ the same person? Are we the same person as we were in our previous life? When a tulku, the reincarnation of teacher, is recognized, is the child the same person as the teacher in his previous life?

If the I of a previous life were inherently the same person as the I of the present life, they should have exactly the same personalities and the same body. But they don't; they have different sets of aggregates. If we were the same person in each lifetime, then since we've been born in all six realms of existence, all six persons—hell being, hungry ghost, animal, human being, demigod, and deva (celestial being)—would be one person. The human being we are today would also be the animals and devas we were a few lives ago. In the case of identifying tulkus (the next birth of a well-respected Buddhist teacher or yogi), if the previous teacher and the current child were one and the same, they would have the same personality, but this is not the case. The thirteenth Dalai Lama was known to be rather stern, while I'm cheerful.

On the other hand, if our former and later selves were inherently distinct, there would be no relationship between the person of one life and the person of the next. It could not be said, "Tsultrim has been reborn as a deva," because the human being Tsultrim of one life and the deva of the next life would be totally unrelated, like a rock and a towel. In addition, if the former and later selves were disparate, it would not be necessary for the former person to have died for the later person to be born.

Many faults like these ensue if we assert inherent existence. This forces us to investigate our conceptions about how the person exists. If we are the same person in both lives, there would be a permanent self that goes from one life to the next. Personal growth and development would be impossible.

We may think that the person is superficially impermanent, but on a deeper level, there is an unchanging self that is intrinsically "me" that continues after death. This would mean that the person has two contradictory attributes—it is both permanent and impermanent. But this is also impossible.

On the other hand, if the selves of the previous and the later lives were inherently different, karma could not function. Actions done in one life would not affect future lives. Tendencies cultivated in one life could not influence the next life.

If we abandon the notion of an ultimately existent I and look at conventional existence, we often use the words "person" or "I" in a general sense, in a way that includes all rebirths of a single mental continuum. This general I is a "part-possessor," and its parts or instances include the I's of each life.

The general I covers all these instances of I, which are called "specific I's" in one person's continuum. When the Buddha said, "I was King Māndhātṛ in the past," he was referring to the I in general that exists in all rebirths of that continuum and goes on to awakening.

A specific I is imputed in dependence on the aggregates of a particular life. In one continuum, one specific I is Gayle in one lifetime and another specific I is Tashi in another lifetime. Neither Gayle nor Tashi is the general I; after Gayle dies Gayle no longer exists, although the general I that she was an instance of continues. After that continuum is reborn as Tashi, Tashi is the specific I of that new life.

The specific I can also refer to the I of a particular day. There's today's I, yesterday's I, and tomorrow's I. In this way, it is acceptable to say "I'm different than when I was a child" because the child's I ceased and the adult I exists now. The senior citizen I will exist in the future. These specific I's are different because we aren't exactly the same person in those three periods of our life. But they aren't inherently different, because one I arises in dependence on the previous I. They are related to each other because the child I is the cause of the adult I.

In the meditation on all sentient beings having been our mother, the focus is on our general sense of I and the general sense of the I of others. Although only one sentient being is the mother of our specific I of this life, all sentient beings have at one time or another been the mother of other specific I's in the same continuum as our present I. When saying that they were our mothers in the past, we do not mean that their specific I of this life was our mother, but that another specific I in the same continuum was. The specific I's in the same continuum are all parts of that general I.

The general I is impermanent; it changes over many lifetimes. A specific I in that continuum—let's say the I of this life—is also impermanent; it changes moment by moment in this life. This life's I is a specific I in relation to the general I designated in dependence on the entire continuum. This life's I is also a general I in relation to its parts—this morning's I, this afternoon's I, and this evening's I. Even within one day, we change; the person of this morning is not the same as the person of this afternoon.

If we hold that all the specific I's in one continuum are inherently one, we fall to the extreme of absolutism. In that case, the person could not change moment by moment and would be permanent. If we hold that all the specific

I's in one continuum are inherently separate, we fall to the extreme of nihilism because they would be totally unrelated. The Buddha in the *Descent into Lanka Sūtra* says (LC 3.291–2):

> Do you think that the person in that lifetime was someone else?
> Do not look at it that way.

Here the Buddha emphasizes that the person in the previous life and the person in the present life, although different instances of the same general I, are not inherently different; they are related in that the I of the previous life is the cause of the I of the present life. The previous and later I's are both imputed in relation to the same mental continuum that changes in every moment. Both I's are parts of the same continuum of I in a general sense. When we say, "I remember this and that," it refers to the general I.

If the specific I's in one continuum were inherently disparate, as soon as one specific I died, the continuum of the person would cease. There would be no rebirth.

The five-year-old I and twenty-year-old I are not the same nature, because to be the same nature, two things must exist at the same time at least at some point. However, the younger and older I's are different, and they have the relationship of cause and effect; the younger I is a cause of the older I. These two I's are part of the same continuum, each being a part of the same general I that spans from beginningless time to buddhahood and beyond. The specific I of one life is not the same as the specific I of another life in the same continuum. Nāgārjuna clarifies this (MMK 27.3):

> "I was born in the past"
> is an untenable claim.
> It is not this very person
> who was born in those earlier lives.

I (Chodron) believe that understanding this can help people suffering from guilt, self-hatred, and depression due to a destructive action they did in the past. Their grasping an inherently existent I is strong, and they incorrectly believe that they are the same person as the one who did that harmful action years ago. If they understood that their present self is not the exact same person who inflicted harm on another being in the past, they could see that they have changed. The person they are today regrets those actions, so they can forgive themselves. They could extend compassion and forgiveness for the person they used to be because they know how confused that person was and how much pain they were in that they thought harming someone else would relieve their misery.

Still, because the present I and the I at the time of that action are parts of the same continuum, the person needs to purify the karma created so their future self does not experience the suffering result of the past action.

Similarly, people who were severely abused as children or who suffer from wartime post-traumatic stress disorder may suffer from flashbacks and feel that they are the same person who experienced the initial trauma. That view interferes with healing. However, if they understood that there is no permanent or inherently existent person, they could see that the tragedy occurred to the specific self that existed at the time of the event but that neither that specific self nor the traumatic event exist now. Knowing that who they are now is not the same as the confused child or distressed soldier would help them on the path to healing.

Since the self lacks inherent existence, it can change. Various instances of the I arise and pass away. The self can function, performing actions and experiencing events precisely because it exists only nominally and lacks a findable intrinsic essence. We can say "I did that destructive action" but not hate ourselves for it because we know we are no longer the exact same person who did it. We have grown and are more mature now. We can regret, reveal, and purify our previous destructive actions, because we know that a future nominally existent I in the same continuum will experience the result of those actions in the future.

To summarize the important points regarding the specific I's and general I that pertain to one continuum: The basis of designation of the general I is the aggregates of the person in general. The self that is the observed object of the view of a personal identity is the mere I. It exists now and will exist without cessation in the future, even though the view of a personal identity that incorrectly grasps it will be eliminated on the path to buddhahood. The person who transmigrates in the three realms is the general I that covers all the different times in the continuity of that person.

When it's said that the person creates karma and the person experiences the result, this refers to the general I of a continuum. The continuum of the person exists at the time of creating the karma and at the time of experiencing the result. Another way to express this is a specific I of one life in a continuum creates the karma and another specific I in a later lifetime of that continuum experiences the result. This is possible because both specific I's are instances of the same continuum. When we say "I will become a buddha in the future," or "I must have created a lot of merit in my previous lives to have a precious human life now," we are referring to the general I, which pervades all specific I's of that continuum.

At death, the self of this life disappears; it does not go to the next life, nor does it go to buddhahood. The person who comes from previous lives and goes on to buddhahood is the general I. The specific I that exists only in this life is the maturation of karma; it is a deva, asura, human, animal, hungry ghost, or hell being. This specific I ends with the exhaustion of the maturation karma that caused that particular rebirth or when an untimely karma ripens, bringing an early death to that specific I.

b. *Our actions bring results*

Second, if the self arises and disintegrates inherently so that there is no continuity of the I from moment to moment, our actions would not bring results. Some people think that the person exists inherently and the existence of this independent self enables us to experience the results of actions we did in the past, either earlier in this life or in previous lives. However, this would be impossible if the self existed inherently, because each moment of an inherently existent I is not related to its preceding or subsequent moments in a continuum. In that case, when a person who created a particular karma died, either the result of that karma would never be experienced or an unrelated person would arise who experiences the result. In short, the law of karma and its effects could not operate and our actions would be wasted.

Even within this life, we see that actions bring results and do not go to waste. Take, for example, a Western child who grows up in India and learns to speak Hindi. As an adolescent, she returns to her own country and forgets Hindi. Yet, some years later, upon returning to India, she finds she can speak it easily, while her friend, who has never learned Hindi, cannot. The child who learned Hindi is not the same person as the adult who speaks it, nor is she totally different and unrelated. Yet the adult experiences the result of what the child learned.

This example is similar to a person creating a constructive or destructive action in one lifetime and experiencing its result in another due to the continuum of the general I in the two lifetimes. The functioning of the law of karma and its effects involves the general I. The specific I that creates the cause and the specific I that experiences the result in a later lifetime are neither inherently the same nor inherently different. They exist as parts of the same continuum, which is nominally called the general I.

c. *We experience the results of our own actions, not the actions of others*

Third, if the self arose and disintegrated inherently, we would experience the results of actions we didn't create. As explained above, an inherently existent person cannot be part of the continuum that is the general I. If that were the case, the system of karmic cause and effect would be thrown into chaos, such that we could experience the karmic results of another person, who was not part of our continuum. If inherently existent Jim created the cause to be born in the human realm, after he died, he could experience the result of an action created by a person who is not in his continuum.

Even in this life, if the child Harry and adult Harry exist inherently, they would be unrelated. An unrelated person, Susan, learned to speak Spanish as a child, but Harry didn't. Still the adult Harry could speak Spanish because the child Susan learned that language. The child Harry and the child Susan would be equally unrelated to the adult Harry who could experience the results of karma created by either child or by any other person for that matter, because they are all equally unrelated to the adult Harry.

Our daily experiences show that cause and effect operate in a systematic way. If Carol takes medicine, she will be well in the future. It is not the case that Carol takes the medicine and Sam gets well. Sometimes when we're pressed for time, we wish another person could sleep for us so that we would feel refreshed, but it doesn't work that way! Sleeping, like practicing the Dharma, has to be done by ourselves in order for us to receive the resulting benefit.

In addition, if earlier and later moments of the self were inherently different, the later self could arise without the former one ceasing. Dekyi could be born before her previous life as Tashi died, and Tashi would still exist even after he had been reborn as Dekyi. Nāgārjuna confirms (MMK 27.10–11):

> If this self were [inherently] different from that of an earlier life,
> it would arise even without the other having existed.
> Likewise, that earlier self could remain there in that life;
> without that self dying, this self could be born.
>
> There would be absurd consequences
> such as the severing of the continuum, the wasting of actions,
> and each person experiencing the effects
> of actions performed by others.

If former and later moments of the same continuum are unrelated—that is, earlier moments are not the cause of later moments—the absurd conclusions we just examined arise: recalling past lives would be impossible because the continuum of the person would be severed, karmic causes would not produce their results, and we could experience the results of actions we did not perform.

The important point is that things that are inherently different cannot be parts of the same continuum because they would be disconnected. Things that are inherently one cannot be part of the same continuum because all the different moments of the continuum would be completely the same, occurring at the exact same time. If the person you were in your previous life and the person you are now were inherently one, you would be identical in all ways, but that is impossible. Your previous I and the present I are parts of the same continuum. They are different—you are not the same person you were in your previous life—but they are not inherently different. They are related: the previous I is the cause of your present self. Because they are related as cause and result, your previous I must cease for the person you are now to be born. A cause and its result cannot exist simultaneously.

If the previous self and the later self were inherently different, they would be completely independent of each other. Existing under its own power, each self would not depend on causes to come into existence and would be permanent. Since this contradicts what we know to be true, the I cannot exist inherently.

Nevertheless, we do exist conventionally and relatively. Thus a person later in that continuum experiences the results of the actions of former persons in that continuum and can remember the lives of those former persons if he possesses the mental clarity and concentration necessary to do so. The former and later selves are specific selves of individual lifetimes. In dependence upon these, the general self is designated and we say, "I remember" or "I'm experiencing the result of what I did before." There is a constantly changing stream of conditioned aggregates, and depending on how we conceive and impute them, we speak of the specific self of a previous or later life or the self in general. In this constantly changing continuum of a person, nothing exists under its own power with its own inherent findable essence.

Examining the Mental Consciousness and the Clear-Light Mind in Particular

Several Buddhist tenet systems mistakenly identify the mental consciousness as being the self. If it were, which mental consciousness would be the person? First examine the various moments of the mental consciousness to see if any of them is a person. Is the mental consciousness of yesterday the person? The mental consciousness of today? Of tomorrow? If it is the mental consciousness of today, is it the mental consciousness in the morning? Afternoon? Evening? The mental consciousness is momentary, never remaining the same in the next instant; the present moment is difficult to pinpoint. We may snap our fingers and say, "This moment is the present moment," but that moment has already ceased. Even if we could freeze that particular moment and make it a permanent present moment, it would still have a beginning portion, a middle portion, and a later portion. Part of that moment of mind could have already ceased and be the past, while another part of that moment of mind has yet to arise and is the future. Even the middle portion of a moment has a beginning, middle, and later portions.

It isn't possible to pinpoint one moment of mind that is the real present mental consciousness. On the other hand, if all the moments of mental consciousness together were the person, there would be many selves. Because that is the situation, it isn't possible that the mental consciousness is the person either conventionally or ultimately.

Next examine if any of the various mental states could be the person. Is the self the consciousness in the waking state? Or is it the dream consciousness, which is more subtle? Or is the self the mind of deep sleep, an even subtler state of consciousness? In this way, examine each succeeding state of ever more subtle consciousness until you arrive at the subtlest clear-light mind. Is this the real I? Is that who you really are?

But considering the clear-light mind to be the self is also problematic. First, there are times when the clear-light mind is manifest and times when it is dormant. However, the self is always present, so these two cannot be one and the same. In addition, we say, "My clear-light mind," indicating a person that is the possessor and the clear-light mind that is the possessed object. In this case, the person and the clear-light mind would be two different things.

If the person were inherently existent, it would have to be either inherently identical or inherently different from the clear-light mind. These two options have already been refuted in the example of the chariot.

Furthermore, if the clear-light mind were an inherently existent person, then the specific self of this life would continue to the next life because the continuity of the clear-light mind is present in the next life. But that too is untenable. The *Guhyasamāja Tantra* explains the sequence of arising and dissolution of the subtle and gross levels of consciousness. The clear-light mind of death arises only after the cessation of the earlier three moments—the white appearance, red increase, and black near attainment. After the clear-light mind of death, the person of the previous life has ceased and the person of a new life arises. The continuity of consciousness goes on into the next life but the person of this life does not. There is no soul or permanent self that connects one life to the next. In my case, Tenzin Gyatso will no longer exist after the clear-light of death of this life has ceased. A new person—the one of my future life—will be present instead.

Such are some of the difficulties that arise if we equate the body, the mind, or the collection of mental and physical aggregates with the person. Although these reasonings may be unfamiliar and even seem strange to us initially, if we reflect on them repeatedly, we will come to understand them, and they will dispel our wrong views. How you see yourself will be more realistic, and your enthusiasm to create virtuous causes now will increase. In addition, the quality of your virtue will become more refined and purer.

REFLECTION

To summarize, the self and the aggregates are not inherently the same because of the following reasons. Slowly reflect on each reason, making examples that demonstrate its infeasibility.

1. Asserting a self would be unnecessary.
2. Either the self would be many or the aggregates would be one.
3. The appropriated aggregates and appropriator (the I) would be the same.
4. Recalling events from past lives would be impossible.
5. Our actions would not produce results.
6. We could experience the results of actions we did not do.

Is the Person Inherently Different from the Aggregates?

We are investigating how the I exists. If it existed inherently, it should be findable, either as one with the aggregates that are its basis of designation or as totally separate from the aggregates. After the above investigation, it's clear that the self isn't one and the same as the aggregates either conventionally or ultimately.

On the conventional level, the self and the aggregates are different. They have different names and appear differently to the conceptual mind. Are they inherently different? The addition of the qualification "inherently" changes the context because such a self would be independent of all other factors such as causes and conditions and parts. It would not be related to the aggregates in any way whatsoever.

If the self were inherently different from the aggregates, various faults would arise. First, the self and the aggregates would not have the same characteristics. Nāgārjuna says (MMK 18.1cd):

> If it [the self] were different from the aggregates,
> it would not have the characteristics of the aggregates.

If the self and the aggregates had different characteristics, many of the conventions we take for granted would be incoherent. For example, we could not say "I am male/female" in dependence on our body because the I could be one gender and the body another. Nor could we say "I am young/old" or "I am short/tall," because the I and the body would not have similar characteristics. The body could die without the person dying, or the person could die and the body continue to live. Our body could be sick, but we would be well. Similarly, the person could be permanent and unchanging, but her mind, perceptions, thoughts, and emotions could change. This contradicts our daily experiences. For example, we say "I'm not feeling well" when our body is ill and "He's more mature" when a person's thoughts have changed over the years. This shows we know the self and the aggregates are related.

Furthermore, if the self and the aggregates were inherently different, they could be apprehended separately. In that case, we could see a person's body without seeing her. Or a person's body and mind could be in one place while that person was in a different place. We could say that Margaret is here without her body being present or that Margaret is meditating when her mind is daydreaming. Clearly this is not so. To say we see a person, we must apprehend some part of her aggregates. Nāgārjuna ponders (MMK 27.7):

> It is not feasible that the self
> be other than the appropriated [aggregates].
> If it were other, it could be apprehended
> without the aggregates, whereas it is not.

Do the Self and the Aggregates Exist Inherently in Any Other Way?

The other five ways of the self and aggregates existing—the self inherently being the support of the aggregates, the aggregates inherently being the support of the self, the self inherently possessing the aggregates, the collection of the aggregates being the self, and the arrangement of the aggregates being the self—can be subsumed in the first two alternatives—the self and the aggregates being either inherently identical or inherently different. The other alternatives were explored in depth in chapter 6 of the *Supplement* where Candrakīrti investigates the relationship between the self and the aggregates, which is similar to the relationship of the car and its parts. The points regarding the two ways of support and supported are cases of the self and the aggregates being inherently different, and the points regarding the collection and the arrangement of the parts are cases of the self and the aggregates being inherently one.

The point of possession has two possibilities: if the self inherently possesses the aggregates like a person possesses a table, they would be inherently different, whereas if the self inherently possesses the aggregates like a person possesses her hand, they would be inherently one.

It is tempting to think the collection of aggregates is the person. However, since the self appropriates the collection of aggregates, they cannot be the same, otherwise the appropriator (the I) and appropriated (the collection of aggregates) would be identical. This cannot be, for agent and object are different. In addition, the collection of aggregates cannot be the person because the collection of aggregates is the basis of designation of the self, and the self is the designated object.

Furthermore, since each of the individual aggregates is not the self, how could the collection of aggregates be the self? A group of things, each of which is not a person, cannot be a person. For example, an orange is not an apple, so a collection of oranges is also not an apple.

Likewise, since the collection of the aggregates isn't the self, the continuum of the aggregates cannot be the self. The continuum is also a collection—the collection of moments of the aggregates. Also, the continuum is a basis of designation of the self, so it cannot be the self.

Furthermore, of the five aggregates, only the body has shape. If the self were the shape of the aggregates, it would not have mental aggregates at all because mental aggregates don't have shape.

When we use analytical wisdom to search how the I exists, we come to understand that the inherently existent self, me, and I—which we have consistently assumed are so real—become untenable. This I that we strongly feel exists objectively and in its own right becomes questionable. When we analyze and try to find something that possesses existence in its own right, we come to a point of being completely perplexed. Previously the existence of a findable I was not in dispute. Now, when we search for exactly who I am, an identifiable self is not to be found.

The Tathāgata Is Empty Yet Exists

It is tempting to refute the inherent existence of seeds and sprouts and undesirable situations, but to accept that the Tathāgata—the Buddha, our object of refuge who has eliminated all defilements and actualized all excellent qualities—does not exist from his own side is more difficult. After all, the Tathāgata is no longer subject to the twelve links of dependent origination, and his pristine wisdom of emptiness realizes emptiness like water mixed with water. Shouldn't someone like that be beyond the vagaries of dependent existence and exist in his own right? Nāgārjuna points out that if we subject the Tathāgata to critical analysis and search for the essence of the Awakened One and the true referent for the name "the Tathāgata," it cannot be found. He explains (MMK 22.1):

> Neither [one with] the aggregates, nor different from the aggregates;
> the aggregates are not [based on] him, nor is he [based on] the aggregates.
> The Tathāgata does not possess the aggregates.
> What is the Tathāgata?

Even the Tathāgata, whom we revere as supreme among all beings, is empty of inherent existence. When we search for exactly who the Tathāgata is, we cannot pinpoint anything specific. The Tathāgata is not found either in his aggregates or totally distinct from them.

If he were inherently one with the aggregates, asserting a self would be redundant: there would be either one aggregate or many selves, the agent and the object would be the same, and he would inherently arise and disintegrate. In the latter case, recalling events from previous lives would be impossible, his actions would not bring results, and he could experience the results of actions done by others.

If he were inherently distinct from his aggregates, the Buddha could exist separate from his body and mind. But like all beings, the Buddha has five aggregates, although his are purified and are not under the control of afflictions and polluted karma. The Buddha is designated in dependence on his body and mind—the purified aggregates of the enjoyment body and emanation bodies—and does not exist separate from them.

The aggregates are not [based on] him means that the aggregates are not inherently supported by the Tathāgata; *he is not based on the aggregates* means he is not inherently supported by the aggregates. These two possibilities were disproved in the previous chapter. Similarly, the Tathāgata doesn't possess the aggregates like a person possesses either a dog or his nose. This too was disproven in chapter 2. Not existing in any of these ways, the Tathāgata does not exist independent of his aggregates or as identical with them. Rather, he depends on his causes (the collections of merit and wisdom), his parts (the purified aggregates), and the mind that conceives and designates "Tathāgata." The Tathāgata is merely designated in dependence on the aggregates. He lacks ultimate existence and exists only nominally, dependently.

Nāgārjuna continues (MMK 22.2):

> If the Buddha depended on the aggregates,
> he would not exist through an [inherent] nature (*svabhāva*).
> How could something that does not exist with its own [inherent] nature
> exist through the nature of another (his aggregates)?

Dependent existence and inherent existence are contradictory. The Tathāgata, who is designated in dependence on the aggregates that are his basis of designation, lacks any inherent existence and has no inherent nature. Since this is the case, the basis of designation—the unpolluted aggregates of the Tathāgata—must also be empty of inherent existence. Nāgārjuna continues (MMK 22.3):

> Whatever is dependent on the nature of another,
> its selfhood is not tenable.
> How could that which lacks selfhood
> be a tathāgata?

Whatever phenomenon it may be, if its identity can be posited in dependence on other factors, it cannot exist with its own inherent nature or selfhood. Since the Tathāgata is designated in dependence on his aggregates, he too is devoid of inherent nature. If the Tathāgata was a self-enclosed entity that existed under its own power, what need would there be to identify him in dependence on other factors, such as his form body and truth body? It would be possible to point to his inherent nature to identify him. However, no inherent nature or essence can be found in the Tathāgata. Given that there is not an independent self, how could the inherently existent Tathāgata exist?

Although the Tathāgata has abandoned defiled aggregates such as those of sentient beings, his five purified aggregates exist. These are free from the pollutants of ignorance and afflictions, their seeds and latencies, and all polluted karma. Such pure aggregates are the basis of designation of the name "Tathāgata." It is by means of being merely designated in dependence on these purified aggregates that the Tathāgata exists.

There are only two possible ways something could exist—dependently or independently. These two are mutually exclusive and directly contradictory. There is not a third option. Since the Tathāgata is dependently designated in relation to other factors such as the purified aggregates, he cannot exist independently with an inherent nature. Thus even our objects of refuge and the goals of our practice—liberation and full awakening—lack inherent nature. Nāgārjuna declares (MMK 22.15):

> Those who develop elaborations with regard to the Buddha—
> the unextinguished one who has gone beyond all elaborations—
> and are impaired by those cognitive elaborations,
> fail to see the Tathāgata.

The Tathāgata is called the "unextinguished one" because he has not ceased to exist upon attaining nonabiding nirvāṇa. This contradicts the assertions of the Vaibhāṣikas and Sautrāntikas who claim the Tathāgata inherently exists. As a result of that belief, they assert that when his polluted body ceases at the time of parinirvāṇa, the continuity of the Tathāgata also ceases, with nothing remaining. However, the five aggregates that are free from two obscurations arise, and the Tathāgata is designated in dependence on them. There is no counterforce that can extinguish the continuity of the pure aggregates, so the Tathāgata continues to exist, working for the welfare of all sentient beings for as long as space endures.

Those who conceive the Tathāgata to exist inherently are obscured by the elaborations of inherent existence—self-grasping ignorance. Unable to realize profound emptiness, they fail to see the Tathāgata as he actually is. The quality that makes him the Tathāgata is nonabiding nirvāṇa—the purified aspect of the emptiness of the mind that is forever free from all obscurations. Nonabiding nirvāṇa is the actual Tathāgata. Someone who has not understood profound emptiness cannot fathom nonabiding nirvāṇa and is unable to understand the Tathāgata. These people also fail to actualize in their own mindstreams the Tathāgata's pristine wisdom that is able to perceive the two truths simultaneously. The Buddha said in the *Diamond Cutter Sūtra* (*Vajracchedikā Sūtra*, OR 450):

> Whoever sees me as material form
> and those who know me as sound—
> who discard me through distortions—
> such people do not see me.
>
> The buddhas should be seen as reality,
> and the guides should be seen as the truth body (*dharmakāya*).
> Reality is not an object of [dualistic] wisdom;
> it is impossible to comprehend it [as it is].

While grasping notions of true existence, it is impossible to comprehend the Buddha's wisdom, which lies beyond the conceptual ability of ordinary beings. Here *dharmakāya* means reality seen as it actually is. Having the nature of lacking objective existence and existing by mere imputation is not unique to buddhas. This is also the nature of sentient beings, although at present sentient beings—which includes arhats and high-level bodhisattvas—do not fully realize this. Nāgārjuna says (MMK 22.16):

> Of what nature is the Tathāgata,
> of that nature is this world.
> The Tathāgata is without [inherent] nature,
> this world is without [inherent] nature.

A beautiful passage from the *Ratnākara Sūtra* (OR 296) illustrates that the Buddha lacks any inherent nature and yet is able to liberate sentient beings from saṃsāra and lead them to nirvāṇa, which both lack inherent existence.

> All phenomena are presented as selfless.
> Through guiding sentient beings, the world is liberated.
> He himself is liberated from transmigration and transmigrators are liberated;
> though he has passed beyond, he has not crossed over.
>
> The Great Sage has passed beyond saṃsāra;
> that which has passed beyond is not found.
> Neither the other shore nor this shore exists;
> "gone beyond" is also said to be mere words.
>
> He who expresses words does not exist;
> the words that are expressed do not exist;
> they to whom they are expressed are also not found;
> he who knows this also does not exist.
>
> Through being wrongly conceived by the power of attachment,
> all transmigrators wander here.
> Whoever sees the peaceful Dharma
> sees the self-originated Tathāgata.
>
> The peaceful supreme Dharma is understood;
> obtaining bliss, beings are satisfied.
> Having conquered the afflictions, he is victorious;
> having become victorious, he does not endure.
>
> Thus, the Victor's awakening is realized;
> having achieved awakening, he awakens transmigrators.

In the verses above, "not exist" means does not inherently exist. Why do sūtras and sages often omit that word so that it sounds like they are saying someone or something does not exist at all? Since we sentient beings tend more toward the extreme of absolutism than the extreme of nihilism, saying "does not exist" jars us and wakes us up so that we investigate the difference between non-inherent existence and nonexistence as well as the difference between inherent existence and existence.

Looking again at Nāgārjuna's verse at the beginning of this section, substitute I for "Tathāgata" so the verse reads:

> Neither [one with] the aggregates, nor different from the aggregates;
> the aggregates are not [based on] me, nor am I [based on] the aggregates.
> I do not possess the aggregates.
> What am I?

Remember to begin with identifying the object of negation of I-grasping, the inherently existent I that you believe you are. That I appears separate from the physical and mental aggregates, yet mixed in with them. The innate grasping of self is strongly felt when we are in danger and think, "I'm going to die." That mind doesn't innately grasp the body or the mind as I. At that time, self-grasping is not grasping or conceiving the I or any of the aggregates as being inherently identical (one) or inherently separate (different). To conceive sameness and difference, the mind has to be involved in making these distinctions, and it is not doing that at that time. It's just grasping the I to exist inherently. That is, you're not thinking that your body or mind will be injured, you're only thinking "I'm going to die." The I that appears at that time is the object of negation. It appears very clearly because there is strong grasping to it.

There are many degrees of strength of the self-grasping of I, ranging from weak to strong. When someone is extremely happy and excited—for example, if they win a gold medal in the Olympics—self-grasping is very strong then and the I that is the object of negation appears very clearly.

If an inherently existent I existed, its relationship with the physical and mental aggregates would have to be either that of inherently one or inherently different. When both of these possibilities have been disproved, any basis for assuming a self that exists in its own right is undermined, and the emptiness of true existence of the self is realized.

REFLECTION

To investigate how the I exists as explained in the verse immediately above:

1. Identify the I that is the object of negation of I-grasping as explained immediately above..
2. Ascertain that if the I that you cherish, cling to, and seek to protect exists inherently, it would have to be either one with the aggregates or inherently different from them.
3. Investigate as explained in the last two chapters if the I is either of these.
4. Investigate if the I exists in any other way: Are the aggregates the base of the I or is the I the base of the aggregates? Do you possess the aggregates in either of the two ways?
5. Sit with the question "What am I?" and when you can't find anything that is the real, independent you, rest the mind in emptiness.

4 | The Person Is Not the Six Elements

WE SPEAK ABOUT *my* body, speech, and mind, but who is the I that possesses them? The I appears to exist in and of itself, as if it had a core identity. But when we investigate, we can't pinpoint who or what is the self. The self exists, but not inherently. Similarly, our body, speech, and mind exist, but not inherently.

The mantra *oṃ svabhāva śuddhāḥ sarva dharmāḥ svabhāva śuddho 'haṃ* is recited before dissolving into emptiness in tantric sādhanas. It means *all phenomena by nature are pure; by nature I am pure. All phenomena* refers particularly to the aggregates, which are pure by nature in that they have always been and will always be empty of inherent existence. Likewise, the I who is meditating is empty.

Nāgārjuna: How Is the Self Related to the Six Elements?

Another way in which Nāgārjuna disproves the inherent existence of the person is by showing that the self is neither inherently one with nor different from the six elements that compose the person—earth, water, fire, wind, space, and consciousness. While refuting the person's inherent existence, he also establishes the person's conventional existence. In addition, he indicates the six elements are also empty. In the *Precious Garland* Nāgārjuna says (RA 80–82):

> A person is not earth, not water,
> not fire, not wind, not space,

not consciousness, and not all of them [together].
What person is there other than these?

Just as a person is not real
because of being a composite of six elements,
so each of the elements also is not real
because of being a composite.

The aggregates are not the self, nor are they based on the [self];
nor is the [self based on] the [aggregates]; but without them the [self] cannot exist.
The self and aggregates are not mixed like fire and fuel.
Therefore how could the self exist?

This analysis is in terms of a being with a body in the desire realm. The body is composed of the physical elements of earth, water, fire, wind, and space, the latter being the vacuity within the body. The sixth element is consciousness. Together these six constitute a person and are the basis of designation of the person. Usually it is said that the five aggregates are the basis of designation of the person, but claiming these six elements as the basis of designation of the person is not contradictory. The first five elements—earth, water, fire, wind, and space—comprise the first aggregate, the body. The body's solidity is the earth element, its cohesiveness is the water element, its heat is the fire element, and its motility is the air element. The space inside bodily cavities—in the stomach, intestines, and so on—is the space element. The sixth element, consciousness, consists of the four mental aggregates—feelings, discriminations, miscellaneous factors, and consciousnesses.

The self is not any of these six elements individually nor is it the collection of them. By negating the self being the consciousness, Nāgārjuna discredits the position of some Buddhist schools that identify the mental consciousness or the continuity of consciousness as the self.

Nāgārjuna makes the point that the person cannot be any of the aggregates that are its basis of designation. The basis of designation (the six elements) cannot be the designated object (the I). There is nothing whatsoever in or about the elements that is a person. In that case, what person is there? This implies that the person cannot be found independent of the aggregates either, thus negating the view of non-Buddhist schools that postulate the person is independent of the aggregates and of a different nature than the aggregates.

When meditating on emptiness, we search to see if the person inherently exists. If a person existed inherently, it would have to have certain characteristics. We then investigate to see if the person has those characteristics or not by examining if the person who comes and goes, who reads and eats, who experiences happiness and pain, is inherently the elements individually or is their collection, or if it exists separately from them.

Although an inherently existent person is an object of negation in the meditation on the emptiness of the person, and the first step in meditating on emptiness is to identify the object of negation, we can't realize an inherently existent person with a reliable cognizer because it does not exist. Rather, we think of what such a person would be like if it did exist and hold a conceptual appearance of an inherently existent person in our mind. Such a person would be totally independent of causes and conditions, parts, or any other factors, including name and conceptuality. Then we investigate whether the person actually exists like that or not. The person isn't any one of these elements, nor is it the collection of them. Separate from these six elements, no person can be identified. What person is there other than these? These few lines have tremendous meaning; understanding them requires deep contemplation.

Nāgārjuna does not immediately conclude that the person does not exist. In the second verse he says that the person depends on the composite of the six elements. Using the reason that the person is dependent on the collection of elements, Nāgārjuna then concludes that the person is empty of independent or true existence. This can be expressed in the form of a syllogism: "Consider a person; it does not inherently exist because it depends on the collection of six elements."

Negating the person being either one with or totally separate from the aggregates avoids the extreme of absolutism. Identifying the person as being merely designated in dependence on the collection of the six elements avoids the extreme of nihilism. The person exists and depends on its parts, even though it is not its parts and cannot be found among them. The only way a person could exist is by being merely designated in dependence on its basis of designation. Although nothing can ultimately be identified as the person, the person exists nominally. This is the true meaning of the Middle Way, free from both extremes of absolutism (inherent existence) and nihilism (total nonexistence).

Whereas the first two lines of the second verse establish the selflessness of persons, the last two lines establish the selflessness of phenomena. Just as the person does not truly exist because it depends on its parts—the six elements—each element does not truly exist because it depends on its parts. Just as the person exists by being merely imputed in dependence on its basis of designation—the six elements—each element exists by being merely imputed in dependence on its basis of designation—the collections of its parts or attributes.

For example, the earth element doesn't inherently exist because it depends on the collection of its parts. The earth element cannot be found in any of its parts individually, in the collection of its parts as a whole, in the continuity of its parts, or separate from the collection of its parts. What other earth element could there be? The only other reasonable alternative is that it exists by being merely imputed in dependence on the collection of its parts that is its basis of designation. This argument can be applied to the other elements and to all other objects as well. Once we understand this reasoning well in terms of one thing, we can easily apply it to others.

In the third verse, Nāgārjuna returns to the selflessness of the person by analyzing the person in relation to its parts, the aggregates. The aggregates are not the same as the person; the person is not separate from the aggregates, which it would have to be if either the aggregates were the base of the person or the person were the base of the aggregates. But without the aggregates, the person does not exist, so the person and the aggregates must be related, but not inherently related. Furthermore, the person does not inherently possess the aggregates.

Furthermore, the person and the aggregates are not related in an ambiguous, inexpressible way—for example, saying fuel and fire have an inexpressible relationship because when fuel burns, it is indistinguishable from fire. In the realm of inherent existence, two things must be either inherently one or inherently different; there is no other inexpressible choice. The fire arises by depending on its substantial cause, the fuel. It is not the fuel nor is it unrelated to the fuel. By weaving dependent arising in with this refutation of inherent existence, Nāgārjuna illustrates the compatibility of emptiness and dependent arising.

Phenomena Are Empty but Exist Nominally

The third verse has great meaning. Although neither the person nor other phenomena such as the aggregates have the slightest inherent existence, they are posited by nominal convention and exist conventionally. Nāgārjuna asks in *Sixty Stanzas of Reasoning* (YK 37):

> Since the buddhas have stated that
> the world is conditioned by ignorance,
> why isn't it reasonable to assert that
> this world is [a result of] conceptualization?

Conceptualization has different meanings depending on the context. Here it means grasping true existence. The world is conditioned by true-grasping ignorance in that we, our environment, and the sentient beings in it arise in dependence on ignorance, the first of the twelve links of dependent origination. The first link, ignorance, gives rise to other afflictions, which lead to creating the second link, formative actions or karma. When craving and clinging nourish the seeds of this polluted karma, it ripens in our taking rebirth in saṃsāra.[13]

The world and other sentient beings appear to us to exist inherently and we appear to ourselves to exist that way as well. In addition to their appearing to exist inherently, we ignorantly assent to that appearance and grasp them as inherently existent.

However, persons and phenomena do not exist the way they appear, for they are dependent. Dependent existence precludes independent or inherent existence. When we realize that the conceived object of self-grasping ignorance (inherently existent persons and phenomena) does not exist, we realize that the person and other phenomena such as the aggregates do not inherently exist. However, the mere person and mere phenomena, which are the observed object of both self-grasping and reliable cognizers, exist nominally, as mere name, by mere concept.

Refuting the inherent existence of an object does not negate the nominal or conventional existence of that object. Phenomena could exist in only two ways: either inherently (ultimately) or nominally (conventionally). When inherently existent objects are refuted, dependent objects that exist as mere name and convention are implied. Since things lack existence from their own side and do not have their own essence, the only possible way they could exist is by mere dependent designation. This is the essential meaning of the Middle Way. Because it is difficult to understand, this important point is repeated often.

In general, understanding that phenomena exist by being merely designated does not arise automatically from understanding emptiness. Rather, prior to having an inferential reliable cognizer of emptiness, you must contemplate many reasonings that disprove inherent existence. One of these reasonings is dependent arising, which not only refutes inherent existence but also establishes dependent existence. Of the various levels of dependency, dependence on being merely designated by term and concept is the most subtle, so it is helpful to start familiarizing yourself with this early on. Later, after you have familiarized yourself with emptiness by means of an inferential cognizer that realizes emptiness, because you have repeatedly contemplated existence by mere name and concept in the past, after arising from meditative equipoise on emptiness, emptiness will dawn as the meaning of dependent arising. That is, while your mind is still informed by the previous meditation on emptiness, when you turn your mind to other objects an awareness that they are dependent designations will automatically arise. Then when going about your daily activities, you will know that phenomena are like illusions in that they appear to exist inherently although they do not.

After you realize emptiness, the ease with which you are able to realize that all phenomena exist as mere designations depends on the extent to which you have contemplated this topic beforehand. This is why spiritual mentors encourage you to "plant the seeds of realizations" by studying particular topics and doing certain practices now. Those seeds will ripen later when your mind is more mature in the Dharma.

The Middle Way harmony of emptiness and dependent arising is subtle, and except for the Prāsaṅgikas, proponents of the lower systems—including masters like Bhāvaviveka—do not understand that phenomena can be empty of inherent existence and still exist conventionally as mere name, mere convention. But when we deeply understand dependent arising, we can't find any type of existence apart from dependent designation. Knowing that phenomena are dependent, we will not reject emptiness; knowing that they arise through being merely designated, we will not reject conventional existence. Although it requires much contemplation on our part in order to understand this, it is the key to freedom from saṃsāra and its duḥkha.

If something exists by mere conceptual designation, it exists; if it does not exist by mere conceptual designation, it does not exist. However, this doesn't mean that whatever is conceptually designated exists. I heard that there is a tale in the West called "The Emperor's New Clothes." Although the entire populace—except for one little boy—was talked into thinking that the emperor was wearing splendid new clothes when he was actually naked, their saying this didn't make it so, as the young boy pointed out. We can conceptualize many things such as our enemy's many bad qualities and evil actions, when actually there was a misunderstanding that can be rectified by an open-minded discussion.

All existents are merely designated by term and concept. There is no other way for them to exist, since existence from their own side is impossible. A young child in Amdo was designated the Dalai Lama in 1939 or 1940. Aside from that conceptual designation, there is nothing in these aggregates that is the Dalai Lama.

When the physical and mental aggregates appear, we conceive a person and designate "I." In fact there is nothing within the aggregates that is Me or I, let alone being inherently Me or I. One aggregate is not the person; the collection of the five aggregates is not the person. No part of an aggregate is the person; the continuity of the aggregates is not the person. If we search apart from the aggregates, we cannot find the I. Look as we may, there is no I to be found. The I is merely imputed by conception. In the same way, all phenomena exist by being merely designated by thought.

REFLECTION

1. Consider that the world is conditioned by true-grasping ignorance in that we, our environment, and the sentient beings in it arise in dependence on ignorance, the first of the twelve links of dependent origination.

2. Consider that ignorance apprehends persons and phenomena to exist independent of all other factors, whereas in fact they depend on causes and conditions, their parts, and being designated by term and concept.

3. They are empty of independent or inherent existence, but they still exist dependently.

Pāli Tradition: The Six Elements Are Not the Self

The roots of many of Nāgārjuna's arguments in his *Treatise on the Middle Way* lie in the sūtras of the eighteen early schools. So it is not surprising that the above argument regarding the six elements not being the self is also found in the Pāli canon. Nāgārjuna was familiar with the early sūtras that were commonly studied at his time, and he often expanded on their reasoning.

The Pāli sūtra the *Exposition of the Elements* says (MN 140.8):

> This person consists of six elements. So it was said. And with reference to what was this said? There are the earth element, the water element, the fire element, the wind element, the space element, and the consciousness element.

In explaining this passage, the *Commentary on the Majjhima Nikāya* says (MN 1346 n1268):

> Here the Buddha expounds the reducibly-found by way of the irreducibly-found.[14] The elements are reducibly-found, but the person is not irreducibly-found. This is meant: "That which you perceive as a person consists of six elements. Ultimately there is no person here. 'Person' is a mere concept."

Here what is "irreducibly-existent" is contrasted with what is conceived. According to the Pāli Abhidharma, the six elements are real phenomena and irreducibly exist, whereas conventional things, such as the person, exist due to conceptualization. The elements are fundamental properties of phenomena; they exist apart from mental conceptualization, and in that sense they actually exist. The elements can be discovered on their own, in contrast to things that are mentally constructed through conceptualization. Being fundamental properties does not mean that the six elements are not dependent. Rather it means that they are natural elements of which other things can be composed. The six elements are dependent, conditioned, and impermanent. The person is imputed or conceived dependent on the six elements.

In this way, the commentary expounds the imputedly-existent person by way of discussing the irreducibly-existent elements that comprise the person. Ultimately there is no person because when searched for, a person cannot be found. Only the six impersonal elements are there, and there is nothing about any of them that is a person or is personal. The earth, water, fire, and wind elements are the properties of solidity, cohesion, heat, and mobility. The internal space element is the unoccupied space in the body: the nostrils, the auditory canal, the space in the mouth, in the esophagus, and inside the intestines and colon. The external space element is any unoccupied space. Proper wisdom sees these five physical elements as "this is not mine; this I am not; this is not my self." In this way insight into the material aspects of our existence is cultivated, and we become disenchanted with these elements and dispassionate toward them.

The sixth element, consciousness, consists of the six consciousnesses—visual, auditory, olfactory, gustatory, tactile, and mental—as well as feelings, discriminations, and all mental factors in the aggregate of miscellaneous factors. Although we may believe that the consciousness is the I, it too is impersonal. When we examine any of the six consciousnesses or the mental factors, no person can be found among them. There is nothing in fleeting thoughts, feelings, or emotions that is an enduring self. Feelings and thoughts are dependent on many factors; they cannot be an independent self. There is a continuous flow of dependently arisen mental events from one moment to the next without there being a self that holds them together to become an individual person.

Because it is easy to consider consciousness with its thoughts, feelings, moods, and opinions to be the person, it is worthwhile to examine this notion more closely. The Buddha clearly states that consciousness is not the self. In the *Greater Sutta on the Destruction of Craving*, he calls Bhikṣu Sāti and questions him about his wrong view that the consciousness is the self. The following dialogue ensues (MN 38.5):

> (The Buddha): Sāti, is it true that the following pernicious view has arisen in you: As I understand the Dhamma taught by the Blessed One, it is this same consciousness that runs and wanders through the round of rebirths, not another?
>
> (Sāti): Exactly so, Venerable Sir. As I understand the Dhamma taught by the Blessed One, it is this same consciousness that runs and wanders through the round of rebirths, not another.
>
> (The Buddha): What is that consciousness, Sāti?
>
> (Sāti): Venerable Sir, it is that which speaks and feels and experiences here and there the result of good and bad actions.
>
> (The Buddha): Misguided man, to whom have you ever known me to teach the Dhamma in that way? Misguided man, have I not stated in many discourses consciousness to be dependently arisen, since without a condition there is no origination of consciousness?

Sāti's view is that consciousness exists in and of itself, independent of conditions. Saying the self is that which speaks shows the I as an agent of the action of speaking. Saying the self feels is the notion that the I is a passive subject that experiences. "Here and there" indicates the self as a transmigrator that remains unchanging as it passes through many rebirths. This consciousness or self goes from life to life, creating karma and experiencing its results, but not being transformed or changing in the process. It has an unchanging identity that remains the same as it experiences one event after another and goes from one life to the next. In short, Sāti views the consciousness as an *ātman* or Self.

The commentary explains that Sāti was an expert in the *Jātaka Tales*, in which the Buddha recounts his previous lives, saying, "At that time, I was King Goodness the Great" or "During that life I was the deer." Sāti apparently misunderstood the Buddha's conventional usage of the word "I" and thought there is an unchanging consciousness or self that continues from life to life.

To guide him away from this wrong and dangerous view, the Buddha begins by explaining that there are six consciousnesses. In doing so, he discusses the specific types of consciousness, indicating that consciousness has parts and is not an abstraction, such as a universal, all-pervading cosmic consciousness. Rather than talk with fanciful conceptions about an ethereal consciousness, the Buddha speaks about the consciousnesses that are our experience.

The Buddha proceeds to explain the dependent arising of consciousness in three different ways. First is the conditionality[15] of consciousness—consciousness arises as a result of the coming together of a sense faculty, an object, and an immediate condition, which is the previous moment of consciousness. All six types of consciousness have the same function: to cognize and know objects. They are differentiated and designated according to the sense faculties through which the act of knowing takes place. As discussed previously, the eye, ear, nose, tongue, and tactile sense faculties are a subtle type of matter, invisible to the eye and located within the gross physical organs.[16] They have the capacity to respond to particular types of sense data: the eye faculty connects with colors, the ear faculty with sounds, and so forth. Each faculty produces its own distinct consciousness: the visual consciousness, auditory consciousness, and so forth. The mental sense faculty differs from the others in that it has a broader range of objects that include those perceptible to the other five senses. Although the visual consciousness sees only colors and is activated only by the eye faculty, the mental consciousness knows a greater number of phenomena and has the capacity to plan, imagine, remember, and think about them. The mental consciousness is activated by the mental faculty.[17]

Each consciousness is dependent upon its particular conditions. The Buddha gives the example of a fire that burns logs being called a log-fire and a fire that burns straw is a straw-fire. When the logs are consumed, the log-fire ceases, and when the straw is exhausted, the straw-fire ceases. One fire does not become the other. By saying this, the Buddha emphasizes that each sense consciousness is distinguished individually according to its object and sense faculty. For example, a consciousness arising dependent on the eye sense faculty and visual forms is called the visual consciousness. Since consciousness does not go from one sense to the other in this life, it is even more mistaken to think of it transmigrating unchanged from one life to another.

Furthermore, the mental aggregates of each life arise in dependence on their particular conditions. There are many types of consciousness and all of them are impermanent. Thinking that there is one, unchanging consciousness that transmigrates from one life to another is incorrect.

The second way that the Buddha explained the dependent nature of consciousness is by pointing out that although conscious experience appears to be one unitary thing, in fact it is composed of different mind-moments. What appears to us as one experience—for example, the knowing of the color yellow—is in fact a series of very brief mind-moments that are arising and passing away extremely rapidly. An experience can be dissected logically, separating it into smaller moments that together compose the whole. But with deep mindfulness and strong concentration, each individual mind-moment can be vividly experienced in meditation. It is said that millions of mind-moments occur during the duration of a flash of lightning or a finger snap. Along with each moment of consciousness comes a group of associated mental factors that are also in momentary flux. The objects of the sense consciousnesses also undergo extremely rapid change, arising and passing away in each moment. What appears to be one state of consciousness or one material object is in fact a series of different moments arising and ceasing.

What makes these different moments of consciousness into a continuum instead of disconnected, chaotic events that make no sense? This leads to the third way in which consciousness is dependent. Each moment of consciousness is conditioned by its preceding moment and in turn conditions the subsequent moment. Even though each moment or act of consciousness is distinct, there is continuity and consistency because each moment arises dependent on its preceding moment of consciousness and influences its subsequent moment of consciousness. In short, three factors condition an act of consciousness: its sense faculty, object, and the preceding moment of consciousness, which is the immediate condition.

The same process of one mind-moment conditioning the next occurs at the time of death as well. According to the Pāli Abhidhamma system, a passive stream of subliminal consciousness called the *bhavaṅga* exists on all occasions when a clearly cognizing consciousness is not present. When an external object "strikes" a sense faculty or when a mental object appears, the bhavaṅga stops and a procession of clearly cognizing states of consciousness arise according to the nature of the object (sight, sound, and so forth). When that process ceases, the bhavaṅga arises again and continues until another sensory object appears. At the time of death, the bhavaṅga gives way to the death consciousness. In the very next moment and depending on the new physical organism, the rebirth consciousness of the next life arises.

A mental consciousness with its own inner object, the bhavaṅga continues throughout a lifetime, serving as the underlying thread that maintains the continuity of consciousness when no clear cognition is occurring. The bhavaṅga is not a single consciousness that retains its identity throughout time. Like all other states of consciousness, it consists of a series of mind-moments that arise and cease in every nanosecond.

As the mind that takes rebirth in the next life, consciousness—the third link of dependent origination—arises dependent on the first two links, ignorance and formative actions. Due to ignorance, polluted actions are created. These actions condition the consciousness, which is drawn toward a particular rebirth in saṃsāra. This consciousness does not exist under its own power but arises due to preceding conditions.

In summary, consciousness cannot be an independent self because each moment of the various types of consciousness arise as a result of causes and conditions. They are dependent on their own sense faculty, object, and a preceding moment of consciousness. What appears to be a single conscious experience is actually a series of mind-moments, each arising and passing away very rapidly. Conscious experience is dependent on its parts; being conscious is nothing more than a series of similar mind-moments. The consciousness that takes rebirth is conditioned by previous moments of mental consciousness and also by the ignorance and formative actions that preceded it in the cycle of dependent origination.

Nowhere in the Pāli canon or Pāli commentaries is the mental consciousness or the collection of aggregates said to be the self. No phenomenon (dharma) whatsoever is posited as the self or person. Although some Buddhist schools have posited something that is the person that carries the karmic seeds—the collection of aggregates, mental consciousness, foundation consciousness, and so forth—there is no such notion in the Pāli tradition. Based on the Pāli sūtras and their commentaries, Theravādins regard the person as a conceptual notion imputed dependent on the basis of the five aggregates.

From whichever way we look at it, neither a self that is one and the same as the six elements nor a self that is completely different from them can be found. Still, the self is designated dependent on the six elements and the words "I," "you," "he/she/they," and so on—words that are conventions we use to communicate.

The Emptiness of Mine

The view of a personal identity grasps the inherent existence of I and mine. Like all other existents, I and mine exist conventionally but not ultimately or inherently. When someone says "this is mine," they are referring to the aggregates or an external object. Here "mine" does not explicitly refer to a person; however, we cannot say "mine" without implying a person who is the possessor. The view of a personal identity grasping mine focuses only on mine, not on the objects that are mine. "Mine" is a personal pronoun, so the notion of a person is implicit in it. Mine is not separate from I; it is the same nature as I, although it is nominally different. Grasping the objects that are mine as inherently existent is self-grasping of phenomena, whereas grasping mine as inherently existent is included in self-grasping of persons.

When you get a new car, you say "this is mine," and conventionally that is true. But if you then grasp a truly existent mine, your feeling changes because now it seems you have real ownership of the car: "This is mine! You can't use it unless I give you permission." As soon we impute something as *mine* or say it is *my* possession, the object takes on new meaning. The car on the showroom floor is not mine, so I don't care if it gets damaged. But if I buy it and think of it as mine, I become very upset if even a small scratch appears on it.

We put a lot of energy into procuring and protecting our possessions. We can see from the above example that grasping an inherent mine can make our life and our relationships complicated and painful. Realizing an inherent mine does not exist relaxes the mind and releases the grasping. For practical purposes in daily life, we still refer to things as mine or yours because that is an accepted convention in society.

The erroneous view grasping an inherently existent mine is dispelled by negating an inherently existent I. Nāgārjuna says (MMK 18.2):

> If the self does not exist,
> how could there be mine?

> By pacifying the self and mine,
> there will be no grasping to I and mine.

Here Nāgārjuna asks: If there is no I, how could there be an I that owns things? When we have negated the inherent existence of the I, by simply turning our attention to mine, we will know there is no inherently existent person that possesses the aggregates or anything else. Free from the pain of defending an inherently existent I and of clinging to *my* body, protecting *my* reputation, and procuring *my* possessions, our lives will be less stressful and being generous with our possessions will be easier.

Candrakīrti's sevenfold analysis is one of the main ways to refute an inherently existent person and to consequently destroy the self-grasping ignorance that conceives the person to exist inherently. By reflecting on these points repeatedly, your sense of self will begin to change, and you will feel more relaxed, less defensive, and more in harmony with others and your environment.

Innate Self-Grasping Ignorance

Although innate self-grasping was discussed in the previous volume, *Searching for the Self*, a review of this topic is useful, for it will help us to identify the conceived object of self-grasping ignorance. This conceived object is subtle: it appears to be mixed with the aggregates yet able to stand alone; it appears to exist from its own side without depending on anything else.

In observing how the mind sees the relationship of the I and the aggregates, sometimes it seems as if we grasp the I to be one of the aggregates. For example, we say "I am ill" when our stomach hurts and "I can't think straight right now" when our mind is confused. But if we innately grasped the I to inherently be the body, as in the first example, we would never wish to exchange bodies with someone who had a more attractive body than ours. And if we innately grasped the I to inherently be the mind, the wish to exchange our temperament with that of someone who is calmer and friendlier would not arise. Grasping the I to be either inherently one with or inherently different from the aggregates is not an innate grasping. All people, no matter their belief system, have ordinary conventional consciousnesses that see the self and the aggregates as related, not as so completely distinct that we could actually exchange our body and mind with those of others.

Similarly, innate self-grasping doesn't grasp a cause and its effect, such as a seed and the flower that grows from it, to be inherently unrelated. In the summer when we look at a flowering garden, we say, "I planted those flowers in the spring," when in fact we planted the seeds, not the flowers. That shows that we think of the seed and the flowers as related, not as inherently separate.

Understanding the conceived object of innate self-grasping is important, because without this we risk not identifying the object of negation correctly. For example, if we slip while walking near a cliff, a strong sense of an inherently existent I springs up. We might think that this is the object of negation, but it is not because it grasps the body as being an inherently existent I. The I whose safety we fear for is not an inherently existent I; it is a notion of I that is associated with the body. Similarly, when the thought arises that I may have an unfortunate rebirth, there is a strong feeling of I, but that I is associated with the mind—it is not the object of negation that is mixed with the collection of aggregates but stands alone.

If the innate mind does not grasp the self and the aggregates to be either inherently one or inherently separate, why do we spend so much time refuting inherent existence by using the seven points? If the self existed inherently, it would have to exist as either inherently one with or inherently different from the aggregates. There is no third alternative, because if inherently existent phenomena existed, they would be independent of all other factors, including parts, causes and conditions, and term and concept. If the I is neither inherently one with the aggregates nor inherently separate from them, then the I cannot exist inherently, and the person is empty of inherent existence.

Grasping the self and the aggregates to be inherently one and grasping them to be inherently separate are both acquired conceptions, ones we learned or fabricated in this life. Without relinquishing these false acquired conceptions, it is not possible to realize emptiness and eradicate the innate self-grasping. Refuting these erroneous alternatives enables us to get at the meaning of emptiness and refute the innate grasping.

In short, grasping the I to be either inherently one with or inherently separate from the aggregates is not the meaning of grasping the I to exist inherently. Along the same line, if the I existed inherently, it would be permanent because inherently existent things are not dependent on other factors and thus cannot change. But permanence is not the meaning of inherent existence, although it is an unwanted consequence of grasping functioning things as inherently existent.

Believing things—such as a soul—to be permanent, unproduced, and independent of parts are coarse misconceptions that are acquired afflictions. They are not the root of saṃsāra. Nevertheless, if phenomena existed in the way they appeared to us—as truly existent—they would have these qualities. Seeing that they don't exist in those ways leads us to understand their emptiness.

In conclusion, refuting the seven possibilities that Candrakīrti set forth discredits the notions of self asserted by non-Buddhists and the lower Buddhist tenet systems. Many non-Buddhist philosophies and religions assert a permanent, unified, and independent self or soul. Among Buddhist schools, the Pudgalavādin (Vātsīputrīya) Vaibhāṣikas asserted an enduring person who is neither the same as nor different from the mental and physical aggregates; this is the person who is reborn in saṃsāra and later attains nirvāṇa. The Saṃmitīya Vaibhāṣikas say the collection of the aggregates is the self, whereas the Kashmiri Vaibhāṣikas and the Sautrāntika Scriptural Proponents assert the continuum of mental and physical aggregates is the self. The Sautrāntika Reasoning Proponents, Yogācāra Reasoning Proponents, and the Sautrāntika-Svātantrika Mādhyamikas accept a subtle mental consciousness is the self, and the Yogācāra Scriptural Proponents assert a foundation consciousness (*ālayavijñāna*) is the self. Yogācāra-Svātantrika Mādhyamikas assert the continuum of the mental consciousness is the self. Only Prāsaṅgika Mādhyamikas say the person is merely designated in dependence on the aggregates.

The seven points prove that a self as propounded in any of the above ways is untenable because, when subjected to ultimate analysis, all those selves cannot be found as either one with or completely different from the aggregates. By refuting these views, the Prāsaṅgika Mādhyamikas say the self is the mere I imputed in dependence on the four or five aggregates (all five aggregates are not necessary because beings in the formless realm do not have a body).

Meditation: The Four Essential Points

Nāgārjuna's five-point analysis and Candrakīrti's seven-point analysis can be condensed into the reasoning of the four essential points, which is another way to meditate on the selflessness of persons. When used to refute the inherent existence of the person, this meditation employs the syllogism: "Consider the I, it does not inherently exist, because it does not exist as inherently one with the aggregates or as inherently separate from and unrelated to the aggregates." The four essential points used in this meditation are:

1. Identify the object of negation, the inherent existence of the I.
2. Ascertain the pervasion that whatever does not exist as inherently one with or inherently separate from its parts (in this case the aggregates) does not exist. If the I existed inherently, it should be findable either as inherently one with the aggregates or inherently separate from them; there is not a third option.
3. Ascertain that the I does not exist as inherently one with the aggregates individually or with their collection.
4. Ascertain that the I does not exist inherently distinct from the aggregates.

For this and the preceding refutations to have an impact, the practitioners contemplating them should not be strongly attached to the view that the I inherently exists and should have some doubt whether the person inherently exists or not. When such suitable vessels have examined these four points and penetrated their depth, they can safely conclude that the I does not exist inherently, or expressed another way, that an inherently existent I does not exist at all.

1. Identify the object of negation

The first point is to identify the object of negation, the inherent existence of the self that we believe exists. As ordinary beings, whatever appears to our mind seems to exist from its own side, independent of thought. We accept how this object or person appears to us as if that were its actual mode of being.

When we examine our sense of self, we instinctually feel that in addition to our body and mind, there is a third element—a self that is the master and owner of the physical and mental aggregates that constitute the individual. We use conventions such as "my body" and "my mind," and we assume that over and beyond the body and mind there is an independent entity called "self," something that unassailably is really Me.

Identifying this "solid" self that we're sure exists is the first step in this meditation. If you proceed with the other three steps without having a clear experiential feeling of an inherently existent I, the meditation will remain on the intellectual level and its impact on you will be minimal. To bring up the image or feeling of an inherently existent I, the masters suggest remembering an emotionally charged situation—for example, when you were wrongly accused in front of a group of people by someone shouting: "You ruined this event! You're the one who made the horrible miscalculation." Suddenly the thought roars in your mind: "*I* didn't do that! Don't blame *Me*!"

Then while one part of your mind holds that feeling of I, with a corner of your mind examine how the self appears at that moment. Does this I that you cherish and need to defend seem "solid"? Do you doubt its existence at all or are you 100 percent sure that this real I truly exists? Don't recite a verbal description mimicking a text that describes the object of negation, but rather observe how the I appears to exist. Does the I depend on anything else or does it appear to exist and operate under its own power? Does it seem to exist in its own right? Observing the sense of I, be aware of how the mind innately apprehends the I as inherently existent. Spend as much time as needed to get a sense of what the I would be like if it inherently existed.

If the sense of I diminishes, remember the emotionally charged situation again so that the sense of a real I appears. This sense of I is so strong that you feel: if this doesn't exist, what does? The corner of your mind that observes this sense of I must be very discreet. If it is too strong or prominent, the sense of a solid I disappears.

The grasping of the inherent existence of the I that arises when you are falsely accused is a comparatively coarse grasping, but it is easier to identify than the innate grasping, so begin with this. Over time as you become more adept at identifying the various ways you grasp the I and the conceived object of that grasping, you will be able to identify subtler forms of grasping the false I. Eventually you will be able to identify the object of negation of the innate grasping—anything more than what is merely designated by conception. That is that subtle object of negation. The fifth Dalai Lama described it (HSY 132–33):

> Sometimes the I will seem to exist in the context of the body. Sometimes it will seem to exist in the context of the mind. Sometimes it will seem to exist in the context of feelings, discriminations, or other factors. At the end of noticing a variety of modes of appearance, you will come to identify an I that exists in its own right, that exists inherently, that from the start is self-established, existing undifferentiatedly with the mind and body, which are also mixed like milk and water.
>
> This is the first step, ascertainment of the object to be negated in the view of selflessness. You should work at it until deep experience arises.

Those who have received many teachings on the object of negation know the words describing the object of negation—inherent existence—but that doesn't mean we recognize grasping inherent existence when it arises in our own lives. For this reason, the fifth Dalai Lama compassionately counsels us to be persistent until we are able to identify the object of negation in our own experience.

2. Ascertain the pervasion

The second point is to determine if the self exists in the way it appears—as able to set itself up without relying on anything else. There are only two possible ways it could exist: as either inherently one with the mental and physical aggregates or as inherently different from the aggregates.[18] If the person truly existed as it appears to—under its own power and independent of any other factors—it should be found upon a search for its real identity. There should be an objectified basis that could be identified as being either inherently one with the aggregates or inherently separate from them. There is no third alternative. If, to exist inherently, something need not exist in either of those two ways—if there were a third way it could exist—then disproving these two options would not prove that the I was empty of inherent existence.

It is important to note that we are not looking for an inherently existent I on or in the conventional I. The conventional I, the sense faculties, and sense consciousnesses by themselves do not generate suffering. Even arhats possess these. Rather, the troublemaker is the mind that grasps these to exist from their own side, inherently. For example, instead of searching to see if the I is inherently one or inherently different from the aggregates, you simply investigate if the I was findable inside or outside the body, or in the lower or upper parts of the body, or somewhere else. Not finding the I anywhere, you then conclude that the I is nonexistent. In this case, you would fall to the extreme of nihilism. The reason for this error is that you are searching for the conventionally existent I.

Why is being either inherently one with or inherently different from its parts the only two options for how the I could exist if it existed inherently? Even conventionally, anything that exists must exist as either one with or different from its parts; likewise in terms of inherent existence, anything that inherently exists must be either inherently one with or inherently different from its parts. For us to investigate this, the I and aggregates would have to be inherently objective entities. When they appeared to a consciousness, they would have an unchanging appearance. That is, a person and his body conventionally appear as one to a sense consciousness, but they do not appear inseparably one to a conceptual mental consciousness; we can think about a person without thinking about his body. Such disparity is feasible conventionally. But if the I and the aggregates existed inherently, then the way they appear to a sense consciousness and to a conceptual mental consciousness would have to be exactly the same. However, this is not the case, because to a sense consciousness they appear as one but to a conceptual consciousness they appear as separate. For example, you can think of Tashi and his foot separately.

Take time to clearly ascertain the pervasion that if the I existed inherently, it must be either inherently one with the aggregates or inherently separate from them; these are the only two options. If the I doesn't exist as either inherently one with or inherently separate from the aggregates, it cannot exist inherently. If this point isn't clear, your subsequent investigation will not lead to the correct conclusion.

After ascertaining this pervasion, search for how the I exists by employing the third and fourth points.

3. Ascertain that the I is not inherently one with the aggregates

The third point commences the actual investigation to discover if the person exists in either of the two ways. Now we will examine the first: If the I were inherently one with the aggregates, it must be identical to the aggregates in all aspects. There would be no discernable difference between them. Investigate if the I is identical in all aspects with any part of your body. Do not search to find the I in the body; rather, examine if the I is inherently one with the body or any part of the body.

Begin by mentally dissecting your body, examining each organ, limb, tissue, and so forth to see if it is identical to the self. Some people find it helpful to visualize a replica of themselves and mentally dismantle the body into its parts to do this examination. Other people find it more effective to be "in" their body, examining each part: Are the eyeballs identical to Me? Is the brain one and the same as the person? After examining one part of the body and not finding your self as identical to it, investigate if the I is identical to the next part. At the end, you may have a strange feeling of not being there. That means your meditation has been effective.

Then investigate if your mind is one and the same as your self. The mind has many aspects, so examine each of them. Am I identical to a primary consciousness, such as one of the sense primary consciousnesses or the mental primary consciousness? Am I identical to a particular mental factor? Which mental factor? Am I identical to my anger? Is compassion identical to the I? Is the thought of I the same as the I? Is a virtuous mind identical to the I? Investigate each sense consciousness as well as each thought, mood, emotion, perception, or conception to see if you can find one mental event that can be isolated as being identical in all aspects to a person.

Examine each mind: the waking mind, the dreaming mind, the mind of deep sleep. Is it identical to the I, so that everything the I does that consciousness also does? Are any of the subtle consciousnesses that manifest when the winds are being absorbed in the central channel—the white appearance, red increase, or black near attainment—one and the same as the I? Is the clear-light mind identical to the I? Be aware that each mind and mental factor is impermanent. Its continuity doesn't last long and another mental state quickly replaces it. Can any of these fluctuating mental states be an independent self?

Then examine if an independent I is identical to the collection of the aggregates. None of the parts are identical to the person, so how could a collection of non-persons be a person?

If you could find one aggregate or part of an aggregate that is identical in all aspects to the self—for example, if you found your brain to be one and the same as the person—then everything the person did, the brain would also do. When you graduated from high school, your brain would graduate from high school. When you walked on the platform to receive the diploma, your brain would walk on the platform. In fact, there would be no need for two words "I" and "brain" to indicate a person, because these two terms would be synonymous.

While doing this examination, keep the appearance and feeling of an inherently existent I in the back of your mind. Investigate very thoroughly, and at the end reach the firm conclusion: I searched to see if any aggregates or part of any aggregate is inherently identical to the self and found that none of them are. Therefore the I is not inherently one with the aggregates.

4. Ascertain that the I is not inherently separate from the aggregates

Since the I is not inherently one with any of the aggregates or with the collection of aggregates, the only other way the I could exist inherently is as inherently separate from the aggregates. Conventionally, the aggregates and the person are different, but they are one nature in that the I is imputed in dependence on the aggregates. If the I existed as inherently different from the aggregates, the I and the aggregates would be totally separate and unrelated. They could not be related as basis of designation (the aggregates) and designated object (I).

Check if an inherently existent I can be found apart from the aggregates. Examine if there is something the I does that does not depend on the body or mind. Can you find a self that walks, talks, feels, creates karma, experiences the result, is reborn, and will attain awakening that is totally separate from the psychophysical aggregates? Is the I doing this investigation separate from the body and mind?

Clearly the self is not an external phenomenon such as a tree or stone. What else could it be? Do you have the sense of the I being some amorphous mass that is separate from the body and mind, some vague mass that floats up out of your body when you die? If so, examine what that amorphous mass is. You feel it exists, but what exactly is it? When you think of this mass as

Me, don't the subject and the object become confused? How could the I, who is an amorphous mass, investigate an amorphous mass that is separate from me and think that it is me?

If the I is completely unrelated to the aggregates, then the body could die but I wouldn't die. The aggregates could be in the room but I could be outside the room. That certainly doesn't make sense.

Since an inherently existent I could not depend on any other factors such as causes and conditions, it would be permanent. If the I were unchanging, you could not change over the years. The self would be the same person, with the same exact traits, and the same unchanging body and thoughts, from the time you were conceived in your mother's womb until your death. That certainly contradicts your experience.

Or perhaps the I is unchanging but parts of you change. That is, one part of you is permanent and one part is impermanent. Is that possible? Would you have two selves with mutually contradictory attributes? Your thoughts and emotions could change but you wouldn't change. Your body would age, but you wouldn't. Finding yourself entangled in a mass of contradictions, ascertain that the I is unfindable as something completely separate from and unrelated to the body and mind.

Having examined if the I is identical to the aggregates in all aspects or inherently separate from the aggregates and finding that the I is neither, conclude that the I does not exist inherently. There isn't a findable objective locus that is the I. Therefore the I cannot exist inherently. In the second of the four steps, we established the criteria that an inherently existent I should fulfill, but such an I does not exist in any of those ways. In your meditation, the appearance of the I as inherently existent now disappears and its emptiness—the complete absence of inherent existence—appears as your meditation object.

Through this process of inquiry, it becomes clear that if the I—or anything else—existed inherently, it would be a self-enclosed entity that was findable by ultimate analysis inquiring into its ultimate mode of existence. But an inherently existent thing would be a frozen object that could neither change nor interact with anything else, and nothing exists in that way. Every phenomenon exists in relation to other phenomena.

The observed object in our analysis is the conventional self, the mere I. Self-grasping ignorance and the wisdom realizing emptiness have the same observed object—the mere I—but they apprehend it in opposite ways. The conceived and apprehended objects of ignorance are an inherently existent I, whereas the apprehended object of the wisdom realizing emptiness is the emptiness of the I, the non-inherent existence of the I.

The last two points of the four-point analysis are the first two of the seven points in Candrakīrti's analysis. The other five points constitute an expanded method of considering if the I and the aggregates are inherently the same as or inherently different from the aggregates. Elaborating on the two main points by adding five more reinforces the fact that an inherently existent I cannot be found. For that reason, we examine: Does the I inherently possess the aggregates? Is the I inherently based on the aggregates? Are the aggregates inherently based on the I? Is the I inherently the same as the collection of the aggregates? Is it inherently the shape or arrangement of the aggregates? By investigating in this way, our experience of the I changes. It no longer feels so solid or real, and our attachment to it declines.

Approach this inquiry with a sense of curiosity, free from the expectation of reaching a predetermined conclusion. After examining all the possibilities where an inherently existent I could exist but where it is not found, the only possible conclusion is that the I does not inherently exist. There is a sense of vacuity and a profound sense of wonderment because previously you had a strong sense of an independent, findable I that you now discover is nowhere to be found. Sometimes a sense of fear may arise: "I don't exist!" Don't be alarmed, that is a sign that your meditation is touching home and having a good effect. The I that is merely designated still exists.

Fear arises because the sense of an inherently existent I has been confused with the conventionally existent mere I, so when the sense of an inherently existent I vanishes, there is fear that the I has disappeared altogether. That is not the case, because ultimate analysis cannot destroy the conventionally existent I. The fifth Dalai Lama commented that people who are new to emptiness may have a sense of loss when they initially understand it (EY 253):

> If you have no imprints for emptiness from a former life, it seems that a thing that was in the hand has suddenly been lost. If you have imprints, it seems that a lost jewel that had been in the hand has suddenly been found.

Meditating on emptiness requires fortitude because the experience of emptiness is so radically different from our usual way of thinking and perceiving that confusion and fear may arise as your seemingly solid I and the world around it dissolve. However, those who have imprints from studying, reflecting, and meditating on emptiness in previous lives have a certain familiarity with it so that understanding emptiness in this life is joyful, like finding a jewel that had been lost.

The third phase of the path of preparation is called "fortitude" because it marks the attainment of fortitude in the face of emptiness. This fortitude continues to gain strength as the realization of emptiness deepens and as the meditator progresses through the paths and grounds until the eighth ground is attained. At that time, fear no longer arises in the face of emptiness because grasping inherent existence and its seeds have been completely and forever eradicated.

After completing the analysis, stay in the experience of emptiness for as long as possible. When the experience fades, meditate on dependent arising. Although the I does not inherently exist, it does exist dependently, by being merely designated by term and concept in dependence on its basis of designation. Meditate that the I exists dependent on causes and conditions, parts, and the mind that conceives and designates it. As Candrakīrti notes in the *Supplement* (MMA 6.158):

> [The person] is not established ultimately
> or in the world in the seven ways.
> But without analysis, through worldly convention,
> it is imputed in dependence on its parts.

The ultimate or inherent existence of the person and all phenomena is refuted through analyzing the seven possibilities; if the person—or anything else—existed ultimately, it should be findable in one of the seven ways, but it is not. However, that doesn't mean it is nonexistent. When we do not analyze, things still appear to us and they exist by being merely designated by worldly conventions. All of us agree that a crunchy, round, red edible fruit of the rose family is called an apple. This name is imputed in dependence on the parts of that fruit. That fruit functions according to the definition we have given to the word "apple."

Meditating sometimes on the emptiness of the I and sometimes on the I as a dependent arising helps to ascertain both the emptiness and the dependent existence of the person. Meditation on the person as dependent prevents the mistaken notion that it exists inherently, independent of all other factors. Meditating that the person arises prevents the erroneous idea that it doesn't exist at all. The person both exists and is empty. Conventional existence and being empty of inherent existence are not contradictory. In fact, it is because the person is empty that it exists and functions. If we were inherently existent, we could not function at all. A person has an empty nature and a dependent nature; these two are mutually dependent attributes of the person.

Checking Your Realization

As we've seen, there are different levels of objects of negation related to the person: a permanent, unified, and independent self; a self-sufficient substantially existent person; and an I that exists inherently. The existence of a permanent, unified, and independent self is refuted by examining if a permanent I could function; if the I were one monolithic, partless whole; and if the I were independent of the body. The self-sufficient substantially existent person is refuted by examining if the I can be identified without identifying any of the aggregates. The chief way to refute the inherent existence of the I is by ultimate analysis investigating if the I is inherently identical to or inherently separate from the aggregates. Although there are different refutations for each level of the object of negation related to the person, when grasping inherent existence has been overcome, so have all coarser graspings as well as all afflictions that are rooted in self-grasping ignorance.

Realizing the nonexistence of a self-sufficient substantially existent person is a helpful step that takes us in the direction of realizing the emptiness of inherent existence of the person. But we should not confuse the two, because negating a self-sufficient substantially existent person alone will not lead to liberation. To differentiate them, when the sense of an objectively existent I vanishes after meditating on the fourfold, fivefold, or sevenfold reasoning, turn your attention to your body or some part of your body. If your sense of it being objectively existent disappears, you have succeeded in negating the inherent existence of the person. However, if the force of the reasoning doesn't immediately have the same impact when applied to your body, then you have negated a self-sufficient substantially existent person, not an inherently existent I.

About fifty years ago I was meditating on the point in *Ocean of Reasoning*—Tsongkhapa's commentary to the *Treatise on the Middle Way*—that the I is neither one with nor different from the aggregates. I experienced a feeling as if lightning had struck my heart and a strong awareness of the absence of the I followed. To check whether my understanding was of an inherently existent person, I changed the focus of my meditation to the body. But the experience of emptiness was not the same. At that point, I understood that I had realized coarse selflessness, the lack of a self-sufficient substantially existent person. While it is powerful, understanding the absence of a self that is the controller or overlord of the aggregates is not the realization of the emptiness of an inherently existent person.

Nāgārjuna said (RA 35ab):

> As long as one grasps the aggregates,
> one will also grasp the I with regard to them.

Seeing that the force of my understanding weakened when I turned my attention to my body, I understood that my understanding of the selflessness of persons was not complete. It is crucial to reduce grasping the aggregates in order to realize the subtle selflessness of the person—the person's emptiness of inherent existence.

In his writings Dodrupchen warns that someone may think he is practicing Dzogchen, but in reality he's meditating on the conventional nature of the fundamental mind, rigpa. In the same way, someone could think she is meditating on the emptiness of inherent existence of the I when in fact she is refuting only a self-sufficient substantially existent person. For that reason, changing the basis of the negation from the person to the aggregates as mentioned above is useful to ensure our meditation is on track.

Let's back up for a moment and question: If a person is neither the body nor the mind, nor the collection of these two, nor something other than them, then what is the I that exists? The great masters tell us it is a dependent I or person. When we aren't experiencing a strong emotion, attitude, or view, the I that appears to us is the mere I that exists by being merely designated in dependence on the aggregates. Mixed in with the appearance of this dependently arisen I is the appearance of an inherently existent I. Similarly, when we have a neutral state of mind and perceive any other external and internal phenomena, the appearance of the dependently arisen object is mixed with the appearance of an inherently existent object. This happens due to the latencies of grasping inherent existence on our mindstream; these are cognitive obscurations. For this reason all consciousnesses of sentient beings—even those of arhats and pure-ground bodhisattvas—except āryas' meditative equipoise directly perceiving emptiness—are mistaken with respect to what appears to them in that everything still appears inherently existent. Their minds may be right about the general object—they can correctly identify a table as a table—but mistaken in that the table has an overlay of the appearance of inherent existence.

Correctly identifying the object of negation is a process that takes time. During your daily life, observe your sense of I; see how it changes depending on the situations you experience and the emotions that arise in response to them. Question if the I that appears to you exists as it appears.

By doing this, you will gradually deepen both your ability to identify an exaggerated sense of self and the instability of its foundation. You will also start to distinguish between the I that exists and the I that doesn't. As you do so, take care to avoid the extreme of seeing everything as solid entities that exist by their own power and the opposite extreme of thinking that people and things don't exist at all. They do exist; analysis is trying to get at how they exist. As you continue, contemplate that people and things exist dependently. This will stimulate you to pay closer attention to how people and things appear and will loosen your belief that things exist as they appear.

Realizing emptiness is not quick or easy. If it were we would all have become buddhas a long time ago. But if you keep observing and analyzing, your understanding will grow. The non-finding of the object of negation is the object's emptiness. By keeping at this process, your understanding will become a correct assumption; then it will get deeper and become an inferential realization of emptiness and later a direct perceiver of emptiness. As you understand emptiness better, your ability to identify the object of negation will increase, and as that becomes clearer, your ability to prove to yourself that an inherently existent person and inherently existent phenomena cannot possibly exist also increases. This will challenge you to understand how they do exist, and that will turn your mind to dependent arising.

REFLECTION

1. First identify the I that is the object of negation. Then proceed with the remaining points of the fourfold, fivefold, or sevenfold analysis to refute it.
2. When the sense of an I that exists from its own side vanishes, change the object of analysis to your body or a part of your body.
3. Does the sense that your body inherently exists vanish due to the force of the previous analysis?
4. If not, this indicates that you had refuted a coarser level of the object of negation.

Does the Person Exist Inherently on the Conventional Level?

Candrakīrti fleshes out the meaning of emptiness when he claims that a person when searched for on its basis of imputation cannot be found either conventionally or ultimately. Using the example of a chariot, he says (MMA 6.158):

> Although the chariot does not exist in any of the seven ways
> both in terms of suchness as well as worldly [convention],
> through worldly [conventions] alone and without analysis
> it is designated in dependence on its parts.

A chariot cannot be found when searched for on its basis of imputation either conventionally or ultimately. A chariot can only be established on the level of worldly convention, where its mode of existence is not examined with analysis.

Saying that the person, when searched for on its basis of imputation, can be found neither on the conventional nor the ultimate level emphasizes the subtle distinction of Candrakīrti's and Buddhapālita's understanding of Nāgārjuna on the one hand, and Bhāvaviveka's understanding of Nāgārjuna on the other.

According to Bhāvaviveka and his fellow Svātantrikas, for something to be imputedly existent, its basis must be substantially existent.[19] Since the person, for example, exists imputedly, its basis of imputation must be substantially existent. This compels the Svātantrikas and proponents of the other lower tenet schools to find something that is the real person. Depending on the school, they point to the mental consciousness, the mental continuum, a foundation consciousness, and so forth as being the person. The Prāsaṅgikas, however, do not need the support of a substantially existent basis of imputation to establish the existence of the person. They assert that the person exists by being merely designated in dependence on the aggregates.

Thus, although Bhāvaviveka and his fellow Svātantrikas accept that all persons and phenomena lack true existence and inherent existence on the ultimate level, they maintain that all phenomena must possess some degree of objective reality on the conventional level. Because terms refer to objects, there must be something substantially existent on the side of an object that serves as the referent of that term. If there weren't, Bhāvaviveka says, any object could be called by any name and that would make it function as that phenomenon. If there weren't something inherently existent that makes a giraffe a giraffe, designating a giraffe with the term "chipmunk" would make the giraffe become a chipmunk. In short, all forms of conventional communication among people in society would break down, and there would be no agreed-upon meanings and notions through which people could relate.

Bhāvaviveka and the Svātantrika Mādhyamika masters identify the mental consciousness itself or the continuum of consciousness to be the true referent of the term "person"—that is the person in the final analysis. Although inherent existence is negated on the ultimate level, an objectified basis of the term "person" remains conventionally. If the person didn't possess some degree of objective existence, things couldn't function on the conventional level and establishing conventional existence would be impossible.

Candrakīrti points out that Bhāvaviveka asserts that the person exists inherently on the conventional level because he is not satisfied with understanding veiled truths as only mere appearances. He believes that there must be something more than nominal existence and existence on the level of appearance. Therefore, although he negates inherent existence ultimately, he posits inherent existence conventionally.

Although we may wonder how such intelligent Madhyamaka masters could advocate this position, we can sometimes see the same tendency toward reification within ourselves. The ignorant mind desperately wants something to grasp; it wants something that is real, findable, solid, and stable; it craves something that possesses its own essential nature to hold on to. Existence on the level of appearance or by mere name can frighten us, so we adopt a subtle absolutist position. We think that if everything existed by mere imputation, conventional existence would be chaotic. A horse could be called a tank and it would become that, and a person could be designated the moon and she would become that. There must be something in food that makes it inherently eatable, otherwise we could eat a chair to remove our hunger. In this way, we too could slip into grasping inherent existence on the conventional level and become a proponent of Svātantrika tenets.

Because of this distinction among Nāgārjuna's followers regarding whether or not phenomena exist inherently on the conventional level, Tibetan commentarial traditions distinguished them into two camps: one accepting some notion of self-defining characteristics and inherent existence, the other rejecting these even conventionally. The former are called Svātantrika Mādhyamikas, the latter Prāsaṅgika Mādhyamikas.

In the *Supplement*, Candrakīrti refutes the Svātantrika view that negates true existence but accepts inherent existence conventionally.[20] He says that accepting any degree of inherent existence whatsoever serves as the basis for further grasping, which keeps us circling in saṃsāra. To refute Svātantrikas' assertion that because phenomena exist inherently on the conventional level, the appearance of inherent existence to everyday consciousnesses is accurate, Candrakīrti reveals four absurd consequences. Three of the consequences are found in his *Supplement* (6.34–36), and one is in its autocommentary. The four are also mentioned in Tsongkhapa's *Essence of Eloquence*. If phenomena existed inherently, there would be four absurd consequences:

1. An ārya's consciousness of meditative equipoise realizing emptiness, which knows things as they actually exist, would destroy phenomena because it does not perceive the inherently existent things that Svātan-

trikas say exist. "Destroy" means something formerly existed and later ceases. Candrakīrti says (MMA 6.34):

> If the inherent characteristics of things were to arise
> dependently,
> things would be destroyed by denying them; [175]
> emptiness would then be a cause for the destruction of things.
> But this is illogical, so no real [inherently existent] entities exist.

If conventional phenomena existed inherently, they would appear to and be established by an ārya's meditative equipoise on emptiness that knows them as they actually are. However, since veiled truths don't appear to the meditative equipoise that directly perceives emptiness, that wisdom must have destroyed them. That is absurd because ultimate wisdom does not have the ability to destroy veilings.

2. Veiled truths would be able to withstand ultimate analysis because their inherent existence could be found. For example, when we search for the ultimate existence of the person, if we found the mental consciousness, then the person could withstand ultimate analysis. However, the person is not found under ultimate analysis. Candrakīrti explains (MMA 6.35):

> Thus, when such phenomena are analyzed,
> nothing is found as their nature apart from suchness
> (emptiness).
> So the veiled truths of the everyday world
> should not be subjected to thorough analysis.

Since veiled truths, such as the person, exist merely by social conventions and not inherently, they should not be subjected to ultimate analysis that tries to find an inherent essence in them. If they did not exist by mere designation and social conventions but existed from their own side, they would be found by ultimate analysis.

3. Ultimately established arising could not be refuted because sense consciousnesses would be reliable cognizers of the ultimate nature. In that case, arising from the four positions presented in diamond slivers—arising from self, other, both, or causelessly—could not be refuted. Candrakīrti states (MMA 6.36):

> In the context of suchness, certain reasoning disallows arising
> from self or from something [inherently] other, and that same reasoning
> disallows them on the conventional level too.
> So by what means then is your arising established?

This question is addressed to those who accept arising from a cause that is inherently other than its result—that is, to Svātantrikas. Neither ultimate nor conventional reasoning can establish the existence of inherently existent phenomena. Thus inherent existence is negated on both the ultimate and conventional levels.

4. The scriptural statement that phenomena are self-empty (T. *rang stong*)—that is, empty from their own side—as opposed to other-empty (T. *gzhan stong*) would not be feasible. In the *Kāśyapa Chapter* (*Kāśyapaparivarta*) of the *Heap of Jewels Sūtra*, the Buddha said (GR 262):

> Furthermore, Kāśyapa, [when] the Middle Way correctly [and]
> individually analyses phenomena, [it sees] that emptiness does not make
> phenomena empty; phenomena are themselves empty.

When wisdom critically analyzes form, for example, it discovers the ultimate truth of form, its emptiness of inherent existence. Form is not made empty by the realization of emptiness because form itself is empty. Saying that *emptiness does not make phenomena empty* rules out other-emptiness. Saying that *phenomena are themselves empty* affirms self-emptiness.

I frequently reflect on these points because they reinforce the fact that phenomena must lack inherent existence. Doing this ensures that my meditation on emptiness progresses correctly. Reflecting on these four points clarifies the difference between the Prāsaṅgika and the Svātantrika perspectives regarding the object of negation and the ignorance that is the root of saṃsāra. Since liberation and awakening depend on realizing selflessness, understanding this difference is crucial to our meditation practice.

How Does the Body Exist?

In a previous reflection, we examined how the I exists; that is a meditation on the selflessness of persons. To meditate on the selflessness of phenomena, we will now use the body as an example. Our body is an object of strong attachment, so investigating how it exists can have an impact. The steps to contemplate are below.

REFLECTION

1. Identify the object of negation, an inherently existent body. Let the sense arise that a real body that exists in its own right is here. Feel that if the body as you are currently apprehending it didn't exist, you don't know what would. The stronger the sense of an inherently existent body is at the beginning of the meditation, the greater the impact of not being able to find it after searching for it.
2. Determine that if such an inherently existent body existed, it should be findable either as inherently one with its parts or inherently separate and distinct from them.
3. Investigate: Is the body inherently one with its parts—the arms, legs, belly, brain, and so forth? Examine each part of the body to see if it is the body.
4. Is the body inherently different from the parts? Can you find the body in one place and the parts of the body in another?
5. Is our body inherently the base of its parts?
6. Are the parts inherently the base of the body?
7. Does the body inherently possess its parts?
8. Is the body the collection of its parts?
9. Is it the shape or arrangements of its organs and limbs?
10. Conclude that the body does not exist inherently. Since the inherently

existent body that you were so certain existed cannot be found in any of the above ways, it does not exist.

11. Feel your attachment to the body decline and a sense of relaxation that is freedom from grasping an inherently existent body increase.
12. Contemplate that although the body lacks any inherent existence whatsoever, it does exist conventionally, nominally, relatively. It exists by being merely designated in dependence on its basis of designation—the parts of the body.

The same meditation can be done to examine if the mind inherently exists. Here investigate if the mind is inherently one with or different from its parts, the parts being the earlier and later moments of mind. Examine if it is inherently one with or different from its two distinguishing characteristics, clarity and awareness. In addition, investigate if the mind is one of the primary consciousnesses—visual, auditory, olfactory, gustatory, tactile, or mental. Or does the mind exist entirely separate from the primary consciousnesses? Is the mind one of the miscellaneous factors—a particular attitude, emotion, or view? Is it a feeling or a discrimination? Understanding that our object of analysis does not exist inherently as either one with or different from its parts, we can then conclude that it does not exist inherently.

Then, in the break times between meditation sessions, practice seeing the I, body, or mind as illusion-like in that they appear inherently existent but do not exist that way at all. Maintain this awareness of all persons and phenomena being like illusions as you do virtuous actions throughout the day. That is, an illusion-like I does illusion-like prostrations, makes illusion-like offerings, and converses with illusion-like people. Reflecting in this way repeatedly over time will increase your understanding of emptiness, nominal existence, and their compatibility.

5 Ultimate Analysis and Conventional Existence

ĀRYADEVA (second to third century CE), an Indian scholar and sage who possessed great acuity in debate, is often quoted in this volume. I'd like to tell you an interesting story about him, versions of which are found in both Tibetan and Chinese literature. In ancient India, public debates were held in which two parties from divergent groups debated philosophical assertions in the presence of the monarch, other spiritual practitioners, and the general public. These debates were popular and much was invested in their results. Often the loser converted and became a disciple of the winner; other times more drastic results occurred, such as the loser cutting off his tongue.

Āryadeva was renowned as the "defeater of the heterodox" because he traveled throughout India refuting non-Buddhists and defending the Buddhist doctrine in public debates. More than twelve years had passed since the Buddhist monks in Pāṭaliputra had won a debate. They were so discouraged that they had ceased challenging others to debate. Āryadeva asked his teacher Nāgārjuna for permission to go there to debate the non-Buddhists and restore Buddhism. Doubting if Āryadeva was a match for the Brahminical scholars of North India, Nāgārjuna trained him for seven days. During this time Nāgārjuna argued the heterodox position while Āryadeva argued the Buddhist position. Finally, Āryadeva was able to win the debate and Nāgārjuna gave him permission to go north to debate the Brahmins. According to the Chinese story, Āryadeva defeated them in less than twelve days, to the delight of the king and the monks.

The Tibetan version tells us that at Nālandā Āryadeva in particular debated the non-Buddhist Mātṛceṭa, who was a follower of the deity

Maheśvara. Whenever Mātṛceṭa engaged in debate, he was known to bring a parrot, his sister, and a piece of magic chalk to the debate ground. Āryadeva surmised that the parrot and sister were manifestations of Maheśvara and his consort and knew that he could not win the debate if the parrot and sister were feeding the deity's answers to Mātṛceṭa. To counteract these interferences, Āryadeva brought a foul-mouthed layman, a cat, and some oil to the debating ground. When the debate began, the layman insulted the sister, who was offended and fled. The cat went after the parrot, who flew away, and Āryadeva poured oil on the ground so the magic chalk could not write on it. Without these aids Mātṛceṭa was defeated. Disgraced, he flew up in space, but Āryadeva chased him, returned him to earth, and locked him inside a Buddhist temple.

There, Mātṛceṭa began to read the Buddhist scriptures, one of which prophesied his role in propagating the Buddhadharma. Shocked at this discovery, Mātṛceṭa immediately confessed his negativities and previous behavior, took monastic ordination, and became a great Buddhist scholar-practitioner. The words he used in his confession became the commonly recited confession prayer in Tibetan Buddhism that begins "Woe is me!"

Refining Our Understanding of the Object of Negation

As we learn and practice meditation on emptiness, we refine our understanding of the object of negation in several ways. In meditation we examine if the I exists in the way it appears to self-grasping ignorance. In other words, does the I exist inherently? Our search is not to see if the I exists but to determine if it exists inherently. In other words, we are not searching for the mere I that does exist; if we were, we would be incorrectly applying ultimate analysis to the conventional I. Doing that runs the risk of falling to nihilism, because we can't find the I as either one with or separate from the aggregates and would erroneously conclude that the I doesn't exist at all. However, when analysis is done correctly we understand that the I does not exist inherently. It exists dependently. Understanding the I as it actually is on both the ultimate level (empty) and the conventional level (dependent), we are more encouraged to do the practices to create the causes for buddhahood.

Identifying the object of negation involves contemplating what inherent existence would be if it existed. Through this, we gain a conceptual appearance of what the I or the body, for example, would be like if it existed inherently. Here we are called to differentiate the appearance of inherent existence from inherent existence itself. The appearance of inherent existence exists and is known by reliable cognizers, whereas inherent existence doesn't exist at all. For example, if we imagine flowers in the sky, the conceptual appearance of flowers in the sky exists, whereas those flowers do not. If the difference between these two is not clear, we might conflate the appearance of inherent existence with inherent existence and negate the former, which is an existent object. But existents are not the object of negation. By negating existents, we negate too much and fall to the extreme of nihilism.

What makes this challenging is that before finding the correct Middle Way view, we are unable to distinguish the mere I and the inherently existent I with a reliable cognizer. We do it first with a mind of correct assumption by relying on a term generality. A term generality appears to the mind when someone describes something we have never seen—in this case, inherent existence—and an image of it appears to our mind.

Although it is difficult to distinguish between inherent existence and the appearance of inherent existence, doing so is important. First, it ensures we negate the actual object of negation and not an existent phenomenon when we meditate on emptiness. Second, it enables us to better understand what buddhas perceive, in that inherent existence does not appear to buddhas' minds from their own side because buddhas have abandoned cognitive obscurations. But buddhas do perceive the appearance of inherent existence that appears to sentient beings' minds because that appearance is an existent, and all existents are known by the buddhas' omniscient minds.

How does emptiness appear to a mind that ascertains it? If our understanding of emptiness is incorrect and we equate emptiness with a vacuity that is nothingness, we have not ascertained emptiness. It could also happen that with analysis, we generate a correct understanding of emptiness, but lose it later in the meditation session so that we begin to meditate on nothingness. This could happen because of a lack of concentration or because our initial understanding was a correct assumption, not ascertainment, of emptiness. In another situation, we may ascertain the meaning of emptiness but think, "This is emptiness." Here we are not apprehending emptiness, but instead know the existence of emptiness, which is a conventionality. This, too, is not ascertainment of emptiness. If we ascertained emptiness, only the mere negation—that is, the emptiness of true existence—appears to the direct reliable cognizer perceiving it. In the case of an inferential reliable cognizer, a conceptual appearance of emptiness appears to the mind. This is according to the Sūtra system; in the context of deity yoga in Tantrayāna, the deity, which is the basis of emptiness, appears to the inferential realization of emptiness.

Reasoning Analyzing the Ultimate

In *Commentary on the Awakening Mind* (57) Nāgārjuna says:

> Just as sweetness is the nature of molasses
> and heat the nature of fire,
> likewise we maintain that the nature
> of all phenomena is emptiness.

How delightful it would be to rest the mind in the nature of all phenomena, emptiness! That would be a true vacation that would let us relax and return refreshed and with more capacity to skillfully benefit sentient beings. The ultimate nature of all phenomena is present here and now all the time; our task is to realize it. This is done through employing probing awareness and reasoning analyzing the ultimate.

As discussed in *Searching for the Self*, when identifying the object of negation and meditating on emptiness, it is of utmost importance to avoid both the extreme of absolutism that superimposes inherent existence and the extreme of nihilism that negates conventional existence. In the former, inherent existence is left untouched, and in the latter, conventional existence is denigrated. To avoid the two extremes it is crucial to differentiate two distinct types of analysis—ultimate analysis and conventional analysis—as well as their distinct domains—ultimate truths and veiled truths.

The *ultimate mode of existence* is the deepest or final mode of existence, how phenomena actually exist—their emptiness of inherent existence. *Reasoning analyzing the ultimate* (T. *don dam dpyod byed kyi rigs pa*) and ultimate analysis (T. *don dam pa'i dpyad pa*) are used to investigate the final mode of existence. It has the same implication as "probing awareness analyzing (or looking into) the ultimate" (T. *mthar thug dpyod pa'i rigs shes*). Both of these lead to the correct view of emptiness.

For example, what is the referent of the term "helicopter"? Does Tenzin exist from his own side? Can an inherently existent Tenzin be found as one with or separate from his body or mind? When we are not satisfied with mere nominal existence, we use reasoning analyzing the ultimate to find what something actually is. Reasoning analyzing the ultimate differs from *conventional reasoning* (T. *tha snyad dpyod byed kyi rigs pa*), which is used to examine conventional topics such as fouls in soccer games, government policies, the workings of a computer, and personal relationships.

If something existed inherently, it would be able to withstand reasoning analyzing the ultimate. That reasoning would be able to find an inherently existent thing. However, when we subject a person, ocean, or democracy to the reasoning analyzing the ultimate, it cannot withstand that reasoning. An inherently existent person or thing cannot be found. We cannot isolate a specific, independent object that any word refers to. Ultimate analysis finds only the lack or emptiness of an inherently existent thing.

By apprehending Tenzin's emptiness of inherent existence, reasoning analyzing the ultimate eliminates the elaboration of inherent existence on Tenzin. Eliminating elaborations on an object—in this case, Tenzin—does not mean that the conventional object is found to be nonexistent. It means the object does not have an inherent essence. Ultimate analysis can determine only whether something exists ultimately or not; it cannot determine whether that object exists conventionally.

In the past, some early Tibetan scholars, such as Ngok Loden Sherab (1059–1109), erroneously thought that emptiness is not a knowable object—it is not an existent—because it cannot bear analysis by reasoning analyzing the ultimate. Other early Mādhyamikas, such as Chaba Chokyi Senge (1109–69), thought that emptiness must be inherently existent because it is found by reasoning analyzing the ultimate and is seen by an ārya's pristine wisdom of meditative equipoise. All of these so-called Mādhyamikas did not find the Middle Way view, although they saw themselves as Mādhyamikas.

So-called Mādhyamikas who negate too much say that since the phenomena analyzed by probing awareness (T. *rigs shes*) are not found, they do not exist at all. When ultimate analysis cannot find an inherently existent Tashi, they confuse emptiness and total nonexistence and think the object doesn't exist. They think this way not only regarding conventional things like yarn and thread but also regarding emptiness, the ultimate truth. They believe that if emptiness existed, it should be found by probing awareness, but since it is not found, it does not exist. Thus these so-called Mādhyamikas say that nothing can be established as an ultimate truth; there is no āryas' meditative equipoise on emptiness because there is no ultimate truth to be perceived. For them, "elaborations" does not refer to the object of negation—inherent existence—but to all existence, and "freedom from elaborations" means not apprehendable by mind as either existing or nonexisting. It is a freedom from elaborations in which nothing at all is established.

Mādhyamikas say that "freedom from elaborations" refers to the elimination of dualistic appearances for a particular mind. The object of probing awareness—emptiness or reality—is the apprehended object of that consciousness, and thus it is a phenomenon that is realized by a reliable cognizer. This nonaffirming negative is found—that is, realized—by probing awareness; emptiness is an object of mind, it is not mere nothingness.

Not being able to bear analysis by reasoning analyzing the ultimate (T. *rigs pas dpyad mi bzod pa*) is not the same as being *negated by that reasoning* (T. *rigs pas gnod pa*). Although Tashi cannot bear analysis by the reasoning analyzing the ultimate, his conventional existence is not undermined or negated by that reasoning. Why? Because the purview of the reasoning analyzing the ultimate is just an object's ultimate nature. That reasoning does not examine a thing's conventional existence and thus does not have the ability to establish that thing as conventionally existent or nonexistent. An ārya's reasoning analyzing the ultimate finds only ultimate truth, emptiness. It does not find veilings such as tables and persons, and thus can neither establish nor negate their existence. For example, since our visual consciousness does not know the sound of music, it cannot negate the existence of a melody because sound is not within the purview of what a visual consciousness can apprehend.

Furthermore, existence is not posited from the viewpoint of the ultimate, so not finding something when searched for with ultimate analysis does not negate that thing's conventional existence. Ultimate analysis examines if an object exists inherently and refutes its inherent existence. It does not search for mere phenomena. Nothing can withstand or bear reasoning analyzing the ultimate, and therefore nothing inherently exists. Nevertheless, phenomena still exist conventionally. They are established by the conventional reliable cognizers that cognize them. Conventional reliable cognizers are consciousnesses that correctly realize the conventional existence of an object without analyzing its ultimate nature. For example, our visual consciousness is a conventional reliable cognizer: it sees the table in this room and establishes its existence.

Similarly, *not being found by a probing awareness* (T. *rigs shes kyis ma rnyed pa*) and being *refuted by a probing awareness* (T. *rigs shes kyis bkag pa*) are not the same. When a probing awareness searches for an inherently existent Tenzin, it does not find such a person. It finds only the emptiness of Tenzin. Because that mind's purview is only the ultimate nature of Tenzin, it does not refute the conventional existence of Tenzin, only his ultimate existence.

In summary, do not confuse the following:

1. *Not being able to bear ultimate analysis* and *being undermined or refuted by that analysis.* A dog cannot bear ultimate analysis, but its conventional existence is not negated or undermined by that analysis. An inherently existent dog cannot bear analysis and its existence is refuted by that analysis.
2. *Not being seen (known) by an ārya's pristine wisdom of meditative equipoise* and *being seen (known) as nonexistent by that wisdom.* A buffalo is not seen by an ārya's wisdom of meditative equipoise, but it is not seen as nonexistent by that wisdom because veiled truths are not within the purview of that wisdom. An inherently existent buffalo isn't seen by an ārya's pristine wisdom of meditative equipoise and it is seen as nonexistent by that wisdom.
3. *Not being found by reasoning analyzing the ultimate* and being *found as nonexistent* by that reasoning. A politician is not found by ultimate analysis, but he or she is not found to be nonexistent by that analysis.

Similarly do not confuse:

1. *Being established by reasoning analyzing the ultimate* and *being able to bear analysis by that reasoning.* The emptiness of Brian is established by the ultimate analysis searching for Brian's ultimate mode of existence,

but neither the emptiness of Brian nor Brian is able to bear analysis by that reasoning.

2. *Being seen or known by an ārya's pristine wisdom of meditative equipoise* and *being seen or known as ultimately existent by that wisdom*. A grapefruit's emptiness is seen by an ārya's wisdom of meditative equipoise, but it is not seen as ultimately existent by that wisdom.
3. *Being found by reasoning analyzing the ultimate* and *being inherently existent*. The emptiness of the lamp is found by ultimate analysis searching for the lamp, but that emptiness is not inherently existent.

Although āryas' pristine wisdom knows emptiness and finds emptiness, that does not make emptiness inherently existent. Emptiness is found by reasoning analyzing the ultimate, but it is not found to be inherently existent by that reasoning. Emptiness is established by that reasoning, but cannot bear analysis by it. In short, after searching to see if the person inherently exists, that reasoning does not find an inherently existent person. It finds only the lack of inherent existence of the person—the emptiness of the person. If we subject emptiness to ultimate analysis, it too cannot withstand analysis, but that doesn't mean it is nonexistent. The emptiness of emptiness is found.

If veilings were proven to be nonexistent by reasoning analyzing the ultimate, there would be no purpose in trying to free ourselves from saṃsāra or in practicing the path to attain liberation, for they would both be nonexistent. However, the existence of both saṃsāra and nirvāṇa are established by conventional consciousnesses, which are more powerful than faulty reasonings that try to refute the existence of things that conventionally exist. Please note: although emptiness is known by wisdom analyzing the ultimate, the existence of emptiness is established by a conventional reliable cognizer.

Yogācārins' reasonings dispute the existence of external objects, but conventional reliable cognizers establish their existence, thus showing those reasonings are erroneous. Prāsaṅgikas emphasize the importance of accepting what is conventionally established in the world. That doesn't mean everything the world accepts exists, because some erroneous ideas and cognitions are widespread in society. Yogācārins proclaim that no external objects exist and that all phenomena are one nature with the mind perceiving them—that is, that the perceiving consciousness and the perceived object arise from the same latency on the foundation consciousness. This assertion of Yogācārins can be refuted by conventional reliable cognizers that apprehend conventionally existent external objects such as tables and chairs. Just because a particular tenet system uses its version of ultimate analysis to negate something, it doesn't mean that its ultimate analysis is correct. Faulty analysis cannot establish the nonexistence of external objects. If something is established by a correct worldly consciousness, it exists.

Someone questions: How can you say that nothing is found when searched for by an analytical mind? At the airport we search for our friend after her plane arrives and find her. Doctors run tests and diagnose illnesses. These are reliable minds that find what they are searching for.

Conventional analysis and the analysis done by probing awareness are different. A probing awareness searches for ultimate existence, whereas a conventional knower searches for the conventionally existent thing. Tsongkhapa clarifies the difference between conventional and ultimate analysis (OR 39–40):

> This conventional analysis is *not* as follows: Not being satisfied with just the conventional imputation of arising and going, one employs a method of analysis searching for the way in which the object of conventional imputation exists.

The analysis described in this chapter is ultimate analysis, not conventional analysis. It searches for ultimately existent phenomena, and such phenomena cannot be found under this type of analysis. That analysis refutes their existence. If ultimate analysis is used to search for a conventionally existent thing, it cannot find it either. But since conventional existence is not in the purview of the reasoning analyzing the ultimate, it does not negate its existence. In other words, a probing awareness cannot find either an inherently existent grapefruit or a conventionally existent grapefruit. Although that mind can refute the existence of the inherently existent grapefruit, it cannot refute the existence of the conventionally existent one.

Phenomena cannot withstand ultimate analysis—examination of their ultimate mode of existence. Ultimate analysis is done by investigating whether an object is inherently one with its basis of imputation or inherently different from it; it examines if impermanent things are produced from self, other, both, or causelessly. Nevertheless, appearances—that is, veiled truths (conventional truths)—are posited from the viewpoint of conditionality without analysis or investigation. Saying that they are posited without analysis or investigation does not mean that veiled truths are beyond the worldly analysis or conventional investigation that we do in our daily lives. Such analysis and investigation apply to questions such as: Has the electric bill been paid? Is this person guilty or innocent of the crime they are accused of committing? Rocket science, artificial intelligence, and the best way to grow broccoli are in the realm of conventional analysis. Whether the rockets and broccoli exist from their own side and whether they exist by being merely imputed—such questions are in the realm of ultimate analysis. So conventional phenomena and veiled truths are neither figments of the imagination nor beyond logical reasoning, because conventional analysis is useful in our lives. It is also used to refute a permanent self and a permanent cosmic substance out of which everything is created. Because refutation of these latter two topics does not involve an understanding of emptiness, the reasoning used to negate them is considered conventional analysis. Only analysis that is seeking phenomena's deepest mode of existence, which is beyond their conventional appearances, constitutes ultimate analysis.

The Buddha said "They see in the manner of non-seeing" and "Not seeing is the supreme seeing." This doesn't mean that buddhas don't see veiled truths or that they consider veiled truths nonexistent. Rather, if veiled truths existed inherently, the pristine wisdom of meditative equipoise on emptiness would see them because that wisdom sees the ultimate mode of existence of all phenomena. But this wisdom has exhausted all possible ways that phenomena could exist inherently and knows inherent existence to be nonexistent. This pristine wisdom perceives only emptiness, which is the supreme seeing.

The way āryas' pristine wisdom of meditative equipoise on emptiness knows emptiness is compared to knowing space. The *Verse Summary of the Perfection of Wisdom* says (FEW 353):

> The Tathāgata teaches that one who does not see forms,
> does not see feelings, does not see discriminations,
> does not see intentions, does not see consciousness,
> mind, or sentience sees the Dharma (suchness).

Analyze how space is seen as in the expression
by sentient beings in the words "Space is seen."
The Tathāgata teaches that seeing the Dharma is also like that.
The seeing cannot be expressed by another example.

Emptiness is seen by not seeing inherent existence and not seeing veiled truths such as the aggregates that are the base of emptiness. In the example, space is the absence of tangible obstruction, which would be known if it were present. The not knowing of tangible obstruction (the unseen) is the knowing of space (the seen). In the perspective of āryas' wisdom directly realizing emptiness, neither veiled truths nor inherent existence is seen. However, this does not mean veiled truths do not exist; they are known in post-meditation time by conventional reliable cognizers. Do not think that buddhas perceive only emptiness; they know both truths.

REFLECTION

1. Review the differences between:
    - Not being able to bear ultimate analysis and being undermined or refuted by that analysis.
    - Not being seen (known) by an ārya's pristine wisdom of meditative equipoise and being seen (known) as nonexistent by that wisdom.
    - Not being found by reasoning analyzing the ultimate and being found as nonexistent by that reasoning.
2. Review the differences between:
    - Being established by reasoning analyzing the ultimate and being able to bear analysis by that reasoning.
    - Being seen or known by an ārya's pristine wisdom of meditative equipoise and being seen or known as ultimately existent by that wisdom.
    - Being found by reasoning analyzing the ultimate and being inherently existent.

Objects Negated by the Path and Objects Negated by Reasoning

In *Searching for the Self* we discussed objects negated by the path and objects negated by reasoning.[21] To review, objects negated by the path are existent phenomena, and most of them are consciousnesses that misapprehend their objects—for example, consciousnesses that grasp true existence and afflictions that are based on this grasping. By realizing impermanence, emptiness, and so forth, these erroneous minds are gradually overcome. Reliable minds such as bodhicitta, the inferential realization of impermanence or emptiness, and the visual consciousness seeing yellow are not negated by the path.

Objects negated by reasoning are nonexistents, such as a permanent person, a self-sufficient substantially existent person, inherent existence, existence by its own characteristics, ultimate existence, true existence, and so on. These have never existed. Reasoning does not eradicate inherent existence; it refutes or discredits it. Here we see the importance of differentiating the mind grasping inherent existence and inherent existence. The mind grasping inherent existence exists. It is negated by the path; its antidote is a wisdom mind whose mode of apprehending its object is the opposite of the way such grasping apprehends objects. Inherent existence, on the other hand, has never existed; it is shown to be nonexistent and is an object negated by reasoning.

Reasoning analyzing the ultimate does not discredit the existence of objects negated by the path, for these things exist conventionally and what exists cannot be disproven by reasoning. Reasoning analyzing the ultimate disproves objects negated by reasoning such as inherent existence. The probing awareness analyzing the ultimate overcomes erroneous consciousnesses that are objects negated by the path by replacing them with correct consciousnesses that perceive phenomena as empty. It does this gradually, like the brightening of the sky at dawn. The brighter the light becomes, the more the darkness declines. Similarly, as the wisdom realizing emptiness increases, the self-grasping ignorance gradually weakens until it is completely eradicated. The process of generating this wisdom in our mindstream requires enthusiasm and continuous effort that are well worth our time and energy.

Phenomena established by conventional consciousnesses are not negated by reasoning analyzing the ultimate. Similarly, the emptiness known by the reasoning analyzing the ultimate is not refuted by conventional consciousnesses. Probing awareness analyzing the ultimate and conventional reliable cognizers have different purviews. Conventional reliable cognizers establish veiled truths; they do not examine their ultimate nature. Reasoning analyzing the ultimate investigates their ultimate nature; it neither establishes nor refutes veiled truths. Because it does not find phenomena to exist ultimately, reasoning analyzing the ultimate establishes their emptiness of ultimate existence; it does not apprehend their conventional nature. Although ultimate analysis does not find forms and so forth, it does not negate their existence either.

Although everything in saṃsāra and nirvāṇa is empty of inherent existence, it still exists. How does it exist? It exists conventionally. Our experiences arise due to karma as well as present conditions. Our sense faculties, bodies, and consciousnesses are maturation results of karma and arise dependent on karma. The objects they contact arise dependent on their own causes and depend on natural laws such as the laws of biology, chemistry, and physics. Our experiences are produced as results of the interaction of an object, a sense faculty, and a previous moment of consciousness. Even though our sense faculties, consciousnesseses, and their objects do not inherently exist and cannot be found when examined by ultimate analysis; they do dependently exist, arise, and function to produce results.

Phenomena can exist and produce effects without being inherently existent or findable by ultimate analysis. For example, although the people on a TV screen are not real people, we experience various emotions when we see them. By seeing the false appearance of elephants on television, we learn about their habitat and behavior. Although no real elephants are present in the television, we cannot deny their appearance on the screen. Although all phenomena are empty of inherent existence, they still appear and exist conventionally.

Two Kinds of Self

We talk of two kinds of self: (1) a self that is negated, such as an inherently existent self, and (2) a self that exists, a self that is merely designated by term and concept. Negating the inherently existent self and proving that it is nonexistent is done in relation to the self that exists. Trinlay exists by being merely designated in dependence on a set of aggregates. This merely designated Trinlay is the *basis of negation*, and an inherently existent Trinlay is the *object of negation*. Trinlay is empty of inherent existence. The merely designated Trinlay and Trinlay's emptiness of inherent existence both exist. They depend on each other; one cannot exist without the other.

The appearance of an inherently existent person exists although an inherently existent person does not. When we look at Trinlay and when he thinks of himself, an inherently existent person appears to the consciousness apprehending him. When Trinlay analyzes whether he exists inherently or not and over time gains a direct realization of the emptiness of the I, the appearance of an inherently existent I subsides while he is in meditation. To this mind of meditative equipoise on emptiness, it is as if no person remains. Once an inherently existent person is refuted, there seems to be nothing left.

But something does remain. This is the mere I that exists by mere designation, mere name. Once Trinlay arises from meditation and goes about his daily activities, the I again appears to his mind as inherently existent. However, as long as his mind is still influenced by the meditation on emptiness, he knows this appearance is mistaken and sees his I as like an illusion. But once the influence of the mind meditating on emptiness ceases, grasping the I as inherently existent may again arise. The inherently existent I that he grasps is itself the object of negation.

There is a self that is observed (T. *dmigs pa'i bdag*) as well as an inherently existent self that is the object of negation (T. *dgag bya'i bdag*). They appear mixed, and differentiating them in our own experience is an extremely subtle and difficult process. When we ordinary beings refer to the body and mind, it seems that an inherently existent I immediately appears in relation to them. We're convinced there is an independent person who is distinct from yet blended in with the body and mind. In fact, no such independent I exists. But trying to distinguish "this much of what appears is the object of negation and this much is the self that exists" is very difficult, no matter how well we intellectually know the words to describe it. For this reason, refuting the inherently existent self that is the object of negation while preserving the self that is observed—the merely imputed self—is an extremely delicate venture.

The Mere I

In the previous chapter, we discussed the general I and particular I's. When speaking in terms of the general I, it is correct and understandable to say, "I did this action and I experienced this result." But when speaking in terms of the particular I's, the I that creates a karmic cause is not the same I that experiences its effect. These two I's exist at different times, with the former being the cause of the latter. Since this life's I and a previous life's I are different, you may wonder why we experience the results of actions done by someone else in a past life. Although the two particular I's are different, they are not inherently different or totally unrelated. They exist within the same continuum; they are parts of the same general I.

Similarly, the I that goes to school is different from the I that is employed after graduation, although they exist in the same continuum. The person who studied hard created the cause for the future I in his continuum to receive a job. In the same way, a person who gives generously in this life creates the cause for a future person in the same continuum to receive wealth. Here, the time between the creation of the cause and experience of the result is longer and the change of aggregates is more pronounced, but the idea is the same. By thinking of the general I, the link between actions we did in the past and results we experience in the present becomes clearer. The person who will experience the result in the future may not look like or have the same personality as the present self, but that person—our future I—will want happiness and not suffering.

Each person or general I has his or her own continuum. Your body and my body, your mind and my mind, are parts of different continuums. Our general I's are not the same either; they exist in different continuums. For this reason the I that remembers your past is not the same I that remembers mine. In the future I will not experience the results of the karmic causes that you have created. Although you and I are equal in not existing inherently, our conventional selves are different. Each of us experiences the results of our own actions.

According to highest yoga tantra, the subtlest mind and wind are the same nature, and they exist continuously, without interruption throughout all our lives and into buddhahood. The subtlest mind-wind is the subtlest basis of designation for the I. However, it is not a soul or a permanent, unified, and independent self. When sought with ultimate analysis, the mere I cannot be found in the subtlest mind or subtlest wind or separate from them. Furthermore, the subtlest mind-wind is constantly changing. Since it is not a permanent, inherently existent basis of designation, the I designated in dependence on it isn't permanent or inherently existent. Nevertheless, while we are alive in a particular body, that coarse body and mind are the coarse basis of designation of that life's I, and in the intermediate state, a subtler mind and body are the basis of designation of the intermediate state I.

The continuum of the subtlest mind-wind, like all other phenomena, is empty of inherent existence yet exists conventionally. When it manifests at the time of death, the subtlest mind is without thought in that there is no subjective sense of self at that time. However, from the viewpoint of another person, there is a person, and this self is designated in dependence on the clear-light mind.

This is similar to a yoginī in meditative equipoise that directly perceives emptiness. At that time there is no thought "I am in meditative equipoise" or "I am perceiving emptiness." In meditative equipoise directly realizing emptiness, only emptiness appears to the mind—no other object, including a sense of self appears—and emptiness is perceived nondually. Nevertheless, another person may think that this yoginī is perceiving emptiness now. Upon arising from that meditative equipoise, the yoginī looks back on her experience in equipoise and knows that she realized emptiness nonconceptually.

The mere I is designated in dependence on the collection of a body and a mind. When the body and mind are of the human realm, the self or the person is a human being. When that body ceases to function and the mind separates from it, that human being has ceased because the term "human being" is used only when human mental aggregates are associated with a human body. According to Sūtrayāna, the mental consciousness is the basis of designation of the mere I in the bardo, and the coarse body and mind are the basis of designation in the next life. According to highest yoga tantra, the inseparable subtler mind and body of the bardo state is the basis of designation of the person in the bardo. According to Sūtrayāna, beings in the formless realm do not have a form aggregate, so the self of a formless realm being is designated in dependence on the four mental aggregates. But from a Tantric perspective, beings in the formless realm have a subtle body in that the subtlest mind-wind is present.

What Carries Karmic Seeds?

The question of who or what carries karmic seeds from one life to the next has been a challenge to all Buddhist and non-Buddhist tenet systems. Non-Buddhist schools assert that a permanent, unified, independent self or soul performs this function, but an unchanging permanent self is fixed in time and cannot carry karmic seeds. Such a self is roundly refuted by all Buddhist tenet systems.

The lower Buddhist schools resolve the dilemma of what or who carries the karmic seeds from one life to another by asserting that the I is one of the aggregates or a collection of them. Kashmiri Vaibhāṣikas assert that the continuum of the mental consciousness allows for actions created in one life to produce results in a later life. Other Vaibhāṣikas assert that an abstract composite called "acquisition" (obtainer, *prāpti*) or another abstract composite called "non-wastage" (*avipraṇāśa*) connects actions to their results. Acquisition and non-wastage are likened to a voucher that guarantees a loan preventing loss to the lender in that they prevent the forfeiture of the result of an action. Sautrāntika Reasoning Proponents and Yogācāra Reasoning Proponents say the mental consciousness is the I, and it is the carrier of karmic seeds.

Yogācāra Scriptural Proponents assert eight consciousnesses—the six consciousnesses commonly accepted by all Buddhist schools, as well as two more consciousnesses: the afflictive consciousness and the foundation consciousness (*ālayavijñāna*). They say that since the person is in a state of non-mentation[22] during the meditative absorption of cessation, deep sleep, and death, a separate consciousness that is the repository for karmic seeds must exist. This is the foundation consciousness, which is a neutral undefiled consciousness. Phenomena appear to the foundation consciousness, but it does not ascertain them. It is a beginningless, manifest, ever-present consciousness that carries the karmic seeds from one life to the next. It is the person, and it transmigrates from one life to another.

Svātantrikas refute this, saying that Yogācāra Scriptural Proponents created the idea of a foundation consciousness by their own thought, not through empirical investigation. Because these Yogācārins assert that consciousnesses and their objects truly exist, they need to posit a truly existent stable basis—the foundation consciousness—that carries the karmic seeds from life to life. Svātantrikas state that it is not necessary to posit a foundation consciousness as a real, stable repository, for it is only the coarse six consciousnesses that do not function during the meditative equipoise of cessation, death, and so forth. A subtle mental consciousness exists during those times, and it carries the seeds. Furthermore, say the Svātantrikas, difficulties arise as soon as a truly existent consciousness that is the person is asserted: Is that person truly one with or different from the foundation consciousness? If the foundation consciousness exists truly, it could not change, so how could it accept new seeds and "lose" old ones when they ripen?

Avoiding these problems, the Svātantrikas posit an inherently existent self that is findable within the aggregates; the continuum of the mental consciousness is the person that carries the karmic seeds. Without such an I, the transmission of karmic seeds from one life to the next cannot be explained. However, this assertion is also problematic, because in the uninterrupted path of the path of seeing, a meditator passes into a nondual state that is free from any polluted consciousness, and an unpolluted consciousness is not suitable to be a repository for seeds of polluted karma. The mind in meditative equipoise that directly realizes emptiness is totally unpolluted and is so pure that it cannot be the basis for or carrier of seeds of polluted karma.

The underlying problem with all the above assertions is that they hold that the I exists inherently and is findable among the aggregates. But as we've seen, this notion is refuted because an inherently existent I doesn't depend on any other factors such as causes and conditions and would thus be permanent. A permanent I cannot carry the karmic seeds.

Prāsaṅgikas avoid all these difficulties by asserting that since the five aggregates are appropriated by the self, the self cannot be one of the aggregates or the collection of them.[23] The appropriator and the appropriated must be different, so the mental consciousness cannot be the self. On the other hand, a self apart from the five aggregates cannot exist. They conclude that the self is designated in dependence on the four or five aggregates, and therefore the I exists by mere name, by merely being designated. "Mere" does not refute the basis of designation of the self or the conventional self. It precludes the inherent existence of the self.

To resolve the dilemma of what carries the remaining seeds of polluted karma when an ārya is in meditative equipoise directly realizing emptiness, Prāsaṅgikas say that while karmic seeds accumulate on the continuity of the mental consciousness, the mere I is also the carrier of karmic seeds. That is, although an ārya's mental consciousness directly realizing emptiness is unpolluted, the mere I is polluted because it is designated in dependence on the polluted and unpolluted aggregates. Thus it is suitable to carry the karmic seeds, be they polluted or unpolluted.

In this way, Prāsaṅgikas posit two repositories of karmic seeds, one temporary, the other constant. The continuity of the mental consciousnesses that functions during our lives is the temporary basis of karmic seeds. The mere I is the constant basis. Existing even during the uninterrupted path of the path of seeing, deep sleep, and death, the mere I carries the karmic seeds. Nonetheless, the mere I exists only by designation; it is not findable under analysis.

Some interesting issues arise here. For example, a mind that is the uninterrupted path of the path of seeing abides in meditative equipoise on emptiness and is in the process of eradicating the acquired afflictions and their seeds from the root. This mind is unpolluted—it is not under the influence of ignorance—because it has no appearance of or grasping to inherent existence. However, the innate afflictions and the cognitive obscurations haven't yet been eradicated. What is the basis of the seeds and latencies of these obscurations to be abandoned by the path of meditation? That uninterrupted path of the path of seeing doesn't have the latencies of ignorance that cause mistaken dualistic appearance because it is unpolluted. The latencies don't abide on the sense consciousnesses because sense consciousnesses don't function during meditative equipoise. The mere I carries these latencies. This conventional I is not imputed *on* the aggregates or *to* the aggregates, but simply in dependence on them. It exists merely nominally. Understanding this solves many problems.

To look at another example, a śrāvaka ārya who is born in the peak of saṃsāra, the highest division of the formless realm, is still a transmigrator in saṃsāra. The mind of the peak of saṃsāra is too subtle to realize emptiness directly, so he has to descend to the meditative absorption of the level of the formless realm immediately below—the mind of the base of nothingness—to meditate on emptiness. At the time he is in meditative equipoise on emptiness, his mental consciousness is unpolluted. He has no other consciousnesses; because beings in the formless realm don't have a body, they don't have sense consciousnesses. Nor is there a coarse mental consciousness. Is there a transmigrator in saṃsāra at that time? That unpolluted mind isn't a transmigrator. But not all the afflictive obscurations have been eliminated, so we can't say there isn't a transmigrator. The mere I is still present, and it is the transmigrator. In which realm is this transmigrator? The person is a transmigrator of the peak of saṃsāra because that is the realm of his rebirth, even though his mind at that time is a mind of the base of nothingness.

CHART: THE PERSON ACCORDING TO VARIOUS TENET SYSTEMS

TENET SYSTEMS	WHAT THEY ASSERT IS THE PERSON
Non-Buddhist systems	Permanent, unitary, and independent self that is separate from the aggregates
Vaibhāṣikas[24]	Collection of four or five aggregates Mental consciousness Inexpressible as either one with or separate from the aggregates
Sautrāntika Scriptural Proponents	Continuum of the aggregates
Sautrāntika Reasoning Proponents	Mental consciousness
Yogācāra Scriptural Proponents	Foundation consciousness
Yogācāra Reasoning Proponents	Mental consciousness
Yogācāra-Svātantrika Madhyamaka	Continuum of the mental consciousness
Sautrāntika-Svātantrika Madhyamaka	Subtle, neutral mental consciousness
Prāsaṅgika Madhyamaka	Mere I

In general, Prāsaṅgikas say that the mere I is what carries karmic seeds from one life to another. In highest yoga tantra, it is said that the subtlest mind carries the seeds. This difference in presentations occurs because the explanation of the subtlest mind is not found in Sūtrayāna or the three lower tantric classes. Although Pāramitāyāna and the lower tantras speak of a subtle consciousness, it is a neutral consciousness that is present only occasionally. Since they do not speak of a subtlest mind that is present in states of non-mentation, they say that when a person is in states such as deep sleep or a faint, there is no manifest consciousness and the mere I carries the karmic seeds. The highest yoga tantra, however, says that the subtlest mind is present during these times, and it is the basis on which the karmic seeds rest. Saying the subtlest mind is the carrier of the karmic seeds and saying that the mere I is the carrier of the karmic seeds are not contradictory because during times of unconsciousness, the mere I is designated in dependence on the subtlest mind-wind.

REFLECTION

1. What would an inherently existent I be like if it existed?
2. What is the mere I?
3. What is the difference between them? What can the mere I do that an inherently existent I can't?

6 The Selflessness of Phenomena: Diamond Slivers

NĀGĀRJUNA'S *Treatise on the Middle Way* is one of my favorite texts, and I love to read and ponder its meaning. I often begin with chapter 26, "Examination of the Twelve Links of Dependent Origination," because it teaches causality in terms of the twelve links that show the causal process leading to rebirth in saṃsāra and the causal process of ceasing such rebirth. In doing so, Nāgārjuna explains the functioning of cause and effect and the existence of veiled truths, and on that basis he establishes emptiness. Since the weak point in the twelve links is first-link ignorance, I next read chapter 18, "Examination of the Self and Phenomena," which explains that the only weapon to destroy ignorance is understanding ultimate reality, the emptiness of true existence. What is this emptiness? This is elucidated in chapter 24, "Examination of the Four Truths," which contains arguments of those who assert true existence and Nāgārjuna's systematic refutation of them. Here he clarifies that the meaning of emptiness is dependent arising. Dependent designation shows that saṃsāra and nirvāṇa, as well as the law of causality, make sense and function within the fact that everything lacks inherent existence, whereas they are not tenable when seen from the perspective of inherent existence. Here too Nāgārjuna shows that emptiness and dependent arising are compatible and come to the same point. Remembering this is important when studying the other chapters in his treatise that principally focus on negating inherent existence.

Then I read chapter 22, "Examination of the Tathāgata," which contains a thorough explanation of dependent designation. It takes me several days to contemplate these chapters in this sequence, and doing this is very rewarding.

In this and the following chapters, I will often quote this precious text by Nāgārjuna. I encourage you to study it and to reflect and meditate on its meaning. Buddhapālita's commentary on the *Treatise on the Middle Way* entitled *Buddhapālitavṛtti* is wonderful, as is Tsongkhapa's commentary *Ocean of Reasoning* (*Rtsa shes tik chen rigs pa'i rgya mtsho*).

Nāgārjuna's work is not easy to understand. If I were compelled to give a commentary on the entire *Treatise on the Middle Way*, it would be similar to an old person without teeth eating food—he chews what is soft and swallows the hard parts! When some people give teachings on this text, their rhetoric is fantastic. They state that all the important points have been fully established by means of hundreds of reasonings. However, when they give the actual teaching, it is only a series of citations.

Persons are either buddhas or sentient beings—human beings, animals, āryas, and all other ordinary beings of the six classes. The inherent existence of persons is refuted by meditating on the selflessness of persons. The bases of designation of persons are phenomena—the five aggregates, the six constituents (earth, water, fire, wind, space, and consciousness), the six sense faculties (visual, auditory, olfactory, gustatory, tactile, and mental), and so forth. We refute the inherent existence of these by meditating on the selflessness of phenomena. By refuting the inherent existence of persons and their bases of designation—the psychophysical aggregates—the ignorance that binds us to uncontrolled existence in saṃsāra crumbles.

There are several different methods for refuting the self of phenomena. We have discussed Candrakīrti's seven points; now we will explore the method called "diamond slivers," which examines the way things exist from the viewpoint of their cause. These teachings originated with the Buddha, were expounded by Nāgārjuna in his *Treatise on the Middle Way*, and were further explained by Candrakīrti and other sages of the Nālandā tradition. These teachings were disseminated in India, China, Tibet, Mongolia, and elsewhere and are still studied and practiced today because no matter the historical period, they give us the key to liberation and awakening.

Refuting Inherently Existent Arising

What is the object of negation? Does it exist? These questions are crucial because if inherent existence existed, the ignorance that grasps it would be a correct consciousness that could not be eliminated by wisdom. Afflictions would exist inherently, without depending on causes and conditions. In that case they could not be completely overcome by stopping their causes or temporarily abandoned by stopping their conditions. Attaining liberation and full awakening would be impossible.

Tsongkhapa defines the object of negation for examining the ultimate nature of things (impermanent phenomena) (OR 97):

> When such things as seeds and fuel are seen or heard to be performing the action of giving rise to such things as sprouts and fire respectively, grasping the object of negation is to grasp both cause and effect not as merely nominally imputed or as the objects that are the bases of nominal imputation, but as inherently existent produced and producer.

"Nominal imputation" means designated by name and concept. When both the causes—such as seeds and fuel—and the effects—sprouts and fire—are held to have their own essence, independent of everything else, including mere nominal imputation, they are grasped as inherently existent.

If a thing exists inherently, it must arise inherently either from a cause or without a cause. If it arises from a cause, its effect must be (1) inherently the same as the cause (arising from itself), (2) inherently different from the cause (arising from other), or (3) both (arising inherently from both self and other). Only these four options exist—arising from a cause in one of these three ways or arising without a cause; there are no other alternatives. Various philosophical systems—both Buddhist and non-Buddhist—assert one or another of these four types of arising as proof of inherently existent arising. Prāsaṅgikas use contradictory consequences—*reductio ad absurdum* arguments (*prāsaṅga*)—to refute these four possible ways of inherent arising. By refuting these four, any possibility of inherent arising is negated without negating the nominal, conventional, dependent arising of effects from their causes.

Diamond slivers—so-called because just as even a fragment of a diamond is strong and can easily cut a hard object, each of its four reasons decisively contradicts inherent existence—is one of the foremost reasonings disproving the inherent existence of phenomena other than persons. This reasoning refuting the four extremes of arising is a fourfold negation (*catuṣkoṭi*) that refutes four hypothetical ways a result could arise inherently. Indicative of its importance, this argument is the first verse of the first chapter of Nāgārjuna's *Treatise on the Middle Way* (MMK 1.1):

> Neither from itself nor from another,
> nor from both,
> nor without a cause
> does anything anywhere ever arise.

Here Nāgārjuna asserts that nothing ever, anywhere, and in no philosophical system in the slightest arises inherently from itself, another, both, or without a cause.

This reasoning has its roots in both Pāli and Sanskrit sūtras. *The Extensive Play Sūtra* (*Lalitavistara Sūtra* 13.103) says:

> For instance, there is sprout when there is seed. That which is seed is not itself the sprout. Neither is it other than that, nor is it that itself. Thus, the reality (*dharmatā*) is not annihilated and not eternal.

The Rice Seedling Sūtra (*Śālistamba Sūtra*) says:

> This sprout, whose cause is a seed and which arises, is not created by itself, not created by other, not created by both, nor arisen without a cause, nor arisen from God (*Īśvara*), time (*kāla*), atoms (*aṇu*), nature (*prakṛti*), or self-being (*svabhāva*).[25]

A similar argument is found in the Pāli sūtras (SN 12.17 and 12.67). We'll look at this in the next chapter.

Candrakīrti unpacks this argument in his *Supplement to "Treatise on the Middle Way"* by constructing the syllogism "Consider a sprout, it does not inherently arise because it does not (inherently) arise from self, other, both, or without a cause." A sprout arising from itself, from both itself and other, and causelessly do not exist conventionally, let alone ultimately. In addition, in the option of arising from other Candrakīrti reads "other" as an inherently separate other. Since the notion of an inherently real other is already implied, he does not include the word "inherently" when he lays out the four possibilities for the sprout to inherently arise:

1. A thing does not arise from itself.
2. A thing does not [inherently] arise from other.
3. A thing does not arise from both itself and other.
4. A thing does not arise without any cause.

Taken together these four statements are reasons proving the thesis that a sprout does not inherently exist. They refute all possible options for inherently existent arising. By ascertaining these four theses, which are nonaffirming negatives, we can draw the conclusion that a sprout does not inherently arise and does not inherently exist.

If a thing existed inherently, it would have to inherently arise from itself, from another thing, from both itself and other, or causelessly. *Arising from itself* means a thing—for example, a sprout, suffering, the body, a relationship, or realization of the path—arises from causes that are the same nature as itself. The ancient Indian philosophical school of the Sāṃkhyas accepts this type of arising in which the cause and effect share the same nature in the primal substance. *Arising from other* is an inherently existent effect arising from an inherently existing cause that is other than it. Non-Buddhists, as well as Buddhist essentialists, assert this. *Arising from both* means something arises from both itself and other. Followers of the Jain religion in India (Nirgranthas) accept this type of arising. They cite the example that both the clay and the potter are causes of a pot. The clay is the same nature as the pot and the potter is an inherently different nature. *Causeless arising* is accepted by the Materialists (Cārvākas), who say that some things arise randomly without any cause.

Although some of the views of these philosophical systems may initially seem unusual to us, some people today adhere to similar beliefs. Those adhering to an external independent creator believe that the world and the beings in it were created by an inherently existent other, whereas reductionists and cynics, who say that happiness and suffering occur haphazardly, support causeless arising. Some people may believe in a kind of predetermination whereby the result already exists in the cause and just needs to manifest.

Most of us have never examined how we think things' arising occurs. In one way, we accept it without analysis. This is fine, for in fact arising occurs only conventionally and cannot bear ultimate analysis. On the other hand, if someone pushed us to state how arising occurs, we may find that we have one of these four views.

Does the Effect Exist in the Cause?

Before delving into this refutation, some background is helpful. In classical Indian philosophy in general, there are two ways that two objects can be related: either they are the same nature (same entity) or they are cause and effect. If two things are the same nature, they are related in that if one exists, so must the other at some point in time. Two things that are equivalent or synonymous are one nature—for example, impermanent phenomena and functioning things. Two cups that look alike are not one nature because they are separate objects that are not related to each other. Something that is a part or quality of another thing is one nature with it—the wood that forms a table is *one nature with* the table. However, we don't say the wood and the table are one nature. An apple and an orange are different natures.

Two things that are related as cause and effect do not exist at the same time and are not the same nature. The cause must cease for the effect to arise, and the cause must have the ability to produce that effect. A barley seed is the cause of the barley sprout that grows from it. Parents are the causes of their child. A wall is not the cause of a grapefruit.

The Indian Sāṃkhya school believes that all phenomena except the person arise from a primal substance (*prakṛti*) that pervades all of them. Thus Sāṃkhyas' notion of nature is very different than the Buddhist notion; Sāṃkhyas say that a cause and its effect share the same nature—the nature of the primal substance. In other words the primal substance is the nature of all its creations. The nature of a barley seed, for example, is the same nature as the barley sprout that arises from it. These are the same nature as the conditions—water, fertilizer, and the proper temperature—that enable the seed to give rise to the sprout.

Before the world arose, everything existed in an unmanifest form in this primal substance, as one nature with it. At that time, the world was unrevealed, but later when conditions such as water and heat were present, things were revealed—they were made manifest. The primal substance merely manifests as those things that are already existing within it.

Sāṃkhyas accept that the seed and the sprout are different and do not say that the sprout arises from itself. However, because they say the nature of the seed and the sprout are the same and that the sprout arises from the seed, the sprout must arise from its own nature. Therefore at the time of the seed, an unmanifest sprout that has the same nature as the seed must exist. Since things are already present in the primal substance, which merely brings them to manifestation, they should arise from themselves.

After suitable conditions such as water and sunshine are present, the unmanifest sprout arises in the manifest form that we can see. The sprout exists not only at the time of the seed that is its direct cause, but also at the time of the tree that produced that seed, which is the sprout's indirect cause. The sprout would also be present at the time of the tree that grows from it, and all of these share the same nature of the primal substance. Sāṃkhyas state that things arise from themselves or are self-arisen because they exist within their principal cause prior to their arising.

If the sprout existed in the seed, then the seed and the sprout would not be related as cause and effect. That would mean, for example, that an old man (the effect) would exist in an unmanifest manner in a newborn baby (his substantial cause). However, if a fully formed result existed at the time of its cause yet it still needed to arise, several unwanted consequences would follow:

1. The sprout, which is the effect, would exist at the time of its cause, the seed. Since they are related and exist at the same time, the seed and sprout would be the same nature, and the sprout wouldn't need to arise because it would already exist. Its arising would be senseless because arising means something new comes into existence, but the sprout already exists. Buddhists tease Sāṃkhyas, saying that since excrement is the effect of food, it would exist inside the food since cause and effect would exist at the same time. In that case, when we eat food, we're actually eating excrement!
2. If cause and effect exist simultaneously such that a sprout exists inside a seed, then even after the sprout arises, the seed would still exist. Usually the cause needs to cease for the result to arise, but now they exist

simultaneously so that there's no need for the seed to cease for the sprout to come into being. In that case, the seed could continue to produce sprouts, one after the other endlessly, because the seed would never cease when its result arose.

3. According to the Sāṃkhyas, the seed already exists but needs to arise again by being made manifest; that is, something that has already arisen must arise again. Thus the same seed would keep reproducing itself without interruption, and no condition could stop the seed from arising repeatedly. In this case, there would be no opportunity for the sprout to arise and grow.[26]
4. We would be able to see the seed and its resultant sprout at the same time.
5. The producer (seed) and its product (sprout) would be exactly the same. If the sprout were inherently one nature with the seed, they would be exactly the same. In that case, we could not differentiate the seed from the sprout.
6. If the seed and the sprout are one nature and exist at the same time, then just as conventionally the seed cannot be apprehended after the sprout arises, so too the sprout should not be apprehended after it arises.

Our everyday experience invalidates each of these consequences. We don't see a cause and its result at the same time; we know that a seed must cease for a sprout to arise. It is impossible for a cause and its effect to exist at the same time and to be the same nature. Arising from itself doesn't exist even conventionally, let alone ultimately. Candrakīrti concisely says (MMA 6.12):

> Because the effect can be seen when the cause is no more,
> even ordinary people do not accept that the two are the same.
> Thus the postulation that things originate from themselves
> is untenable ultimately as well as in everyday experience.

When we gain the correct understanding of these reasonings, we will come to avoid at least two wrong views: The first incorrect view holds that all phenomena, such as a cause and its effect, are distinct phenomena yet share the same ultimate nature—the nature of the primal substance. If this were correct, a cause and its effect would be one, which they clearly are not. Another incorrect view holds that the ultimate nature of the cause is itself the ultimate nature of its effect. In this case, cause and effect would exist simultaneously, so either the effect arising from the cause would be impossible or the cause would produce its effect without end.

We may not hold the Sāṃkhyas' view, but some people nowadays hold views that resemble arising from itself—for example, thinking the future is predetermined and already exists in an unmanifest form in another plane. Or they may think there is a universal substance or energy in which everything exists fully formed before it arises. Contemplating the faults of arising from itself dispels these views.

REFLECTION

1. We may speak a lot about the laws of cause and effect, but to what extent do we live our lives as if we believed in it?
2. Think of some areas of your life that have been troublesome to you: school, career, friendships, relationships, Dharma practice, ethical conduct, making difficult decisions, and so forth.
3. Before deciding on a course of action, do you think of the possible results that could come from various options?
4. Do you consider the conditions that must accompany the principal cause to bring that specific result? Do you ask yourself if you are willing and able to create those causes and conditions?
5. Is there an aspect of wishful thinking in your mind? Perhaps there's a cause or condition that is necessary to bring the desired result, but not wanting to do that work you hope that somehow you can get around it.
6. Determine to reflect more on cause and effect, and observe how your life changes when you do.

Do Things Arise from an Inherently Existent Other?

Non-Prāsaṅgika Buddhist tenet systems assert that effects arise from causes that are inherently other than them. On the nominal level, cause and effect are other—after all, the cause is not the effect and the effect is not the cause. However, these tenet systems don't leave it at that, but instead say that the seed and the sprout exist inherently so that the difference between them is inherent within them. It is not a difference that arises due to causes and conditions. A sprout arises from a seed, and these two are objectively different from each other since each one exists inherently.

Prāsaṅgikas refute this saying that if the seed and sprout are inherently other, they would be totally unrelated and different. The sprout would then have the same kind of relationship with the seed that it had with an elephant because the seed and the elephant are equally other than the sprout. In that case, anything that was not the sprout could be the cause of the sprout. A sprout could arise from a telephone because the telephone is inherently other than the sprout just as the seed is inherently other. Alternatively, if the telephone wasn't the cause of the sprout then the seed couldn't be either. Cause and effect would be nonsensical: darkness could arise from a lamp and happiness could come from nonvirtue. In short, anything could arise from anything because there would be no particular relationship between a result and its causes, since all things would be the same in being inherently other and thus totally unrelated. Nāgārjuna's *Treatise on the Middle Way* (20.20cd) says:

> If cause and effect were [inherently] different,
> causes and non-causes would be alike.

And Candrakīrti says (MMA 6.14cd):

> Anything could arise from anything else because
> all nonproducers would be equivalent in that they are other.

As mentioned, one defect of asserting arising from an inherently existent other is that everything that was other than the effect would be equally other. In that case, either the sprout could arise from anything other than it or, just as a sprout can't arise from a car, it couldn't arise from its seed either.

Another unwanted consequence of the sprout arising from a cause that was inherently different from it is that the seed and sprout could not be of the same continuum. Conventionally, an effect depends on its cause and is in the same continuum as its cause. A peach tree is in the same continuum as the peach seed that was its cause. But if they were inherently different, the effect need not depend on its cause to arise, and cause and effect would not be in the same continuum. Candrakīrti tells us (MMA 6.61.cd):

> Things different from each other by their own characteristics
> could not logically be part of the same continuum.

We may think: A seed and a sprout are part of the same continuum, so the sprout must inherently arise from the seed. However, this is not the case. If things existed inherently, they would be completely independent from all other factors—such as their causes and conditions. Each thing would exist by its own characteristics and under its own power, without depending on anything else. In that case, effects would not depend on their causes and would not exist in the same continuum as their causes.

Would an inherently existent cause and its effect meet or not? That is, does the time that the cause—a seed—exists "touch" or connect to the time that its result—a sprout—exists? Alternatively, does the cause totally cease without any continuity arising from it such that in the next split-second a sprout immediately arises out of nothing? Or do the time that the seed exists and the time that the sprout exists overlap so that the seed and the sprout exist at the same time? If the time of the seed doesn't connect to the time of the sprout so that the seed discontinues before the sprout arises, how could the sprout arise from the seed? There would be intervening time in between the existence of the seed and the existence of the sprout.[27] On the other hand, if they did meet, they would be present simultaneously. In that case, how could the seed produce the sprout? The sprout would already be there so there would be no need for it to arise from a seed. When we think deeply about inherent existence, these kind of quandaries arise.

Conventionally, while the seed exists, we often speak of the sprout that is about to arise from it. When we plant carrot seeds, even before anything appears above the ground, we say "I planted carrots." In fact, we didn't plant carrots; we planted their cause, carrot seeds. When the seed is watered in the summer, a carrot sprout is in the process of arising while the carrot seed is in the process of ceasing. At that time, does the sprout exist? If it existed, it would have its own nature and it would exist at the same time as the seed. That isn't possible because cause and effect cannot occur simultaneously. The result arises only when the cause has ceased. Although the seed is in the process of ceasing at the same time the sprout is in the process of arising, only the seed exists at that time. If the sprout was already present, it wouldn't need to arise again.

Conventionally, a seed transforms into a sprout. We see it all the time. However, if things existed inherently, this could not happen. Something that exists inherently is self-enclosed. It has its own essence that cannot be influenced by other things and therefore cannot change. It would be permanent. But something that is permanent cannot be either a cause or an effect.

Furthermore, a sprout that is in the process of arising and that is inherently other than a seed would already exist because anything that has an independent essence has attained its own entity and is evident. We would be able to see the sprout that is about to arise before it has arisen. But we cannot. Therefore the sprout does not inherently exist.

If a sprout exists at the time of its seed, then it shouldn't need to arise because it already exists. But if someone says that it still needs to arise, then its arising would be endless because being inherently existent, the seed would never cease and would continuously produce sprouts.

Furthermore, if the seed or the sprout existed inherently, it would be impossible for them to have the relationship of cause and effect. This is because inherently existent things are independent of and unrelated to all other factors. They exist in isolation, by themselves, without needing to be produced. Candrakīrti says in *Clear Words*:

> If things—miscellaneous factors, sprouts, and so forth—have [inherent] nature, then what need have those existing things for causes and conditions?

Such are the faults of asserting arising from an inherently existent other. Here we see that arising necessitates a dependent relationship between the cause and its effect, with the former being in the process of ceasing while the latter is in the process of arising. Although we speak of the seed and the sprout at this time, the sprout does not yet exist; it has not "attained its entity." The seed, however, exists at that time; it is in the process of ceasing.

Philosophers may debate how a sprout arises from a seed, but ordinary beings see plants growing all the time. Farmers know that seeds produce sprouts, although they do not inquire beyond the conventional appearance of seeds and sprouts to ask how the sprout arises. Does it arise from itself, from an inherently existent other, both, or causelessly? The analytical process investigates how arising occurs. It reveals that ultimate arising from other is not possible, although conventionally a sprout arises from a seed that is other than itself.

The causal process of a sprout arising from a seed makes sense only conventionally. It cannot be explained within a framework where things possess inherent nature. In a world where phenomena lack inherent existence, these activities are possible, and we can talk about a seed producing a sprout without insisting that the seed, the action of arising, and the sprout exist simultaneously.

Upon close investigation, identifying one exclusive moment when the sprout arises is impossible. Language is a concise and effective way to communicate with each other and to understand the world; it is an approximation of how things function conventionally. Within a conventional framework we can talk of a sprout arising from a seed without pinpointing the exact moment that happens and without analyzing whether they exist simultaneously or not.

Someone may give the example of the two sides of a balance, saying: Look, the actions of the cause and the effect exist at the same time. Just as one side of the balance goes up while the other goes down, an inherently existent seed is in the process of ceasing while an inherently existent sprout is in the process of arising.

While this analogy may seem to work at first, the same problem exists as before: If the sprout exists at the time of the seed, the arising of the sprout from the seed would be useless. Or if the sprout still needs to arise even though it's already attained its entity, its arising would be endless.

In addition, this analogy does not fit what is to be explained. The two sides of the balance exist simultaneously, whereas the sprout that will arise doesn't exist at the time of the seed.

Conventionally, although the actions of the seed ceasing and the sprout arising are simultaneous, the seed and the sprout do not exist at the same time. The seed exists in the present, while the sprout will exist in the future. Although the sprout does not exist in the present, the causes exist for it to arise in the future so we can speak about the future sprout. As long as things are accepted on the level of appearance without analyzing how the sprout exists or what the sprout really is, the arising of the sprout at the same time as the ceasing of the seed makes sense. But when we are not content with conventional existence and grasp the seed and sprout as inherently existent, then they should be findable when searched for with ultimate analysis. However, when inherently existent seeds and sprouts are sought with ultimate analysis, they cannot be found. They are empty of inherent or ultimate existence.

Cause and effect are designated in dependence on each other. Not only does the effect depend on the cause, but the cause depends on the effect in that they are dependently designated. Something is called a cause because it has the potential to produce an effect, and something is called an effect because it arises due to a cause. In the world of veilings, things exist by being designated in dependence on other things; they do not exist on their own, independently.

Although seeds and sprouts are used as examples, don't think that this is a lesson on gardening! Once you understand how these reasonings work to refute inherent existence, think about how your body arose and how results arise from the karma we create. Apply this to the twelve links of dependent arising to understand how rebirth in saṃsāra arises, how your feelings of pleasure and pain arise, and so forth.

In the *Treatise on the Middle Way*, Nāgārjuna points out many shortcomings and unwanted consequences of asserting arising from inherently existent other. To summarize some of them:

- A sprout could arise from anything because all other phenomena would equally be inherently other just as the seed is inherently other than the sprout.
- A sprout that is in the process of arising and that is inherently other than the seed would already exist at the time of the seed, making cause and effect simultaneous. While conventional things can be other and not exist at the same time, inherently existent things would have to

exist at the same time to be considered other. This is because anything that has an independent essence has attained its own entity—it already exists.

- Furthermore, a sprout that is in the process of arising and that is inherently other than a seed would already exist and should be perceptible although it hasn't yet arisen.
- A sprout that is about to arise and that is inherently other than a seed does not need to arise because it has already attained its entity.
- An inherently existent sprout that does not exist in the present cannot have a cause that is inherently other because for two things to be inherently other, they would have to exist at the same time.
- An inherently existent sprout could never arise because the seed, being unaffected by causes and conditions, would be permanent and unchanging.
- If the seed were permanent, it would not cease after producing the sprout, so it would continue to produce more and more sprouts. Or if the seed did not produce anything because it was permanent, then it could never produce a sprout.

Three of the modes of arising spoken of in the reasoning refuting the four extremes of arising—from itself, both, and without a cause—do not exist conventionally, let alone inherently. Ultimate analysis is not needed to refute them. However, effects do arise from causes that are other and that are conventionally different from them. A daisy and the daisy seed are other; they are different. The daisy arises from the daisy seed, but only conventionally, not ultimately or inherently. Our examination refutes arising in which the cause and effect are inherently other. Therefore, qualifying this particular statement with "inherently" is important; a sprout does not inherently arise from a seed. If we simply stated that a sprout does not arise from a seed that is different from itself, we would be very ignorant!

In the *Ocean of Reasoning* (OR 67) Tsongkhapa first quotes Buddhapālita regarding arising from other and then explains the meaning:

> Buddhapālita says: "Nor do things arise from others, because then anything could arise from anything."

Here the reason why the absurd consequence "if there were arising from another, anything could arise from anything" is presented is that the "other" in "arising from another" is not just something that is different by virtue of being the referent of a different noun, but something that is inherently different. If it existed in that way, then the sprout's depending on the seed would be inconsistent; thus their relation would be refuted. If it were to arise from another unrelated object, then it could arise from anything!

Sūtra quotations also illustrate nonarising from inherently existent others. The *Ratnākara Sūtra* says (OR 95):

> Just as mountains are immovable,
> phenomena are unshakable,
> without [inherently existing] death, transformation, or birth:
> so the Victor has presented all phenomena.

Saying that *phenomena are unshakable* means that phenomena cannot be separated from their ultimate nature, emptiness. Their emptiness does not arise or cease due to causes and conditions; it is immutable, so phenomena always lack inherent existence. Sentient beings and all other conditioned phenomena are not inherently born, do not go through an inherent process of change, and do not experience inherently existent death. All these processes occur conventionally, nominally, without any fixed or independent nature of their own.

Contemplating this is helpful to relieve anxiety regarding dying and death. When thinking of death, most ordinary beings fear that they will cease to exist or that they will experience much suffering in the death process. This derives from self-grasping. However, when we realize that there is no inherently existent person who dies, just as there was no inherently existent person who was born, the mind relaxes. The *Ratnākara Sūtra* continues (OR 96):

> Phenomena are neither born nor come into existence,
> nor die, nor transform, nor age.
> The lion among men (the Buddha) has shown this
> and has led hundreds of sentient beings to see this.

While arising, transforming, aging, and dying all exist conventionally as processes dependent on their agents and dependent on being designated in relation to each other, they do not exist from their own side. Rather, they exist dependent on causes and conditions, parts, and being designated by concept and term. By teaching this, the Buddha has led countless sentient beings to liberation. When we follow his instructions, we too can attain liberation and full awakening by realizing that emptiness and dependent arising are not contradictory but are mutually complementary. Then we will be capable of guiding others to awakening and engaging in compassionate activities as the buddhas do.

REFLECTION

Look at your house plants, or sit in a garden, park, or forest and look at the plants and trees around you.

1. Ponder how that plant arose from its cause. Considering the biological system of cause and effect, if the plant existed inherently, could it arise?
2. Did the fully formed plant exist in the seed? Is that possible?
3. Did the plant arise from a cause that existed inherently? If cause and effect were inherently existent, they would have to exist at the same time. Can the plant arise from a seed that exists at the same time? Can one moment of the plant arise from the previous moment if they existed simultaneously?
4. Did the plant arise without any causes or conditions?
5. If the seed and the plant existed nominally and conventionally, how would the growth of the plant occur?
6. Use the above questions to investigate how your body arose from the sperm and egg of your parents.
7. Also contemplate how a bad mood arises. Does a bad mood come from nowhere? Can you trace some of the causes and conditions that led to it? Is that mood permanent? Or does it too act as a cause for a future result?

Refuting Arising from Both Itself and Other

The Jains, whose founding teacher Mahāvira was a contemporary of the Buddha, believe that things arise from causes that are both inherently the same and inherently other than them. They say, for example, a clay pot arises from clay, which is inherently the same as the pot, and a potter, who is inherently other than it. Buddhists, too, say a clay pot arises from clay and from the potter's efforts. However, neither the clay nor the potter is inherently the same as or inherently other than the pot.

The Jains have an interesting way of explaining that a person arises due to causes that are both itself and other. Since Jampa has been born in the present life due to having existed in previous lives with life force, she arises from herself. This is because Jampa and her life force are not separate; since the life force goes from one birth to the next, so does Jampa. Jampa also arises from another in that she was born from parents and previous karma. For this reason, she arises from both herself and other, and the individual refutations of arising from itself and arising from other do not apply.

For arising from both itself and other to be tenable, arising from itself would have to be possible, as would arising from other. Since both of them have already been refuted, arising from the two together cannot occur either conventionally nor ultimately. Candrakīrti says (MMA 6.98):

> Arising from both [itself and other] is not logical,
> for it is vulnerable to the objections already raised.
> This is found neither in the world (conventionally) nor accepted in
> terms of suchness (ultimately),
> for arising is untenable in terms of either pole of itself or other.

In short, in whatever way we search for an inherently existent object such as a chariot, a car, or a person, we cannot find it either conventionally or ultimately.

Do Things Arise Randomly without a Cause?

Some people claim that effects arise without causes. They do not refute obvious cause and effect, such as a sprout arising from a seed. However, since they cannot explain the causes for some things, such as the color design of a peacock's feathers or the roundness of peas, they say these arise without any cause. In ancient India, proponents of the Materialist philosophical school (Cārvāka) held such beliefs.

Nowadays some people believe that miraculous experiences occur without causes. Other people believe that some events occur randomly or haphazardly without any cause—for example, that somehow without any cause consciousness randomly emerged from the inanimate cells during the evolutionary process.

However, all functioning things arise from causes that have the ability to produce those results. When the causes are unknown to us, we may term an event random, miraculous, or mysterious. When we don't know the specific conditions that support a cause to bring its result, we may say it was a random occurrence. Certain causes and conditions may be out of our current range of knowledge at the moment, but as human beings gain more knowledge, and as individuals we develop our mental capacity, concentration, meditative abilities, and wisdom, these causes will become apparent. Our not knowing the dependently arising history of something owing to our limited abilities does not mean that thing came about without any causes and conditions whatsoever. Centuries ago people thought insects were spontaneously born in hot weather without any cause. Later we were able to discern the microscopic eggs that were their cause. Nowadays, scientists know that DNA causes the colors of a peacock's feathers and the roundness of peas, even though they may not yet know the exact mechanics of how this happens.

Several faults would occur if things arose without causes:

1. Nothing would arise, because there would be nothing to cause it to come into existence. Everything would be frozen in time.
2. Things would arise chaotically and unpredictably. What arises at one time and in one situation could arise anytime and anywhere, because the arising of a thing would not be constrained by requiring causes that have the ability to produce it. Flowers could grow in ice, and everyone would know rocket science without ever having studied it. The fact that things arise in some places and at some times but not others indicates that they depend on a variety of causes and conditions. However,

while we may not always know what the causes are for certain events, they definitely have causes.

3. All efforts to attain certain goals would be useless because things would come about causelessly or randomly. Farmers wouldn't plant seeds to grow crops, children wouldn't learn the alphabet in order to read, and people wouldn't work to earn a living because all these results could happen without causes. However, this is not the case and we have to go to work!
4. There would be no way to stop undesirable results by eliminating their causes and conditions. Fire prevention would be useless because fires would arise without causes.

After examining these points, conclude that nothing can arise without causes that have the capacity to produce them.

REFLECTION

Diamond slivers can be used to explore frequently asked questions—for example, is there an absolute beginning to the universe before which nothing existed? This belief is based on accepting inherent existence; we assume that there was a unique, definable moment in which an inherently existent universe appeared.

1. Is a findable, inherently existent beginning caused or uncaused?
2. If an inherently existent beginning has no cause, then how did the universe arise? Contemplate the consequences of causeless arising.
3. If causeless arising isn't tenable and the universe must have had a cause, did it arise from itself? Was it already present before the Big Bang? The universe arising from a permanent, inherently existent cosmic substance would be an example of arising from itself.
4. Was the universe arising caused by something other—for example, a divine creator?
5. Did it arise from both itself and other?

Apply the previous refutations and consider the logical consequences of an absolute beginning to the universe. If you can't arrive at clarity on this topic, ask a teacher for help in understanding and applying the reasoning. Doing this will help clarify your thoughts on this subject.

Benefits of Meditating on Diamond Slivers

Diamond slivers uses seeds and sprouts as examples of causes creating effects and effects arising from causes. We may wonder why there is so much commotion about how a sprout arises when we can see with our eyes that a sprout grows from a seed when it is watered, the soil is fertile, and the weather is the right temperature. Seeds and sprouts are a comparatively easy example to understand. The same analytical process applies to examining how our happiness and suffering arise, the process through which we are born in saṃsāra, and how certain Dharma practices lead to specific results. Diamond slivers shines light on our preconceptions and mistaken ideas of how happiness and suffering, ourselves, and the world around us come into being. It helps us identify realistic ways in which things arise and dispel wrong views that limit our spiritual growth. It also leads us to understand the nature of reality, the realization of which brings the peace of nirvāṇa.

When you first learn the reasonings contained in diamond slivers, they may seem convoluted or even superficial. Thinking about them, however, will lead you to ask yourself: How and when does a cause turn into its result? You'll question: How do things come into existence? What makes them change and cease? Remember to consider how inherently existent arising would function if it existed. Correctly identifying the object of negation is especially important before refuting arising from other, since of the four theses, this one explicitly presumes inherent existence and thus requires ultimate analysis.

If we think deeper about the difference between ultimate and conventional arising, the arguments presented here will make more sense to us. It is useful to reflect: What is conventional arising? What would ultimate arising be like? How are these two different? Are both possible or just one? What does it mean to say that a result and its cause are nominally (or conventionally) different but not inherently different?

A practical way to apply this analysis is to ask ourselves to what extent and in what areas do we live our lives with knowledge of cause and effect, and to what extent and in what areas of our lives do we deliberately or unconsciously disregard the operation of cause and effect or are ignorant of it.

REFLECTION

To prepare to meditate on diamond slivers, review the material above and make a list of the unwanted consequences if an effect arose from itself, other, both, or causelessly. This list will form the basis for meditation on point 3 below.

To meditate on emptiness by employing diamond slivers, choose an example of arising that is clear to you. It could be trees growing from seeds; poverty arising from miserliness in a previous life; consciousness arising dependent on an object, sense faculty, and the preceding moment of consciousness; knowledge arising from study; anger arising from an unpleasant feeling; or any other cause and effect sequence.

1. Identify the object of negation by seeing how you think of both the cause and the effect as existing from their own side and having their own independent, inherent nature.

2. Gain certainty that if causes and effects existed under their own power, an effect arising from its cause must occur in one of four ways—from itself, another, both, or causelessly. There are no other possibilities for arising.

3. Then examine those causes and effects to determine if they actually exist as self-enclosed entities, the way they appear to. Reflect on the unwanted consequences if a result were to arise from itself by referring to the list you made and conclude that things cannot arise from themselves. Then reflect on the unwanted consequences if results arose from an inherently existent other by referring to your list and conclude that such arising is not tenable. Do the same for arising from both and causelessly.

4. After seeing that any of these four ways of arising is impossible, release all grasping at inherently existent arising.

By understanding that things do not arise inherently from itself, other, both, or causelessly we draw the conclusion that because things do not arise inherently in any of the four ways, they are empty of inherent existence. In other words, after examining each of the four theses, it is evident that inherently existent arising isn't possible. Tsongkhapa says (OR 29): "The lack of ultimate existence of the arising of the sprout is the emptiness of the sprout." That is, by negating the inherent existence of the arising of the sprout, the inherent existence of the sprout itself has been negated and the emptiness of the sprout has been ascertained.

Try to prolong whatever experience you have of emptiness by abiding single-pointedly without doing further analysis. If you lose awareness of emptiness, resume analysis so that the experience of emptiness will again arise. When it does, remain in that experience as long as you can.

Results Arise Dependently

After reflecting as above, contemplate that causes do give rise to effects—we see that apple trees grow from apple seeds; we know that realizations of the path come from learning, reflecting, and meditating on the teachings. How do these things arise and exist? Dependently—they rely on a multitude of causes and conditions.

A proper awareness of causality is essential to living a good life. Since causes and effects do not exist inherently, they must exist dependent on nominal convention—there is no other choice. Tsongkhapa says (OR 98):

> Since ordinary people are thoroughly habituated to positing producer and produced as existing through their own characteristics, when this is refuted they find it awkward to posit them as existing merely through the force of nominal convention. However, since there are only these two modes of positing them, and since the first one is untenable, one should steer one's mind in the direction of the second one, since it is inevitable.

Initially it may seem difficult to posit conventional existence after refuting inherent existence. This is because your mind has conflated the two so inextricably that you think if inherent existence is negated, conventional existence also doesn't exist. However, on the basis of seeing that things lack inherent existence, train the mind to recognize what exists after the negation—this is conventional existence. This point is very subtle.

Here are some other ideas for how to meditate using diamond slivers. Once you understand the basic principles regarding the impossibility of an effect arising from itself, other, both, or causelessly, apply this to karma and its results. Do the results of your actions inhere in the action itself or in karmic seeds? Is the result inherently different from and unrelated to its causal action? Could karma (the initial action) and its results exist at the same time?

Meditate on the twelve links in this way too, examining how each link produces the next and how each link arises from the preceding one.[28] This will lead you to a correct understanding of the dependently arising nature of conditioned things.

Then contemplate: If one link ceases, the following link will too. This is the way to cease rebirth in saṃsāra. There are two main points where we can cease the chain of twelve links. The first is by ceasing first-link ignorance. Without it, formative actions will not be produced, and without formative actions, consciousness would not arise, and so on.

The other possible point to disrupt the cycle is between seventh-link feeling and eighth-link craving. Try to train your mind to simply experience a feeling—be it pleasant, painful, or neutral—without reacting by craving for a pleasant feeling to continue and increase, by craving to be free of an unpleasant feeling, or by craving for a neutral feeling not to cease. As you develop that ability, feeling is robbed of one of the necessary conditions to trigger craving. Without craving, destructive afflictions cannot arise. Observe what happens as you gradually train your mind not to immediately respond to feelings with craving. What changes in your mind and your life occur when you do this?

Nāgārjuna devotes a chapter to the examination of duḥkha and how it arises. The chapter begins with (MMK 12.1):

> Some maintain that duḥkha is self-created;
> some maintain that it is created by another;
> others that it is created by both, or that it arises without a cause.
> Such creation is impossible.

The remainder of the chapter clarifies that the creation of duḥkha in any of the four ways is untenable. In the concluding verse of this chapter, Nāgārjuna expands this reasoning to refute not only the inherent existence of the inner world of sentient beings, such as our duḥkha, but also all other phenomena as well. He draws us into examining how anything and everything—internal or external—arises (MMK 12.10):

> Not only does duḥkha not exist
> in any of the fourfold ways,
> no external entity exists
> in any of the fourfold ways.

When to Qualify with "Inherently"

As we've seen, to avoid the two extremes, distinguishing emptiness (non-inherent existence) from nonexistence and distinguishing existence from inherent existence are important. In each of those pairs, one of the terms has "inherently" and the other doesn't. In which cases do we add the words "inherently"?

When speaking of a nonexistent, such as a rabbit's horn or flowers growing in the sky, we do not need to specify that it does not inherently exist. Simply saying it does not exist is sufficient. When speaking of the lack of things that exist at some times and places but not at others, we also do not need to affix "inherently." Simply saying "flowers don't grow in winter" or "democracy is not practiced in a dictatorship" conveys our point. With respect to objects accepted by essentialists that Mādhyamikas say are not established conventionally, we again do not need to affix "inherently." Saying "there is no permanent soul" or "partless particles do not exist" is sufficient. Ultimate analysis is not required to negate those. Negating inherent existence is not necessary when proving that these things do not exist.

When speaking about the ultimate mode of existence of conventionally existent objects, such as tables and chairs, we must add "inherently": tables do not inherently exist and rebirth does not inherently exist. Why must "inherently" be added here? When examining how phenomena actually exist, we are not trying to negate their conventional existence or say that they do not exist at all. Veiled truths, such as flowers and rebirth, exist and cannot be negated by another conventional reliable cognizer or by reasoning analyzing the ultimate. On the conventional level, saying "rebirth exists" is true, but if someone asserts that plants and rebirth exist inherently, Prāsaṅgikas refute that. Adding "inherently" to the object of negation in this context is extremely important, for without it we could not distinguish conventionally existent objects from nonexistents.[29]

Establishing conventional existence and refuting inherent existence are equally important, for things could not exist conventionally if they existed inherently. Conventionally we say "the dish broke," "she generated bodhicitta," and "the Buddha is awakened." Since these things do not exist inherently, their qualities of arising and ceasing do not exist inherently either. However, all these objects and their qualities exist and function conventionally. We should not think that dependent production and disintegration on the one hand and the lack of inherent production and disintegration on the other are contradictory. In fact, they are mutually complementary.

In the reasoning refuting the four extremes of arising, affixing "inherently" is not necessary when we say "a sprout does not arise from itself, it does not arise from both, and it does not arise causelessly," because even conventionally things do not arise in any of these three ways. However, we must add "inherently" to the second alternative and say "a sprout does not arise from a seed that is *inherently* other." A sprout, in fact, arises from a seed that is other than it, but that seed is not an inherently existent other. If it were, it would be totally unrelated to the sprout and could not be the cause of the sprout, or the seed could be the cause of everything. Since the seed and the sprout exist as cause and effect, they are related conventionally; thus only inherent arising from other, not conventional arising from other, is refuted.

In the sūtras, commentaries, and treatises, the Buddha, Nāgārjuna, Āryadeva, Śāntideva, Buddhapālita, Candrakīrti, and others sometimes affix "inherently" to the object of negation. However, they do not do it every time because that would make for cumbersome speech. They assume that their followers will note the pattern and affix this qualification whenever needed. In the *Heart Sūtra*, the conventional existence of eyes, ears, the four truths, and so forth is not negated, only their inherent existence. The phrase "do not inherently exist" is used early in the sūtra indicating that it applies to all phenomena, so "no eyes, no ears . . ." means "no inherently existing eyes, no inherently existing ears. . . ."

Similarly, when these authors say in the context of ultimate reality "When analyzed, this does not exist," they mean, "When analyzed by reasoning analyzing the ultimate, this does not inherently exist." The Buddha explains in the *Descent into Lanka Sūtra* (*Laṅkāvatāra Sūtra*):

> Mahāmati, thinking that they do not arise inherently, I said that all phenomena do not arise.

Here the Buddha clearly states that when he says that phenomena do not arise, he means that they do not arise inherently. If something did exist inherently, it should become more evident when searched for with ultimate analysis. However, the opposite occurs and we find only its emptiness of inherent existence.

Conclusion from the Reasoning of Diamond Slivers

Without clarifying that inherent otherness, not conventional difference, is negated by the reasoning of diamond slivers, people could mistakenly conclude that conventional arising is nonexistent. They would then fall to the extreme of thinking that karmic actions don't lead to results and erroneously conclude that there is no reason to restrain from destructive actions and to live ethically because happiness arises randomly. Such a belief would be extremely damaging for these individuals as well as for society in general. It is important to remember that establishing the correct view of emptiness does not nullify the conventional functioning of cause and result and in fact reinforces it.

Three of the four views—that things arise from itself, both itself and others, and without cause—are acquired views that result from exposure to incorrect philosophical systems. Things do not arise from itself, both, or causelessly even conventionally, and a conventional reliable cognizer is capable of realizing this. These views are not so difficult to refute.

Arising from a cause that is inherently other than the effect is also an acquired wrong view. We do not naturally grasp cause and effect to be inherently separate. For example, when working in the garden, we say "I'm planting flowers," although we are planting the seeds. Students think "I'm writing an essay" while they are researching a topic. Candrakīrti says (MMA 6.32):

> Ordinary people say, "By sowing this seed (semen)
> I caused the birth of this child," and think
> "I have planted this tree." Therefore there is no
> arising from [inherently existent] other even according to ordinary people.

These common thoughts illustrate that we do not innately hold cause and effect to be totally unrelated, as they would be if the flowers arose from seeds that were inherently other. Although we do not innately grasp an effect to arise from an inherently existent other, we still grasp seeds, flowers, virtuous paths of karma, and upper rebirths as inherently existent. For this reason, it is important to refute the possibility of arising from other. If flowers did exist inherently, they would have to arise from itself, other, both, or causelessly. Since they don't exist in any of those ways, they do not exist inherently.

Similarly, we do not innately grasp the I and the aggregates to be inherently one nature or inherently different natures. We say, "I hurt my toe," indicating that I and our toe are related. We say, "I am the one who thinks," illustrating a relationship between I and our mind. But we do innately grasp the I as inherently existent. If the I existed inherently, it would have to be either inherently one with or inherently different from the aggregates. On examination we find it is neither and conclude that therefore the I doesn't inherently exist.

Since the only point of the four that is really in question is arising from other, is refuting it sufficient to conclude there is no inherently existent arising? A person who has learned incorrect views may believe that arising exists in one of the other three ways. All wrong views about arising need to be refuted to realize the absence of inherently existent arising. Taken together, refuting arising from itself, other, both, and causelessly undermines all possible incorrect beliefs people could have about how things arise and exist.

Realizing that the sprout does not arise from a cause that is inherently different from itself overcomes the acquired belief that it arises from a cause that is inherently other. But that does not mean that realizing that the sprout does not arise from a cause that is inherently other is the realization of the sprout's emptiness. To realize the sprout's emptiness, it is necessary to refute all four alternatives.

In the homage in *Treatise on the Middle Way*, Nāgārjuna describes nirvāṇa as "peaceful and free from conceptual elaborations." "Conceptual elaborations" refers to grasping the inherent existence of eight characteristics of dependent things: their ceasing, arising, discontinuation, permanence, coming, going, difference, and identity. While not comprising all characteristics of dependent things, these eight are key areas in which ignorance grounds its grasping; it adheres to the notion that each thing has real characteristics that define it and inhere in it.

After examining the process of effects arising from their causes, we conclude that such self-defining characteristics are untenable. If the arising of an effect from a cause possessed essence, when we search in the effect to determine if it has a cause that is identical to itself, other than itself, both, or if it arises causelessly, we would be able to identify it. However, we cannot pinpoint any inherently existent essence that connects the two in either the cause or its effect; nor can we isolate a particular moment in which the cause becomes the effect. These things are nominally imputed; they do not inhere in the cause or the effect themselves. Nevertheless, causes and their effects exist: some are beneficial, some are detrimental. Thus they must have some level of existence. Although they cannot be found when searched for with probing awareness, they nevertheless exist conventionally.

7 Does the World Exist Objectively?

TIBETANS HAVE A SAYING, "THE Buddhadharma says this, but…," the implication being that we must still live our lives, and to be successful in a worldly way, we may "need" to go beyond the Buddha's guidelines for ethical living. Thinking like this indicates that our Dharma understanding is at the level of listening or learning. We need to develop experience of the teachings that transforms our mind. Monastics studying in the monasteries have a good understanding of the Dharma based on learning, but not so many have experience based on reflection, let alone meditation. We must work hard and use this precious human life to gain actual experience. Doing this will benefit us personally and contribute to the long-term existence of the Buddha's teachings in our world.

Four Possibilities of Arising as Presented in the Pāli Canon

Nāgārjuna relied heavily on the reasonings in the early sūtras when formulating the arguments in the *Treatise on the Middle Way.* In doing so, he drew out their implications in a way that had not been previously done. Some of those sūtras are in the Pāli canon, where we find a forerunner to Nāgārjuna's tetralemma. In the *Sheaves of Reeds Sutta* (SN 12.67), Bhikkhu Mahākoṭṭhita questions Śāriputra about birth (*jāti*), which is a form of arising:

> Is birth created by oneself, or is it created[30] by another, or is it created both by oneself and by another, or has it arisen fortuitously, being created neither by oneself nor by another?

Śāriputra replies that birth is not created in any of these four ways but with tenth-link renewed existence as the condition for eleventh-link birth. After refuting birth by itself, other, both, and neither, he establishes birth as dependent, similar to the way in which Mādhyamikas refute arising in any of the four ways but establish it as a dependent arising. When Mahākoṭṭhita questions the arising of each of the other links of dependent arising, Śāriputra responds that they too are conditioned by the link preceding them as well as by other factors.

The Sanskrit term *svabhāva* (P. *sabhāva*)—now translated as "inherent existence"—was not used at the time of the Buddha; it appeared first in Abhidharma texts where it was translated as "own-being." Later, for example in Nāgārjuna's rebuttal, it came to mean inherent existence. Several sūtras in the Pāli canon refute arising from itself, other, both, and causelessly. In them, "itself" refers to oneself as the agent who is acting, as in the conversation between the naked ascetic Kassapa and the Buddha (SN 12.17):

> "How is it, Master Gotama: is dukkha created by oneself?"
>
> "Not so, Kassapa," the Blessed One said.
>
> "Then, Master Gotama, is dukkha created by another?"
>
> "Not so, Kassapa," the Blessed One said.
>
> "How is it then, Master Gotama: is dukkha created both by oneself and by another?"
>
> "Not so, Kassapa," the Blessed One said.
>
> "Then, Master Gotama, has dukkha arisen fortuitously, being created neither by oneself nor by another?"
>
> "Not so, Kassapa," the Blessed One said.
>
> "How is it then, Master Gotama: is there no dukkha?"
>
> "It is not that there is no dukkha, Kassapa; there is dukkha."
>
> "Then is it that Master Gotama does not know and see dukkha?"
>
> "It is not that I do not know and see dukkha, Kassapa. I know dukkha, I see dukkha."

Confused, Kassapa asks the Buddha for clarification. The Buddha explains:

> Kassapa, [if one thinks,] "The one who acts is the same as the one who experiences [the result]," [then one asserts] with reference to one existing from the beginning, "Dukkha is created by oneself." When one asserts thus, this amounts to absolutism.
>
> But, Kassapa, [if one thinks,] "The one who acts is one, the one who experiences [the result] is another," [then one asserts] with reference to one stricken by feeling: "Dukkha is created by another." When one assert thus, this amounts to nihilism.
>
> Without veering toward either of these extremes, the Tathāgata teaches the Dhamma by the middle: "With ignorance as condition, formative actions [come to be]; with formative actions as condition, consciousness [comes to be]; the remainder of the twelve links are described here, with each one serving as the condition for the arising of the next link.... Such is the origin of this whole mass of dukkha. But with the remainderless fading away and cessation of ignorance comes cessation of formative actions; with the cessation of formative actions, cessation of consciousness.... Such is the cessation of this whole mass of dukkha."

The duḥkha of saṃsāra arises from karma. How karmic seeds are transmitted from one lifetime to the next has been a topic of discussion for millennia among Buddhists and non-Buddhists who believe in rebirth. What is the relationship between the person who creates the cause and the person who experiences the result? Are they the same, different, both, or does duḥkha arise without a cause?

The first alternative—duḥkha is created by oneself—is absolutism because it believes the agent who creates the cause for duḥkha and the one who experiences the resultant duḥkha to be one and the same. This rests on the belief that there is a permanent self or soul that continues through time that is both the agent of the karma and experiencer of the result. The Buddha refutes the existence of a permanent self because such a person can neither change nor act as a cause for something else.

The second alternative—duḥkha is created by another—is nihilism. That is, one thinks the creator of the cause ceases at death and has no connection to the person who experiences the result in a future life. If someone accepts rebirth, he may think, "The person who created the karma for the duḥkha

I'm experiencing now is a completely different person than I, the one experiencing the results." This person does not see the continuity between the agent and the experiencer, between cause and result. He thinks that the person who created the causes was completely annihilated at the death of the previous life and someone new, who is totally unrelated, is born.

Another person may think, "An external, unrelated agent, such as an independent supreme being, is the one who determines my duḥkha and happiness. I am not responsible for what I experience because I did not create the causes for it." The Buddha refutes duḥkha arising from an independent, separate agent because that would entail no relationship between cause and its result. In that case, anything could arise from anything, and a person could abdicate any and all responsibility for their actions and the results these produce.

The third alternative—that duḥkha is caused by both itself and other—would be thinking, for example: The supreme being created me and the potential for my actions, but I act and experience the results of my actions. Thinking that a supreme being created oneself is holding arising from other and thinking that one acts and experiences the results oneself is holding arising from itself. This view has the faults of both of these views.

The fourth view is that there is no cause or condition for our experiences. Mādhyamikas refer to this as the extreme of nihilism, while in the Pāli tradition it is called spontaneous or chance arising (P. *adhicca-samuppanna-vāda*). If this were the case and everything were up to chance, we would not eat in order to stop our hunger and students would not go to school to get an education. The Buddha's teachings on dependent arising disprove this alternative.

People adhere to one or the other of these four alternatives based on conceiving a real self to exist. When all four options are disproven, the only option is to conclude that a real, independent self does not exist.

After negating these incorrect views, the Buddha expounds the Middle Way that is free from the extremes of absolutism and nihilism: Causes produce their results that concord with them. Without the cause ceasing, its result cannot arise. Duḥkha is not produced by a permanent cause, by someone completely distinct from the one experiencing the result, or by both. Duḥkha is not fated or predestined, nor does it occur haphazardly. Instead, the Buddha traced the evolution of our duḥkha and our saṃsāra through the series of causes and effects of the twelve links of dependent origination. He similarly traced the cessation of duḥkha and saṃsāra to the cessation of each link in this chain of causes. The resulting freedom is liberation.

The Buddha did not explicitly state in the sūtra what kind of real self he was refuting: a permanent, unitary, independent self, a self-sufficient substantially existent person, or an inherently existent person. It is up to the reader or the commentator to determine that. The refutation is the same for all of them, so what the sūtra means to us will depend on what type of real self we aim to disprove.

Nāgārjuna states the same in *Praise to the World Transcendent* (LS 19–20):

> Dialecticians assert that suffering arises from itself,
> arises from another, by both itself and another,
> or that it has no cause at all.
> You have stated it to be dependent arising.
>
> That which originates through dependence,
> this you maintain to be empty;
> that no independent entity exists,
> You, the Peerless One, proclaimed in a lion's roar.

In the *Book of Causation* the non-Buddhist wanderer Timbaruka has a similar exchange with the Buddha regarding the arising of pleasure and pain. The Buddha responds to him (SN 12.18):

> Timbaruka, [if one thinks,] "The feeling and the one who feels it are the same," [then one asserts] with reference to one existing from the beginning: "Pleasure and pain are created by oneself," I do not speak thus. But Timbaruka, [if one thinks,] "The feeling is one, the one who feels it is another," [then one asserts] with reference to one stricken by feeling: "Pleasure and pain are created by another." Neither do I speak thus. Without veering toward either of these extremes the Tathāgata teaches the Dhamma by the middle: "With ignorance as condition, formative actions [come to be]; with formative actions as condition, consciousness.... Such is the origin of this whole mass of dukkha. But with

> the remainderless fading away and cessation of ignorance comes cessation of formative actions; with the cessation of formative actions, cessation of consciousness. . . . Such is the cessation of this whole mass of dukkha."

Here, the topic of discussion is the feelings of pleasure and pain, and Timbaruka is confused about their causes and results. The first position—that a feeling and the one feeling it are the same—is the extreme of absolutism because he thinks that feeling is created by feeling itself. In this case, the feeling would have to exist in the past, before it arose.

The second position—that a feeling is one thing and the one feeling it is another—is nihilism. This person thinks that the feeling was created by another—a person in the past who is unrelated to the present person experiencing the feeling. That is, the feeling of the person in the past has ceased totally, and another person experiences the results of his deeds. This view holds that the person who created the cause of the feelings completely ceases to exist at the time of his death and a totally different person who will experience the resultant feeling is born in the future.

Pleasure and pain are not created by both themselves and another because that would have both of the above faults; nor are they created randomly without cause at all. The Buddha does not negate the existence of pleasure and pain, but instead teaches Timbaruka dependent origination, beginning with ignorance as the first of the twelve links. He also teaches the cessation of ignorance as leading to the peace of nirvāṇa and the end of birth and death. Feelings are produced by impermanent causes that produce impermanent, concordant results. When the causes are ceased, polluted feelings no longer arise. The person who creates the karma to experience certain feelings is in the same continuum as the person who experiences the resultant feelings. Understanding this, Timbaruka took refuge in the Three Jewels and became a lay follower of the Buddha.

In the *Sūtra for Bhūmija*, the monk Bhūmija asks Śāriputra, the Buddha's disciple who is foremost in wisdom, how pleasure and pain arise (SN 12.25):

> Friend Sāriputta, some ascetics and brahmins, proponents of kamma, maintain that pleasure and pain are created by oneself; some ascetics and brahmins, proponents of kamma, maintain

> that pleasure and pain are created by another; some ascetics and brahmins, proponents of kamma, maintain that pleasure and pain are created by both oneself and by another; some ascetics and brahmins, proponents of kamma, maintain that pleasure and pain have arisen fortuitously, being created by neither oneself nor by another. Now, friend Sāriputta, what does the Blessed One say about this? What does he teach? . . .
>
> (Sāriputta): Friend, the Blessed One has said that pleasure and pain are dependently arisen. Dependent on what? Dependent on contact.

Śāriputra clarifies that the Buddha does not accept any of the four alternatives because the people who propound them are thinking in terms of a substantial self. Since such a self does not exist, none of the four alternatives are acceptable. Instead Śāriputra relays that the feelings of pleasure and pain arise dependently. Specifically, the teaching on dependent origination says that seventh-link feelings are caused by sixth-link contact, which, in turn, is caused by fifth-link six sense sources, and so on. Here dependent origination is used to refute the mistaken notion of a substantial self that exists through time as the creator of feelings.

Not clearly seeing the cause of duḥkha, people form many incorrect assumptions, the theory of causeless arising being one of them. Some non-Buddhist renunciants and brahmins at the time of the Buddha purported (MN 60.21):

> There is no cause or condition for the defilement of beings. Beings are defiled without cause or condition. There is no cause or condition for the purification of beings. Beings are purified without cause or condition. There is no power, no energy, no manly strength, no manly endurance. All beings, all living things, all creatures, all souls are without mastery, power, and energy; molded by destiny, circumstance, and nature, they experience pleasure and pain in the six classes [of beings].

This view sounds somewhat similar to a view held today that we are hard-wired to be selfish, angry, and greedy because these qualities served our species well in the past by enabling us to fend off harm. The most we can expect is to modify the excesses, because vengeance and avarice are an inextricable part of human nature. These defilements have always been part of human beings and there is no way to purify ourselves of them.

To this the Buddha responds that there are causes and conditions for both the defilement and purification of beings (SN 22.60):

> If this form (body) [feeling, discrimination, miscellaneous factors, consciousness] were exclusively dukkha, immersed in dukkha, steeped in dukkha, and if it were not [also] steeped in pleasure, beings would not become enamored with it. But because form is pleasurable, immersed in pleasure, steeped in pleasure, and is not steeped [only] in dukkha, beings become enamored with it. By being enamored with it, they are captivated by it, and by being captivated by it they are defiled. This is a cause and condition for the defilement of beings; it is thus that beings are defiled with cause and condition.

The Buddha does not posit an external creator of our duḥkha, nor does he say it arises causelessly or from discordant causes, such as from itself or from truly existent other factors. Rather, he presents a psychological approach, showing that by operating in a distorted manner the ignorant mind creates misery. Our body, feelings, emotions, and so on are not inherently and exclusively painful. Some pleasure is experienced from them. Experiencing that pleasure, we delight in it and crave for more, and in this way we become ensnared by craving and clinging. This is the manner in which sentient beings are defiled and saṃsāra continues.

The Buddha also notes that a person who nihilistically disbelieves causality will likely create great nonvirtue. While alive, that person will be censured by the wise as an immoral person. If at the time of death there is no rebirth, he is safe enough. But if rebirth exists, he will experience unfortunate future lives. However, someone who accepts causality will have right view and right intention and practice ethical conduct. While alive, they will be praised by the wise, and after death, if rebirth exists, they will have fortunate rebirths, whereas if there is no rebirth, they have not lost anything.

The cause and condition for the purification of beings also exists (SN 22.60):

> If this form [feeling, discrimination, miscellaneous factors, consciousness] were exclusively pleasurable, immersed in pleasure, steeped in pleasure, and if it were not [also] steeped in dukkha, beings would not become disenchanted with it. But because form is dukkha, immersed in dukkha, steeped in dukkha, and is not steeped [only] in pleasure, beings become disenchanted with it. By being disenchanted, they become dispassionate, and through dispassion they are purified. This is cause and condition for the purification of beings; it is thus that beings are purified with cause and condition.

Just as the mind creates the causes for duḥkha, it can also create the causes and conditions to be free from duḥkha. Because our body, feelings, emotions, and so forth are not inherently pleasurable, we experience pain and misery. That duḥkha spurs us to question the nature of our saṃsāric body and mind. Seeing that they cannot provide continuous and enduring pleasure, we become disenchanted and disillusioned with them. This leads to losing interest in them and not passionately clinging to them as true happiness. Then, employing wisdom to separate ourselves from craving and clinging to the polluted aggregates, we will be free from them and attain nirvāṇa, the deathless state.

This discussion may seem philosophical, but it is intimately related to our lives. When we feel pain or pleasure, to what do we attribute it? Do we think the person we are today created the cause for it in the past? Do we think our duḥkha is others' fault? That it is a punishment from a supreme being? That it happens randomly because of "bad luck"?

When we experience happiness, do we trace its origins or do we simply assume it is our due? Do we believe there is a way to cease duḥkha altogether and attain a state beyond sorrow or do we just shrug and go about our day without contemplating these deeper issues? All of these teachings are food for thought on our spiritual journey.

Sometimes we may wonder, Why was I born who I was? Why wasn't I born as someone else? In asking this question, we assume there is a separate self from the circumstances of our life, a doer apart from karma and result. Yet such an agent does not exist, nor do causes and results exist as substantial entities. In the *Path of Purification*, Buddhaghosa quotes the ancients, the early Indian and Sinhalese commentators, as saying (Vism 19.20):

> There is no doer of a deed
> or one who reaps the deed's result;
> phenomena alone flow on—
> no other view than this is right.
>
> And so, while kamma and result
> thus causally maintain their round,
> as seed and tree succeed in turn,
> no first beginning can be shown.
>
> Nor in the future round of births
> can they be shown not to occur:
> non-Buddhists, not knowing this
> have failed to gain self-mastery.
>
> They assume a being, see it as
> eternal or annihilated,
> adopt the sixty-two wrong views,
> each contradicting the other.
>
> The stream of craving bears them on,
> caught in the meshes of their views;
> and as the stream thus bears them on,
> they are not freed from dukkha.
>
> A monastic, disciple of the Buddha,
> with direct knowledge of this fact
> can penetrate this deep and subtle
> empty conditionality.

There is no kamma (cause) in result,
nor does result exist in kamma (cause);
though they are empty of one another,
there is no fruit without the kamma.

As fire does not exist inside
the sun, a gem, cowdung, or yet
outside them, but is brought to be
by means of its component parts,

So neither can result be found
within the kamma, nor without;
nor does the kamma still persist
[in the result it has produced].

The kamma of its fruit is empty;
no fruit exists yet in the kamma;
and still the fruit is born from it,
wholly depending on the kamma.

For here there is no Brahmā god,
creator of the round of births;
phenomena alone flow on—
cause and component their condition.

REFLECTION

1. Slowly contemplate the above verses.
2. Get a sense of how persons and phenomena can exist dependent on other factors without having their own fixed essence.

Refutation of the Arising of Existents and Nonexistents

Diamond slivers focuses on examining the cause: Does something arise from a cause that is inherently itself, another, both, or without a cause? Another reasoning—the refutation of the arising of existents or nonexistents—focuses on the effect, investigating if an effect is inherently existent, nonexistent, both, or neither. Nāgārjuna queries in *Praise to the World Transcendent* (13):

> An existent thing does not arise;
> nor does a nonexistent, nor do both;
> neither from itself nor from another,
> nor from both; how can there be arising?

Āryadeva suggests this meditation for practitioners who have contemplated the refutation of one and many. In the *Four Hundred* he says (CŚ 346):

> The approach of existence, nonexistence,
> both existence and nonexistence, and neither,
> should always be applied by those
> with mastery of oneness and so forth.

Candrakīrti presents this refutation in the context of one of the four diamond slivers, refuting arising from an inherently existent other (MMA 6.21):

> If the cause is a producer that produces something other [than itself],
> is what it produces existent, nonexistent, both, or neither?
> If existent, what need is there for a producer (a cause)? If nonexistent, what can a producer do?
> If both, again, what use is it? If neither, what use does a producer serve?

This verse becomes the following syllogism: "Consider a sprout, it does not inherently arise because (1) an existent does not inherently arise, (2) a nonexistent does not inherently arise, (3) what is both existent and nonexistent does not inherently arise, and (4) what is neither existent nor nonexistent does not inherently arise." These are the only options in which an inherently existent effect could arise. When these four are refuted, we can firmly establish the absence of inherent arising. Let's examine them individually:

1. An existent does not inherently arise. An inherently existent effect would be a self-enclosed entity unaffected by other factors. Whatever arises inherently would always exist and would not need a cause to produce it. An inherently existent grasshopper could arise without a cause. If the grasshopper did not always exist, it would never exist and could never arise. Or it would exist before it arose, but this is problematic because a cause and its effect cannot exist simultaneously. The cause must cease for the effect to arise.

2. A nonexistent does not inherently arise. If a nonexistent could arise, then a turtle's moustache and a healthy disease could arise. However, a nonexistent cannot arise because it lacks a cause; nothing can produce it. A turtle's moustache has no cause, and if it arose anyway, what would it look like? An inherently existent healthy disease would exist before it arose, while it was approaching production, and after it ceased.

3. Whatever is both existent and nonexistent does not inherently arise. There is nothing that is both existent and nonexistent because things cannot possess two contradictory natures. Āryadeva comments (CŚ 351):

> If what does not exist at the last [moment of its cause] is produced,
> how can the nonexistent be produced?
> If what exists from the outset is produced,
> how can that which exists be produced?

4. What is neither existent nor nonexistent does not inherently arise. Here, too, something that is neither existent nor nonexistent cannot arise because there is no such thing. If it were to arise anyway, any causes or conditions would be superfluous.

When these four options are refuted, a vacuity that is the absence of an inherently existent grasshopper appears to the meditators' mind. They know that an inherently existent effect, such as a grasshopper, does not exist and their mind dwells in emptiness. When they arise from this meditation, they know that things exist dependently, by mere designation.

In short, saying that an existent grasshopper inherently arises or that a nonexistent grasshopper inherently arises presents problems. Āryadeva comments (CŚ 265):

> For those who assert effects exist,
> and for those who assert they do not exist,
> adornments like pillars and so forth
> for a home are purposeless.

Since the arising of an inherently existent home, a nonexistent home, a home that both inherently exists and does not inherently exist, and a home that neither inherently exists nor does not inherently exist is impossible, you don't need to be concerned with decorating it!

Nāgārjuna agrees (MMK 20.21–22):

> If an effect is inherently existent,
> To what could a cause give rise?
> If an effect is inherently nonexistent,
> To what could a cause give rise?

Dependently Arising Causes and Effects

The lower schools assert arising from inherently existent other. Since arising from itself, both, and causelessly do not make sense and since flowers are other than their seeds, they say things must arise from causes that are other than themselves. These schools also assert inherent existence, so they say that effects must arise from causes that are inherently other than them. Prāsaṅgikas say, on the other hand, that although it is true that a seed produces a sprout and the seed is other than the sprout, the seed is not inherently other than the sprout. If it were, it would be totally unrelated to the sprout—because if things inherently existed, they would be independent of all other phenomena, in which case the effect would be unrelated to the cause.

If inherent arising existed, it should be findable. It should be able to bear ultimate analysis. Dependent or nominal arising, however, does not need to withstand ultimate analysis because it exists only conventionally. In the *Supplement* Candrakīrti says (MMA 6.114–15):

> Because things do not arise causelessly,
> from causes such as a divine creator
> or from itself, other, or both [self and other],
> they arise dependently.
>
> Because things arise dependently,
> these mistaken conceptions cannot bear scrutiny.
> Therefore, the reasoning of dependent arising
> cuts all the entanglements of bad views.

The reasoning of dependent arising disproves arising from itself, other, both, and causelessly. It also prevents us from misunderstanding how things arise. For example, someone could confuse non-inherent arising and no arising whatsoever and mistakenly believe that refuting arising in the four ways negates not just inherent arising but also all arising and thus all existence. With such thought, he falls to the extreme of nihilism. However, when he understands dependent arising, he knows that something that arises dependently is empty of inherent arising and yet still exists conventionally.

Dependently arising products are like the reflections of a face in a mirror; they are false in that they appear to exist in one way although they exist in another. But they are not nonexistent. A real face in a mirror does not exist, but the appearance of a face does. Similarly, inherently existent effects do not exist, but conventional ones that are only appearances do exist. Although a reflection is false, it arises dependent on its causes—a mirror, the face, and light. In the same way, veiled truths are false in that they appear inherently existent although they are not; they exist dependently and arise from their causes, which are similarly false. Because veiled truths do not exist the way they appear, they exist falsely. Nevertheless they function and produce results.

The appearance of inherent existence exists although inherent existence does not. The appearance of inherent existence is a false appearance. When meditating on emptiness, we do not negate the appearance of an inherently existent I—that appearance exists—but we do negate the inherently existent I that appears; such an I is nonexistent.

Some scientists are interested in the idea that things do not exist the way they appear. Many years ago, the atom appeared to be one unit and scientists thought it was the tiniest unit of material. But that appearance was false, and with further research they discovered that an atom consists of many parts, and those parts are composed of parts as well. In addition, those parts—electrons and other subatomic particles—are constantly changing. An atom still appears to be one thing, but where is that one, independent item? What is it really? I believe that some Buddhist ideas could help scientists in their exploration. Already the dialogue between Buddhists and scientists has been very productive for both parties.

Every functioning thing arises from its own specific causes, not from other, unrelated causes. In other words, a cause and its result must be concordant. From rice seeds rice grows, not cabbage. And from positive actions happiness results, not suffering. Why do the great scholar-adepts repeatedly emphasize these points? Because imprinting them in our mind will prevent us from falling to nihilism in the future when we realize emptiness. Our understanding of karma and its effects will be robust so that we will avoid the pitfall of thinking that because everything is empty there is no good and no bad, so tantric yogis can do whatever they like. In actuality, tantric yogis and others who have realized emptiness have a stronger conviction in the law of karma and its effects than ordinary beings.

Statements in sūtras such as "Whatever has arisen from conditions has not arisen" do not mean things do not arise at all. Rather, they indicate that they do not arise from inherently existent causes. Although the word "inherently" is not affixed in every place in a sūtra, because it is mentioned in one place, it is inferred in other places. Otherwise, such sūtra statements would appear to be a mass of contradictions that people could interpret to mean whatever they like. This is precisely the mistake made by those who negate too much and why they differ from true Mādhyamikas.

When meditating on the four parts of the diamond slivers, apply this reasoning to understand the emptiness of duḥkha, the emptiness of anger and other emotions, and the emptiness of the path to awakening. Tsongkhapa encourages us (OR 72):

> If we understand the nonexistence of inherent arising as the meaning of the verse, "Nothing ever in any way arises from itself, from another, from both, or without a cause," we will not be bereft of things to meditate on when contemplating the meaning of suchness. Therefore, those who aspire to meditate by understanding the reality of one's own mind as nonarisen should focus their practice on just this point.

If we aspire to know the nature of our own mind, we should meditate on it not arising in any of the four ways. In this way, our wisdom will realize the mind's ultimate nature—its emptiness of true existence—and our saṃsāra will shatter.

When we understand well that the mind and all other phenomena arise dependently, we will also understand that they are empty. These understandings as well as the practitioners who gain them also do not arise in any of the four ways, nor do they produce inherently existent results. So many sages throughout the centuries praise and respect the Buddha for having taught the complementary nature of emptiness and dependent arising.

The Order of Realizing the Selflessness of Persons and of Phenomena

In some scriptures the selflessness of persons is presented first, in others the selflessness of phenomena. Which one should we focus on first? In what order are they realized?

The *Great Treatise on the Stages of the Path* recommends meditating on the selflessness of persons first. This is the case in the *Condensed Perfection of Wisdom Sūtra* (*Prajñāpāramitāsañcayagāthā Sūtra*) as well, where the Buddha first explains the selflessness of persons and then says that the same contemplations should be applied to all other phenomena, especially the aggregates that are the basis of designation of the person.

This mirrors the recommendation of most spiritual mentors to meditate on the selflessness of persons first because it is said to be easier to understand than the selflessness of phenomena, although there is no difference in subtlety between the two. Why is this? One reason is that even people who do not accept that the I exists by being merely designated—such as proponents of the lower systems—accept that it is imputed. By using their comparatively coarse understanding of the meaning of "imputed" or "designated" and expanding on it, the subtler understanding of the Prāsaṅgikas can be revealed. Another reason is that the designated object—in this case the person—is less "concrete" than its basis of designation, the aggregates. According to our common perception, the basis of designation seems to be more real than the object designated in dependence on it.

The lower systems speak of the self as imputed, although their definition of "imputed" differs from that of the Prāsaṅgikas. Nevertheless, the idea of the self, the person, as a construct is present. In the taxonomy of existents,[31] there are three types of impermanent phenomena—form, consciousness, and abstract composites. The person is included in the third category, indicating that it is an abstract construct and thus seems less real and true than things like tables, mountains, and bodies.

According to the lower systems, something is imputed if it cannot be identified without some other phenomenon appearing to the mind. To apprehend Dechen, we must hear her voice or see her body; only then do we know Dechen is here. Understanding how the self is imputed according to the lower systems facilitates understanding the subtler meaning of existing by mere designation as asserted by the Prāsaṅgikas. If we deepen our understanding of the person as an imputed construct according to the lower schools and then draw out the implications of this, eventually we will arrive at the Prāsaṅgikas' deeper understanding of the imputed nature of the self.

According to the Prāsaṅgika view, the person and the aggregates have the relationship of the designated object (the person) and the basis of designation (the aggregates). The designated object is always less "solid" because it depends on its basis of designation; it is designated in dependence on its basis of designation. For this reason, initially realizing the selflessness of persons is considered easier than realizing the selflessness of phenomena.

How do we reconcile this with Nāgārjuna's statement in *Precious Garland* (35ab)?

> As long as one grasps the aggregates,
> One will also grasp the I with regard to them.

As long as we grasp the aggregates as inherently existent, we will grasp the I as inherently existent, because the aggregates are the basis of designation of the I. When we refute the inherent existence of the aggregates, grasping the I designated in dependence on those aggregates is subdued.

However, a doubt arises. The order of generating grasping inherent existence is we first grasp the aggregates and then the I as inherently existent, but the order for realizing their emptiness is the opposite: first we realize the emptiness of the I and then the aggregates. How can we realize the emptiness of the I without having first realized the emptiness of the aggregates? As Nāgārjuna says, so long as there is grasping the aggregates as inherently existent there will be grasping the I as inherently existent.

There are two levels of grasping inherent existence: innate and acquired. *Innate* grasping has been with our mindstream beginninglessly; it doesn't depend on learning erroneous philosophies and reasonings. *Acquired* grasping is supported by many reasons that try to prove inherent existence and comes from learning incorrect philosophies in this life. While we are actively thinking that the aggregates are inherently existent and use various incorrect reasonings to support this, realization of the emptiness of the I will elude us. Thus Nāgārjuna's statement means that as long as acquired self-grasping is actively holding the aggregates to exist inherently, we will be unable to dismantle grasping an inherently existent I with regard to them.

However, it isn't necessary to completely eliminate acquired grasping of the aggregates from our mindstream to realize the emptiness of the I; it is sufficient that it is not manifest and active at that time. But Candrakīrti makes it very clear that if the conceived object of true-grasping of the aggregates—the basis of designation of the person—is not disbelieved, the fully-qualified selflessness of persons cannot be realized.

Emptiness of the Mind

Meditating on the selflessness of phenomena mainly centers on refuting the true existence of the mind. Of all the infinite phenomena, why is the mind the most prominent? One reason is that in both Sūtra and Tantra, the mind is the final basis of designation of the person. Among the Madhyamaka thinkers, Bhāvaviveka identified the continuum of consciousness to be the true referent for the term "person" or "I" in the final analysis. In *Blaze of Reasoning* (*Tarkajvālā*), his autocommentary on his *Heart of the Middle Way* (*Madhyamakahṛdaya*), Bhāvaviveka says, "We refer to consciousness as the true referent of the person because it is consciousness that takes rebirth." Haribhadra also identified the continuum of consciousness as the true referent for the identity of the person. While Prāsaṅgikas refute that consciousness is the true referent of the person—that is, consciousness *is not* the person—they maintain that consciousness *is the final basis of designation* of the person. Similarly, in Tantra, although the subtlest mind-wind is not considered to be the person, it is the deepest basis of designation of the person. Because we tend to identify our self more with the mind than with the body, realizing there is no truly existent mind easily stops the thought that there is a truly existent I.

Although it is possible to have a nondual experience of the emptiness of any inanimate object, the direct realization of the emptiness of the mind has a strong impact because the mind is seeing its own ultimate nature. The experience of the "same taste" is especially powerful when the apprehending subject—the wisdom mind—and the apprehended object—the emptiness of that mind—are fused nondually. This has a much stronger effect on the meditator than when the mind directly apprehends the emptiness of any other object. Here the mind is apprehending its own emptiness and is fused with its emptiness like water poured in water. In the meditator's experience, the mind and its own nature are indistinguishable.

Moreover, this mind is what will attain buddhahood; the continuity of our present mind will become the wisdom truth body of a buddha, and the emptiness of our present mind allows for the nature truth body of a buddha. Thus, thinking about and meditating on the emptiness of the mind has tremendous significance and force.

Tantra stresses meditation on the emptiness of the mind. In the *Great Treatise on the Stages of Tantra*, Tsongkhapa explains the meaning of the mantra *Oṃ śūnyatā jñāna vajra svabhāvātmako 'haṃ*, which appears in the Yamāntaka sādhana as well as many other tantric sādhanas. Here *śūnyatā* refers to emptiness, *jñāna* indicates the pristine wisdom (T. *ye shes*) that understands emptiness, *vajra* connotes the inseparability of emptiness and the pristine wisdom that directly realizes emptiness, *svabhāva* means nature, while *atmako 'haṃ* means "it is me." Together, the syllables of the mantra can be translated as "Om, I have an essential nature of indivisible emptiness and pristine wisdom."

The pristine wisdom that realizes emptiness cognizes the emptiness of that very wisdom mind. It directly perceives its own lack of inherent existence. When the mind realizes its own emptiness, it merges with that emptiness, perceiving it nondually; in that way it becomes indistinguishably of the same taste with its own fundamental nature. This is the meaning of *Ka* and *Śrī* in the passage from the "Yoga of the Three Purifications" mentioned below.

In other scriptures and texts, the order of presentation of the two selflessnesses begins with the selflessness of phenomena. The *Heart Sūtra* speaks mainly of the selflessness of phenomena, saying that the five aggregates, six objects, six sense faculties, eighteen elements, twelve links, four truths, and all attainments of the path are empty of inherent existence. The selflessness of persons is implied by the word "also" at the beginning of the text when it says Avalokiteśvara was "looking at the emptiness of inherent existence of the five aggregates *also*."

The "Yoga of the Three Purifications," from the Heruka Cakrasaṃvara sādhana, presents the selflessness of phenomena first, followed by the selflessness of persons:

> *He* is the selflessness of phenomena—the emptiness of the mind that has been imputed as the source of everything.
>
> *Ru* is the selflessness of persons—the emptiness of the self fabricated by the web of conceptual thoughts grasping the self of persons.
>
> *Ka* is nonduality—the object and subject of ultimate reality not being discordant.
>
> *Śri* is the meaning of *Evaṃ*—the object emptiness and the nondual pristine wisdom abiding in exactly the way emptiness exists.

The first line explains the meaning of *He*, which is meditation on the emptiness of the mind, the selflessness of phenomena. It is followed by meditation on *Ru*, the selflessness of the person. In *He* the mind that is seen as empty is the continuity of the subtlest mind, which is one nature with the subtlest wind. If even this subtlest innate mind of clear light lacks inherent existence, what need is there to speak of the absence of inherent existence of the person who is designated in dependence on that continuum? From here, one proceeds to meditate on *Ru*, the emptiness of the person whose deepest basis of designation is the subtlest mind-wind.

Āryadeva's *Lamp for Integrating the Practices* (*Caryāmelāpakapradipa*), a meaning commentary on Nāgārjuna's tantric text *Five Stages*, also presents the selflessness of phenomena more prominently. When explaining the practices of isolated mind, Nāgārjuna and Āryadeva emphasize the importance of cultivating the wisdom understanding the emptiness of mind. The completion stage of Guhyasamāja Tantra focuses on the selflessness of the mind, especially in the stage of isolated mind and fourth-stage clear light. In both Mahāmudrā and Dzogchen, the key practice is meditating on the emptiness of the mind itself.

In general, people begin with meditating on the selflessness of the person followed by the selflessness of phenomena. However, for some individuals the reverse order is more appropriate. In the end, the emptiness of both person and phenomena must be realized.

The Emptiness of Permanent Phenomena

There are two broad divisions of phenomena: (1) Impermanent phenomena (things) are products that arise due to causes and conditions and change in every nanosecond. They include material objects, people, the environment, mental states, and abstract composites. (2) Permanent phenomena do not arise dependent on causes and conditions and are static and unchanging. In general, they are the absence or negation of impermanent phenomena. Permanent phenomena include unconditioned space, analytical and nonanalytical cessations,[32] emptinesses, conceptual appearances, and nonaffirming negatives.

So far, we have been focusing on the emptiness of impermanent phenomena because our attachment and anger predominantly arise in reaction to them. The reasonings of diamond slivers and other reasonings that analyze causality pertain to impermanent phenomena. Dependent arising, the reasonings that analyze the relationships between an object (whole) and its parts, and those analyzing the relationship between an object and its ultimate nature can also be applied to permanent phenomena.

Although permanent phenomena do not depend on causes and conditions, they exist dependently, for they rely on their parts, their bases of designation, and the term and concept that impute them. Permanent phenomena also depend on negating an object of negation. For example, unconditioned space depends on negating obstructability, and emptiness depends on negating inherent existence. Because permanent phenomena are the absence of an impermanent phenomenon (such as obstructability), or in the case of emptiness, the absence of a nonexistent (inherent existence), they are neither self-established nor independent.

All Mādhyamikas assert that permanent phenomena depend on their parts. Unconditioned space depends on its parts—the north part, the west part, and so forth. Emptiness, too, depends on its parts—the emptiness of the table, the emptiness of the person, and so on. In dependence on these, the general term "emptiness" is designated. In addition, there is the emptiness apprehended by the first moment of mind realizing emptiness, the emptiness apprehended by the second moment of mind realizing emptiness, the emptiness apprehended inferentially, the emptiness apprehended directly, and so on. In dependence on all these instances of emptiness, the general term "emptiness" is imputed.

Furthermore, unconditioned space and all other permanent phenomena are established in dependence on the reliable cognizers apprehending them. They also exist in relation to their definitions. Being mutually dependent with their reliable cognizers and their definitions, space and so forth do not exist under their own power or from their own side.

Analyzing whether a permanent phenomenon is inherently one with or different from its parts leads to understanding its emptiness. Unconditioned space is neither inherently one with nor inherently separate from its parts, and it exists in dependence upon them and in dependence upon the term and concept that imputes "unconditioned space." Similarly, emptiness depends on its basis of designation, but it is neither inherently one with nor inherently different from it or from the various emptinesses that compose it.

An emptiness exists in dependence on a veiled truth that is empty of inherent existence—the emptiness of the chair is dependent upon the chair;

the emptiness of the person depends on the person. If the chair and person didn't exist, we couldn't speak of the existence of their emptiness. In addition, emptiness is established by a reliable cognizer—either an inferential cognizer or a direct, nonconceptual perceiver—apprehending it and thus depends upon that consciousness.

In *Precious Garland*, Nāgārjuna explains emptiness of the permanent phenomenon, unconditioned space (RA 99ab):

> Since it is merely the absence of form,
> space is merely a designation.

Unconditioned space is a nonaffirming negation that exists by being merely designated in dependence on the absence of obstructing form. Space is understood by negating obstructing form; it is posited in relation to obstructing form. Because obstructing form, which is an impermanent phenomenon, does not exist inherently but exists in mere name, space too must lack inherent existence and exist in mere name.

The realizations of the emptiness of impermanent and permanent phenomena occur in a sequence. Tsongkhapa said (GR 180):

> Once this absence of true existence of conditioned things is established, one can also negate, with the very same reasoning, the true existence of the unconditioned. For example, one must admit that even unconditioned space pervades some material objects, and thus there must be parts that pervade the east and parts that extend in other directions.

Since all phenomena are either impermanent or permanent, and having negated the true existence of both, we now know that all phenomena lack true existence.

8 The Selflessness of All Existents: Dependent Arising

NĀGĀRJUNA COMMENCES THE *Treatise on the Middle Way* with a now famous homage that draws out the implications of dependent arising. It does this by praising the Buddha for teaching that whatever is dependently arisen does not inherently exist.

> I prostrate to the perfect Buddha,
> the best of all teachers, who taught that
> that which is dependent arising is
> without ceasing, without arising,
> without discontinuation, without permanence,
> without coming, without going,
> without difference, without identity,
> and peaceful—free from [conceptual] fabrication.

Here dependent arisings refer to all phenomena because all of them come into existence dependently, be it by causal dependence, mutual dependence, or dependent designation. Dependent arisings are the basis that lack having the inherent nature of ceasing, arising, discontinuation, permanence, coming, going, difference, and identity. Their emptiness of having such inherent characteristics is the object of the unpolluted wisdom of meditative equipoise. "Ceasing" (disintegrating every moment) and "arising" (becoming that thing) refer to the nature, the development and degeneration, of things. "Discontinuation" (annihilation of the previous continuum) and "permanence" (continuation through time) demonstrate time. "Coming" (coming closer from a distant place) and "going" (moving further away) refer to destination or place. "Difference" (diversity between objects) and "identity" (sameness of objects) show the relation of things. Although these eight characteristics exist conventionally, the wisdom directly knowing the ultimate truth cognizes their emptiness.

"Peaceful—free from [conceptual] fabrications" means that when dependent arising is perceived the way it actually exists, all conceptualization has been stopped; when the ultimate truth is known as it really is, it is cognized without any conceptual thought that it is this and not that. The rest of the *Treatise on the Middle Way* unpacks the meaning of this homage. Many commentaries have been written on this in India, Tibet, and China.

Nāgārjuna was a great sage who possessed the profound eye of wisdom that sees profound reality—suchness—as it is. With the intention of explaining the meaning of suchness based on profound dependent arising, and with the hairs on his body standing on end and his eyes filled with tears of devotion and faith in the Buddha, Nāgārjuna places his palms together on the crown of his head and bows to the Buddha. His purpose for composing the *Treatise on the Middle Way* is to help spiritual trainees to attain their ultimate aspiration of buddhahood. May we, too, come to have the same faith in the Three Jewels—confidence that is based on a deep understanding of the complementary nature of emptiness and dependent arising. Like Nāgārjuna, may we, too, cultivate the sincere aspiration to lead sentient beings to full awakening through the teachings on suchness and dependent arising.

It is not easy to be Nāgārjuna's student. His profound and sophisticated writings have subtle implications. We need to think deeply about these teachings over time and use them as a tool to understand our mind and to correct its way of apprehending phenomena. I encourage you to reflect on emptiness and dependent arising every day, implementing analytical meditation to probe their meaning deeply. By doing so, day by day, month by month, year by year, your understanding of and conviction in these teachings will increase, bringing immense benefit to yourself and others.

Dependent Arising: The Monarch of Reasonings

The reasoning of dependent arising is often called the monarch of reasonings because of its power to dispel the two extreme views of absolutism and nihilism that obstruct realizing the view of the Middle Way. Compared to other types of reasonings such as diamond slivers or one and different, the reasoning of dependent arising not only leads the meditator to the unfindability of an object when sought with ultimate analysis but also makes dependent existence evident right from the beginning. Several sūtras support this. *Questions of Sāgaramati* says (EMW 269):

> Those which arise dependently
> are quiescent of inherent existence.

"Quiescent" refers to natural nirvāṇa, the natural emptiness of our mind that is present right now and will become a factor of the nature truth body of a buddha. *Questions of the Nāga King Anavatapta Sūtra* (*Anavataptanāgarājaparipṛcchā Sūtra*) confirms (EMW 270):

> Those which are produced from [causes and] conditions are not produced;
> they have no inherent nature of arising.
> [Therefore] those that rely on [causes and] conditions are said to be empty.
> [A person] who knows emptiness
> is conscientious in [overcoming the unpeacefulness of afflictions].

The third line, "those that rely on [causes and] conditions are said to be empty," says that dependence and reliance on conditions is the meaning of emptiness, so the emptiness of inherent existence is the meaning of dependent arising. Nāgārjuna supports that dependent arising is the key to realizing emptiness (HSY 50):

> Through what is emptiness known?
> It is known through seeing dependent arising.
> Buddha, the supreme knower of reality, said
> what is dependently arisen does not inherently arise.

The reason of dependent arising dispels the two extremes of absolutism and nihilism. To understand this, let's look at the syllogism in which dependent arising is the reason used to prove the emptiness of inherent existence. To realize the meaning of the syllogism "Consider the sprout, it is empty of inherent existence because it is a dependent arising," three criteria must be ascertained:

1. The reason applies to the subject (*pakṣadharma*)—the sprout is a dependent arising.
2. The pervasion (*anvayavyāpti*) is whatever is the reason is the predicate—that is, everything that is dependent arising is empty.
3. The counterpervasion (*vyatirekavyāpti*) is whatever is not the predicate is not the reason—everything that is not empty does not dependently arise.

To begin, we must understand the basics of causal dependence—that things arise due to causes and conditions that have the ability to produce them. We know that sprouts will arise in dependence on the presence of their causes (seeds) and conditions (water, fertilizer, and the proper temperature). Thus we know the first criteria, the reason applies to the subject. This understanding dispels the view of nihilism, since we know that the sprout exists because it arose dependent on causes and conditions.

The pervasion is that whatever is a dependent arising is necessarily empty of inherent existence. This point is more difficult to understand and is the point that proponents of the lower tenet systems have not ascertained. Although they know that the sprout arises dependently, they have yet to understand that whatever arises dependently is empty. They find this difficult to understand because it contradicts their belief that everything that arises dependently exists inherently. Because they confuse existence with inherent existence and emptiness with total nonexistence, they think that if something exists, it must exist inherently, and if it doesn't exist inherently, it does not exist at all.

To eradicate these wrong views, Prāsaṅgikas extensively discuss the compatibility of emptiness and dependent arising and emphasize that being empty does not contradict arising dependent on other factors. They explain that the existence of the sprout and the sprout's emptiness of inherent existence are compatible. By deeply contemplating the Prāsaṅgikas' extensive explanations over time, proponents of the lower schools will come to understand the pervasion that whatever is a dependent arising is necessarily empty of inherent existence. The understanding of this pervasion dispels absolutism by proving that the sprout lacks inherent existence.

When the pervasion of a syllogism is true, the counterpervasion is also true. Still, it is helpful to individually ascertain this. In this syllogism, the counterpervasion is whatever is not empty is not a dependent arising. Whatever is not empty refers to all inherently existent items—items that are self-enclosed, independent entities unrelated to all other phenomena. Clearly such things cannot exist dependently because dependent and independent are mutually exclusive. This establishes the counterpervasion. Since all three criteria have been established, the syllogism is correct.

Does that mean that we have realized emptiness? Understanding the syllogism by having a general idea of what it is saying is a correct assumption. This correct assumption needs to be further enhanced through repeated reflection so that it will lead to a correct inference, which is an unwavering conviction. The three criteria need to be unequivocally ascertained, not just believed, in order to realize the meaning of the syllogism. With more study, reflection, and meditation, as well as purification and creation of merit, such profound knowledge will arise.

Dependent Arising Proves Emptiness

As a result of the latencies of ignorance on our mindstream, everything appearing to our mind appears to exist inherently although it does not. We assent to this false appearance, grasping it as true without realizing that our perceptions are deceptive. For example, when a face reflected in a mirror appears to a baby, the baby does not know that the reflected face appearing to be a real face is from the perspective of his mind, and that it doesn't exist in the way it appears. Instead, the child believes the reflected face is a real face. Similarly, when we apprehend something, we aren't aware that the appearance of inherent existence is from the perspective of our mind, and instead we mistakenly accept it as being the object's true nature. In fact, it is a false appearance, and the object doesn't exist inherently.

Things appear to exist under their power, to exist by their own entity (*svabhāvatā siddhi*), to exist by their own nature (*svabhāvatā siddhi*), and to exist independently (*svairīsiddhi*).[33] They appear not to depend on any other phenomena and to exist as they appear. Nor do they appear to exist by being merely designated by mind, even though that is how they exist. In short, we believe our ordinary perception of inherently existent things is true; we believe the object of negation—inherent existence—actually exists.

However, looking at the world around us, it is clear that things exist dependently. Effects depend on causes. Farmers plant seeds in order to grow crops; students go to school to learn. Dependency in terms of causes producing effects is all around us. As human beings, we depend on one another to learn, to have food, to be cared for, and to care for others. Whatever is dependent cannot be independent. Phenomena cannot have their own inherent nature that is unrelated to anything else. For this reason, they are dependent and cannot exist inherently. Āryadeva emphasizes in the *Four Hundred* (CŚ 348):

> Anything that arises dependently
> is not independent.
> All these are not independent;
> therefore there is no [inherently existent] self.

Whereas the lower systems use dependence to establish inherent existence, Prāsaṅgikas use it to refute inherent existence. Prāsaṅgikas establish emptiness by employing ultimate analysis to determine that inherent existence is not feasible, but their main argument to prove emptiness is dependent arising. By so doing, the faults of asserting either inherent existence or nonexistence do not accrue to them. While asserting the total lack of inherent existence, they accept illusion-like existence, conventional existence, and nominal existence.

Levels of Understanding Dependent Arising

Dependent arising (*pratītyasamutpāda*) can be understood on multiple levels. Etymologically *prati* means meet, rely, and depend; all three terms apply to all phenomena and all presentations of dependent arising. *Samutpāda* means arising; it can also refer to existing (*sat*) and established (*siddha*).

There are several ways to present dependent arising. Here we will speak of a threefold presentation of dependence on causes and conditions, parts, and dependent designation; a twofold presentation that consists of causal dependence and dependent designation, where dependent designation has two further subdivisions; and other presentations of dependent arising.

These various presentations are not contradictory. Rather, each one has its own flavor and emphasizes particular points or perspectives. For example, the threefold presentation emphasizes an object's dependence on its parts, not only because these parts compose it, but also because they are its basis of designation. The twofold presentation draws out the implications of mutual dependence by listing it as a branch of dependent designation. One presentation emphasizes the dependent arising of external factors, whereas another presentation emphasizes the inner dependent arising of the twelve links of dependent arising. Contemplating a topic from such diverse perspectives enhances our understanding of it.

Threefold Presentation of Dependent Arising

One presentation of dependent arising speaks of three levels: (1) arising in dependence on causes and conditions, (2) existing in dependence on its parts, and (3) designated dependently by being merely imputed in dependence on its basis of designation.

Dependence on causes and conditions

Dependence on causes and conditions (causal dependence) is also called dependently arisen (T. *brten nas skyes pa*) and refers to effects arising from causes. Pertaining only to impermanent things, this type of dependence is commonly accepted by all Buddhist schools and traditions.

Nevertheless Mādhyamikas and the lower systems see this type of dependent arising differently: the lower systems believe it indicates that truly existent effects arise from truly existent causes. Mādhyamikas, on the other hand, assert that a cause and its effect as well as the process of effects arising from causes do not exist independently, under their own power, but exist by mere designation. For them, a thing's dependence on causes and conditions proves its emptiness of true existence.

There's a big difference in the syllogisms asserted by the two parties; the lower schools say, "Consider impermanent things, they exist truly because they arise (only) dependently," whereas Mādhyamikas assert, "Consider impermanent things, they are empty of true existence because they arise (only) dependently." For the lower systems, to exist means to truly exist, and truly existent causes produce truly existent effects. The idea that dependence proves non-true existence sounds nonsensical to them.

Some people object to calling causal dependence "meeting," saying that if cause and effect meet, they would be simultaneous. In that case, the effect would not depend on its cause because it would already exist at the time of the cause and its arising would be superfluous. For example, when the cause is approaching cessation, the effect is approaching arising. So don't cause and effect exist simultaneously since they are both the agents of their respective actions? While the seed is germinating and transforming into a sprout, it is in the process of ceasing. At the same time, the sprout is gradually arising and coming into being.

According to the lower systems the seed and the sprout truly exist, in which case they must both be present while performing their respective actions. But if both the seed and the sprout exist at the same time, there would be no arising because the sprout would already exist. In that case, the seed couldn't be the cause of the sprout. But if you say that the sprout doesn't exist at the time the seed is ceasing, then what is arising? There must be an agent performing the action of arising.

Someone proposes a solution to this dilemma by saying that it's like two ends of a balance—they exist simultaneously, and while one (the seed) descends, the other (the sprout) ascends.

But this too is refuted because the seed and sprout aren't like the two ends of a scale. A sprout is presently approaching arising in that it is in the process of being produced. It does not exist at this time, although it will exist soon. Its approaching arising is imputed in dependence on the seed germinating due to the assembly of all conditions conducive to its growth. The seed exists while it is ceasing, but in the following moment it will not. The sprout does not exist while it is arising, but will exist as soon as it has arisen. In short, the "meeting" happens between the cause's approaching cessation and the effect's approaching production, although the cause and effect do not exist simultaneously and do not actually meet.[34] The sprout that is in the process of arising is a future sprout that is imputed in dependence on its principal cause (the seed) when all the conditions for its arising have not yet assembled. Effects definitely arise from their causes; they arise dependently, not inherently, and when no analysis is made, arising is like a magician's illusion—arising occurs but we can't pinpoint it.

Dependence on parts

Dependence on parts, often called "dependent establishment" (T. *brten nas grub pa*), emphasizes that all phenomena exist in dependence on their parts. They "attain their identity"—that is, they come into being—in reliance on their parts. Applying to all phenomena, both permanent and impermanent, dependent establishment is broader than dependence on causes and conditions, which applies only to impermanent products.

Conditioned phenomena have parts: an apple depends on its core, seeds, pulp, and skin; a school depends on classrooms, a playground, administrative offices, an area where the students eat, and a lounge for the teachers. Unconditioned phenomena such as unconditioned space and emptiness also depend on their parts. Since unconditioned space pervades all material objects and those objects have parts, the space pervading them also has parts that are conceptually distinct. Thus unconditioned space in general has many parts: the space in the east, west, north, south, and so forth. Similarly, emptiness pervades all phenomena, so the emptiness of the table, the emptiness of the person, and so on—which are conceptually distinct—are parts of emptiness in general. The emptiness apprehended today and the emptiness apprehended tomorrow, which are conceptually distinct, are also parts of emptiness in general.

Applying to both permanent and impermanent phenomena, dependent arising in terms of dependence on parts is accepted only by Mādhyamikas. Svātantrikas favor using this level of dependence as the reason to prove emptiness. Āryadeva also liked this reasoning.

Dependent designation by mere imputation

Dependent designation (*upādāyaprajñapti*, T. *rten nas btags pa*) is also called dependent imputation. It indicates that all phenomena exist as mere imputations designated by conceptuality in dependence on their basis of designation. Without the conceptuality that designates phenomena, their existence could not occur. This level of dependence is accepted only by Prāsaṅgika Mādhyamikas and is the unique meaning of dependent arising for the proponents of that system.

Despite being merely imputed, phenomena appear to us as if they had their own independent essence. They appear to exist objectively, to exist in and of themselves, and to exist from the object's side toward the perceiving consciousness. They don't appear to be imputed by consciousness toward the object, when in fact they are. It's as if we designated phenomena and then forgot that we designated them, and then instead believe that they exist objectively there on their own, waiting for our consciousness to come along and perceive them.

After outlining the three levels of dependent arising in his *Middle Treatise on the Stages of the Path to Awakening*, Tsongkhapa concludes (FEW 91): "Those are two presentations of the reasoning of dependent arising." The two presentations are dependence on causes and conditions and dependent designation by imputation. Here dependent designation includes dependence on parts, which are the basis of designation. In dependence on that basis of designation, an object is imputed by term and concept. For example, the aggregates are the parts that form the basis of designation, and the person is imputed by term and concept in dependence on them. This indicates that both impermanent and permanent phenomena come into existence (attain their own identities) in reliance on their parts and dependent on being merely imputed in dependence on their basis of designation.

Different Ways to Understand "Causes and Conditions" and "Arising"

Since these are the three meanings of dependent arising, how do we make sense of Candrakīrti's statement in *Clear Words* (EMW 275):

> Hence, the arising of things in reliance on causes and conditions is the meaning of dependent arising.

Although this quotation seems to limit dependent arising to meaning only causal dependence, later scholars saw more nuance in Candrakīrti's words and explained multiple meanings of the words, phrases, and passage.[35] When "causes and conditions" means the substantial cause (seed) and cooperative conditions that assist in the production of an object (fertilizer, water, and the right temperature), and "arising" means production of things by their own concordant causes, that is the first level of dependent arising, causal dependence. If conditioned things existed inherently, they would be able to set themselves up, in which case they wouldn't depend on causes and conditions. In this way, the first level of dependent arising proves emptiness.

When we take "causes and conditions" to mean an object's parts that form its basis of designation, and "arising" to mean exist, it refers to the second level of dependent arising whereby both conditioned and unconditioned phenomena attain their own identity—that is, they come to exist in reliance on their respective parts. If both impermanent and permanent phenomena existed inherently, they would be monolithic wholes. But phenomena are not imperishable wholes, they depend on their parts—a puzzle depends on the pieces of a puzzle, a box of crackers depends on many crackers and a box. Thus they lack inherent existence.

When we take "causes and conditions" to mean the basis of designation and the conceptuality that imputes the object, and "arising" is taken to mean the condition or situation that allows the positing of an object so that it exists, that is the third level of dependent arising, dependent designation. This refers to the establishment of all phenomena as mere designations in dependence on their basis of designation and a designating consciousness. If phenomena existed inherently and autonomously, they would not need to be imputed in dependence on a basis of designation. Because that is not the case, they are empty of inherent existence.

Therefore when Candrakīrti speaks of dependence on causes and conditions, he is also referring to dependence on parts, dependence on the basis of designation, and dependence on an imputing consciousness. In this way "meet," "rely," and "depend" are equivalent, so that all three terms refer to phenomena's existence by being merely designated by term and concept.

These three levels of dependent arising set forth three reasonings that refute inherent existence. The chart below summarizes the expanded meaning of "arising due to causes and conditions" to include an object's existence in dependence on parts and on being merely designated on its basis of designation.

CHART: THREE WAYS TO UNDERSTAND THE MEANING OF "CAUSES AND CONDITIONS" AND "ARISING"

THE MEANING OF "CAUSES AND CONDITIONS"	THE MEANING OF "ARISING"	LEVEL OF DEPENDENT ARISING AND WHAT IT APPLIES TO	WHY IT PROVES THE EMPTINESS OF INHERENT EXISTENCE
Substantial cause and cooperative conditions	Production of things by their own causes and conditions	Causal dependence (conditioned things)	Things that arise due to causes and conditions cannot exist without the cause ceasing and the effect arising.
Parts (that form its basis of designation)	Come into existence (attain their identity)	Dependence on parts and on the collection of parts (conditioned and unconditioned phenomena)	Phenomena that have parts cannot set themselves up.
Basis of designation and conceptuality that imputes	Situation that allows the positing of an object so that it attains its own entity	Dependent designation (all phenomena)	Without being posited by conceptuality, phenomena cannot attain their own entity.

In general, Candrakīrti explains mere conditionality (*idaṃ pratyayatā*) as dependence on "causes and conditions." Conventional things arise due to their causes and conditions, not by arising from itself, other, both, or causelessly. But now Candrakīrti expands the meaning of "mere conditionality," and thus the meaning of "arising dependent on causes and conditions" so that they are not limited to cooperative conditions enabling the substantial cause to bring its result. These terms now include factors that allow the positing of an object, such as the parts that form its basis of designation, other things in relation to which it is posited, and the conceptuality that designates the object. In addition to indicating production, "arising" is expanded to mean existence and establishment.

In short, inherent existence is an entity of phenomena that doesn't rely on being posited by conceptuality. If being established by its own power meant depending on causes and conditions, then there would be no need to establish this for the essentialists because they already accept that. But that meaning of dependent arising isn't the Middle Way view, where existing by its own power is understood as being able to set itself up by its own entity, right in the object—that is, existence that is independent of conceptuality, existence without being posited through the force of consciousness.

In conclusion, "arising dependent on causes and conditions" refers not only to causes and conditions such as seeds and fertilizer, but also to an object's parts, which are its basis of designation, and to the conceptual consciousness that imputes or designates that object. In this reading "arising" doesn't mean just production of an effect from a cause, but also existence and establishment. It is said that all phenomena are dependent existents or dependent arisings. They exist conventionally by mere conditionality, not by being established from their own side.

Emptiness doesn't mean things are frozen in time and space; it doesn't negate things being able to perform their functions. When the understanding of the Middle Way is complete, things are seen as empty of inherent existence *and* able to perform functions. These two seemingly incompatible qualities are found to be noncontradictory. In fact, emptiness does not inhibit the conventional functioning of things. Rather, it is necessary for them to function and for causes to produce their results. Candrakīrti in his *Commentary on the Four Hundred Stanzas* says (RSS 58):

> A pot and so forth are not found to exist on application of the fivefold analysis to determine whether they are one with their "cause" [i.e., their basis of designation] or other than their basis of designation. Nonetheless, as dependent imputations, they are capable of such functions as holding and dispensing honey, water, milk, and so forth. How amazing is this!

Twofold Presentation of Dependent Arising

This can be expressed as:

1. *Causal dependence* is the dependence of effects on their causes and conditions. Happiness depends on and is caused by virtuous actions. Rebirth depends on its main cause, ignorance. This type of dependence applies only to impermanent phenomena.
2. *Dependent designation* (*upādāyaprajñapti*, T. *brten nas btags pa*) has two aspects. Both apply to impermanent and permanent phenomena.

- *Dependent designation of mutual establishment* (T. *phan tshun bltos grub*) is the mutual dependence of long and short, parent and child, healthy and sick, basis of designation and designated object, and so forth, where two or more things are designated and established in relation to each other.
- *Dependent designation that is mere designation by term and concept in dependence on a basis of designation* is the subtlest form of dependent arising and demonstrates how all phenomena exist in relation to the mind.

Dependence on causes and conditions is accepted by all Buddhist traditions and all vehicles. This meaning of dependent arising serves as the foundation to understand the deeper meaning of dependent arising—dependent designation.

In his commentary to Nāgārjuna's *Treatise on the Middle Way*, Buddhapālita raises the question: When teaching the four truths during the first turning of the wheel of Dharma, the Buddha explained the cause-and-effect relationship between duḥkha and its origin. He elaborated on this by teaching the twelve links of dependent arising, in which each subsequent link is dependent on its cause, the preceding link. Since the Buddha had already explained dependent arising in terms of effects arising in dependence on their causes and conditions, why was it necessary for him to present dependent arising again in the Perfection of Wisdom sūtras in the second turning of the Dharma wheel?

Buddhapālita responds to his own question: In the public discourse on the four truths, the meaning of dependent arising is explained in terms of causal dependence. However, the teaching on dependent arising in the Perfection of Wisdom sūtras is more profound. Here the meaning of "dependent" is explained not only in terms of causes and conditions but also in terms of dependent designation.

Dependent designation has two aspects: The first is mutual dependence—phenomena being posited in relation to each other: an object and its parts, cause and effect, agent and action, innocent and guilty. The second aspect is phenomena's existence by being merely designated by name and concept in dependence on their basis of designation. Here dependent arising indicates that phenomena exist by mere name; they have no self-nature at all.

This is the profound meaning of dependent arising that Nāgārjuna emphasized in the *Treatise on the Middle Way* and to which only the Prāsaṅgika Mādhyamikas subscribe. All other systems mistakenly fear that if phenomena existed by being merely imputed by mind, then anything could be called any name and become that thing; that just giving something a name would make it exist; and that there would be no conventional reality that acts as a standard in society.

The level of understanding of dependent arising differs among the various tenet systems. For Vaibhāṣikas, Sautrāntikas, and Yogācārins, dependent arising refers only to causal dependence and applies only to impermanent things. For Svātantrikas, it also refers to mutual dependence in that phenomena depend on their parts. Such dependence applies to all phenomena, impermanent and permanent. Only Prāsaṅgikas accept dependent designation in terms of being merely imputed by conceptuality, which applies to all phenomena.

Causal Dependence

The Pāli and Sanskrit traditions both stress causal dependence, especially in terms of the twelve links of dependent origination and karma and its effects. Dependent origination is explained in chapters 7 and 8 of *Saṃsāra, Nirvāṇa, and Buddha Nature*; you may want to review it. Dependence on causes and conditions is accepted in the Śrāvaka, Solitary Realizer, and Bodhisattva Vehicles. Nāgārjuna emphasizes causal dependence in chapter 26 of *Treatise on the Middle Way*, and the Buddha expresses the essence of causal dependence in the Pāli *Sutta on the Many Kinds of Elements* (MN 115.11):

> When this exists, that comes to be;
> with the arising of this, that arises.
> When this does not exist, that does not come to be;
> with the cessation of this, that ceases.

Although the example of a seed producing a sprout is often used to express the principle of causal dependence, the Buddha's true purpose is to explain the evolution and cessation of saṃsāra. All the undesirable duḥkha we experience in countless lifetimes arises from causes. It does not arise causelessly, due to a permanent cause, or as the result of a discordant cause. The main cause is ignorance, the first link of dependent origination. Each subsequent link arises as the result of its preceding link, as the first two lines of the above verse state.

To cease our saṃsāra, ignorance must be ceased through the realization of selflessness. When ignorance no longer exists, the second link of formative actions does not come to be. In that way, the cessation of each link means that its subsequent link will not arise. Through this process, liberation is attained. Understanding dependent origination gives us the power to act to cease our duḥkha and the confidence that by correctly generating all the elements of the path, saṃsāra can be brought to an end.

Furthermore, through meditation on the causal relationship of the four truths, we come to see that saṃsāra itself is empty of true existence. Each of the twelve links is not a self-existent entity that exists independently, under its own power. It exists only because the causes and conditions for it exist. By generating the wisdom realizing emptiness, we can overcome the principal cause of saṃsāra, ignorance, and by practicing other aspects of the path, we can cease unfavorable conditions that interfere with cultivating that wisdom.

Contemplating causal dependence enables us to be more practical. When our wishes are frustrated, it's because we didn't create the complete causes and conditions for them to be fulfilled. When external conditions block our happiness in this life, it is related to causality in the external world as well as to the karmic causes we created or didn't create in this or previous lives. Understanding karmic causality enables us to change unfavorable conditions by living in ethical conduct; understanding social and political causality helps us to work to transform society and overcome structural inequalities and cultural prejudices. Knowledge of and belief in causal dependence gives us the confidence and fortitude to affect events in a constructive way. For example, we Tibetans became refugees because of karmic causes as well as political and cultural conditions. Instead of just attributing fault to others, we are doing our best to create the causes for a better future.

Causal dependence applies to all conditioned phenomena—everything that is impermanent and produced. Compared to dependent designation, dependence on causes and conditions is a coarser form of dependence. However, meditating on it profoundly affects our mind and how we view the world and our possibilities in it. We should not neglect thinking and meditating on causal dependence in the name of meditating on a more profound form of dependent arising. Rather, contemplating each level of dependent arising brings its own benefits and naturally leads to deeper understanding of the other levels.

Grasping ourselves, other people, and the world around us to exist inherently contradicts causal dependence. Nāgārjuna says (MMK 24.16):

> If you regard all things
> as existing by virtue of their essence,
> then you will regard all things
> as being without causes and conditions.

If things have an inherent essence, the law of cause and effect would be mute. Nothing could function; everything would be frozen in time. As the reasoning of diamond slivers explains, if a cause existed inherently, it would have to be a cause at all times. It could not change and produce an effect. Or, if it did produce a result, it still would not cease and would thus continue to produce effects endlessly. However, causes cease and effects that are different from them arise.

A profound understanding of causal dependence is a powerful right view that shatters extreme views. Tsongkhapa says (OR 232):

> Thus, essencelessness is established just by reasoning from dependent arising. Thus, just by ascertaining causality one destroys all apparitions grasped as truly existent. From that point on, reification and nihilism, elaboration and deprecation—all of the antitheses of the right view—are cut off.

In the context of the twelve links, causal dependence explains the evolution and cessation of saṃsāra, whereas in the context of investigating the ultimate nature of phenomena, it becomes a proof that inherent existence is impossible. Whatever exists inherently would have its own independent nature and could not exist in relationship to anything else. It would not arise from causes; it would not change or produce effects; it would not depend on parts.

In short, causal dependence applies to many areas of life: the evolution and cessation of our saṃsāra, the karmic causation of virtue bringing happiness and nonvirtue causing suffering, our effectiveness in social engagement, and as the proof of the emptiness of inherent existence.

Mutual Dependence

Causal dependence is evident; we observe effects arising from causes frequently in our lives—children are born from parents; knowledge arises from study; athletic, artistic, and musical abilities increase through practice. This is the dependence propounded by all Buddhist tenet systems: a result depends on its cause; but there is no mention of causes depending on results.

Although a cause is not produced by its effect, the identity of something as a cause depends on its having the potential to produce an effect. A seed becomes a cause because it has the potential to produce an effect, a sprout. Without there being a sprout, we cannot say that the seed is a cause—even if that sprout has not yet arisen. The very identity of a seed as a cause is posited in relation to its effect. Only Prāsaṅgikas accept that causes depend on effects. Similarly, the identity of something as an effect depends on there having been a cause that produced it; cause and effect are mutually dependent.

To give another example, we know that a cake depends on its causes and conditions, which include the baker. But how does the baker depend on the cake? When a person bakes cakes for a living, she becomes a baker. She is not inherently a baker; her identity as a baker depends on the cakes she bakes. In this way, the cause (being a baker) depends on the result (producing a cake). On the basis of observing causal dependence, deeper reflection will lead us to recognize the mutuality of the relationship: Not only does the effect depend on the cause, but also the cause being a cause depends on the effect. Things have no inherent identity as either a cause or an effect; they are made so depending on their relationship with other things.

But what if the seed becomes rotten and doesn't grow into a sprout or the cake batter burns and is inedible? Is the seed still considered a cause? Is the person who bakes still called a baker? Yes, they both produced results—even though a rotten seed and a burned cake weren't the desired results!

Many things exist in mutual dependence on one another. Nāgārjuna gives some examples (RA 48–49):

When there is this, that exists,
just as when there is long, there is short.
When this is produced, that arises,
just as when a lamp's [flame] is produced, light arises.

When there is long, there is short;
they do not inherently exist;
and when a lamp's [flame] is not produced,
the light also does not arise.

These verses speak of causal dependence—when this is produced, that arises. They also speak of mutual dependence—when there is this, that exists, just as when there is long, there is short. Other examples of mutual dependence are agent and action, whole and parts, an object (the qualified) and its attributes (its qualities), teacher and student, leader and follower, and definition and definiendum. These are posited in relation to each other. So are east and west, high and low, employer and employee, suffering and happiness, goer and going, designated object and basis of designation, ultimate truths and veiled truths, slow learner and fast learner, spiritual practitioner and path.

Some examples of pairs that are mutually dependent are also causally dependent, such as seed and sprout; however, the way the effect depends on the cause in causal dependence is different from the way it depends on the cause in mutual dependence. There are also many examples of things posited in relation to each other that are not causally dependent, such as our social identities. Someone becomes an employer only because he or she has employees, and someone becomes an employee only in relation to there being someone who employs them. Someone becomes the spouse of another person only because that other person is his or her spouse. None of these roles are self-existent from the side of the people involved; they mutually depend on each other.

Some actions are termed "constructive" and others "destructive" not because they are inherently so. They become so in relation to the results of happiness or suffering they produce. Here "constructive" and "destructive" are posited not only in relation to each other but also in dependence on the type of results they bring. When sentient beings experience happiness, the

Buddha called its causes "constructive actions," and when they experience suffering, those causes were termed "destructive actions."

REFLECTION

A simple exercise will give you a sense of mutual dependence. Be aware that everything you encounter in your daily life is posited in relation to other things.

1. Your car is posited in relation to the parts of the car, and car parts are posited in relation to the car.
2. The borders of one nation are established in relation to the borders of its neighbors.
3. One political party is posited in relation to other political parties.
4. Beautiful and ugly; wealthy, middle class, and poor; grandparents, parents, and children—all of these exist in dependence on the others.
5. Consider that these are not hard and fast, truly existent categories; the borders of countries change, the members of various political parties as well as the positions of those parties change, and the teacher of a particular student may become the student of that person who then becomes a teacher.

When we think of perceiving an object, we typically think that the object—let's say a petunia—is out there waiting to be perceived, and our consciousness is "in here," waiting to perceive an object. We see an object and a consciousness as inherently existing entities that are unrelated to each other—they exist from their own side with no relationship to each other. We think the petunia is a real visual object regardless of whether a visual consciousness perceives it. And we think there is a visual consciousness even when a visual object is not being perceived. However, it's not like that. A visual reliable consciousness is posited in dependence on an existent visual object, and a visual object is certified as existent in dependence on being cognized by a visual reliable consciousness. A reliable cognizer and an existent object are established in mutual dependence on each other. In *Clear Words* Candrakīrti says (FEW 128):

> Those are established through mutual dependence. When reliable cognizers exist, there are things that are the objects of comprehension. When there are things that are objects of comprehension, there are reliable cognizers. However, neither reliable cognizers nor objects of comprehension exist inherently.

In the meditation to equalize self and others,[36] we reflect that imputing one set of aggregates "I" and another set "other" depends on our vantage point, just as imputing one side of the valley "this side" and the other side "that side." Self and other are mutually dependent. The aggregates that we call "I" are validly designated "other" by other people, and the aggregates that they designate "I" we call "other." Without there being "other," our aggregates could not be called "mine," and without calling these aggregates "mine," another person's aggregates couldn't be called "other." Seen in this way, making such concrete distinctions between self and others becomes silly. This leads Śāntideva to remark that suffering is to be eliminated no matter whose it is because the demarcations between self and other depends on our perspective; self and others are not hard and fast categories.

Agent, action, and object of action are mutually dependent on one another. Without an action there is not an agent who is acting. Without an agent and action, there is no object of action. These are designated in relation to one another and are mutually dependent. When we say, "I talked to my friend," someone being the agent who is speaking depends on the action of talking, the words being spoken, and the friend who is listening. The action of talking exists in relation to a speaker, listening, and spoken words. Sounds are designated "words" because someone says them with an intended meaning and another person understands the meaning. None of these things have their own independent identities as agent, action, and object; they exist in mutual dependence with one another. Being dependent in this way, they are empty of independent existence. Nāgārjuna says (MMK 8.12, 8.13cd):

> A doer depends on doing,
> and doing depends on the doer as well.
> Apart from dependent arising,
> we cannot see a cause for their existence. . . .
>
> Through action and agent
> all remaining things should be understood.

Tsongkhapa clarifies (OR 231):

> Devadatta's being an agent depends on action; that is, it comes into existence depending on that. That which an agent does not perform is not an action. Thus, not only is the agent dependent, but also the action arises—that is, comes into existence—in dependence on the agent. But apart from that, no inherently existent cause or means is seen.

It is not the case that an independent doer (agent) comes along and does an independently existing action (doing). Rather someone becomes a doer by virtue of doing, and the action becomes doing because there is a doer. The two exist dependent on each other. Each one is designated in dependence on something that is not itself—the doer is posited in relation to the doing and the doing is posited in relation to the doer. The doer and doing are related to each other because neither of them can be established in and of itself, without the other. They are empty of inherent existence because they are dependent, and they are dependent because they lack inherent existence.

Whole and parts also depend on each other. A whole—that is, something we consider one object, such as a tree—is dependent on its parts: the roots, trunk, branches, twigs, and so on. Those being parts of the tree depend on the tree. A car and car parts are also an example of the mutual dependence of the whole (the car) and its parts (the wheels, engine, gears, and so forth). The car and car parts are mutually designated in relation to each other. We may think that since the wheels, engine, and so forth exist before the car is built, they don't depend on the car. However, they are established as car parts in dependence on the car. Although the car has not yet been manufactured, we know the wheels, axle, trunk, engine, and so forth are parts that will soon be assembled to form a car.

Another example of mutual dependence is the relationship between a universal category and a particular instance. For the lower schools, a particular (specific) is related to a universal (generality), but a universal is not related to its particulars. For example, they assert that the particular, a yellow hat, is related to the universal, hat, but not vice versa. This is so because without a yellow hat, the larger category of hats would still exist, but without the universal "hat," the yellow object put on your head to protect you from the heat or cold could not be a yellow hat. From the Prāsaṅgika viewpoint, however, the particular yellow hat and the universal hat are mutually dependent. The generality, hat, is posited in dependence on many hats—the yellow one, blue one, big one, and so forth—and those particular hats depend on the universal, hat, to be known as hats. Furthermore, both the individual hats and the generality "hat" lack true existence but exist by mere designation.

Social roles such as leader and follower, president and populace, and employer and employee are also mutually dependent. In chapter 4 of the *Four Hundred*, Āryadeva tears into the conceit and pomposity of a leader by saying a leader is dependent on followers and is thus actually their servant (CŚ 80):

> When a ruler seems to be the protector
> of his people, as well as protected,
> why be proud because of the one?
> Why not be free from pride because of the other?

A leader—a president, monarch, CEO, admiral, and so forth—may feel superior because he or she protects the people, but the leader is protected by the people. Without the people assenting to that person to lead them, someone would not have the title or position of a leader. In fact, the leader is the servant of the people who employ him to protect them and the country, businesses, labor unions, religious groups, and so on. Seeing this, how could a leader be arrogant?

Students of history know that leaders and followers are dependent on each other. A person goes from being a follower to a president after an election or a coup because other followers agree to that and give him or her that job. When a president's term is complete, he or she returns to being a follower. Neither of these positions exist in and of itself; they exist in mutual dependence and by the power of dependent designation—that is, by a majority of people giving someone that title.

A sprout can be a cause and an effect in relation to different phenomena: a sprout is an effect in relation to its seed and is a cause in relation to the plant that grows from it. Here it is evident that there is nothing inherent in the cause that makes it a cause; it is a cause owing to conceptual designation. When the term "cause" is imputed, there is nothing in that basis that objectively justifies it as a referent for the term "cause." Even if the sprout were dissected into tiny pieces, nothing there could denote it as being a cause or a sprout. They exist as such in reliance on conceptual designation.

Mutual dependence also applies to permanent phenomena. The space in the east exists in relation to the space in the west, north, and south. Emptiness is dependent on the basis of emptiness—the object that is empty. The emptiness of the person depends on the person; it is established in relation to the person.[37] Why are these considered dependent arisings when space and emptiness are permanent and do not arise like impermanent phenomena do? Not all phenomena that are mutually dependent are causally dependent; arise can also mean "exist" or "established."

In chapter 2 of the *Treatise on the Middle Way*, Nāgārjuna analyzes the dependent nature of a goer, the area gone over, and the action of going to show that they lack inherent existence. Such analysis can be applied to other activities and agents as well. If any of these mutually dependent aspects existed inherently, they should be findable with ultimate analysis.

Since we all like to talk, let's use that as an example and investigate it. To be a talker, someone must do the action of talking and have a topic to talk about. Who begins to talk? Does a talker begin to talk? A talker is already talking, so there's no purpose in her beginning to talk. But a non-talker also cannot begin to talk because a non-talker doesn't talk.

What does a talker talk about? There is no sense in a talker talking about what they have already talked about. Does a talker talk about the topic currently being talked about? If so, which part of the topic being talked about? The topic being discussed has many parts and aspects. Can you isolate one that is the topic being discussed? If so, which sentence is it? And which word in the sentence is the topic being discussed? A talker certainly can't talk about the yet to be talked about—the future topic—because it isn't being talked about.

If the talker, the action of talking, and the topic talked about existed inherently, these questions would have clear-cut answers because anything that exists inherently should be findable under analysis. We would be able to point to a talker regardless of whether he was talking, and the action of talking would exist without a talker or a topic. But none of the elements of talking can be isolated as independent elements. They are imputed in dependence on one another. There is no inherently existent talker; if there were, that person would always be talking, night and day, because his being a talker wouldn't depend on his having a topic or doing the action of talking! An inherently existent topic is impossible to find because the talker talks about many different things to make a point. Which one is the topic? An inherently existent action of talking cannot be found. If such a thing existed, it would not necessitate there being a person who is talking because the action of talking would be independent of all other factors, so nothing could interrupt or hinder it.

Failing to understand mutual dependence leads to incorrect views. For example, some Vaibhāṣikas and Sautrāntikas say that only parts—the smallest particles of material and smallest moments of consciousness—really exist and that wholes—a table or an hour—are mere imputations. Other people say there are only processes and no agents; for example, there is only the process of continual cognition but no mind that cognizes. From a Prāsaṅgika viewpoint, these views are erroneous because their proponents fail to see that parts and wholes as well as actions and agents can only be established in dependence on each other.

Some people think that only words and concepts are mutually dependent, not the things themselves that are their referents. Tsongkhapa clarifies that not only are the words and concepts—"fire" and "fuel"—mutually dependent, but the referents of the words are as well. Fuel depends on the fire that burns it or has the potential to burn it for its identity as fuel. It could not function as fuel or be called "fuel"—the substance consumed by fire—without the existence of fire. Similarly, fire could not function as fire—the agent that burns fuel—without the existence of fuel. To be what they are, fire and fuel mutually depend on each other.

If fire and fuel had inherent nature, they would have to be either inherently one with or inherently different from each other. If they were one, they could not be distinguished as agent (fire) and the object (fuel). In that case, fire could burn itself because it would be one and the same as fuel. On the other hand, if fire and fuel were inherently different, fire could burn without fuel. Furthermore, if fuel existed inherently as that which is burned by fire, then before it was burned and after it was burned it would not be fuel because at those times it was not being burned. But at the time the fuel is burning, it is already fire, so it would not be fuel then either.

Similarly, not only are the words "cause" and "effect" mutually dependent, but so are the referents of those words. Fire, as the cause of smoke, is posited in dependence on smoke, which is its effect. This is so because unlike other systems that claim fire does not depend on smoke, for Mādhyamikas neither fire nor smoke exist ultimately.

Dependence on Mere Designation

Dependent designation in general encompasses mutual dependence, dependence on parts, and imputation in dependence on a basis of designation. When speaking of dependence on mere designation, "mere" emphasizes that neither the object nor its basis of designation exist inherently—they exist by mere imputations without any existence from their own side.

Generally speaking, not all phenomena are mutually dependent, whereas all phenomena exist by mere dependent designation. Left and right are mutually dependent but pot and pillar are not; however, all of them are dependently designated. Designated object and basis of designation as well as car and car parts are mutually dependent and dependently designated.

Causal dependence—dependence on causes and conditions—is easier to understand than mutual dependence, which is easier to understand than mere dependent designation. However, reflection and meditation on them need not be done in sequence; you can go back and forth among them. The three differ in terms of subtlety—mere dependent designation is subtler than mutual dependence, which is subtler than causal dependence.

Causal dependence is evident in our daily lives. We initiate particular actions because we know that with the proper conditions they will bring the desired effect. Mutual dependence emphasizes that to posit one object or quality, another one must be posited as well. For up to exist, so must down; for someone to be a leader, followers must exist. Mere dependent designation goes deeper: when we see someone's body, we say, "There is Tashi." We give a name although we may not say it verbally. This is subtler because in dependence on the basis of designation an object is imputed; the object has no self-instituting power or existence from its own side. The understanding of mere dependent designation brings the full understanding of the correct view of emptiness in that it eliminates the two extremes of absolutism and nihilism.

Reflecting on mutual dependence flows into contemplation on dependent designation. We think "I" from our own perspective, and that leads to differentiating ourselves from others. Although I and others are established as mutually dependent, we still feel that this I exists independent of others. If it did, then everyone would look at us and think "I." But they don't, they see us as others. It's like this and that side of the valley. The side where we stand is called this side, and the other side is that side. But when we go to the other side of the valley, it becomes this side, and the side where we previously stood is that side. From this we understand this and that, I and other, are not established independently. Our way of thinking of I and others is false; we are not independent, unrelated entities but are mutually dependent and designated in relation to each other. We can't talk about I without an awareness of other, we cannot call one side of the valley "this side" without calling the other side "that side."

Since I and others are not independent entities, they must be dependent. Specifically, they are mutually dependently designated based on our perspective. Here, understanding I and others as mutually established has a different flavor than understanding them as mere dependent designations, although the former understanding leads to the latter.

As we delve deeper into the meaning of "dependence," it becomes evident that phenomena exist by being merely designated in dependence on their basis of designation. There is the designated object—let's say a table—and its basis of designation—the collection of parts. The mind conceives the object in dependence on the collection of parts and gives it the name "table." If we try to find the essence—the true referent of the term "table"—nothing can be found. There is nothing in the parts that can be objectively identified as the table; there is no intrinsic nature that makes it a table independent of all other things. The table exists by mere designation. For Prāsaṅgikas "merely" or "mere" eliminates any objective existence from the side of the object. Tsongkhapa says (FEW 202–3):

> . . . all phenomena are also described as posited by conceptuality, like the imputation of a snake to a rope. [The rope's] speckled color and mode of coiling are similar to those of a snake, and when this is perceived in a dim area, the thought arises with respect to the rope, "This is a snake." As for the rope, at that time, the collection and parts of the rope are not even in the slightest way positable as an illustration of a snake. Therefore, that snake is merely imputed by conceptuality. In the same way, when the thought "I" arises in dependence on the aggregates, nothing in terms of the aggregates—neither the collection that is the continuum of the earlier and later [moments], nor the collection [of the parts] at one time, nor the parts of those [mental and physical aggregates]—is even in the slightest way positable as an illustration of that I.

In a dimly lit place, we see a long, coiled, speckled object in the corner, and thinking that there is a snake, we are terrified. But when we turn on the light and see it is only a rope that we have mistakenly imputed to be a snake our fear vanishes and we chuckle at our error.

Let's go back to when we imputed "snake" and were certain a snake was there a few feet in front of us. If we examine how this "snake" exists, we find there is no snake in or on the rope. Although a snake appears, there is no snake there. Similarly, when we examine the mental and physical aggregates, there is no person in or on those aggregates. There is nothing whatsoever there that can be located or found to be a person, even though an inherently real person appears to us.

When "snake" is erroneously imputed to a coiled, speckled rope in a dimly lit area, there is nothing on the side of the rope that is a snake. When "snake" is imputed to a coiled, speckled body of a snake, we know a dangerous animal is nearby, but still there is nothing on the side of that sentient being's body that is a snake. We may say, "Wait a minute, there must be something that is a snake from the side of the snake body for it to function like a snake and to be correctly imputed as a snake. If there isn't something from the side of the snake body that makes it a snake, then there is no reason for that to be a snake and for the rope not to be a snake."

This is the view of the Svātantrikas, who assert that although the person is imputed, there is something on the side of the aggregates that makes them a valid basis of imputation of the person. That is, within the basis of designation there is something that is the object. However, if we search for what that findable essence is that makes that sentient being with a long, coiled body a snake, there is nothing in the individual parts or in the collection of parts that is its basis of designation that we can pinpoint.

Just as a snake cannot be found in the rope or in any parts of the rope, I cannot be found anywhere in the aggregates. For this reason, it is said that objects are mere names. This does not mean that they are words or sounds. If a tree were a sound, it couldn't grow leaves. Being mere names means that phenomena exist by being merely conceptually designated; they have no findable essence of their own.

REFLECTION

1. Imagine being in a dimly lit place and unexpectedly seeing a snake just a few feet away. Startled, you feel afraid.
2. Then you turn on the light, and relief floods you because you realize it's only a rope. There is no snake there.
3. Now think "I am here" and feel the strong sense of I.
4. Reflect that just as there is no snake in or on the rope, there is no I in or on the aggregates. There is simply the appearance of a person, but no inherently existent person exists.

Three Criteria for Conventional Existence

Despite there not being a person in or among the aggregates, in our daily life we say "I" and people know who we're talking about. What makes designating "snake" in dependence on a sentient being with a long, coiled body or designating "I" in dependence on the aggregates valid, whereas designating "snake" in dependence on a rope is erroneous? The snake designated on the rope does not exist at all—it cannot perform the function of a snake—whereas the I designated in dependence on the aggregates does exist and can function as a person who walks, smiles, and thinks. Even though the I cannot be found in the aggregates or separate from them, it still exists because it fulfills the three criteria for conventional existence.

1. The person is commonly known in the world; that is, it is known to a conventional consciousness. Without doing any investigation as to what a person is, we look over there and recognize that a person is sitting in a chair.
2. The existence of that person isn't contradicted by another conventional reliable cognizer. Other people with nondeceptive senses see a person and agree that there is a person, not a robot. This conventionally existent person goes here and there, has various opinions, and has a family.
3. The existence of that person isn't contradicted by reasoning analyzing the ultimate nature. Although reasoning analyzing the ultimate can negate the existence of an inherently existent person, it cannot negate the existence of a conventionally existent person because veiled truths are outside of its purview.

The existence of a snake on a rope, on the other hand, can be disproved. First, a rope is not commonly accepted in the world to be a snake and does not function like a snake. Second, people with unimpaired senses in a brightly lit room do not see a snake; they see a rope. Third, reasoning analyzing the ultimate doesn't contradict a snake being there, since that mind isn't analyzing the ultimate mode of existence of that object. In this example, the first two criteria are sufficient to discredit a rope being a snake. The third criteria comes in only when the object is apprehended as inherently existent.

What is the relationship between a word and its referent—the object it refers to? There is not an inherent bond between them. Nāgārjuna paraphrases the Buddha's perspective on that (LS 7):

> If a word and its referent are not different,
> [the word] "fire" would burn one's mouth.
> If they are different, there will be no comprehension.
> This you, the speaker of truth, have stated.

Terms—for example, the word "fire"—apply to their referent object, in this case that which is hot and burning. The term itself is not the actual thing that is referred to; however, there is a relationship between the two. If the term and referent object were the same, the word "fire" would burn our mouth. On the other hand, if the term and the object referred to were independent and unrelated, we could not explain why a term refers to a particular object and not to another referent. The word and its referent are neither one and the same nor totally separate. Neither the word nor the referent object exists apart from the interrelationship of the two.

From Nāgārjuna's point of view, the existence of things can be understood only at the level of name and designation. This does not mean that apart from words and language there are no objects of reference. In *Ocean of Reasoning*, Tsongkhapa was adamant that the expression "mere name" does not negate the conventional existence of things other than linguistically.

An attractive person or a colorful sunrise, as well as all other phenomena, appear to exist from their own side, but when we examine if there is something in that collection of parts that is that object, nothing can be found. Although things appear to exist in their own right, we can't come up with any reason to prove they exist in that way.

We see the world as filled with objective entities, but when we think about it, human beings created the situation we live in. We created the economic system that can bring both benefit and hardship. Our mind created the notions of race, ethnicity, citizenship, countries, socioeconomic class, religion, family, war, peace, and so forth. None of these things are a given; they did not arise by themselves and do not exist under their own power. They depend on name and concept.

Physical objects and mental events also exist in dependence on name and concept. Temples, businesses, trees, treaties, and birthday parties also exist by dependent designation. As for mental events, destructive and constructive emotions are not "solid." Anger, for example, is merely a name given to some mental states that have the common quality of being based on the projection or exaggeration of negative qualities and the wish to strike at what appears to be their source. Apart from what is merely designated as "anger" or any other emotion on the basis of a group of mental states with common attributes, there is no anger, greed, compassion, love, or so on. Āryadeva tell us (CŚ 178):

> Apart from conceptuality,
> desire and so forth have no existence.
> Who with intelligence would hold [that there are]
> real objects [imputed by] conceptuality?

Candrakīrti's commentary on this verse affirms that phenomena do not exist from their own side but exist only by conceptuality (HSY 188):

> Those that exist only when conceptuality exists and do not exist when conceptuality does not are undoubtedly ascertained as not established by their own nature, like a snake imputed to a coiled rope.

Although things are empty of inherent existence, they exist. However, they do not exist in the way they appear or in the way we usually grasp them to exist. It is by way of their functioning and producing results—for example, helping and harming—that consciousness imputes them. They exist through the power of the mind and the power of conventions—general agreements about basic principles, procedures, rules, and functions in society. No one legislates these conventions; they are simply what is commonly known or done, although not everyone may follow them. The *Questions of Upāli Sūtra* (*Upālipariprcchā Sūtra*) says (OR 233):

> The world is fabricated by conception.
> By grasping what they perceive, fools are identified.
> Neither grasping nor non-grasping occurs;
> they are completely conceptualized, like an illusion or a mirage.

After hearing that things exist by being merely designated, we may think that before something exists we personally must conceive and designate it.

It would be very strange to assert that before knowing any object we must have a thought designating it at that moment. One visual consciousness perceives so many things in a moment that there wouldn't be enough time to conceive and designate all of them. In addition, visual consciousnesses are nonconceptual and do not designate things. If everything existed because we personally designated it, we would be faced with the unwanted consequence that when we aren't conceiving or perceiving an object, it would cease to exist. But we know that when all the occupants of a building leave, the inside of the building is still there!

But who designates things? Is there one person who conceives and designates all phenomena, and the world exists because of that being? Who could that person be? We may think it is the Buddha because he is omniscient, but the Buddha doesn't have conceptual consciousness. Everything exists by being merely designated, but we can't identify one person or a specific group of people who do all the designating.

It seems that the meaning of the world being established by conceptual thought is that without depending on a consciousness, objects cannot establish their existence right within themselves. They don't exist as self-enclosed or self-powered phenomena that exist independent of consciousness.

From this perspective we say that the world—both persons and things—are established by conceptual thought. When something new is discovered or invented, someone gives it a name, which is a short way of referring to an object so that we don't need to recite a description of it every time we refer to it. Other people then use that name to refer to the object, and in that way the object becomes renowned in society. The Buddha states (HSY 185):

> Here even the various mind-pleasing blossoming flowers
> and attractive shining supreme golden houses
> have no inherently existent maker at all.
> They are set up through the power of thought.
> Through the power of conceptuality the world is established.

Being established by thought doesn't mean that our usual coarse conceptual consciousnesses that use language must designate them. The process of designation and conceptualization is subtler than this. Clearly animals and babies have conceptual consciousnesses—a mother cow and her calf can identify each other. An infant knows that milk will soothe its hunger. In short, people and things must exist as either independent entities that do not depend on other factors or in relation to the mind. Since it is impossible for us to show an illustration of an object that has never been perceived or designated by a consciousness, the only way we can establish the existence of something is in relation to the mind, and in particular to its being conceived and designated by the mind.

The designated object, such as a table, and the basis of designation—the top and legs—are mutually exclusive; there is nothing that is both of them. The designated object cannot be found in the basis of designation nor can it be found separate from the basis of designation. The only conclusion we can draw is that the object is mere name, mere designation. In the same way, the I cannot be found in the aggregates or totally separate from them. The I is empty of inherent existence; it exists by being merely designated in dependence on the aggregates.

While the lower systems talk about some things being designated, they do not say that everything exists by mere designation. Svātantrikas consider the role of the imputing mind, yet they say that in addition to being imputed by mind things still correctly appear to exist from their own side to a nondefective mind. Svātantrikas assert there must be something in the basis of designation that makes it that object; otherwise anything could be anything. In this way, they accept dependent designation with the caveat of things having some objective existence on the conventional level. Prāsaṅgikas counter this by saying that if there were even a speck of inherent existence in an object, then things would be independent of all other factors, and this is impossible. In the example of the rope imputed as a snake, Svātantrikas say that rope is not a valid basis of designation of snake because it does not inherently exist as a snake. Prāsaṅgikas, on the other hand, say the rope lacks the dependently arisen conditions necessary to function as a snake.

Only Prāsaṅgikas speak of dependent designation in its complete sense, as merely or only being designated by term and conception in dependence on a basis of designation. "Merely" eliminates phenomena having the slightest bit of inherent existence. Prāsaṅgikas accept the emptiness of inherent existence because they have realized with reliable cognizers that (1) whatever exists inherently doesn't rely on another, and (2) independent existence and dependent arising are contradictory.

Other Presentations of Dependent Arising

To round out the description of various presentations of dependent arising, we'll now turn to the *Rice Seedling Sūtra*, the source of these well-known words spoken by the Buddha (RSS 3):

> [This] is the result of conditionedness: Whether the tathāgatas arise or not, this nature of dharmas (phenomena) remains.

Causes producing results and results arising from causes is a law of nature. Dependent arising was not created by the Buddha, it exists whether a buddha who teaches dependent arising appears in our world or not. The *Rice Seedling Sūtra* goes on to describe external and internal dependent arising. External dependent arising is fivefold:

1. It is not eternalism, because the seed and sprout are different. Seed and sprout are related but do not exist at the same time. The sprout arises only at the time the seed ceases.
2. It is not nihilism in that the sprout does not arise from a seed that has ceased a while ago, a seed that has not ceased, or a nonexistent. These could be the case if the seed and sprout were not part of the same continuum.
3. It is not transmigration, meaning that the same thing does not go from being a seed to being a sprout. The seed and sprout are other, but they are related as cause and effect.
4. A great result can arise from a small cause indicates that additional conditions also affect the result. With the help of certain conditions, a small seed can produce a huge tree.
5. The result arises from a concordant cause, a cause that has the capacity to produce it; a cause produces a concordant result. A result cannot arise from any cause, and a cause cannot produce any result. A strawberry doesn't grow from a squash seed, and a tomato seed doesn't produce a rhinoceros.

Internal dependent arising refers to the twelve links of dependent arising that describe how we are born in saṃsāra and how we can free ourselves from it. *Saṃsāra, Nirvāṇa, and Buddha Nature* explains this in depth in chapters 7 and 8. Internal dependent arising is fivefold:

1. It is not eternalism, because the aggregates of one life are different from those of the next life. The same aggregates do not go from one life to the next. Because the aggregates of one life cease, the aggregates of the next life can arise. The body as well as the mental aggregates change from one life to the next. This accounts for sentient beings being born in different realms from one life to the next.
2. It is not nihilism in that the new aggregates arise neither from the previous lives' aggregates that have ceased a while ago nor from the previous aggregates that have not yet ceased. Although we speak of new aggregates arising as the old aggregates are dying, it is not until the death of the previous life is complete that the aggregates of the next life arise.
3. It is not transmigration, because a permanent self or a self-sufficient substantially existent person does not transmigrate from one life to the next. This is because such a self does not exist. In addition, the previous life is not necessarily of the same realm as the next life.
4. A great result can arise from a small cause indicates that a powerful or long-lasting result can arise from a small action. If not purified a small destructive karma can result in strong suffering, and if not impeded by anger or wrong views, a small virtuous karma can ripen as great happiness or a rebirth that is very beneficial for Dharma practice.
5. The result arises from a concordant cause in that the result arising from a particular karma accords with that karma. Happiness arises from virtue, never nonvirtue; nonvirtue produces suffering, never happiness.

In the *Sūtra Enumerating Phenomena Called "Discerning the Divisions of Existence and the Rest,"* the Buddha spoke of three causes that constitute dependent arising: (1) arising from a cause that is not a divine creator's thought, (2) arising from many impermanent causes (and conditions), and (3) arising from a cause that has the ability to produce that effect. In the *Rice Seedling Sūtra*, the Buddha added two more: (4) arising from causes that exist—a result cannot arise from a nonexistent cause—and (5) arising from selfless causes—the causes must be empty of any kind of self. "Self" has different meanings according to the tenet system.

The Various Levels of Dependence Are Related

The various levels of dependent arising are intertwined and support one another such that contemplation on each of them leads to understanding the emptiness of inherent existence. It is recommended that we begin by focusing on causal dependence. It is easier to understand because we know causal dependence through the direct experience of seeing flowers grow, children learn, and new situations come about. We know that certain medicines cure particular diseases and that pollution adversely affects sentient beings' health. By reflecting deeply on the observable fact of causal dependence, we will understand that the fact that things possess a dependent nature is what allows for causes to bring effects when the suitable cooperative conditions assemble.

Not only do things arise dependent on causes and conditions (causal dependence), but also their very identity is dependent on others (mutual dependence). They are posited in mutual dependence. Understanding this leads to understanding the deepest meaning of dependent arising, dependence on mere designation. If things existed objectively, without being designated by name and concept, two things would not be mutually dependent. And without being mutually dependent, they could not arise due to their causes.

Going in the other direction, if causes and their effects existed from their own side, they would not attain their identity in relation to each other (mutual dependence), and in that case, they would not be dependently designated. Buddhapālita confirms in *Buddhapālitavṛtti*, his commentary to the *Treatise on the Middle Way* (HSY 193):

> If something exists by its own entity, what would be the need for being posited dependently?

If things had their own inherent nature, that alone should be sufficient to posit their existence. We could say "It is this" and point to a self-enclosed independent entity that didn't rely on anything else. But that doesn't work because everything exists in a network of interdependent factors, including the mind that conceives and designates them. Through critical examination, we see that because everything lacks objective existence, causes produce effects, parts form wholes, dependent relationships exist. On the basis of the observed fact of causal dependence, we go through this chain of reasoning culminating in the realization of the emptiness of all phenomena. This, in turn, enables us to understand that emptiness is the meaning of dependent arising.

The above explanation began with dependent arising and traces how understanding it leads to understanding emptiness. It can go the other way too. How are we to understand the existence of seeds and sprouts, ignorance and karmic formations, and other causes and effects? There are only two possibilities: either phenomena have some degree of objective existence from their own side or they exist nominally, within the framework of conventional language, by mere designation. When probing awareness investigates these two options, it becomes clear that objective existence—phenomena existing from their own side, unrelated to anything else—is untenable. Why? Because if phenomena possessed such a fixed reality, their real identity would become clearer the more we searched for them. However, when we subject things—our parents, the stock market, a frog—to critical analysis, we cannot find them. This indicates that they lack objective existence.

Furthermore, since asserting inherent existence is unacceptable, the only choice is to accept nominal existence that is dependently designated. Phenomena can be established only on the level of mutual dependence and dependent designation.

Because the lower tenet systems contend that there is some degree of objective reality in phenomena, they cannot accept that phenomena are totally relational. They find it difficult to posit the relationship of cause and effect and so on in a world that is devoid of inherent existence. Clinging to the view of inherent existence, they are unable to posit conventional existence. Nāgārjuna mourns (MMK 24.36):

> Those who deny emptiness,
> which is dependent arising,
> undermine all
> of the worldly conventions.

For those who then fall to the extreme of nihilism, thinking nothing exists, Candrakīrti's *Clear Words* clarifies (PSP 109a7):

> We are not saying action, agent, and effect do not exist. What do we mean? We posit that these phenomena have no inherent existence.

In other words, Prāsaṅgikas are not negating all existence whatsoever, only inherent existence. Conventional, dependent existence remains. When we see that emptiness is the meaning of dependent arising, which implies nominal existence, we will not fall to the extreme of nihilism.

REFLECTION

1. Think of a relationship that is important in your life. How do you refer to that person? Are they a spouse, a parent, a child, a friend, a teacher, a pet?
2. Look closely at that person—their body and mind. Can you observe anything there that makes that person warrant the term you call them?
3. Mentally examine if any of their body parts are a parent, spouse, child, friend, and so on.
4. Think of all the various mental states, thoughts, moods, and emotions that person has. Do any of them make them a teacher, companion, coworker, and so forth?
5. Rest in that awareness that none of those roles exist inherently in those people.
6. Contemplate that your relationship with them exists dependent on conceptual designation. Based on certain criteria, we call a relationship parent-child, teacher-student, colleagues, or friends, and people in general accept these designations.

Although emptiness is initially realized based on the reason of causal dependence, as we go deeper we find that for causal dependence to exist and function, things must be empty of inherent existence. That is, things have a dependent nature because fundamentally they are devoid of inherent existence. Their being empty means that they are not frozen, independent realities cut off from everything else. Because they lack inherent existence, causes and conditions can come together and give rise to an effect that is a new phenomenon. Because phenomena are empty, they can be mutually dependent. The I and aggregates, whole and parts, agent and action, and so forth are posited in dependence on each other. In this way, understanding emptiness based on causal dependence will evolve to understanding emptiness in terms of dependent designation.

9 | Gaining the Correct View

WHEN I WAS A YOUNGSTER, the first text I memorized in my philosophical studies was *Ornament for Clear Realization*. That was followed by Candrakīrti's *Supplement*, Vasubandhu's *Treasury of Knowledge*, and others. At times I became quite frustrated during my memorization and studies. In one text, there was a word that was so difficult to understand that I scratched the paper so that the word could no longer be seen! Fortunately, my teachers encouraged me to persevere, and for this I am forever grateful.

Perhaps you feel confused and frustrated about some words too, especially those concerning emptiness. If so, discuss with your fellow students and ask your spiritual mentor. Also, be patient with yourself. It takes time and repetition to familiarize yourself with new terms and ideas. Patience and effort are also required to understand their meaning.

Especially when studying philosophy, maintain a cheerful attitude and a sense of humor. One of my longtime students recalls an episode that reminded him of the importance of being able to laugh at ourselves. Written in his own words:[38]

> During the Kālacakra event in Los Angeles, Richard Gere organized an afternoon reception to introduce His Holiness to the Hollywood community of studio heads, writers, and actors to inform them about the tragedy of Tibet. At the time, my wife and I were heading the U.S. Tibet Committee in Los Angeles, as well as helping to organize the Kālacakra event.
>
> The reception was held in the backyard of a writer's home.

It was very Hollywood. Richard and His Holiness were on the stage; my wife and I mingled in the crowd. Richard gave a short talk about the situation in Tibet. He then saw me standing off to the side and spontaneously asked me to come and say a few words about the U.S. Tibet Committee. I was a bit nervous as I walked up to the mic and stood next to His Holiness.

I said hello and introduced myself as someone from the U.S. Tibet Committee. To my surprise everyone began to laugh. Not knowing what everyone was laughing about, I was embarrassed and started to sweat. I continued, "Our office is located in Redondo Beach." Again, my words brought down the house with laughter. I was now very uncomfortable. Seeing how embarrassed I was made people laugh even more.

For reassurance I glimpsed at His Holiness only to see him playing around with my bald head. Then he played with a pin on my jacket. Because everyone could see that I was not in on the joke, it must have been very funny. To comfort me His Holiness gave me a little hug.

Everyone loved to see His Holiness be so informal. He put everyone at ease—except me! But after I joined in the laughter at his playful antics, I relaxed.

Wrong Views about Emptiness

Some early Tibetan scholars thought that because emptiness could not withstand ultimate analysis, it was nonexistent and not a knowable object. However, not being able to bear ultimate analysis does not mean that something is totally nonexistent. It means that it does not inherently exist; it cannot be found when subjected to reasoning analyzing the ultimate. It may still conventionally exist. Although emptiness is an ultimate truth, it exists conventionally, because conventional existence is the only kind of existence there is: reasoning has refuted ultimate existence or findability when analyzed with ultimate analysis.

Other early Tibetan scholars thought that emptiness was ineffable and therefore unable to be grasped by mind and was thus not a knowable object. If that were the case, nirvāṇa could not be attained. Nirvāṇa is the final true cessation, and all true cessations are emptinesses. If emptiness did not exist at all, then neither would true cessations and nirvāṇa. In addition, if emptiness was not an existent, then generating the wisdom realizing it would be impossible. In that case, eradicating ignorance by means of such wisdom could not occur, and thus there would be no reason to practice the path in order to attain nirvāṇa.

The mode of apprehension of ignorance and of wisdom are completely opposite. Ignorance views a person as inherently existent, and wisdom sees a person as empty of inherent existence. Thus wisdom and ignorance are contradictory. Wisdom sees things as they are; ignorance fabricates a mode of existence that does not exist. Because truth stands on a valid basis, wisdom can overcome and uproot ignorance. If we say that the object of this wisdom, emptiness or non-inherent existence, does not exist, what else could wisdom perceive?

Other early Tibetan scholars thought that because emptiness was found by the reasoning analyzing the ultimate, it must inherently exist. When examining a sprout with ultimate analysis, the sprout is not found but its emptiness is. However, the sprout's emptiness is not the object being searched for by the reasoning analyzing the ultimate nature of the sprout. We are examining if the sprout has an inherent essence; we are not examining emptiness to determine if it has an inherent essence. However, when emptiness is subjected to ultimate analysis, it too cannot bear analysis; it too is not found under ultimate analysis. What is found at that time is the emptiness of emptiness. Thus emptiness is also empty of inherent existence.

Some people think that a permanent phenomenon such as nirvāṇa is truly existent because it is true. They have misunderstood what Nāgārjuna queried (YS 35):

> When the Conqueror stated
> that only nirvāṇa is a truth,
> what wise person would think
> that the rest are not false?

Nirvāṇa is understood in relation to emptiness; it is a type of emptiness. In meditative equipoise directly perceiving emptiness, emptiness appears just as it is to the meditating mind. Thus nirvāṇa is true in the sense that it is nondeceptive. It exists in the way it appears to the direct perceiver perceiving it. However, nirvāṇa and emptiness are not true in the sense of being able to bear ultimate analysis. Since the ability to bear ultimate analysis is the criteria determining if a phenomenon truly exists or not, nirvāṇa, like all other phenomena, does not truly exist. If it did, it would be able to withstand ultimate analysis—that is, it would be found when searched for by ultimate analysis. If nirvāṇa were truly existent, the probing awareness analyzing its ultimate mode of being should find something objective that is nirvāṇa, but it doesn't. Thus although nirvāṇa is unconditioned and isn't produced by causes, it exists dependent on its parts as well as on its basis of designation—the mind that is totally purified of all afflictions. It also depends on saṃsāra in that saṃsāra and nirvāṇa are posited in mutual dependence on each other. Being dependent, neither saṃsāra nor nirvāṇa inherently exist. Nāgārjuna says (YS 6):

> These two, saṃsāra and nirvāṇa,
> do not [inherently] exist.
> The thorough understanding of saṃsāra
> is called "nirvāṇa."

Neither saṃsāra nor nirvāṇa exists inherently. Saṃsāra being empty of inherent existence doesn't mean that nothing exists. The appropriated aggregates are saṃsāra; when they are realized as empty and this is meditated on over time, all afflictive obscurations are ceased, and that true cessation is emptiness. The emptiness of the mind in which afflictive obscurations have been ceased is called nirvāṇa.

In the *Treatise on the Middle Way* Nāgārjuna states (MMK 18.3):

> He who does not grasp I and mine,
> also does not [inherently] exist.
> Whoever sees [the one who does] not grasp I and mine
> does not see [reality].

The first line speaks of a person—let's call him Tashi—who has realized emptiness and thus does not grasp the inherent existence of I and mine. The second line states that if analyzed, Tashi is also found to lack inherent existence. Lines three and four describe another person—let's call her Dechen—who sees Tashi and mistakenly grasps him as existing inherently. In doing so, Dechen does not see reality.

By realizing emptiness and abandoning grasping I and mine, Tashi has a correct realization. Dechen looks at Tashi and respects the emptiness he has realized so much that she grasps emptiness as existing from its own side. She also admires Tashi so much for realizing emptiness that she grasps him as existing from his own side. A contradiction now exists in Dechen's mind: she appreciates emptiness and Tashi who has realized it but grasps both emptiness and Tashi as existing inherently, the opposite of emptiness. This occurred because she did not understand the lack of inherent existence of the emptiness that Tashi realized.

When she comes to understand the emptiness of emptiness, she will not see emptiness as inherently existent. At that time, she will be able to appreciate that Tashi has realized emptiness without grasping him as inherently existent. When Dechen understands the emptiness of Tashi, that will facilitate her understanding that the emptiness he realized is also empty. Although there is no set sequence as to which emptiness Dechen must realize first—the emptiness of emptiness or the emptiness of Tashi—the fact that at present she grasps emptiness as inherently existent indicates that she will also grasp Tashi as inherently existent.

Reifying emptiness and regarding it as an absolute phenomenon unrelated to everything else prevents us from seeing reality as it actually is. Emptiness is discovered by means of critical reasoning, but some people think that since emptiness is the final truth found by critical analysis it must truly exist and be absolute. Yogācārins, for example, assert that external objects are empty of being different entities from the minds perceiving them. They claim this lack of subject and object being different substances is emptiness—the consummate nature—which is truly existent. Here we see the danger in reifying what is found to be the truth and clinging to it as existing with its own independent nature. Grasping emptiness as truly existent indicates that one is completely befuddled. As Nāgārjuna cautions (LS 21):

> Since you (the Buddha) teach the ambrosia of emptiness
> to help abandon all conceptualizations,

one who clings to this [emptiness],
this you have strongly condemned.

The Perfection of Wisdom sūtras explain sixteen divisions of emptiness. Among these are the emptiness of emptiness, the emptiness of nirvāṇa, and the emptiness of ultimate truth. In these, emptiness is the basis that is empty of true existence, just as in other divisions of emptiness a flower is a basis that is empty of true existence. The sūtras speak of the emptiness of emptiness, nirvāṇa, and ultimate truth specifically to prevent us from reifying emptiness and clinging to it as an independent, absolute truth unrelated to all other phenomena.

Mere Nominalities

The emptiness of inherent existence appears directly to the mind of āryas' nonconceptual meditative equipoise—the principal reliable cognizer perceiving it—as a nonaffirming negation. Nothing is affirmed and no conventional objects appear to that mind. This does not mean that nothing exists, only that conventional objects are not in the purview of that meditative equipoise. Mere nominalities—phenomena that exist by mere imputation—are not negated. These mere nominalities—the helper and the helped, the harmer and the harmed, and so forth—dawn to nonconceptual and conceptual consciousnesses of yogis after they arise from meditative equipoise. Those objects, each performing its own function, are not discredited by other conventional reliable cognizers. A dog barks, children do their homework, healthcare workers treat patients, and so on—all these are posited as true relative to the perspective of the world. That is, from the viewpoint of common worldly perception, these things are said to exist and they function in the ways that correspond to their definitions.

Although flying elephants and permanent souls may be spoken about, their appearances depend on superficial causes of error, such as hallucinogenic drugs, faulty sense faculties, and wrong views. Their ability to perform the functions ascribed to them is discredited by the conventional reliable cognizers of people whose minds are not captivated by such hindrances.

Saying that mere nominalities remain after direct realization of emptiness does not mean that the names of things are all that is left. We must be able to establish cause and effect as well as agent, object, and action within their being merely imputed. In the phrases "only nominally imputed," "name only," and "merely designated," the word "only"—or "mere"—negates inherent existence. It doesn't mean that only words exist, nor does it mean that whatever is posited by nominal conventions exists.

When practitioners who have ascertained emptiness during meditative equipoise on emptiness arise from their meditation, in post-meditation time they apprehend what was left unaffected by the negation of inherent existence. At that time, they easily induce ascertainment that mere names such as "me," "body," and so forth remain and that those objects are conceptual imputations, mere nominalities that are designated by conceptuality. Without analyzing how those mere nominalities exist, through their own experience they establish that these merely imputed phenomena have the ability to function: the I creates karma and experiences its results, animals eat and drink, the economy goes up and down. This experiential way of ascertaining the noncontradictory and complementary nature of dependent arising and emptiness is much more powerful and has a stronger impact on the mind than when ascertainment comes while discussing tenets during oral explanations.

It is difficult for a beginner to gain this ascertainment that phenomena lack inherent existence yet exist as merely designated dependent arisings. Nevertheless it is important to imagine what this experience would be like because doing so will plant seeds in our mindstream so that in the future when our understanding is deeper, merit stronger, and purification greater, actual ascertainment will dawn in our mind. Because at present we are so habituated with accepting that things exist under their own power, after refuting that, it isn't comfortable to posit things as mere nominalities. Still, we must move our mind in that direction by thinking that it's logically impossible for things to exist from their own side; the only way they can exist is by the force of nominal conventions.

Impermanence, Dependent Arising, and Emptiness

Meditation on impermanence also supports our efforts to understand emptiness. A correct realization of subtle impermanence involves understanding that all conditioned things are in constant change, never remaining the same in the next moment. What brings about this continuous change? It is the nature of conditioned phenomena; they arise and cease due to their causes and conditions. They do not exist under their own power but are influenced by other factors. Impermanent phenomena cannot be independent—they are thoroughly dependent on things that are not themselves. People, the environment, and events are not isolated, self-enclosed phenomena. In the case of subtle impermanence, the very cause that made something arise is the cause for it to disintegrate and not remain the same in the very next moment. Being dependent upon causes and conditions in this way, impermanent things cannot possibly exist inherently.

This understanding of causal dependence, in turn, leads to understanding mutual dependence in that effects and causes are posited in mutual dependence on each other. Something is not a cause without the possibility of it issuing forth an effect, and something is not an effect unless it arises from a cause. As noted above, understanding mutual establishment leads to the realization that phenomena cannot and do not exist inherently.

REFLECTION

1. Meditate on subtle impermanence of the I for a while. Observe that while the I is arising it is simultaneously disintegrating.
2. Investigate if the I has an inherent essence that goes from one moment to the next moment. Is there an independent essence that makes the person what it is that is passed on? In other words, even though you are changing in each moment, is there something deeper that really is you and that holds the various moments of yourself together as a continuum such that you exist?
3. This view may seem attractive—I'm constantly changing, but at the same time, there is an enduring essence that does not disappear; I'm still the same person. Does this view make sense or does it contain an internal contradiction? Can one part of you undergo change and another part of you remain the same?
4. Rest the mind in the knowledge that because transience is the very nature of conditioned phenomena, it is impossible for them to have any inherent

essence that goes from one moment to the next and makes them what they are.

Other Reasonings Meet Back to Dependent Arising

Two manners of reasoning can establish emptiness. One is called "non-observation of what is necessarily related to inherent existence" and the other is called "observation of what is contradictory to inherent existence."[39] From the reasonings explained in this book, all except the reasoning of dependent arising are examples of non-observation of what is necessarily related to inherent existence, whereas the reasoning of dependent arising is an example of observation of what is contradictory to inherent existence.

The first reasoning, the reasoning of non-observation of what is necessarily related to inherent existence, relies on the knowledge that if one thing exists, something else that is related to it must necessarily be observed. But that second thing is not found, indicating that the first thing also doesn't exist. For example, anything that exists must be either permanent or impermanent. Square tires are neither permanent nor impermanent. Through this, we understand that they do not exist.

The second reasoning, the observation of what is contradictory to inherent existence, relies on the knowledge that the existence of one thing contradicts the existence of another. For example, the existence of a completely clear sky contradicts the existence of a snowstorm.

Diamond slivers, Nāgārjuna's fivefold reasoning, and Candrakīrti's sevenfold expansion of it are examples of the first reasoning, *non-observation of what is necessarily related to inherent existence*. In the case of diamond slivers, this means that if inherent existence existed, we should be able to find a sprout—or our next rebirth—arising in one of the four ways—from itself, another, both, or causelessly. These are the only ways an inherently existent sprout or rebirth could arise. In the case of the fivefold and sevenfold refutations, if things existed inherently, they should be related to their bases of designation in one of the five or seven ways. However, when we search to find such indicators of inherent existence, we discover there are none. An inherently existent tomato does not relate to its basis of designation—its parts, such as its skin, pulp, and seeds—in any of the five or seven ways. We do not observe what must necessarily be present if things existed inherently. Similarly, an inherently existent person is neither inherently the same as nor inherently different from its basis of designation, the aggregates.

The second type of reasoning used to prove the lack of inherent existence is *the observation of something contradictory to inherent existence.* The reasoning of dependent arising falls in this category. Inherently existent phenomena would exist independent of all other factors and would be able to set themselves up under their own power. However, both our experience and reasoning show the opposite, that phenomena come into existence dependent on other factors: houses depend on their collection of rooms, children and parents exist in relation to each other, money has value simply because people have imputed value on certain pieces of paper. Dependent arising contradicts independent existence, and because independent existence and inherent existence are synonymous, dependent arising contradicts inherent existence.

Diamond slivers and the fivefold and sevenfold reasonings come back to dependent arising. The main purpose of these reasonings is to generate in our mindstream the correct view of the Middle Way free from the two extremes of absolutism and nihilism, and the reasoning of dependent arising does that. Candrakīrti explains how diamond slivers relates or comes back to dependent arising (MMA 6.114):

> Because things do not arise causelessly,
> or from Īśvara and so forth as causes,
> or from themselves, from other, or both,
> they arise dependently.

For practitioners who have previously realized emptiness, when they examine how a sprout arises, they ascertain that the sprout does not arise inherently in any of the four ways—from itself, other, both, or causelessly. Because it does not arise inherently, the sprout does not inherently exist. Through its own force, without need of another reasoning, this ascertainment of the sprout's emptiness of inherent existence induces the ascertainment that the sprout exists by mere imputation. This is called "emptiness dawning as the meaning of subtle dependent arising."

Furthermore, when such practitioners ascertain that the sprout is a mere imputation, through its own force without another reasoning consciousness, this ascertainment of dependent designation induces the ascertainment that the sprout is empty of inherent existence. This is called "dependent arising dawning as the meaning of emptiness."

To summarize, for those who have previously realized emptiness, the ascertainment of the sprout's emptiness induces ascertainment of its dependent designation, and the ascertainment of the sprout's dependent designation induces ascertainment of the sprout's emptiness. This demonstrates how the essential point of the diamond slivers refutation meets back to dependent arising.

Candrakīrti also explains that the sevenfold refutation that focuses on the relationship of a phenomenon to its basis of designation comes back to dependent arising. After refuting the existence of an inherently existent chariot, he affirms that the chariot exists by being merely imputed in dependence on its parts by worldly, everyday convention, without analyzing what the chariot really is (MMA 6.158):

> Although the chariot does not exist in any of the seven ways,
> both in ultimate reality and in terms of the world
> we here impute the chariot in dependence on its parts
> without analysis and through everyday convention alone.

If the chariot existed inherently, it should be in one of the seven ways. Finding that the chariot does not exist in any of these ways, we ascertain that the chariot is empty of inherent existence. This in turn induces ascertainment that the chariot is merely designated in dependence on its parts, which are its basis of designation. This shows that ascertainment of emptiness induces ascertainment of dependent arising. But it doesn't stop there. Ascertaining that the chariot is merely designated in dependence on its parts induces ascertainment of its emptiness of inherent existence. This illustrates that the sevenfold refutation meets back to dependent arising.

In short, the two reasonings that are a non-observation of what is necessarily related to inherent existence—diamond slivers and the sevenfold reasoning—induce the observation of something opposite to inherent existence—dependent arising. Dependent arising then becomes another reason to prove emptiness. Here we say, for example: Consider the car, it does not exist inherently because it arises dependently.

Only the non-observation of what is related to inherent existence is explicitly mentioned in the two reasonings (1) consider the car, it is empty of inherent arising because it does not inherently arise from itself, other, both, or causelessly, and (2) consider the stove, it is empty of inherent existence because it is not inherently one with or different from its parts. The emptiness proven by these two reasonings induces an ascertainment of dependent arising. That is, the two reasonings bring realization of the emptiness of, for example, the car and the stove. But that doesn't mean the car and the stove are totally nonexistent. In the aftermath of meditation on emptiness, dependent existence is affirmed; all phenomena exist dependent on other factors that are not themselves.

Dependent arising is said to be the monarch of reasonings because it *explicitly* refutes the two extremes of absolutism and nihilism. Because phenomena are dependent, they do not exist inherently. Because they arise or exist, they are not nonexistent. The reasonings that are a non-observation of what is necessarily related to inherent existence (1) *implicitly* refute absolutism through not finding what is related to inherent existence and (2) *explicitly* refute nihilism through finding an opposite factor, dependent arising.

However, the fact that realization of emptiness induces ascertainment of dependent arising and understanding of dependent arising induces ascertainment of emptiness does not mean that a consciousness realizing one knows the other. Rather, the ascertainment of one induces the ascertainment of the other by another consciousness. The phrase "the compatibility of emptiness and dependent arising" means that the understanding of emptiness and the understanding of dependent arising mutually induce each other for someone who has previously realized emptiness.

This all sounds well and good intellectually, but when we can't find the inherently existent things that we cling to—the self, our dear ones, or our reputation, status, and the praise and approval others give us—our tendency is to leave aside the pursuit of understanding emptiness and grasp onto something to make us feel secure in knowing that we indeed exist. For this reason, saying that everything exists dependently seems to ease our fears when in fact we again fall into grasping inherently existent I and mine. For this reason, Changkya Rolpai Dorje in *Recognizing My Mother: An Experiential Song on the View* comments (RM 10):

> There seem to be among today's scholars
> some, caught in a web of words like
> "thoroughly withstanding" and "true existence,"
> who seek only to negate some creature with horns
> while leaving intact this everyday appearance of solidity.

Refuting the inherent existence that we have adhered to since beginningless time is jarring to our saṃsāric minds that grasp ourselves and all other phenomena to exist inherently. To avoid the discomfort this brings, we discuss emptiness intellectually, but cannot properly identify the object of negation in our own experience. Instead, we think of the object of negation as something external, like a creature with horns that we can chase away or a hat on our head that we can easily take off. Meanwhile, the inherent existence that appears to our every perception is left unquestioned and our self-grasping is not ruffled in the least. Thus, however challenging it may be to understand the teachings on emptiness, with joyous effort we must study and apply what we learn to our own lived experience and refute inherent existence.

Mādhyamikas Differ from Essentialists

Essentialists—adherents to non-Madhyamaka tenets—also refute independent existence by citing dependent arising. Why then do the Mādhyamikas try to prove the emptiness of independent existence to them? Essentialists take independent existence to mean not depending on causes and conditions and use causal dependence as the reason to refute the non-Buddhists' concept of a permanent, unitary, and independent soul or self. For Mādhyamikas, however, "independent" means truly existent. Because of the difference in the meaning of "independent," Mādhyamikas must prove the emptiness of true existence to the essentialists.

The essentialists and Mādhyamikas also define dependent arising differently. To essentialists it means depending on causes and conditions, which falls short of the complete Madhyamaka meaning. For Mādhyamikas, "arising" has two meanings. The first is "to generate," a meaning that applies only to conditioned phenomena that are generated or arise in dependence on their causes and conditions. The second meaning, which applies to all phenomena, is "to come into existence by being dependently designated." This refers to the way such things as agent and action, and ultimate truths and veiled truths, exist by mutual dependence, although they do not cause each other.

By citing a more complete meaning of dependent arising with three levels of dependence, Mādhyamikas—and in particular, Prāsaṅgikas—refute essentialists' assertion that dependently arising things inherently exist. But the issue is a little more complex than this, because essentialists don't just take dependent arising as a reason to prove the absence of independent existence as they define it, they also use dependent arising as a reason to "prove" true existence. According to them, each cause must have its own inherent potential that is capable of producing its unique effect. If it didn't, everything could produce everything. The causes, natures, and effects of things exist, and they have their own self-defining characteristics that allow them to be objectively differentiated. Essentialists assert that since things arise dependently, they exist, and since they exist, they must truly exist. If they did not, they would not exist at all. Thus when essentialists hear the syllogism "Consider phenomena, they are empty of true existence because they arise dependently," they say there is no pervasion and that the reason is contradictory. To them, phenomena are truly existent because they arise dependently.

Non-Buddhists also disagree with the syllogism "Consider phenomena, they are empty of true existence because they arise dependently," but for a different reason. They say that the reason is not established—that is, from their viewpoint, some phenomena do not arise dependently. Rejecting the Buddha's teachings on mere conditionality, they assert that either things arise spontaneously from no cause at all or they arise from a permanent cause. Those who assert that things happen randomly without a cause are Materialists who negate the law of karma and its effects. Those that assert arising from a permanent cause are the Sāṃkhyas who assert that things arise from a universal primal substance and the theists who state that the world and the sentient beings in it were created by an unchanging prior intelligence, such as a creator god or Īśvara. Their minds obscured by wrong views, both Buddhist essentialists and non-Buddhists cannot understand the Buddha's profound teaching on the compatibility of dependent arising and emptiness.

Some of you may agree that all phenomena are empty of true existence because they arise dependently. After all, you have heard those words often and it is easy to repeat them without understanding their profound meaning. For example, you know a cake is produced by causes—butter, eggs, flour, sugar, baking soda, and so forth—and conditions—the baking pan, the oven, and the baker. But if someone says, "therefore the cake is empty of true existence," you may find that difficult to accept. The cake seems to have its own entity that's different from the entity of its ingredients; it appears to have an essence that is above and beyond the collection of its parts. It's as if you think of the cake as having two contradictory qualities: it depends on causes and conditions, but it also has its own essence that doesn't depend on being merely imputed by mind.

Similarly, it's not too difficult to accept that you depend on parts. You know there's a body and mind and that each of them has parts. But there seems to be an independent I in there that possesses them. Again, it seems that you can be dependent and still have an intrinsic essence. In short, like the essentialists, you haven't realized the pervasion that whatever arises dependently is necessarily empty of true existence. The mind still clings to inherent existence. Although there is a correct assumption when you agree that whatever arises dependently can't exist inherently, you have not yet generated a correct inferential understanding, let alone a direct realization.

If you see this in yourself, continue to do purification practices and accumulate merit, as well as study, reflect, and meditate on the compatibility of dependent arising and emptiness in order to penetrate the meaning of the syllogism. While such syllogisms may initially seem to be intellectual verbiage, they in fact touch on very deep layers of innate misconceptions that we have ignorantly cherished since beginningless time.

For Mādhyamikas dependent arising is an important reason proving the emptiness of true existence. Arising dependently and being empty of true existence come to the same point—whatever is a dependent arising is empty and whatever phenomena is empty is a dependent arising. Essentialists consider these two incompatible. In *Questions of the Nāga King Anavatapta Sūtra*, the Buddha explains (FEW 88–89):

> Whatever arises from conditions is not arisen;
> it is not inherently arisen.
> Whatever depends upon conditions is known to be empty;
> one who knows emptiness is conscientious.

Not arisen in the first line is defined in the second as not inherently arisen. That is, whatever arises dependent on conditions does not arise inherently. The third line indicates that *empty* means dependent on conditions. *Empty* does not mean empty of the ability to perform a function; it is not a negation of conventional products that, by definition, perform functions. Someone who understands emptiness correctly is conscientious in observing the law of karma and its effects.

REFLECTION

1. Bring to mind the sense of I when you have a strong emotion and identify the object of negation.
2. Examine if the I could possibly exist in any of the seven ways that Candrakīrti explained. By doing this repeatedly, develop conviction that the I, and by extension all else, does not exist inherently.
3. Now reflect that although the I does not exist inherently, it does exist conventionally. Because it exists dependently, the I can function and produce results. Although you are empty, you still create actions and experience the results of those actions.

The Compatibility of Emptiness and Dependent Arising

When Tsongkhapa was seeking the correct view, he had a vision of Manjushri, the buddha of wisdom, who advised, "If you are serious about gaining the wisdom realizing emptiness, first do three activities: Engage in strong purification of negativities and create great merit, study the great classical treatises and commentaries on the Middle Way, and make fervent supplications to your gurus, buddhas, bodhisattvas, and deities."

After having this vision, Tsongkhapa finished the teaching he was giving and went to a hermitage in Wolkha Valley with eight of his disciples to do retreat. There he did three-and-a-half-million prostrations and many maṇḍala offerings, and studied the great treatises. One night he had a visionary experience of Nāgārjuna surrounded by Āryadeva, Buddhapālita, Bhāvaviveka, and Candrakīrti, who were discussing dependent arising and emptiness. One of them with a dark complexion, whom he took to be Buddhapālita, lifted up a text and put it on Tsongkhapa's head, saying, "You should read this." The next day, someone presented that very same text—Buddhapālita's commentary on the *Treatise on the Middle Way*—to Tsongkhapa. Tsongkhapa began reading it, and as he was contemplating the eighteenth chapter, the "Analysis of Self and Phenomena," all his doubts about meditation on emptiness suddenly vanished and with crystal clarity he ascertained precisely what was negated and what was left unaffected in the meditation on emptiness. In this way, the profound realization of emptiness dawned in his mind. This gave rise to his deep admiration for the Buddha as the teacher of dependent arising and emptiness. To express his gratitude for the Buddha's teachings, Tsongkhapa composed *Praise to Dependent Arising*, where he exclaimed (PDA 20–21ab):

> "All of this is devoid of essence,"
> and "from this arises that effect"—
> these two certainties complement
> each other with no contradiction at all.
> What is more amazing than this?
> What is more marvelous than this?

Emptiness and dependent arising are important threads of the Buddha's teachings and the ability to link them together in a mutually supportive way is the key to the Middle Way view. That these two are compatible and complementary does not mean they are the same. If they were, then just by perceiving a dependent arising—a book, for example—everyone would perceive emptiness. But that is not the case! Realization of emptiness is not realization of dependent arising, and vice versa. They must be realized in such a way that each one dawns as the meaning of the other.

Being empty and arising dependently are two ways of looking at phenomena. The fact that phenomena are empty of true existence does not cancel out conventional distinctions among them or make veiled truths nonexistent. Realizing emptiness does not make everything appear as a blurry, indiscriminate "one." Pens and tables still have their own unique functions, and a person who realizes emptiness can discern these upon emerging from meditative equipoise on emptiness. Āryadeva says (CŚ 326):

> If a thing did not depend
> on anything else at all,
> it would be self-established;
> but such a thing exists nowhere.

By deep examination with probing awareness, meditators realize that all phenomena do not exist from their own side. However, they are not totally nonexistent. How do they exist? Dependently. Just the term "dependent arising" shows that phenomena are empty and yet exist. "Dependent" indicates that they are empty of independent existence. "Arising" means that they come into being and exist. All phenomena are established by conventional reliable consciousnesses, even though they lack their own self-nature.

One who has realized the compatibility of emptiness and dependent arising understands that although everything lacks true existence, it exists in relation to other factors. Cause and effect, an object and its attributes, definiendum and definition, and whole and parts are posited in dependence on each other. The heart of the Middle Way view is expressed by Nāgārjuna in two verses (MMK 24.18–19):

> That which is dependent arising
> is explained to be emptiness.
> That, being dependently designated,
> is itself the Middle Way.
>
> There does not exist anything

that is not dependently arisen.
Therefore, there does not exist anything
that is not empty.

That which is dependent arising is explained to be emptiness indicates that when Mādhyamikas who have refuted inherent existence with reliable cognizers ascertain that phenomena are dependently arisen, that induces an ascertainment of their emptiness. They understand that inherent existence is the same as independent existence, and that independent existence and dependent existence are contradictory. This realization can occur only to meditators who have previously realized emptiness. When they later see, hear, or remember persons, rockets, and roses—things that depend on causes and conditions—that understanding of dependent arising induces the realization that these things lack inherent existence. Even if their realization of emptiness occurred in a previous life, in this life the awareness that all persons and phenomena are dependent arisings may induce ascertainment of their emptiness.

That [emptiness], being dependently designated, is itself the Middle Way indicates that emptiness itself exists dependently. Like all phenomena, it exists by being merely designated in dependence on its parts and lacks inherent existence. In this way, emptiness too is free from the two extremes of inherent existence and total nonexistence.

If dependent arising referred only to causal dependence, the reason of dependent arising would refute the inherent existence of only conditioned phenomena. However, because dependent arising means dependent designation, the reason of dependent arising can establish the emptiness of all phenomena.

That which is dependently designated is explained to be emptiness means that although phenomena are empty of inherent existence, they are not totally nonexistent because they are dependently designated. This understanding—which negates inherent existence on the one hand, and total nonexistence on the other—is the true Middle Way.

Nāgārjuna states in *Refutations of Objections* (V 71):

I pay homage to the unequalled Buddha
who declared emptiness, dependent arising,

and the Middle Way
as having the same meaning.

Emptiness is posited as dependent imputation, and since all phenomena are imputed in dependence on their parts, they do not arise inherently. Emptiness itself is neither inherently existent nor totally nonexistent, and thus is free from the two extremes. It is the Middle Way.

Saying that emptiness, dependent arising, and the Middle Way have the same meaning doesn't mean they are synonymous, for they are not. Rather it indicates that all three establish that all phenomena are free from absolutism and nihilism. Furthermore, the more we penetrate one, the deeper is our understanding of the other two. Although they are different, these three are inseparable and converge at the same point.

The fact that all phenomena are empty of inherent existence doesn't just mean that they cannot be found with ultimate analysis. The true meaning of emptiness must be understood in terms of dependent arising. Emptiness makes it possible for phenomena to have a dependent character, to interact with one another, and to function. If things were not empty—if they existed inherently and from their own side—there would be no way effects could arise from causes. Everything would be frozen in its own independent existence; warm weather, water, and fertilizer would not cause a viable seed to grow. Emptiness enables the workings of our everyday world of dependent arising. Emptiness is the basis that allows for the diversity of phenomena to interact and for causes and conditions to come together to produce effects. Our experiences of suffering and happiness arise within the emptiness of inherent existence. Understanding the complementary nature of emptiness and dependent arising helps us understand that afflictive mental states can be counteracted and the clear and cognizant nature of the mind can be transformed into the mind of a buddha when it meets the right conditions.

Saying that emptiness is the meaning of dependent arising doesn't mean that emptiness and dependent arising are the same thing. They aren't: emptiness is a nonaffirming negation and dependent arising an affirmative phenomenon. It also doesn't mean that dependent arising is the name and emptiness is the meaning, because then we couldn't realize dependent arising without having realized emptiness. This is because to understand the name of something, we first have to know what the object is, its meaning. It also doesn't mean that when dependent arising is explicitly realized, emptiness is implicitly realized, because emptiness can't be implicitly realized by explicitly realizing dependent arising. If it could be, then proponents of the lower systems would have realized emptiness upon realizing dependent arising. Nor does it mean that dependent arising is the definition of emptiness, just like "flat-bottomed water holder" is the definition of pot. If it were, someone who has ascertained dependent arising would understand emptiness with that very mind.

When our understanding of dependent arising is expansive, it will lead to the realization of the emptiness of inherent existence. We will know that because a phenomenon arises dependently, it lacks inherent existence. Similarly, as our understanding of emptiness becomes clearer, our understanding of dependent arising will naturally deepen because we will know that although phenomena lack inherent existence, they depend on many other factors to exist. In this way, one understanding reinforces the other. In the commentarial tradition, understanding the compatibility of dependent arising and emptiness is called "emptiness dawning as the meaning of dependent arising" or "emptiness going as the meaning of dependent arising." And when it goes the other way, it is called "dependent arising dawning as the meaning of emptiness" or "dependent arising going as the meaning of emptiness." The next chapter will expand on this provocative idea.

10 The Path Pleasing to the Buddha

THE PATH PLEASING to the Buddha is the Middle Way path, the most refined view which explains that the understandings of dependent arising and emptiness are not only compatible and complementary but also facilitate and induce each other. To this end Tsongkhapa presents their convergence in a radical way in which emptiness dawns as the meaning of dependent arising and dependent arising dawns as the meaning of emptiness. In *Praise to Dependent Arising* (PDA 2), he says:

> Whatever degenerations there are in the world,
> the root of all these is ignorance.
> You taught that seeing dependent arising
> will undo this ignorance.

Instead of saying that realizing emptiness will counteract ignorance and lead to liberation—which is what we might expect—Tsongkhapa instead points to dependent arising as the crucial factor in freeing us from ignorance. In doing so, he makes the point that dependent arising and emptiness come to the same point, and that understanding both is essential to attain liberation and full awakening. To gain the full understanding of the correct Middle Way view, emptiness must be understood in terms of dependent arising and dependent arising must be understood in terms of emptiness.

Tsongkhapa describes the progressive stages for arriving at a complete understanding of emptiness and dependent arising that is free from the absolutist view grasping true existence and the nihilistic view holding to total nonexistence. In *Three Principal Aspects of the Path* (*Lam gtso rnam gsum* 9–13) he says:

> Even if you have meditated on the determination to be free and
> bodhicitta,
> without the wisdom realizing the ultimate nature,
> you cannot cut the root of cyclic existence.
> Therefore strive for the means to realize dependent arising.
>
> One who sees the infallible cause and effect
> of all phenomena in cyclic existence and beyond
> and dismantles every notion of an objectified basis
> has entered the path that pleases the Buddha.
>
> As long as the two understandings—
> of appearance, infallible dependent origination,
> and of emptiness, the absence of all positions—remain separate,
> then you have not realized the intent of the Sage (Buddha).
>
> When these [two realizations] are without alternation and
> concurrent,
> from only seeing dependent arising as infallible,
> an ascertaining consciousness entirely undermines all modes of
> mental grasping.
> At that time, the analysis of the [profound] view is complete.
>
> In addition, when you understand appearances clearing away the
> extreme of existence
> and emptiness clearing away the extreme of nonexistence,
> and you understand how emptiness dawns as cause and effect,
> you will never be captivated by either extreme view.

In these verses, fleshed out below, he sets out the sequence of steps to arrive at the culmination of the analysis of the profound view.

The Importance of Realizing Profound Emptiness

> Even if you have meditated on the determination to be free and
> bodhicitta,
> without the wisdom realizing the ultimate nature,
> you cannot cut the root of cyclic existence.
> Therefore strive for the means to realize dependent arising.

The first eight verses of the *Three Principal Aspects of the Path* explain the first two principal aspects of the path—the determination to be free from saṃsāra and bodhicitta. The above verse is the first one that deals with the third principal aspect of the path, the correct view. It presents the reasons why realization of profound dependent arising is important and advises all those who aspire for liberation to search for the correct view. In addition, it presents a general overview of the path leading to the culmination of the analysis of the profound view.

Gaining a stable understanding of veiled truths such as the law of karma and its effects and generating a strong determination to be free from saṃsāra form the basis for examining emptiness, the ultimate nature. For bodhisattva-aspirants, a strong feeling for bodhicitta is also essential. Although the aspiration to be free from saṃsāra and the generation of bodhicitta indirectly help to overcome the ignorance that is the root of cyclic existence, they cannot serve as direct antidotes. For that, realization of the emptiness of inherent existence of persons and phenomena is essential.

The root of cyclic existence is the ignorance of phenomena's ultimate nature; this ignorance observes persons and phenomena and misapprehends their ultimate mode of existence, grasping them as inherently existent. The wisdom realizing emptiness also observes persons and phenomena but apprehends their emptiness of inherent existence. Since this wisdom directly contradicts how ignorance grasps persons and phenomena, it is able to overcome and dispel ignorance.

Tsongkhapa exhorts us to "strive for the means to realize dependent arising." It is interesting to note that he does not explicitly encourage us to work at the means to realize emptiness by contemplating diamond slivers, the sevenfold analysis, and so forth, as we might expect. Why is this? It's because the meaning of dependent arising abides in the meaning of emptiness, and the meaning of emptiness abides in the meaning of dependent arising. When we fully understand the mutually complementary nature of emptiness and dependent arising, our analysis of the profound view will be complete.

Of the many reasonings that can lead to the full realization of the Middle Way, dependent arising is called "the monarch of reasoning" because, unlike other forms of reasoning—diamond slivers, the sevenfold refutation, and so forth—understanding the meaning of the phrase "dependent arising" (T. *rten 'byung*) has the power to simultaneously dispel the two extremes of absolutism and nihilism. "Dependent" (T. *rten*) dispels the extreme of absolutism, and "arising" (T. *'byung*) dispels the extreme of nihilism. No other reasoning has this ability. In fact, all other reasonings that establish emptiness function in a negative manner, to refute inherent existence. They do not have an affirmative role of indicating the validity of veiled truths, such as the functioning of cause and effect.

As in all Dharma practices, there are stages of development. The initial inferential realization of emptiness must be nourished over time. When emptiness dawns as the meaning of dependent arising and dependent arising dawns as the meaning of emptiness and we are able, with a reliable cognizer, to establish cause and effect in the wake of the realization of emptiness, the analysis of the profound view is complete. Furthermore, deep meditation is required to gain serenity and insight focused on emptiness. This is reinforced until a direct perceiver of emptiness arises. The mind must become more and more accustomed to emptiness; the realization of emptiness is strengthened over the paths and grounds, enabling it to gradually eradicate all afflictive obscurations, and in the case of bodhisattvas, to dispel all cognitive obscurations as well.

To have a full understanding of the correct view of emptiness such that the analysis of the profound view is complete, understanding emptiness in terms of dependent designation is key. After gaining an initial realization of emptiness, continued meditation on both emptiness and dependent arising is needed to increase the depth and strength of our understanding of the mutually complementary nature of emptiness and dependent arising. The following verses describe the process of bringing the analysis of the correct view to culmination by cultivating the three understandings gained by learning, reflecting, and meditating.

REFLECTION

1. Why is realizing emptiness important?
2. What is the difference between the initial realization of emptiness and the culmination of the analysis of the profound view?

The Initial Realization of Emptiness That Pleases the Buddha

> One who sees the infallible cause and effect
> of all phenomena in cyclic existence and beyond
> and dismantles every notion of an objectified basis
> has entered the path that pleases the Buddha.

This verse explains how to gain the initial realization of emptiness. Here dependent arising is used as the reason to prove that all phenomena lack inherent existence—that is, emptiness is realized in terms of dependent arising. This marks *entering the path that pleases the Buddha.*

A shallow understanding of dependent arising isn't sufficient to bring about this realization of emptiness, however. Knowing that a sprout arises from a seed cannot induce a conceptual consciousness ascertaining emptiness. If it did, all farmers and gardeners would have realized emptiness!

The infallible cause and effect of all phenomena in cyclic existence and beyond refers to all phenomena, both products (impermanent phenomena) and nonproducts (permanent phenomena). *Beyond* refers to nirvāṇa, the state beyond the sorrow and misery of saṃsāra. Nirvāṇa is a permanent phenomenon, so cause and effect do not literally apply to it. However, true cessations occur dependent on true paths, and the ultimate true cessation is nirvāṇa. Although true cessations are not produced by causes as such, metaphorically it is said that they are effects of the true paths. Similarly, because directly realizing emptiness makes one an ārya, it can be said that emptiness is the "cause" of āryas' qualities even though emptiness is a permanent phenomenon. Grasping either saṃsāra or nirvāṇa as inherently existent keeps us bound and is to be overcome. In *Sixty Stanzas of Reasoning,* Nāgārjuna says (YS 5):

Those who do not see ultimate reality
grasp at saṃsāra and nirvāṇa.
But those who see ultimate reality possess
no pretentions of the world and its transcendence.

The infallible cause and effect of all phenomena in cyclic existence refers to the twelve links of dependent origination that describe how we enter cyclic existence. It also refers to the functioning of the law of karma and its effects. *The infallible cause and effect of all phenomena . . . beyond* refers to the causal process of ceasing saṃsāra and attaining nirvāṇa. By ceasing ignorance, formative actions cease; by ceasing formative actions, consciousness ceases, and so forth. In a broader sense, "cause and effect" here can also refer to mutual dependence and dependent designation, which apply to all phenomena, including nirvāṇa.

The path that pleases the Buddha begins with an inferential realization of emptiness according to the view of the Prāsaṅgika Madhyamaka and progresses to a direct nonconceptual realization of emptiness. To actualize that path, we begin with hearing and studying the teachings as well as thinking about and discussing their meaning. From this our wrong views soften and doubt inclined toward the correct meaning—in this case thinking that perhaps phenomena are empty—arises. Our understanding then progresses from doubt to correct assumption. There are many degrees of correct assumption, stretching from the assumption that phenomena are empty because it "seems right" to a firm belief that will soon become an inference.

The deep understanding of causal dependence is cultivated over time, and once cultivated, repeated meditation is essential to realize that if something arises dependently, it must be empty of existing independently by its own power. This is a difficult step, where proponents of the lower tenet systems fall short in that they cannot realize the pervasion—that whatever arises dependently lacks inherent existence. They also cannot realize the counterpervasion—that whatever is inherently existent cannot exist dependently. When that barrier is overcome through more analysis and meditation, Mādhyamikas gain the inferential realization of emptiness during a meditation session on emptiness.

With this initial realization of emptiness, meditators are not yet able to establish phenomena as conventionally existent in the face of realizing their emptiness. Emptiness and dependent arising are not mutually supportive at this time. Nevertheless, this inferential realization brings about a strong change in the meditators' mind; it does not negate too much and fall to the extreme of nihilism by contradicting the cause-and-effect nature of mundane and supramundane phenomena that undeniably bring harm and help. This understanding also does not negate too little and still accept some degree of inherent existence. When emptiness is realized within a nonmistaken understanding of causal dependence, the resulting wisdom, when progressively developed, is capable of overcoming all grasping at inherent existence.

The path pleasing the Buddha is generated by using dependent arising as the reason to establish emptiness. *Mere dependent designation* (T. *brten nas brtags pa tsam*) is very subtle and understanding it occurs *after* realizing emptiness. To gain the initial realization of emptiness, meditating on the reasonings of causal dependence or dependence on parts is sufficient. These lead to the conclusion that phenomena lack any objectified basis, such that when we search for the referent of a term, such as "I," we cannot identify anything that is it.

This inferential realization *dismantles every notion of an objectified basis* in that now meditators are sure that inherent existence cannot possibly exist. Their previous certitude that ignorantly thought phenomena existed inherently has been shattered. They have correctly understood emptiness and are on the right path. However, they have not yet destroyed all false perceptions of phenomena's inherent existence by uprooting the ignorance grasping inherent existence so that it can never return. The process of doing this begins only when they directly and nonconceptually perceive emptiness without the medium of a conceptual appearance that an inferential realization entails. Thus at this point in their practice, it is important for meditators to stay with the negation of inherent existence by repeated meditation and familiarization with it.

Nevertheless, upon arising from meditative equipoise on emptiness, the people and objects in the environment begin to appear like illusions. That is, although they appear to exist inherently, meditators know that appearance is false. Since meditators will have just realized emptiness, these illusion-like appearances are still weak and do not last long. But as their understanding of emptiness deepens, their experience of illusion-like appearances is extended.

Illusion-like appearances will be explained in more depth in the following chapter.

Without understanding that the existence and identity of all phenomena is posited purely in terms of dependence, we are compelled to assert they exist from their own side, as the non-Buddhist schools and lower Buddhist schools do. Because these schools assert some type of inherent existence, they do not accept that inherent existence and dependent existence are contradictory. In addition, they do not assert that the appearance of inherent existence to our sense consciousnesses is mistaken—that things do not exist inherently although they appear to our senses to exist in that way. By making this error, the Svātantrika Mādhyamikas and followers of the lower systems of Buddhist thought *have not realized the intent of the Buddha* and are unable to gain inferential realization of emptiness, let alone enter the āryas' meditative equipoise directly realizing emptiness.

When Appearance and Emptiness Are Grasped as Distinct

This verse makes the important point that as long as we grasp the nature of appearance and emptiness as distinct, we have not and will not realize the Buddha's intent.

> As long as the two understandings—
> of appearance, infallible dependent arising,
> and of emptiness, the absence of all assertions—remain separate,
> then you have not realized the intent of the Sage (Buddha).

The two understandings referred to in this verse are (1) the understanding ascertaining that dependently arisen agents, objects, and actions that appear to conventional reliable cognizers are infallible, and (2) the understanding ascertaining that emptiness itself is free from any assertions, such as the assertions that it is inherently existent or nonexistent. When these two understandings are seen as separate—when they seem to be unrelated and mutually exclusive, and one undermines the other—an obstacle to realizing the Buddha's intent is present. If the understanding of emptiness causes the understanding of dependent arising to fade, or if the understanding of dependent arising interferes with understanding emptiness, the complete correct view still evades these meditators. This disconnect indicates that meditators have not yet understood the convergence of dependent arising and emptiness. To remedy this, they must continue to reflect and meditate on emptiness and dependent arising to bring these two understandings together in a mutually supportive and harmonious way, so that the meaning of one becomes the meaning of the other.

Once a monk was searching for what the word "I" referred to. Suddenly he grabbed his monastic vest (*donkag*) in fear because he felt like he was disappearing into total nothingness. Such fear may arise at this point in the process of gaining the correct view, when practitioners are actually refuting the inherent existence of the I and are about to gain a correct conceptual realization of emptiness. This fear arises due to thinking that because the I cannot be found under ultimate analysis, it is totally nonexistent. The fear is based on confusing emptiness with nonexistence. Such confusion is present when practitioners do not yet know that emptiness and dependent arising come to the same point. They cannot yet correctly establish the nominal or conventional existence of the I and other phenomena within knowing that they are empty. This story emphasizes that the understanding of emptiness must be grounded in establishing the dependent nature of phenomena. Although the wisdom realizing emptiness negates inherent existence, it must be supported by a robust understanding of veiled truth as well as the law of karma and its effects.

The Measure of Having Culminated the Analysis of the View

The next verse presents the criteria for having culminated the analysis of the correct view. This occurs when meditators can understand emptiness in terms of dependent arising and understand dependent arising in terms of emptiness. These two understandings converge like two sides of the same coin. This is expressed in the next verse of Tsongkhapa's poem:

> When these [two realizations] are without alternation and are
>   concurrent,
> from only seeing dependent arising as infallible,

an ascertaining consciousness entirely undermines all modes of mental grasping.

At that time, the analysis of the [profound] view is complete.

At this point in yogis' meditation, the seeming incompatibility of emptiness and dependent arising is resolved. The understandings of emptiness and dependent arising converge, coming to the same point; subtle dependent arising is realized, emptiness dawns as the meaning of dependent arising and dependent arising dawns as the meaning of emptiness, veilings are posited as mere dependent designations in the wake of negating inherent existence, the meaning of mere dependent designation is understood, veiled truths are now known as veiled truths, and the two extremes are overcome. At this time, *the analysis of the profound view is complete.*

The convergence of dependent arising and emptiness

When meditators who have an inferential or direct realization of emptiness have arisen from meditative equipoise and their experience of emptiness has not faded, simply seeing dependently arising people and objects induces the understanding that these phenomena rely on causes and conditions. That understanding, in turn, has the force to induce another mind that ascertains emptiness conceptually. This powerful experience comprehends without a doubt that emptiness and dependent arising come to the same point and are not contradictory. Now emptiness dawns as the meaning of dependent arising and dependent arising dawns as the meaning of emptiness. Tsongkhapa describes this (EMW 222):

> With respect to how these two [emptiness and dependent arising] go as the meaning of each other . . . [it] is a way in which the one bestows understanding of the other in the perspective of the awareness of a proponent of the Middle Way who knows the absence of inherent existence.

The understanding of emptiness and the understanding of dependent arising are two sides of the same coin. Tsongkhapa continues (EMW 261–62):

> That the meaning of "emptiness goes as the meaning of dependent arising" is for Mādhyamikas who have refuted inherent establishment with reliable cognition, but not for others. For such Mādhyamikas, when they explicitly ascertain that internal and external things are dependent arisings contingent on causes, in dependence on the power of just that awareness they will ascertain this as meaning that [things] are empty of inherent existence. This is because they have realized that whatever is inherently existent does not rely on another and have realized with reliable cognition that the two, this [non-reliant inherent existence] and dependent arising are contradictory.
>
> Hence, through dependent arising itself they gain ascertainment of the emptiness that negates inherent existence and therefore they become accustomed—immediately upon seeing, hearing, or being mindful that sprouts and so forth rely on causes and conditions—to contemplating the principle of the absence of inherent existence through just that fact. This being the case, although in another lifetime the emptiness of inherent existence is not explicitly explained, latencies for the view of emptiness will be awakened through just an explanation of the doctrine of dependent arising, like when Upatiṣya (Śāriputra) realized suchness through Aśvajit's merely explaining the dependent arising of the four truths.

When Mādhyamikas, who have previously refuted inherent existence and realized emptiness with a reliable cognizer, explicitly ascertain that things arise dependent on causes and conditions, without another intervening consciousness they can ascertain that things are empty of inherent existence. They can do this because they have realized that (1) whatever exists inherently does not rely on any other phenomena and (2) independent existence and dependent arising are contradictory. Over time, by contemplating this repeatedly, they become so familiar with it that as soon as they see, hear, or are mindful that sprouts, duḥkha, and so forth rely on causes and conditions, their minds ascertain emptiness. Similarly, they become so accustomed to thinking about emptiness that when they contact dependently arisen objects in future lives, latencies of the realization of emptiness will be awakened through an explanation of dependent arising and they will realize emptiness.

The story of how Śāriputra came to be the Buddha's disciple illustrates this. Śāriputra and his friend Maudgalyāyana were disciples of the skeptic Sañjaya Vairātīputra. One day Śāriputra encountered Aśvajit, a disciple of the Buddha, who taught him about causality. Having latencies for the view of emptiness from previous lives, Śāriputra understood the profound implications of this teaching. Due to this, as well as being impressed by Aśvajit's refined conduct, Śāriputra became the Buddha's disciple. Maudgalyāyana and all of Sañjaya's disciples followed him to join the Buddha's Sangha.

When dependent arising is seen as mere dependent designation, all phenomena can be realized as both empty and dependently arisen. All extremes of reification and deprecation—absolutism and nihilism—are abandoned and the Middle Way is realized. This leads Nāgārjuna, in the final lines of *Refutation of Objections* (*Vigrahavyāvartanī*), to pay homage to the Buddha, who said that emptiness, dependent arising, and the Middle Way come to the same point and have the same meaning (OR 505):

> I prostrate to the Buddha who is unparalleled
> and who has given the supreme teaching that
> emptiness, dependent arising,
> and the Middle Way have the same meaning.

Understanding emptiness as the meaning of dependent arising and dependent arising as the meaning of emptiness occur in post-meditation time, when meditators have culminated analysis of the correct view. Here when they cognize a dependently arisen object, without any other intervening consciousness, they ascertain that it is empty of existing independently, under its own power. This counteracts the extreme of absolutism because they know that dependent arisings lack inherent existence. Furthermore, when contemplating emptiness, without any intervening consciousness, they will ascertain that phenomena exist dependently. This understanding opposes the extreme of nihilism because they ascertain that whatever lacks inherent existence exists dependently.

Positing veiled truths in the wake of negating inherent existence

Culmination of the analysis of the view also brings the ability to posit veiled truths as mere dependent designations in the wake of negating their inherent existence. The meanings of subtle dependent arising and mere dependent designation also become clearer.

After refuting the inherent existence of phenomena by the reason of dependent arising, when meditators arise from meditative equipoise on emptiness, they understand that realization of emptiness does not negate the existence of veilings; dependently arisen phenomena remain. In that we establish, through the reason of dependence on something else, or dependent arising, that a phenomenon is empty of existing under its own power, and a dependently arisen phenomenon is left as positable after the refutation. These phenomena exist by being merely designated by term and concept. These dependent arisings are infallible in that their existence by depending on other factors is a fact.

Not everything we designate or impute exists. When we employ the sevenfold reasoning to investigate how a person appearing in a dream and how an actual person we meet when awake exist, we see that both of them do not exist under their power; they are not self-instituting. Although both are equally unfindable under ultimate analysis, this does not mean a dream person can be posited as a person. That would contradict conventional reliable cognizers that know veilings, because after we wake up, a conventional reliable cognizer ascertains that a dream person is not a living person. However, a conventional reliable cognizer cannot damage an awareness that an actual person *is* a person. Not being found when sought through the sevenfold reasoning does not mean the person does not exist; it means the person does not inherently exist. Because the person exists, we know that the I exists not by its own power but by depending on other factors. In this way, the meaning of being empty of existing under its own power comes to mean dependence on other factors.

The reason phenomena are empty is not because they are not seen, smelled, or felt. Their being empty does not mean that they lack the capacity to perform functions or to be perceived. Moreover, the meaning of dependent arising is not that phenomena inherently arise in dependence on causes and conditions. Rather, they arise in dependence on causes and conditions that are like a magician's illusions in that they do not exist in the way they appear.

When we have a good understanding of emptiness and dependent arising, we will understand with respect to one object its infallible appearance as well as its emptiness and will know that these two are not contradictory. Without understanding the convergence of emptiness and dependent arising, we may think that it is impossible to realize the unconditioned reality of emptiness and the conditioned existence of dependent arising with respect to one object.

When an ascertainment of emptiness arises by perceiving a dependent arising without any other reasoning or intervening consciousness, that ascertainment of emptiness does not harm the ascertainment of dependently arisen phenomena and vice versa. At this time, there is no need to alternate the ascertainment of appearances and the understanding of emptiness as if they were unrelated and separate, and the *analysis of the view is complete.* Candrakīrti says in the *Supplement* (MMA 6.160):

> [When] yogis do not find the existence of this [chariot],
> how could it be said that what does not exist in the seven ways exists
> [inherently]?
> Through that, they easily enter also into suchness.
> Therefore, here the establishment of this [chariot] is to be asserted
> in that way.

In other words, now that the meditator has realized emptiness by the reason of dependent arising, the ascertainment of the chariot as empty arises due to the force of ascertaining it as dependently arising, and the appearance of it as a dependent arising is due to the force of ascertaining it as empty. When the meditator sees a chariot, they see it as a dependent arising, and this induces ascertainment that it is empty.

These two ascertainments do not occur at the same time. One consciousness does not cognize both dependent arising and emptiness. Rather, two consciousnesses arise sequentially—one perceiving emptiness, the other knowing dependent arising.

When sought in the seven ways, phenomena cannot be found, yet they are established as existent. Their existence derives not from the object's own power but from the other-power of conceptuality. A thorough understanding of how phenomena are posited conventionally helps to understand their ultimate nature.

Prior to this level of realization, when you gain a little understanding of emptiness, you might wonder whether the activities of cause and effect or of agent, action, and object are possible within emptiness. At that time, consider the reflection of a face in a mirror. It arises when certain conditions come together and vanishes when those conditions cease. Although it is only a reflection of a face and not an actual face, you can still use it to comb your hair. This is an example of the feasibility of functionality within the absence of inherent existence.

In addition, contemplate your experience of help and harm that come from the presence and absence of particular conditions. This will strengthen your conviction in dependent arising. In your meditation practice, if you begin to incline toward reification of existence, reflect on emptiness. If you tend toward nihilism, reflect on dependent arising. With such skillful alternation of contemplating emptiness and dependent arising, by means of analytical meditation and deep concentration, your understanding of both emptiness and dependent arising will deepen, and at a certain point your understanding of appearances and emptiness will become equal. The understanding of the dependent arising of phenomena—which is from the perspective of phenomena's appearance—and the understanding of emptiness—which is the absence of any inherent existence—become simultaneous in the sense that they are not seen as separate and unrelated to one another. Here, *without alternation and concurrent* does not mean at the same time; it indicates that the meaning of dependent arising and the meaning of emptiness converge to the same point. Understanding this indicates that *analysis of the profound view is complete*. The Sakya master Rendawa says (EMW 311):

> At the very time they appear, [phenomena] are realized as empty,
> and when emptiness is realized, appearances are not stopped.
> When ascertainment is found with respect to how these two are
> unified,
> then the intent of the Conqueror has been realized.

At this time, emptiness dawns as the meaning of dependent arising and dependent arising dawns as the meaning of emptiness to a conceptual mental consciousness. This occurs after meditation on emptiness but before the correct view has faded from awareness. At this time, the mind is still informed by the understanding of emptiness. The yogi and scholar Khedrup Norsang Gyatso[40] expresses it this way (EMW 352–53):

> When the analysis of the view is thoroughly complete,
> through the mere dawning to a sense [or mental] consciousness
> of the appearance of its own object, without relying on another reasoning,
> definite knowledge ascertaining its object as empty is induced.
>
> This is like, for example, through the force of previous knowledge
> that a double moon does not exist, just the appearance
> of a double moon to a being whose eye faculty is faulty
> induces ascertainment of the nonexistence of the double moon.
>
> In this way, at the time of generating ascertainment of emptiness,
> when one thinks about the mode in which all conventional phenomena
> —such as actions and their effects and so forth—exist,
> one [knows] they are imputed existents posited as mere names only.

Now meditators know that veilings are mere dependent designations. When they reflect on karma and its effects and the functioning of conventional phenomena, meditators automatically see them as mere imputations, mere designations. They exist and function without having any inherent existence whatsoever. Konchog Jigme Wangpo says (EMW 352):[41]

> [What is to be understood here is] the dawning of emptiness as dependent arising and the dawning of dependent arising as emptiness. That this consciousness realizing external and internal dependent arisings as without inherent existence ascertains—without relying on another awareness—all presentations of cause

> and effect, definition and definiendum, agent and object, and so on, as feasible in the context of mere nominal imputation is the meaning of emptiness dawning as dependent arising. That this awareness ascertaining external and internal things as dependent arisings—as dependent imputations—is able to induce a strong consciousness ascertaining their emptiness of inherent existence without needing to rely upon another awareness is the dawning of dependent arising as the meaning of emptiness. Such dawning is for one who has identified the pure view and not forgotten it; it is not for others. It is even said that when emptiness dawns thus as the meaning of dependent arising, analysis of the view is complete.

The true meaning of emptiness isn't simply that phenomena are not found under ultimate analysis. Rather, emptiness is to be understood in terms of dependent arising: emptiness makes it possible for things to have a dependent nature, and this dependent nature makes it possible for things to be in contact and influence one another. In this way, emptiness allows cause and effect to function; it is the basis that enables the diversity of phenomena, each of which arises from its own causes and conditions, to exist. This shows that the two truths exist and illustrates how and why our experiences of suffering and happiness arise. When we understand emptiness in this way, it is possible to understand that our polluted consciousness can be transformed into the mind of a buddha when the right conditions come together.

Khedrup Gelek Pelzang (1385–1438) in his *Guide to the View: Lamp Dispelling Darkness* says (EMW 366):

> In the perspective of ascertainment [of emptiness] within meditative equipoise, not even a little bit [of appearance of veiled truths] is left over, but when those skilled at maintaining [this meditative view] look at what is left in place of that negation upon rising from this [meditative equipoise] here in subsequent attainment: (1) they have the capacity to readily induce ascertainment that there remain mere names such as I and so forth and readily induce ascertainment also that those names are exhausted as conceptual imputations, only mere nominalities, baselessly associated

> by conceptuality, and (2) not doing any analysis regarding the meanings of those mere nominalities, by engaging in the context of them they establish through experience [that the merely nominal I is] the accumulator and experiencer of karma and has the capacity to perform the actions of eating, drinking, and so forth.

Khedrup continues by saying that this is an experiential mode of ascertaining from the depth of the heart that emptiness and dependent arising are not disparate but are convergent; the understanding of each other mutually enhances the other to the point where emptiness and dependent arising seem to have the same meaning. Here "having the same meaning" indicates that they converge at the same point. This experiential realization is radically different from an intellectual understanding—it affects our worldview and our inner emotional world. Furthermore, in post-meditation times, yogis see that after inherent existence has been negated nominalities—things that exist by mere imputations without any inherently existent basis—remain. These mere nominalities function: a nominally existent person creates actions whose results they experience.

Knowing veiled truths as veiled truths

We know many veiled truths—our friends, stores, math problems, and so on—but we cannot know them *as* veiled truths until after we have realized emptiness. Their ultimate mode of existence is veiled by the obscuration of ignorance that causes them to appear inherently existent. To know phenomena *as* veiled truths or veilings, their inherent existence must be negated. Only then we will know that the way they appear is false. Tsongkhapa explains (GR 224–25):

> Although individual examples of veiled truths, such as a vase and so on, can be obtained even by those who have not found the Middle Way view, to ascertain a particular phenomenon as a veiled truth by means of a reliable cognition, one must first gain the Middle Way view. Because if a given phenomenon has been established as a veiled truth, this would mean that it would be established as false; and to establish something explicitly as false, one first has to negate true existence with respect to that phe-

> nomenon by means of reliable cognition. Therefore, although as suggested by the phrase "through the force of false views," ordinary common people perceive false realities, this does not imply that they establish these phenomena *as* false.
>
> For example, when the spectators at a magic show see conjured horses and elephants, they do see false things, but they do not necessarily establish these perceptions to be false. Therefore the fact obtained through seeing false reality, which defines something to be a veiled truth, refers to that which is obtained by conventional reliable cognition perceiving false and deceptive objects of cognition.

People who have the Middle Way view know veiled truths—sounds, fragrances, sweet and salty tastes, love, anger, and so on—but without first negating their inherent existence according to the Middle Way view, they cannot ascertain these things *as* veiled truths with a reliable cognizer. To establish something as a veiled truth, we must first know it as false, and that depends on having negated its inherent existence. The example of the magic show is helpful here. The spectators see conjured horses and elephants, which are false, but not knowing them to be false, they take the magnificent animals that appear as real. The magician, on the other hand, knows that he conjured them and therefore knows them as false.

Avoiding the two extremes

As explained above, when emptiness dawns as the meaning of dependent arising and dependent arising dawns as the meaning of emptiness, the understandings of dependent arising and emptiness become mutually reinforcing. Individually and together they overcome the two extremes of absolutism and nihilism. Zhamar Rinpoche (1852–1912) explains (EMW 386):

> Regarding the way the two extremes are avoided: ascertainment of dependent arising prevents at its own time the extreme of nihilism, and when through its very functioning ascertainment of the absence of inherent existence is induced, the extreme of permanence [absolutism] is prevented; ascertainment of emptiness prevents at its own time the extreme of permanence, and

> through its force, right afterward the extreme of nihilism is prevented.

Referring to meditators who have realized emptiness, at the time they ascertain dependent arising they affirm that phenomena exist, overcoming the extreme of nihilism, and when that ascertainment of dependent arising induces the ascertainment of emptiness, they overcome the extreme of absolutism because they know that phenomena lack inherent existence.

Similarly, at the time they ascertain emptiness, the negation of inherent existence overcomes the extreme of absolutism that believes phenomena exist inherently. When that ascertainment of emptiness induces ascertainment of dependent arising, it overcomes the extreme of nihilism that believes nothing whatsoever exists. Since the understanding of emptiness and the understanding of dependent arising can follow each other quickly, it seems as if they are concurrent. This explains the meaning of "concurrent" in the first line of the verse, *When these [two realizations] are without alternation and concurrent.* Their being "without alternation" indicates that they are compatible; one understanding does not contradict the other.

To review, there is a distinction between the realization of emptiness and the culmination of the analytic process when the analysis of the profound view is complete. The realization of emptiness, which takes dependent arising as the reason, begins with a correct inference that is a negation of inherent existence. After arising from meditative equipoise on emptiness, when the mind is still informed by that realization of emptiness, meditators are able to induce ascertainment that things exist as mere dependent designations—conceptually imputed names. These nominalities lack any inherently existent basis—they exist and function on the conventional level. These meditators can now establish the law of karma and its effects—that sentient beings engage in actions and experience the results of those actions—without there being an inherently existent person. They understand subtle dependent arising—mere dependent designation—and know subtle veiled truths *as* veiled truths. This resolves the most difficult challenge of Prāsaṅgika Madhyamaka philosophy—maintaining a robust understanding of veiled truths while rejecting any notion of inherent existence even at the conventional level.

The next verse takes us further into the understanding of the convergence of emptiness and dependent arising.

REFLECTION

1. Review the meaning of "emptiness goes as (dawns as) the meaning of dependent arising" and "dependent arising goes as (dawns as) the meaning of emptiness."
2. Why are these understandings important? What is missing if we lack these understandings?

A Unique Feature of Prāsaṅgikas

The next verse presents a unique feature of the Prāsaṅgika understanding of the convergence of dependent arising and emptiness that is unlike all other Buddhist tenet systems. Whereas previously we considered that dependent arising counteracted the extreme of nihilism and emptiness opposed the extreme of inherent existence, from another perspective *appearance* (veiled truths, veilings) dispels the extreme of existence and *emptiness* dispels the extreme of nihilism.

> In addition, when you understand appearances clearing away the
> extreme of [inherent] existence
> and emptiness clearing away the extreme of [total] nonexistence,
> and you understand how emptiness dawns as cause and effect,
> you will never be captivated by either extreme view.

All Buddhist philosophical schools agree on the importance of understanding dependent arising, although their view of the implications of dependent arising differs. Vaibhāṣikas and Sautrāntikas focus on causal dependence as the meaning of dependent arising, limiting its import to causes and their effects, such as the twelve links of dependent origination. Yogācārins also posit the meaning of dependent arising only in terms of conditioned phenomena, although they explain the causes of conditioned phenomena not in terms of the assembly of partless particles or partless moments of consciousness as the Vaibhāṣikas and Sautrāntikas do, but in terms of latencies on the foundation consciousness. Svātantrikas assert that dependent arising applies to all phenomena, permanent and impermanent, in that all phenomena depend on their parts. However, Svātantrikas don't think the reason of dependent arising contradicts inherent existence; in fact they believe that dependent arising must exist inherently or they wouldn't exist at all. Prāsaṅgikas alone state that dependent arising disproves any and all inherent existence whatsoever. Furthermore, dependent arising establishes all phenomena as existing by mere imputation or designation by conceptuality.

Prāsaṅgikas hold the unique view that not only does the realization of emptiness prevent the extreme of absolutism by counteracting inherent existence, but it also prevents the extreme of nihilism by negating only inherent existence, not all existence whatsoever. The realization of emptiness refutes inherent existence; conventional existence still remains. This explains why highly realized tantric practitioners strongly adhere to the law of karma and its effects, contrary to the misconception that due to their realization of emptiness they are beyond karma and ethical restraints.

Dependent arising prevents not only the extreme of nihilism by showing that phenomena exist although they are empty, but also overcomes the extreme of absolutism by validating nominal existence, not inherent existence. Phenomena exist and function on the conventional level as mere dependently arisen appearances that lack inherent existence. In short, by understanding that dependent arising and emptiness come to the same point, we will *not be captivated by either extreme view* and will realize the view of the Middle Way.[42] Ngawang Palden (1797–1864) says (EMW 385):

> For persons who have completed analysis of the view in this way, the way the extreme of existence is avoided through appearance is that as much as they take to mind the meaning of dependent arising, which is merely posited by name and terminology, to that same degree does the force of their awareness grasping inherent existence diminish, and for such persons the way the extreme of nonexistence is avoided through emptiness is that as much as they take to mind the emptiness of inherent existence, to that

same degree does the force of their awareness not believing in the cause and effect of karma and apprehending the cause and effect of karma to be nonexistent diminish.

Refuting inherent existence completely, without any caveats such as those made by the lower tenet systems, and positing those very persons that lack inherent existence as the creators of karma and the experiencers of results is the Middle Way view that is so difficult to realize. The challenge is to refute inherent existence and simultaneously uphold nominal existence. To meet that challenge yogis must demolish their adherence to inherent existence and their disbelief in cause and effect. Applying the reason of dependent arising to negate inherent existence and meditating on this for a long time accomplishes just that.

The existence and functioning of veilings are possible precisely because they are empty. If they existed inherently, they could not function at all because inherent existence entails not relying on any other factors, such as causes and conditions, parts, and the mind that conceives and designates them. If things existed inherently, they could not change; nor could they arise and cease. And even if they could arise and cease, those activities would be random and chaotic, divorced from the laws of causality.

Because the dependent existence of phenomena is feasible owing to emptiness, it is as if dependent phenomena arise from or arise within emptiness.[43] It is in this way that emptiness is said to be the "cause" of dependent arisings, which are its "effects" in that conventional phenomena appear within their being empty of inherent existence. Being a permanent phenomenon, emptiness is not actually a cause, but without emptiness as their ultimate nature, phenomena could not exist and function. Emptiness is regarded as the "cause" of all phenomena in that it is the space in which phenomena exist.

Emptiness is said to "pose in all sorts of ways"—it is the ultimate nature of the buddhas who have extinguished all defects and are endowed with all good qualities, and it is also the ultimate nature of those beings who, having created great destructive karma, are born in the most torturous hell. All varieties of existent pleasant and unpleasant feelings, and of helpful and harmful phenomena, dawn within the sphere of the emptiness of inherent existence. In short, phenomena have the nature of natural quiescence or natural nirvāṇa—that is, by their very nature they lack inherent existence.

Because veilings have this empty nature and arise within emptiness, they are said to be the manifestation, sport, and play of emptiness.

When we meditate deeply on any level of dependence—causal dependence, dependence on parts, mutual dependence, dependent designation, and so forth—we come to see that the way objects appear to us is mistaken. They appear to exist objectively—as stable, monolithic objects that are independent of all other factors, whereas in fact there is a long history of causes and conditions that lies behind them that we do not consider. The impermanent things we grasp as existing from their own side are in fact a series of ever-changing moments that rely on the myriad causes and conditions that came before them.

Seeing the falseness of their appearance moves us in the direction of contemplating their selflessness. According to the Vaibhāṣikas and Sautrāntikas, selflessness is not perceived directly. Rather, the mind explicitly cognizes the momentary aggregates and implicitly knows they are not a self-sufficient substantially existent person. Yogācārins and Svātantrikas assert that selflessness can be known directly by a yogic direct perceiver. However, the selflessness of both persons and phenomena that they assert is not the subtlest selflessness. Only Prāsaṅgikas assert subtle selflessness—the emptiness of inherent existence of all persons and phenomena—and state that it can be realized directly by a yogic reliable cognizer.

When this view of emptiness is practiced in conjunction with the determination to be free from cyclic existence, it acts as a cause of liberation from saṃsāra. When it is cultivated in conjunction with bodhicitta, it serves as a cause for the full awakening of a buddha. Since the view realizing emptiness is a common cause that gives birth to the awakenings of all three vehicles, it is said to be the "mother" of all buddhas and all āryas.

To conclude, the culmination of the analysis of the profound view (T. *lta ba'i dpyad pa rdzogs pa*) brings many understandings—realization of subtle dependent arising (T. *rten 'brel phra mo rtogs pa*), realization of mere dependent designation, realization of subtle veiled truth (T. *kun rdzob phra mo rtogs pa*), realization of phenomena as mere conventions or mere designations (T. *kun rdzob tsam, ming tsam rtogs pa*).

Having brought us to this point of full comprehension of the correct view, Tsongkhapa directs us to the next step. The ultimate verse of *The Three Principal Aspects of the Path* advises:

In this way, when you have realized the exact points
of the three principal aspects of the path,
by depending on solitude, generate the power of joyous effort
and quickly accomplish the final goal, my spiritual child.

The correct inferential realization of emptiness is essential to gain the union of serenity and insight on emptiness and enter the path of preparation. This realization, however, does not uproot the afflictions and free us from saṃsāra. For that we need to realize emptiness with a direct, nonconceptual reliable cognizer. The best setting to do this is in retreat where we are not distracted by external things and events and can practice the teachings we have studied with joyous effort for a long period of time. For that reason, Tsongkhapa now advises us to abide in a place with few external distractions and with joyous effort to meditate on emptiness so that we can know through direct perceptions. By meditating on emptiness in this way, over time we will overcome all afflictive obscurations and cognitive obscurations and attain our final goal, the full awakening of a buddha, in order to benefit all sentient beings.

Summary

There are several steps to realize the intent of the Buddha, the Middle Way view that pleases the Buddha. First we must understand why the realization of profound emptiness is important. Lacking this understanding, we will have no interest in or energy to learn, contemplate, and meditate on it. For those seeking freedom from saṃsāra and full awakening, the wisdom directly realizing emptiness is the only antidote that completely eradicates the root cause of saṃsāra, the self-grasping ignorance that has bound us in the cycle of repeated rebirth since time without beginning. No other Dharma teaching or realization can do this. The first verse above from *The Three Principal Aspects of the Path* explains this.

The second step is to discover the final thought of the Buddha and enter the Middle Way that pleases the Buddha. Using causal dependence as the reason, we employ probing awareness analyzing the ultimate to refute inherent existence and destroy the conceived object of true-grasping. With this inferential realization of emptiness, we are certain that true existence cannot possibly exist and have entered the path that pleases the Buddha.

Third, as we continue to practice, it is important to ensure that our analytical meditation hits the target. When, despite strong aspirations to actualize the path, our understandings of emptiness and dependent arising seem disjointed and we can't reconcile them, we haven't fully understood the Buddha's intention. Although veiled truths appear as infallible dependent arisings, we cannot understand how they can also be empty. And when we have some understanding of emptiness, we are unable to establish the existence of veiled truths. Although we have entered the Middle Way pleasing to the Buddha, we must continue striving to discover the final thought or intention of the Buddha. The third verse above speaks of this.

Fourth is the step of reconciliation when our realization of emptiness induces a deeper understanding of dependent arising, and our understanding of dependent arising induces greater acceptance of emptiness being the ultimate nature of phenomena. Now our understandings of emptiness and dependent arising not only do not damage each other but they also converge on the same point. At this time, the culmination of the analytical process has been reached.

Many understandings arise at this point: emptiness dawns as the meaning of dependent arising and dependent arising dawns as the meaning of emptiness. Subtle dependent arising is realized, and all phenomena are known to exist as mere designations without any inherent existence whatsoever. Veiled truths are now seen *as* veiled truths, reenforcing that they are only "true" from the perspective of ignorance but are actually false. The fourth verse above describes this.

The fifth verse reveals a unique Madhyamaka presentation in which we understand that dependent arising not only vanquishes the extreme of nihilism but also the extreme of absolutism, and emptiness dispels nihilism as well as absolutism. In addition, dependently arisen phenomena are seen as arising within emptiness, such that emptiness is considered the "cause" of conventional phenomena and conventional phenomena dawn as the sport or play of emptiness in that they are manifestations of emptiness. Now we are not captivated by either extreme view.

Reaching the culmination of analysis on the correct view doesn't mean we no longer engage in analytic meditation. Rather, we must reinforce our understanding of the convergence of emptiness and dependent arising with a mind that is the union of serenity and insight on emptiness. By familiarizing our minds with this repeatedly we will progress through the stages and paths of eradicating the various grades of defilements. This results in first removing acquired afflictions and then all afflictive obscurations from the mindstream. Through continued practice combined with further accumulations of merit and wisdom supported by bodhicitta, even the subtlest cognitive obscurations are eradicated and buddhahood attained.

How to Meditate on Emptiness and Dependent Arising

Instead of presenting a short reflection on this important topic, a more elaborate version of the essential points is given below. Although we may not be at the level of the practitioners described above who have realized emptiness and see the convergence of dependent arising and emptiness, it is still helpful to go through the steps of practice that they do. Contemplating the essential points now not only increases our present understanding but also plants the seeds in our mindstreams to gain these realizations in the future.

Begin by reviewing the earlier meditations on the stage of the path, especially focusing on karma and its effects and the duḥkha of saṃsāra. Generate bodhicitta as your motivation for doing this meditation.

Next, develop a correct conceptual understanding of the points of whichever meditation you use to refute inherent existence. This could be Nāgārjuna's fourfold or fivefold analysis or Candrakīrti's sevenfold analysis, both of which include analyzing whether the object is inherently identical or inherently different than its parts. It could also be the refutation of the four extreme ways of arising, and so forth. Select the object whose mode of existence you will investigate: for example, the I, the body, or the mind. As you meditate on the reasoning, you will see that the basis of analysis—the I, body, or mind—cannot be found under ultimate analysis. Experience the non-inherent existence of the object: This inherently existent self, body, or mind does not exist at all.

Contemplate dependent arising as the reason for the I, body, or so forth being empty of inherent existence.

When you come out of your meditation on emptiness, allow the appearance of people and things around you to arise, and remember that although they appear to inherently exist, that appearance is false because they do not exist in that way.

Then focus more on the dependent nature of the object. The fact that it interacts with other things and causes harm and benefit is proof that it exists and functions. Since inherent existence is untenable, it must exist nominally, relationally, dependently—that is the only other option. Contemplate this in terms of the three types of dependence: dependence on causes and conditions, dependence on parts, and dependence on being designated by term and concept. Alternatively, contemplate them in terms of causal dependence, mutual establishment, and mere dependent designation.

The reason of dependent arising refutes phenomena's existing independent of other factors. Everything exists by relying on factors that are not it. When we see a bridge, it appears to be one monolithic, independent object. In fact, there are many diverse parts with different sizes, shapes, and functions that come together to form bridge. None of those parts are the bridge and the bridge cannot be found elsewhere, separate from its parts. Nor is there a bridge that holds all the pieces together to form one object.

Interdependence applies not only to material objects but also to immaterial mental states. Every mental state has many factors acting in tandem: the primary consciousness, the five omnipresent mental factors, other mental factors that perform various functions. It also depends on a sense faculty contacting a knowable object. In dependence on all of these, a mental state arises. If we mentally separate these components, no mental state can be found.

Similarly, the past, present, and future exist, but if we investigate what the present is, we cannot locate it. Each moment of an object has one portion that is closer to the past, another portion that is closer to the future, and another portion that is the present. But that portion that is the present also has an initial portion, a present portion, and a portion at the end. Finding an independent moment that is the present is impossible. Yet without the present, we cannot designate the past and the future. The past and the future depend on the present; the present exists, yet it is unfindable. The present—momentary and fleeting as it is—exists by mere designation, and in the next moment is replaced by a new moment that is the present.

When we do not engage in analysis to identify precisely what something is, the object appears and exists. We use the things around us and talk about them; they cause pleasure and pain. Being empty of inherent existence and existing in dependence on other factors are attributes of each and every phenomenon. They are not contradictory.

If phenomena existed from their own side, we could point to something and say "that is its essence," in which case there would be no need for things to depend on other factors. Everything would be fixed, permanent, and unchanging, immune to the influence of causes and conditions. If things possessed a findable essence, there would be no need for them to be conceived and designated. Everything would be immediately and objectively identifiable; we would not have to learn the names of objects or how they function. Their essence alone would be what they are. If an apple existed inherently, before anyone designated "apple" we would know it was an apple. Children wouldn't need to learn to associate the name "apple" with that red, round, crisp, and tasty thing, because apple would appear from its own side. If things had their own nature, we wouldn't have to ask what country we were in because Germany, Serbia, and Kazakhstan would appear automatically without anyone conceiving of that plot of earth as a country and giving it that name.

If we insist on grounding our understanding of the world on an objective basis, everything breaks down. Since truly existent causes do not exist, the arising of new things and the ceasing of what existed would collapse. Without an inherently existent present moment, time could not function. No one exists under their own power, so agent, object, and action could not function. Such difficulties arise when we insist that phenomena exist inherently. But when we simply let the world be on a nominal level without analysis—when we are content with conventional norms, then causes produce effects, events occur in the present, and people play ball.

Phenomena's ultimate nature—their actual mode of existence—is known by means of ultimate analysis. However, ultimate analysis neither refutes nor establishes the existence of nominally existent dependent arisings. When we use the sevenfold analysis or diamond slivers to analyze a car, a car is not established either conventionally or ultimately. But when we don't analyze and follow worldly conventions, we impute "car" in dependence on the collection of wheels, an engine, axles, and so forth. This establishes the existence of a car that can be used to take us from one place to another.

Through this contemplation, your understanding of dependent arising will increase your understanding of emptiness and your understanding of the lack of inherent existence will enhance your conviction that phenomena arise dependently. In this way emptiness and dependent arising complement each other. As Tsongkhapa said in *The Three Principal Aspects of the Path*, when these two realizations—that appearances are infallible dependent arisings and that emptiness is free of assertions of inherent existence or nonexistence—are seen as compatible, then from the mere sight of infallible dependent arising comes definite knowledge that completely destroys all grasping of inherent existence. Similarly, while the understanding of emptiness is fresh in your mind, you will understand the objects and people you encounter exist dependently. The seventh Dalai Lama, Kalsang Gyatso, expresses the compatibility of emptiness and dependent arising in his *Songs* (EMW 353):

> Look at this wonder
> utterly nonexistent yet dawning in all sorts.
> On the surface of the empty clear sky
> as rainbow figures that are collections
> of many arisings in dependence on causes and conditions
> despite not being truly self-instituting.
>
> See these illusions,
> these mere nominalities in which
> all agents, actions, and objects are feasibly
> imputed to multitudes of causes, conditions, and parts;
> though when analyzed
> there is nothing to be identified as "this."

Dependently arising phenomena exist within emptiness, inseparable from the emptiness that is their ultimate nature. They dawn as the variety of appearances. Appearances arise in the minds of the omniscient buddhas, in the beings in the lowest hells, and in beings of all the realms in between. Since all phenomena have the nature of emptiness and exist within emptiness, they are said to be the sport or play of emptiness, the manifestations of infallible dependent arisings, the display of their empty nature.

11 Illusion-Like Existence

In meditative equipoise that directly and nonconceptually perceives emptiness, only emptiness appears to the mind, no other phenomenon. Once yogis arise from their meditation, they integrate the experience of emptiness with the appearances of objects in daily life by seeing them as like illusions.

In this context, "illusion-like" has a particular meaning. It does not refer to ordinary illusions such as hallucinations due to drugs or fever or to the appearance of water on asphalt on a hot, sunny day. Those colorful or horrible appearances *are* illusions. Rather, illusion-like refers to phenomena's appearance in post-meditation times to yogis who have realized emptiness. Just as an illusion appears to be a real object although it isn't, similarly, veiled truths appear to be truly existent although they are not. Seeing veiled truths as like illusions does not change their nature, it changes how the mind apprehends them.

A Review: The Twofold Meditation on Emptiness

To review, things, such as a cup, exist in dependence on their basis of designation—the bottom, side, handle, and so forth—and a designating consciousness. The cup exists, but it is not its basis of designation, nor does it exist in its basis of designation. Similarly, you and I exist in dependence on our bases of designation—our respective set of five psychophysical aggregates. Although we don't exist truly or inherently, we exist—we are the doers of actions and the experiencers of their results. When emptiness is realized, phenomena, which have always lacked existence from their own side, are understood as empty of existing from their own side. In other words, we have realized what has always been the ultimate nature of phenomena.

Emptiness is not mentally fabricated, it is the nature of all existents. Realizing emptiness doesn't make something that was truly existent lose its true existence and become empty. Nor does the realization of emptiness destroy conventionally existent phenomena. Furthermore, since all phenomena are empty, the lack of existence from its own side isn't a partial emptiness where only certain objects or attributes lack inherent existence. An entire phenomenon as well as all its attributes and parts are empty. Emptiness is an object of mind, it is an existent phenomenon. It isn't a nothingness that can't be realized by the path or about which there is nothing to understand.

Meditation on emptiness is twofold: meditation on space-like emptiness and meditation on illusion-like emptiness. Space-like emptiness refers to the emptiness of true existence that is a nonaffirming negation. This is yogis' object of meditation during meditative equipoise on emptiness. To do this, they first properly identify the object of negation—true or inherent existence—and refute it by means of analysis. They investigate to see how things exist by employing analytic tools such as Candrakīrti's sevenfold analysis, diamond slivers, the reasoning of one or many, and so on. When they realize that persons and phenomena are not truly existent—that no truly existent things can be found because they do not exist—they focus single-pointedly on that emptiness of objective existence. Veilings—people, trees, devices, and so on—are not in the purview of that ultimate wisdom, but that wisdom does not disprove their existence.

In other words, reasoning analyzing the ultimate refutes the superimposition of inherent existence on conventionally existent objects. If it negated all existence whatsoever, that would be the extreme of nihilism. If ultimate analysis refuted all conventional objects, illusion-like dependent arisings—such as agents, actions, and objects, and so forth—would also be negated, but this is not the case. We may wonder, If veilings are like illusions, how can illusion-like words refute inherent existence? Just as someone's wrong apprehension thinking that a magically emanated woman is a real woman can be negated by a magically emanated person who explains the error, the apprehension of inherent existence can be refuted by words that are like illusions.

Veiled truths exist; since they do not truly exist, the only way they can exist is nominally, conventionally. They exist by being merely designated by term and concept, and their existence is affirmed by our own experience—veiled truths function, they can bring benefit or harm. However, the way phenomena appear to exist is false because they appear to truly exist although they do not. The knowledge of illusion-like emptiness is understanding that although things are empty, they appear falsely, as if they were truly existent. In post-meditation time, yogis contemplate illusion-like emptiness. The *Guru Pūjā* summarizes the practice of space-like emptiness and illusion-like emptiness (GP 106–7):

> Inspire me to complete the perfection of wisdom through the yoga
> on space-like emptiness—
> meditative equipoise on ultimate truth—
> which is conjoined with the great bliss arising from pliancy
> induced by discriminating wisdom analyzing suchness.
>
> Inspire me to perfect samādhi on illusion-like emptiness
> by realizing that all outer and inner phenomena
> lack true existence yet still appear,
> like illusions, dreams, or the moon's image on a clear lake.

Despite this false appearance to sentient beings, phenomena still function. Negating the inherent existence of a thing doesn't mean that thing is nonexistent and cannot perform any function in the world. Although an inherently existent car and an inherently existent person do not exist, nominally existent cars and people do. People ride in cars every day, cars are built and destroyed, people are born and die. No one quarrels with these statements.

Space-like emptiness and illusion-like emptiness correlate with the two aspects of the path: wisdom and method. The wisdom side of the path involves meditating on space-like emptiness. The method or conduct side of the path comprises all other virtuous actions—specific spiritual practices such as prostrating, circumambulating, making offerings, meditating on bodhicitta, and practicing fortitude. Method practices also include actions motivated by kindness, compassion, and bodhicitta. Yogis engage in these practices during post-meditation times by viewing all agents, actions, and objects involved in generosity, ethical conduct, fortitude, and so forth as empty and like illusions in that they falsely appear to be truly existent although they are not. This is the contemplation of illusion-like emptiness. Seeing the agent, object, and action of these activities as like illusions also makes these practices supramundane perfections, as distinct from the mundane perfections of generosity and so forth in which agent, object, and action are perceived and conceived as truly existent. In the supramundane perfection of generosity, generosity is the conventional thought that is manifest, and simultaneous with that, the mind perceiving emptiness is present in a latent form. Due to this, those bodhisattvas can clearly see the agent, object, and action as like illusions.

Illusion-Like Appearances

"Like an illusion" has two meanings: (1) Saying that ultimate truths are like illusions means that ultimate truths—emptinesses—are established as merely existent, and their true existence is negated. (2) Illusion-like appearance also occurs outside of the meditative equipoise directly perceiving emptiness. At this time, phenomena appear truly existent but are known to be empty of true existence.

The first meaning of illusion-like emphasizes that emptiness does not exist truly but exists conventionally. Although it may sound strange to say that emptiness, an ultimate truth, exists conventionally, conventional existence is the only existence there is. Nothing exists ultimately because nothing—including emptiness itself—can bear ultimate analysis.

The second meaning of illusion-like (*māyopama*), which will be explained in this chapter, emphasizes that veiled truths, from form up through omniscient mind, appear to sentient beings in a false manner. Because their appearance is deceptive in that they appear to exist truly although they do not, they are like illusions. Everything except emptiness is illusion-like in this way. Emptiness, however, does not appear in a deceptive manner to a reliable cognizer directly perceiving it. It appears as it exists—as empty of true existence.

Two factors are required for illusion-like appearances: the appearance of a veiled truth and the emptiness of its existing the way it appears. Although a rabbit's horn may appear to our imagination, it is not a veiled truth and doesn't exist, so it isn't an illusion-like appearance in this context. Two kinds of awareness are involved with establishing things as like illusions: (1) a conventional reliable cognizer that undeniably establishes the appearance of an object, and (2) a probing awareness that knows with certainty that phenomena lack objective existence. This illusion-like appearance is a composite of appearance and emptiness. Both the conventional reliable cognizer and the probing awareness operate in their own fields and are not present simultaneously. The probing awareness establishes emptiness but it does not establish veiled truths, such as persons and tables. The nondeceptive conventional consciousness establishes the person or table but does not know their emptiness.

Illusion-like appearances are known by the mental consciousness, not sense consciousnesses, and at the time they appear, probing awareness is not manifest. Although probing awareness does not know emptiness during the post-meditation times when the mind perceives things as like illusion, the mind is informed by a previous realization of emptiness.

No specific reasoning is employed to realize them as like illusions. Rather, after practitioners arise from meditative equipoise on emptiness, as long as their experience of emptiness is still strong, things appear as illusion-like. Another separate meditation is not done to know things as like illusions.

This composite of appearance and emptiness is a veiled truth and an affirming negation—a negation in which an affirmative phenomenon is implied after negating true existence. Illusion-like appearances are not the objects of a mind realizing emptiness; a manifest realization of emptiness occurs only in meditative equipoise on emptiness. The stronger one's realization of emptiness is during meditative equipoise, the stronger illusion-like appearances will be in post-meditation time.

For example, how do we know that the face reflected in a mirror is false or illusory, appearing to be a real face although it is not? Our visual consciousness sees a face in the mirror. The reflected face vividly appears as a real face to that visual consciousness, even though the reflected face never has been and never will be an actual face. Then a mental consciousness examines if that face is real or not, and through prior experience with reflections in mirrors it concludes that the face in the mirror is false. Nevertheless, the reflected image of a face is useful when washing our face, even though it is false.

Similarly, in meditation, yogis conclusively determine either inferentially or directly that phenomena do not exist from their own side. At that time emptiness is the apprehended object of their wisdom. When they arise from meditative equipoise on emptiness and the experience of realizing emptiness is still present in their minds, their sense consciousnesses perceive objects—for example a daisy—as they go about their daily lives. Those objects *appear* truly existent to the sense consciousnesses although the sense consciousnesses do not *grasp* them as truly existent. After that, there is a brief moment of mental direct perception of the daisy, followed by a conceptual mental consciousness. The daisy appears truly existent to that consciousness—the appearance of true existence cannot be stopped because that person still has ignorance. However, without applying any other reasoning, the mental consciousness knows that appearance of a truly existent daisy is false and sees it as like an illusion. This is similar to how a magician sees the horses and elephants that he has conjured: they appear real to his visual consciousness, but he knows they are not actual horses and elephants. Tsongkhapa states:[44]

> . . . one should generate firm conviction in the modes of dependent designation, dependent establishment, and dependent production. Every time a strong contemplation in an [unbroken] continuum of equipoise and post-equipoise has been undertaken, by merely recollecting the view in that post-equipoise period, one will see every appearance as illusion-like.

Seeing the daisy as illusion-like does not interfere with the daisy's functioning—it grew from a seed and delights the minds of people who see it. The *King of Concentration Sūtra* (*Samādhirāja Sūtra*) says (LC 3:306):

> Like a mirage, a phantom city, or an illusion, meditation associated with signs is empty of essence. Know that all phenomena are this way.
>
> The moon shines in a clear sky and its reflection appears in a clear lake, yet the moon has not moved into the water. Know that the character of all phenomena is like that.
>
> People in a wooded mountain range hear echoes from song,

speech, laughter, and weeping, but what seems to be there is not. Know that all phenomena are this way.

Although echoes arise from song, music, and even weeping, the tones of those songs and so forth are never in the sound of the echo. Know that all phenomena are this way.

When people who possess a desired object in a dream awake and do not see it, they are fools to desire and cling to it. Know that all phenomena are this way.

When magicians conjure up forms, creating various horses, elephants, or chariots, what appears to be there does not exist at all. Know that all phenomena are this way.

When a young woman sees the birth and death of a child in a dream, she is delighted at the birth but not at the death. Know that all phenomena are this way.

When reflections of the moon appear at night in clear, clean water, they are empty and vain, ungraspable. Know that all phenomena are this way.

A person tormented by thirst, traveling at midday in summer, sees mirages as pools of water. Know that all phenomena are this way.

Although water does not exist in a mirage at all, a deluded being wants to drink it. It is false and undrinkable. Know that all phenomena are this way.

REFLECTION

1. Select a few of these similes and contemplate how their objects falsely appear to be real.
2. When a situation invoking strong emotions occurs in your life, remember these verses and reflect on the event as like an illusion.

What Illusion-Like Appearances Are Not

We may have unusual experiences in meditation or in special situations, but we must be careful not to confuse these with the illusion-like appearances of yogis who have realized emptiness. During meditation, sometimes people may feel that they are floating in space, their body disappears, their sense of self is diffuse, or the things around them are insubstantial. After taking certain drugs or when delirious with fever, people may experience hallucinations in which they see people who aren't there or feel that the environment around them is flowing here and there. After hearing unexpected tragic news, people may feel that everything around them is unreal and like a dream, and people overwhelmed by anger or grief may experience chaotic appearances. None of these is what is meant by meditation on illusion-like emptiness.

Prior to knowing that phenomena are like illusions, yogis must have realized emptiness either inferentially or directly. This depends on correctly identifying the object of negation. Having an incorrect notion of the object of negation—inherent existence—John analyzes if his body is the same as its parts. Not finding his body among its parts, he concludes that there is no body. He then applies the same analysis to himself, the analyzer, and not finding his self in the aggregates, concludes that he also is not here and that therefore no one knows that neither the body nor he as analyzer exists. From this he absurdly concludes that things are neither existent nor nonexistent.

Since he has no way to determine whether things exist or not, the objects around him begin to appear to his mind as shimmering, ephemeral appearances that are like vague, insubstantial drawings. It seems to him that everything lacks solidity and nothing can be identified as either this or that.

Although seeing phenomena as less solid may sometimes be considered a "good" meditative experience, it is not the meaning of phenomena dawning as illusion-like. Rather, these strange appearances arise due to not properly identifying the object of negation and being unable to differentiate existence and true existence on the one hand, and nonexistence and emptiness on the other.

Another misinterpretation of illusion-like appearances occurs when instead of refuting true existence, some meditators negate too much and fall to the extreme of nihilism. The "emptiness" they perceive destroys dependent existence, and the mind doesn't conceive anything at all. When they arise from this meditation, things appear insubstantial like rainbows or light smoke, not solid and obstructive as before. Appearing empty of coarse solidity is not illusion-like appearance; if it were, we wouldn't see rainbows as truly existent. And if the nonexistence of coarse obstructiveness were the emptiness of true existence, when we analyze obstructive objects, we would conclude that the mere lack of solidity would be their emptiness, and thus we couldn't realize their emptiness of true existence. Such experiences are divorced from the realization of emptiness and the experience of illusion-like appearances.

The Way Illusion-Like Appearances Arise

When engaging in ultimate analysis, it is fairly easy to draw the wrong conclusion that phenomena are neither existent nor nonexistent, and in dependence on this, experience shimmering exotic appearances. This happens to people interested in the Middle Way who have heard a few teachings on emptiness. Having heard of the importance of differentiating true existence and conventional existence, they repeat those words but don't really understand the meaning. Instead of using ultimate analysis to refute true existence, they apply it to conventional existence and fall to nihilism. Tsongkhapa warned that if we apply ultimate analysis to examine conventional existence, we will wind up undermining all worldly conventions. Therefore, he counseled, conventions should not be subjected to ultimate analysis.

Conventional analysis is used to understand veiled truths and is valuable in doing so. This analysis enables us to know how planets orbit stars and viruses interact with human and animal bodies. It knows what factors are conducive for a functioning society, and it adjudicates disputes regarding property ownership. However, conventional analysis cannot explore the ultimate nature of any of these things. Their ultimate mode of existence is known through ultimate analysis.

The difficult point is to be able to correctly ascertain the object of negation—true existence—fully negate it, and still posit those persons that lack true existence as the accumulators of actions and experiencers of results. In short, the understanding of the composite of (1) the complete lack of true existence and (2) the conventional existence of persons and things does not occur very often. For this reason, the realization of the Middle Way is difficult to gain. In the *Commentary on Bodhicitta* Nāgārjuna marvels (BV 88):

> Those who understand this emptiness of phenomena
> yet [also] conform to the law of karma and its results—
> that is more amazing than amazing!
> That is more wondrous than wondrous!

The challenge is to refute without exception all existence from its own side and still be able to ascertain with complete confidence that phenomena exist dependently. A person has no existence from its own side whatsoever yet still creates virtuous, nonvirtuous, and neutral actions, experiences their results, practices the path, and attains awakening.

Alternating meditation on emptiness and contemplation of dependent arising will aid in understanding the mutually complementary nature of dependent arising and emptiness. Meditation on dependent arising—causal dependence, mutual establishment, and mere dependent designation—will lead us to understand that phenomena lack any independent essence whatsoever and do not exist from their own side or under their own power. Meditation on emptiness clarifies that phenomena exist only in dependence on other factors.

In short, the understanding of dependent arising will fortify our understanding of emptiness, and the understanding that phenomena are empty will support a deeper understanding of causal relationships, such as the creation of virtue giving rise to happiness and the creation of nonvirtue bringing suffering. The mind that realizes emptiness does not understand dependent arising, and the mind understanding dependent arising does not itself realize emptiness. However, these two minds can induce each other. Then, in the wake of meditative equipoise on emptiness, we will experience illusion-like appearances and will know veiled truths to be deceptive, like magical creations, in that they appear to exist in one way, whereas they exist in another. Candrakīrti in his *Commentary on (Āryadeva's) "Four Hundred"* says (FEW 81):

> When analyzed thus, the inherent existence of things is not established. Hence, just an illusion-like [appearance] remains left over with respect to the individual things [that are analyzed].

True existence is negated and what remains when yogis arise from meditative equipoise on emptiness are illusion-like appearances. The I that appears is mere name; it exists by merely being conceived and designated by thought. Sentient beings and our environment exist, but not truly. They are empty, but not totally nonexistent. The *King of Concentration Sūtra* says (OR 124):

> Beings in cyclic existence are like dreams;
> they are unborn and undying.
>
> No sentient beings, humans, and life are found.
> These phenomena are like bubbles, plantain trees,[45]
> illusions, flashes of lightning,
> [reflections of] the moon in the water, and mirages.
>
> No person who has died in this world
> passes or goes to another life.
> Actions done are never lost;
> when one transmigrates, both positive and negative effects ripen.
>
> [Actions] are neither permanent nor discontinued;
> karma does not accumulate or endure.
> Yet once it is created, never do you not meet with its result;
> nor will you experience the effect of an action created by someone else.
>
> Nothing is transferred; nor is it returned.
> Nothing exists or does not exist.
> Thus engaging with views is impure.

Although there appears to be truly existent people who are born and die, these are like dreams. When left unanalyzed they appear, but when searched for with ultimate analysis, they cannot be found. Phenomena are like bubbles, appearing temporarily and disintegrating due to the slightest condition. They resemble plantain trees that have no core or essence when the surrounding sheaves are stripped away. They are like magical illusions—horses and elephants concocted by a magician that vividly appear but do not exist. Phenomena are like lightning, for they appear and vanish in a moment; there is nothing to hold on to. They resemble reflections of the moon in water: just as the moon falsely appears to have moved into the water, truly existent people appear to go from one life to the next. They are like mirages in that they appear to be truly existent things we can use but are only appearances; there are no truly existent things to use. Despite our inability to pin down phenomena and draw a line around their essence, they still function, interacting with one another and giving rise to new things and events.

When a seal is stamped on wax, an image is seen in the wax although nothing material transferred from the seal to the wax. When a face appears in a mirror, the face did not transfer into the mirror. Yet without the image in the seal nothing could appear in the wax, and without the face no reflection of a face in the mirror could be seen. Things do not arise from their own nature; an inherent, unchanging essence does not continue from a cause to its effect.

Things appear due to the coming together of many causes and conditions. Sentient beings are born and die in dependence on many factors—some biological, circumstantial, karmic, and so on. One factor cannot be pinpointed as the one and only cause of birth or death. There is no truly existent person who came from the past life into this life and no truly existent person who goes from this life to the next. Sentient beings' existence in saṃsāra is like an illusion.

Yet once karma is created, the result will surely come—this dispels the extreme of nihilism. What we do, say, and think matters, it brings results. However, we will not experience the effect of others' karmic actions, nor can the results of our actions be transferred to someone else to experience.

Actions done do not go to waste: they ripen as pleasant and unpleasant effects in this and future lives. These actions are not permanent, they do not endure without changing until they ripen; there is flexibility in the functioning of karma and its effects. Nevertheless, virtue always produces happiness and nonvirtue consistently leads to suffering. Each action produces potentials, and these potentials continue to change until they ripen. If the cause isn't impermanent, it would be unable to produce a result. When the result is present, the cause has ceased. Karma and its effects are neither truly existent nor totally nonexistent. Similarly, the persons who create karma and experience their effects are neither truly existent nor totally nonexistent. The *Ratnakūṭa Sūtra* says (OR 125):

> O worthy ones, where are you going and whence have you come?
> They replied, "Venerable Subhūti, the Transcendent One has explained things as follows: nothing goes anywhere or comes from anywhere."

When contemplated, these verses and passages from the sūtras are very powerful. Reflect on them when you meditate on the twelve links of dependent origination and on the law of karma and its effects. Doing this will help you cultivate the right view of the complementary nature of emptiness and dependent arising early on in your practice.

REFLECTION

1. Identify the object of negation by remembering a situation when you had strong emotion and observe the sense of an independent, objectively existent I.
2. Examine if the I could possibly exist in any of the seven ways that Candrakīrti explained. (See chapters 1 and 3.) By doing this repeatedly, develop conviction that nothing exists independently, under its own power.
3. As you come out of meditation, let the undeniable appearances of yourself, others, and your environment arise as objects of mind.
4. Understand that these appearances of truly existent people and things are false. They resemble illusions in that they appear one way but exist in another.
5. Consider that although the I is like an illusion, it still creates karma and experiences its effects.

6. Contemplate that the person who criticizes or harms you is also like an illusion. What use is it to be upset with an illusion-like person?

Our aim is to develop a wisdom understanding emptiness that is so strong and firm that it influences all aspects of our lives, so that while we engage in daily activities, our mind is imbued with the sense that everything—ourselves as the agent, the actions we do, and the objects we are acting on—is like an illusion. When prostrating, making offerings, visualizing meditational deities, listening to teachings, and engaging with sentient beings, yogis' minds are affected by the understanding that all elements involved in these activities are empty yet appear like illusions. Seeing things as like illusions doesn't mean that objects appear to exist when in fact they do not; that would be nihilistic. Rather, they appear to truly exist although they are empty of this false mode of existence. These practitioners can distinguish existence from true existence and emptiness from total nonexistence. This understanding arises after realizing emptiness inferentially or directly.

For those of us who are not at that level of realization, it is helpful to question how things appear as we go about our daily activities. Seeing things as like illusions dramatically reduces craving, attachment, and animosity, preventing the creation of destructive karma motivated by these afflictions. As an analogy, knowing that the ghost sitting beside us in Disneyland's haunted house is a hologram, we are not afraid of it. Similarly, knowing that the things around us appear falsely, we are not overwhelmed by disturbing emotions in relation to them.

Ideally we want to become so familiar with the reasonings negating true existence that no matter what we're doing, we won't be drawn into accepting appearances as they are. In difficult situations as well as happy ones, we will be able to mentally step back and recognize that veiled truths are false appearances. Doing this will impede activating the exaggerations and proliferations that lead to disturbing emotions, agitated attitudes, and wrong views.

An example from the *King of Concentration Sūtra* clarifies how to use our understanding of emptiness and illusion-like appearances to counteract afflictions (OR 123):

When they see a woman's ornamented face
on the surface of a mirror or a pot of oil,
childish ones develop attachment to it,
then develop desire and pursue it avidly.

The face does not pass on to them,
nor is the face ever found in the image.
Just as that for which these fools develop desire,
so all phenomena should be known.

Illusion-Like but Not Illusions

To yogis who have realized emptiness inferentially or directly in meditative equipoise, the appearance or perception of inherently existent objects arises in post-meditation times. The Tibetan word *snang ba* is usually translated as "appearance," but in this context it can also mean perception. When we say that the world appears truly existent, it sounds as if the problem is coming from the side of the object, the world. In fact, the falsity originates in the subject, the mind polluted by ignorance and its latencies. Due to the latencies of ignorance, all sentient beings' consciousnesses—except āryas' wisdom of meditative equipoise directly cognizing emptiness—are obscured in that they perceive the world as truly existent.

Rather than accept these mistaken appearances/perceptions as true, these yogis know them to be deceptive and false. Nāgārjuna gives us a hint of this experience (YS 25–27):

Those who are learned with respect to the facts
see that things are impermanent,
deceptive, mere shells, empty, and selfless;
they see them as utterly void.

Devoid of locus, there is nothing to objectify;
rootless, they have no fixed abode.
They arise entirely from the cause, ignorance,
utterly devoid of beginning, middle, and end.

> Like a plantain tree, they have no essence;
> they resemble the city of gandharvas.
> Thus this dreadful world, a city of ignorance,
> appears like a magical illusion.

The world and the beings and environments in it have no core, they are fabricated by ignorance. This world in which beings suffer appears to ordinary beings as a truly existent reality when in fact it is like a magical illusion: it appears falsely and does not exist in the way it appears—like a city of gandharvas, nature spirits whose abodes appear real but are actually phantom cities.[46]

Although veiled truths appear like illusions or to be illusion-like in post-equipoise time, they are not illusions. The difference here is subtle. The objects perceived in illusions do not exist at all. There is no face in the mirror, no water on the asphalt, no good-looking person in a TV screen, and no monster in a dream, although their appearances exist. These analogies point to the fact that like the face, water, dream person, and monster, the people and things in our lives appear real although they are not. These are analogies, and their lack of reality differs from the lack of reality of conventionally existent objects. Harsh words spoken to a person on the TV do not hurt that person's feelings; however, harsh words spoken to an illusion-like person hurt that person. If you strike someone in your dream, no one is injured; but if you strike an illusion-like person, they will be severely injured and will experience pain. Seeing things as like an illusion is not an excuse to abandon ethical discipline; in fact, it is more important than ever to avoid harming others and to benefit them as much as possible.

In *Clear Words*, Candrakīrti compares illusion-like appearances to the visual disorder vitreous floaters (myodesopsia), in which the afflicted see specks or falling hairs where there are none (PSP 261.2–4):

> For, just like those who have vitreous floaters adhere to what is merely the unreal—the essence (true existence) of the [falsely perceived] hair and so on—as if it has essence; likewise, because [their] eyes of intelligence are impaired by the eye disease of ignorance, ignorant beings adhere to things that are without essence

> as if they had an essence. As they adhere to [their essence], they speak of [their] characteristics.

Although hairs and floating shapes may appear to our visual consciousness, they do not exist, even though their appearance exists for those with this visual disorder. Similarly, although truly existent phenomena appear to sentient beings whose minds are obscured by ignorance, truly existent phenomena do not exist, even though their appearance exists to sentient beings. Although falling hair and truly existent things do not exist, illusion-like things exist and function. "Illusion-like" does not mean that something that does not exist still appears; it means that things that exist do not exist in the way they appear.

Within this combination of appearance and emptiness in post-meditation, ārya bodhisattvas meditate on bodhicitta, engage in virtuous actions, and purify negativities. This is called integrating wisdom and method combined as a pair.

Seeing things as like illusions changes the way we relate to people and things. Contemplate this passage from Maitreya's *Sublime Continuum* by reflecting that your own experience of afflictions, karma, and their results resemble clouds, dreams, and deceptive apparitions respectively (RGV 137):

> The mental poisons are like clouds;
> karma resembles a dream experience.
> The aggregates produced by the [mental] poisons and karma
> are similar to an illusion or a deceptive apparition.

The twelve links of dependent origination, which describe how our saṃsāra arises and continues, are grouped into three sets: afflictions, karma, and resultant duḥkha. Afflictions and karma are the second of the four truths (true origins); the polluted aggregates are their result, the first truth (true duḥkha). In this verse, Maitreya directs us to understand that all the factors of our saṃsāra lack true existence. Although they appear truly existent, everything about saṃsāra—its causes and its results—is false and adventitious, like clouds, dreams, and illusions.

Until śrāvakas and solitary realizers become arhats and until bodhisattvas attain the eighth ground, the seeds of ignorance still abide in their continuums. After meditative equipoise on emptiness, while their understanding of emptiness is fresh and active, they do not grasp true existence. However, after the impact of the realization of emptiness fades, illusion-like appearances will also dissipate, while manifest ignorance and afflictions may arise in their minds, so they must continue their meditation on emptiness with daily sessions to stabilize and strengthen their realization of emptiness.

REFLECTION

Reflect on the analogies of illusion-like appearances in terms of your own life in saṃsāra.

1. Afflictions are likened to clouds because they adventitiously obscure the open sky-like nature of the mind.
2. The physical, verbal, and mental actions (karma) produced by afflictions are like dreams because they give rise to experiences that do not exist in the way they appear.
3. The polluted aggregates arising due to afflictions and karma appear real but do not truly exist. They are like illusions, holograms, and people on the television screen.
4. Use this understanding to spur yourself to cease grasping afflictions, karma, and their results as existing in and of themselves as solid things to wrestle with. Resolve to have a more flexible and realistic view of the world that will free you from the oppression of afflictions and karma.

An Empty Reflection in a Mirror

The example of a reflection is frequently used to illustrate the illusion-like appearances that arise after realizing emptiness. This example is useful to remember whenever the appearance of veiled truths as truly existent and their emptiness seem contradictory. Although the reflection of a face appears to be a real face, it is not; it is empty of being a real face. This false appearance arises in dependence on a face, a mirror, and the light. Similarly, although all things appear to exist truly, they arise in dependence on their own causes and conditions and on the mind that conceives and designates them. They appear truly existent but are empty of true existence.

Understanding that a reflected face doesn't exist as it appears does not damage grasping true existence because it doesn't negate the conceived object of true-grasping. We know that the face in the mirror is false without understanding the ultimate nature of that reflection. If knowing that the reflected face isn't a real face were the realization of the emptiness of true existence, then an ordinary being who knows nothing about refuting inherent existence would realize emptiness. In that case, ordinary beings would be āryas and wouldn't have to exert effort to realize emptiness.

Young children don't know that a reflected face isn't a real face, so they try to touch the child in the mirror. When they become older, they learn that a reflected face is empty of being a real face. But that knowledge doesn't harm their true-grasping, so they still apprehend a truly existent reflection. To realize something as non-truly existent, ultimate analysis is required. It's not just a question of saying "This doesn't exist as it appears," because there is more than one way in which things do not exist as they appear.

A reflected face is not a real face we can touch; the images of people on the television are not real people; dream people are not actual people who have feelings; and the water of a mirage is not water that can be drunk. This level of false appearance can be easily realized by conventional reliable cognizers; it is the gross illusory nature.

Although we know these ordinary examples are false appearances, we still grasp reflections, television images, dream characters, and mirages to exist truly in the same way as we grasp our friends, ourselves, and everything in our environment to exist truly. This apprehension can be eliminated only through meditation on the emptiness of true existence. After meditation, the appearance of things as illusion-like is their subtle illusory nature.

The emptiness of a reflected face being a real face can serve as an example to help us understand the emptiness of true existence, because it is easier to realize that the reflected image of the face lacks true existence than to realize that our body, mind, external forms, persons, and so forth lack true existence. The contradiction between how a reflected face appears and how it exists is more readily apparent to us. Exploring this leads to knowing that on a deeper level it also does not truly exist.

In short, initially we realize the emptiness of true existence of things commonly known in the world as false—reflections, dreams, holograms, echoes, mirages, magical illusions, people on the TV screen, and so forth. This leads us to realize that things not known as false in the world also lack true existence.

Teachings that instruct us to "view all phenomena as like a dream" refer to realizing their emptiness and subsequent illusion-like appearance. This differs from realizing that the people and apples appearing in dreams are not actual people and apples. Similarly, some practitioners in a dhyāna meditate on bones filling the universe in order to understand the repulsive nature of saṃsāra. Although they apprehend the vivid appearance of bones filling all of space and know these are not actual bones, they haven't realized them to be empty of true existence and like illusions. We need to think deeply about the unique meaning of illusion-like appearance as explained in the definitive scriptures.

Whether a reflection of a face in a mirror is seen by a baby or by a mature person who knows there is no face there; whether magical appearances of horses and elephants are apprehended by someone unfamiliar with magic or by a magician who understands them to be unreal; whether a dream environment is apprehended by someone who is dreaming and doesn't know it's a dream or by that person when he awakes and recognizes the dream environment wasn't real—in none of these examples have people found the correct view of suchness or realized the meaning of illusion-like appearances.

Dissolving into and Emerging from Emptiness

The seventh Dalai Lama, Kalsang Gyatso (1708–57), was a poet who expressed meditation experiences in verses. I contemplate the following three verses he penned in my daily meditation practice, especially in deity yoga sādhanas at the point just before dissolving into emptiness, after reciting the mantras *Oṃ svabhāva śuddhāḥ sarva dharmāḥ svabhāva śuddho 'haṃ* and *Oṃ śūnyatā jñāna vajra svabhāvātmako 'haṃ.*

> All phenomena in saṃsāra and nirvāṇa are merely designated by mind. Mind itself, when investigated, is beyond arising or ceasing. Abiding in the ultimate mode of being, *emaho!* Most wondrous!

> Just as autumn clouds dissipate in the sky, within the sphere of emptiness, emptiness and my mind become indivisible. Within this, all elaborations of experiences [of pain and pleasure] and appearances [of form and so forth] dissolve.
>
> I, an unborn yogi of space, see that nothing truly exists; all things are falsities. I understand the great show of illusion-like sights and sounds. By experiencing the joyous union of appearance and emptiness, I find certainty in the nondeceptive nature of dependent arising.

The first verse shows the meditation to realize emptiness, the second describes the experience of meditative equipoise on emptiness, and the third indicates the meditation on illusion-like appearances that follows meditative equipoise.

Dissolving into emptiness

All phenomena, be they the impure phenomena of saṃsāra or the pure phenomena of nirvāṇa, exist by being merely designated by conceptuality. Being causally dependent, mutually dependent, and dependently designated, they are empty of inherent existence. The meditating mind itself is also dependent and is free from inherent arising and ceasing. Realizing emptiness directly and nonconceptually with a mind that is the union of serenity and insight is joyful and wondrous, as indicated by the expression *emaho!*

Abiding in emptiness

Emptiness is like space, totally open and free from the impediments of duality. Experientially, the subject—the mind—and its object—its ultimate nature of emptiness—become indifferentiable. All dualistic experiences, such as pain and pleasure, and all appearances of veilings, such as the five sensory objects, form and so forth, vanish into nonduality as the mind sees its ultimate nature.

Emerging from emptiness

The meditator is an unborn yogi in the space of emptiness, someone empty of inherent existence who abides in that very ultimate nature. When she emerges from meditative equipoise on emptiness, all objects around appear to exist inherently, but she knows that appearance is false. All veilings are falsities. Rather than existing inherently, they are illusion-like composites of dependent arising and emptiness. Free from attachment and repulsion, the practitioner experiences them like a play or show; they are manifestations of emptiness in that they exist and appear within the absence of inherent existence. Her understanding of the view is complete, for she now can establish dependently arising phenomena within the sphere of the total absence of inherent existence.

REFLECTION

Meditate on dissolving into, abiding, and emerging from emptiness as the seventh Dalai Lama's verses outline.

1. Use one of the analyses explained earlier in this book to understand emptiness. Although most of us won't have even an inferential understanding of emptiness, it is still helpful to imagine what it would be like to release all grasping at the inherent existence of yourself and all phenomena.
2. Imagine abiding in an internal feeling of spaciousness that is the absence of inherent existence. Your mind is completely peaceful; you apprehend only the absence of inherent existence. No other phenomena appear to your mind.
3. Think of your body, I, or another phenomenon and understand that although it appears inherently existent, that appearance is totally false. There is not even a tiny bit of inherent existence there; thus that phenomenon appears as like an illusion.

Nonduality

What is the nonduality that meditators experience in the second step above? Āryas' meditative equipoise that directly and nonconceptually perceives emptiness is a nondual cognizer that is free from four elaborations:

1. The appearance of inherent existence: Since an ārya's meditative equipoise on emptiness directly realizes the emptiness of inherent existence, it is not possible for inherent existence to appear to this mind.
2. The appearance of subject and object: While in meditative equipoise on emptiness, the subject—the wisdom realizing emptiness—and the object—emptiness—are undifferentiable, like water poured into water.
3. The appearance of veilings: Only emptiness—the nonaffirming negation that is the absence of inherent existence—appears to and is cognized by this mind. There is no appearance of veiled truths at all.
4. The appearance of conceptualization: The wisdom directly cognizing emptiness is free from conceptual appearances, which appear only to conceptual consciousnesses.

Contemplating these aspects of nonduality, which are free of elaborations, gives us an inkling of the uniqueness of the ārya's meditative equipoise that directly realizes emptiness. This meditating mind is totally unlike conventional reliable cognizers or conceptual consciousnesses. The metaphor of "water poured into water" is often used to illustrate the experience of the nonduality of the subject—the wisdom realizing emptiness—and the object—the emptiness of inherent existence—that occurs when an ārya directly realizes emptiness. In this mental state the ultimate nature of the mind itself is manifest to this mind. That wisdom does not realize a conditioned object or an external thing; it is directly and single-pointedly realizing its own true nature. Within that experience, the four above elaborations have ceased. The object of the wisdom consciousness realizing emptiness is a mere negation, the mere nonexistence of inherent existence.

The metaphor of water poured into water does not mean that the wisdom realizing emptiness and emptiness have become one, in the sense of being identical. Emptiness is a permanent, unconditioned phenomenon, and wisdom is a conditioned phenomenon, so they cannot become one and the same. However, the experience of duality between subject and object has ceased, and experientially they cannot be differentiated.

Unpolluted wisdom—wisdom that is unaffected by ignorance—in the continuum of sentient beings manifests during meditative equipoise directly realizing emptiness. At that time, other conventional consciousnesses, such as compassion and bodhicitta, are not manifest. After ārya bodhisattvas arise from meditative equipoise, in post-meditation time their wisdom directly realizing emptiness is not manifest. At that time, conventional consciousnesses—those polluted by the appearance of inherent existence—are manifest.

In the first chapter of *Ocean of Reasoning*, Tsongkhapa's commentary on Nāgārjuna's *Treatise on the Middle Way*, he emphasizes that the thesis being proven in the syllogism establishing emptiness must necessarily be a mere negation, a nonaffirming negation. He also explains that the probing awareness realizing the ultimate mode of being apprehends emptiness, but it does not affirm the existence of emptiness. The existence of emptiness is established by a subsequent conventional reliable cognizer that recollects this experience.

To clarify, when realizing emptiness directly, there is no idea or thought in the mind that subject and object are nondual. There is no thought "I am perceiving emptiness" or "What an amazing experience!" The actual experience is one of mere negation—the mere absence of true existence. No grasping or reification are present or experienced. Nonduality can be spoken of only from the perspective of a subsequent consciousness that knows that the meditative equipoise on emptiness was nondual. There is no subject-object duality in the mind directly knowing emptiness; there is no appearance of veilings. In other words, nonduality is a quality of that experience that is attributed only from an outside perspective. The mind directly realizing emptiness knows only ultimate truth. It does not have the ability to establish the existence of veiled truths or even to establish the existence of emptiness. When a practitioner arises from that meditative equipoise and recalls that he or she has realized emptiness, a conventional reliable cognizer affirms the existence of emptiness.

A buddha's wisdom is an exception in that by virtue of having purified all cognitive obscurations, he or she knows both ultimate truth and veiled truth simultaneously.

12 | Self and Selflessness in the Pāli Tradition

INVESTIGATION AND ANALYSIS into the nature of the self is a prominent topic in the Pāli sūtras, which often feature the Buddha debating with non-Buddhist renunciants and questioning his own disciples on their views. Although the Buddha did not engage in formal debate punctuated with the clapping and shouting that occur in the debate yards of Tibetan monasteries today, he used syllogisms to present his ideas and consequences to point out the unwanted implications of others' wrong views.

The Pāli sūtras are similar to the sūtras as found in other early Buddhist schools. Nāgārjuna surely read these sūtras, and he and pandits of the Nālandā tradition built on the Buddha's reasonings to explore the nature of reality. Analytical inquiry is employed to this day as an important tool among practitioners of both the Pāli and Sanskrit traditions.

In this chapter we will delve into the Buddha's message regarding the lack of self-existence of the person and phenomena as described in the Pāli tradition. In doing so, it will become clear that the roots of Nāgārjuna's refutation of inherent existence lie in sūtras of other early Buddhist schools that are parallels to texts in the Pāli canon.[47] The Buddha clearly pointed out the unwanted consequences of asserting that one of the aggregates or the collection of the aggregates is the self. He also demonstrated that whatever arises dependent on other conditions cannot be a substantial self, setting out the untenable consequences if this were not the case. These same arguments were later expanded in Nāgārjuna's seminal work, *Treatise on the Middle Way*.

The Buddha and his [distant] disciple Nāgārjuna shined the light of wisdom on our long-held beliefs about who we are—deeply held notions that we may not have noticed, let alone questioned. Now, for the sake of freeing ourselves from saṃsāra, we will commence the quest to discover the nature of reality, beginning with investigation of the notion of a solid, findable I. Although the I seems to be located in or among our physical and mental aggregates, the body-mind complex cannot be such an independent person because the aggregates that compose it are themselves impermanent, duḥkha in nature, and insubstantial.

The Buddha's Statements about Self

In the *Dhammapada*, the Buddha says (Dhp 279):

> All dharmas [phenomena] are not self.

This may also be translated as "all phenomena are without a self" or "all phenomena are selfless." It is striking that here the Buddha applied the quality of lacking a self to all phenomena. He did not say "the aggregates are not self," meaning the aggregates are not a permanent, unitary, independent self or a substantial self. The Buddha also made numerous comments about whether a self existed in the way we think it does. In the *Discourse on the Simile of the Snake*, he says (MN 22:25):

> Monastics, there being a self, would there be what belongs to my self?—"Yes, venerable sir."—Or, there being what belongs to a self, would there be my self?—"Yes, venerable sir." Monastics, since a self and what belongs to a self are not apprehended as true and established, then the [above] standpoint for views . . . would it not be an utterly and completely foolish teaching?

By saying that a self and what belongs to self—I and mine—are not apprehended as true and established, the Buddha refutes the existence of a permanent ātman or a substantial self. This, however, does not deny the existence of the conventional or empirical person that depends on the impermanent and conditioned continuity of the aggregates. In fact, he used the terms "I," "person," and "self" when encouraging people to take responsibility for their own liberation.

In the *Book of the Six Sense Sources* (SN 44:10), the non-Buddhist wanderer Vacchagotta asks the Buddha if there is a self, and the Buddha remains silent. Vacchagotta then queries, "Is there no self?" and again the Buddha is silent. Puzzled, Vacchagotta departs, and Ānanda asks the Buddha why he did not answer Vacchagotta's questions. The Buddha explains that if he told Vacchagotta there is a self, people would think he agreed with the absolutists, and if he said there is no self people would think he agreed with the nihilists.

The Buddha then asks Ānanda if he had said there is a self, would that be consistent with the insight knowledge that all phenomena are not self (selfless), and Ānanda replied in the negative. The Buddha continues, saying that if he told Vacchagotta there is no self, Vacchagotta would be even more confused than he already is, because he would think that the self he formerly had does not exist now. By remaining silent, the Buddha was not evading the question. Because Vacchagotta clung to a view of self, he would misunderstand the Buddha's reply no matter which answer he gave. Thus, in order not to be inconsistent with his own realization, not to be mistaken as either an absolutist or a nihilist, and not to induce further confusion in Vacchagotta, the Buddha remained silent. Happily, after some time Vacchagotta overcame his wrong views, joined the Saṅgha, and became an arhat.

Wrong Views of the Self

The reified idea of an autonomous self is not a view we have been taught by someone; rather, it springs up spontaneously in our minds. On further examination, we find that this notion of self holds that there is a substantial, immutable, true entity that is truly "who we are." The five aggregates are transitory phenomena that arise and pass away at every moment, yet their continuity creates the appearance of a real self. We then grasp the idea of a self that is identified with the aggregates or regarded as located within the aggregates or above the aggregates. But such a self is nowhere to be found; it is a product of ignorance and clinging to the doctrine of self.

In many sūtras, such as the *Brahmā Net Sutta* (DN 1) and the *Pañcattaya Sutta* (MN 102), the Buddha outlines the multiplicity of wrong views circulating among the brahmins and ascetics of his time. Varieties of these views live on today. These erroneous views demonstrate the extent to which our ignorance constructs and endeavors to validate a real self, a substantial identity that is the person. Many of these views arise based on inappropriate attention directed to the past and future. In the *All the Pollutants Sutta* (*Sabbāsava Sutta*), the Buddha says (MN 2:7):

> This is how he (an untaught ordinary person) attends unwisely: "Was I in the past? Was I not in the past? What was I in the past? How was I in the past? Having been what, what did I become in the past? Shall I be in the future? Shall I not be in the future? What shall I be in the future? How shall I be in the future? Having been what, what shall I become in the future?" Or else he is inwardly perplexed about the present thus: "Am I? Am I not? What am I? How am I? Where has this being come from? Where will it go?"

Human beings have been dealing with these important existential questions for centuries. However, when we reflect on them in an unwise manner, especially by assuming a substantial self that is the topic of these inquiries, we have gone astray. More wrong views then accumulate on top of this basic ignorance. When a person reflects in an inappropriate manner on the nature of the self, the Buddha says one of six wrong views will arise in him and he will be caught in a thicket of views (MN 2:8):

1. The view "self exists for me." This is absolutism.
2. The view "no self exists for me." In other words, the body is the self and since the body is destroyed at death, so is the self. This materialistic view is nihilistic because it holds there is no continuity of the person after death.
3. The view "I perceive self with self." This and the next two views are based on ordinary beings' awareness of a perceiver and an object perceived. Here the perceiver identifies his true nature with both the subject (the perceiver) and the object.
4. The view "I perceive not-self with self." Here the perceiver identifies with the self but not with the object. She does not perceive that she herself is not a true self.
5. The view "I perceive self with not-self." Here the object of observation

is identified with the self, and the subject that observes it is taken not to be a self.

6. A view such as "It is this self of mine that speaks and feels and experiences here and there the result of good and bad actions; but this self of mine is permanent, everlasting, eternal, not subject to change, and it will endure as long as eternity." This is an expanded absolutist view. Here the self is seen as the active one that speaks as well as the passive one that feels or experiences what happens to him. This unchanging self or soul speaks and experiences "here and there," in many lives as it transmigrates, creating karma and experiencing its results.

Dismantling this thicket of views requires intelligent investigation and analysis. To help people do this, the Buddha engaged in discussion and debate with the brahmins and wanderers of his time. He asked them, as well as his own disciples, penetrating questions so that they can determine for themselves if their views correspond with reality. With compassion, the Buddha revealed the fallacies in their wrong views and refuted their distorted arguments. Saccaka, an astute debater and clever speaker, sought to defeat and humiliate the Buddha, but at the end of their discussion he admitted (MN 35:27):

> Master Gotama, we were bold and impudent in thinking we could attack Master Gotama in debate. A person might attack a mad elephant and find safety, yet he could not attack Master Gotama and find safety [for his wrong views]. A person might attack a blazing mass of fire . . . [or] a terrible poisonous snake and find safety, yet he could not attack Master Gotama and find safety.

Saccaka later respectfully invited the Buddha and the Saṅgha to a meal at his home and the Buddha accepted.

More Wrong Views of the Self

At the beginning of the *Great Discourse on Causation* (*Mahānidāna Sutta*), the Buddha explains the origin of wrong views as not understanding and realizing dependent origination (DN 15:1):

> This dependent origination, Ānanda, is profound and appears profound. Because of not understanding and penetrating this doctrine, this generation has become like a tangled skein, like a knotted ball of thread, covered as with a blight, tangled like coarse grass, unable to pass beyond saṃsāra with its planes of misery, unfortunate births, and lower realms.

After describing the links of dependent origination, to illustrate the tangled skein the Buddha describes the self in relation to the form aggregate. This is done in four ways (DN 15:23): (1) my self has material form and is limited, (2) my self has material form and is infinite, (3) my self is immaterial and limited, (4) my self is immaterial and infinite.

1. *My self has material form and is limited.* According to the commentary, this is the view of someone who thinks the unextended kasiṇa sign is the self. Meditating on kasiṇas is one way to attain the dhyānas.[48] An unextended kasiṇa sign is the sign (P. *nimitta*) of one of the elements, colors, or so forth appearing in a limited, circumscribed way to the mind, for example as the conceptual appearance of a circle of color in front of oneself. The meditator thinks that since the kasiṇa sign is based on form and is of a limited or circumscribed size, the self too is material form and limited.

2. *My self has material form and is infinite.* Here a meditator holds an extended kasiṇa sign to be the self. He describes the self as having material form and being infinite in size because the sign is based on material form and has been extended in his mind so that it appears to fill all of space.

3. *My self is immaterial and limited.* This person removes the unextended kasiṇa sign and then apprehends as self either (1) the area that was formerly covered by the sign, or (2) the four mental aggregates occurring there, or (3) the mere [mental] consciousness. To progress to the next meditative absorption, a meditator may withdraw the sign and contemplate the empty space that it used to occupy. Here, someone with this wrong view considers

the space where the sign previously appeared, or the four mental aggregates that are present, or just the mere mental consciousness as the self. The self is described as immaterial because the kasiṇa sign has been withdrawn, and the self is seen as limited because previously the sign was a limited size and so is the area after the sign has been withdrawn.

4. *My self is immaterial and infinite.* The person withdraws the extended kasiṇa sign and sees either the limitless area that was previously covered by the sign, the four mental aggregates there, or the mere mental consciousness as the self. This self is described as vast and immaterial because it is based on having withdrawn an extended sign.

In the ultimate sense, no self exists. The self grasped in the four ways above is only a mental fabrication of meditators who proliferate wrong views of the self.

The four people holding these four wrong views may hold them in three ways. The three ways in which someone describes the self as material form and limited is an example: First, this person thinks the self that is material form and limited exists only in the present and totally ceases at the time of death—this is a nihilistic view. Second, he sees the same fabricated self as existing eternally in the future without ever perishing or changing in any way—this is an absolutist view. Third, he thinks, "That which is not thus, I will convert toward the state of being thus"—here a nihilist thinks to convert an absolutist to his way of thinking or the absolutist seeks to convert the nihilist to his view. In these three ways the person has a "settled" view of self as having form and as limited. This view is "settled" in that it has not yet been abandoned by the path. It has the ability to manifest again when conducive causes and conditions are present.

Wrong views come about through various means. Some are generated in the minds of meditators who have attained either the dhyānas or the formless absorptions; some exist in the minds of those who rely on incorrect reasonings that they believe to be correct. Furthermore, people who encounter teachers or lineages of teachings that espouse wrong views easily accept and adopt them themselves. For this reason, it is important to investigate well the views we hear and not simply accept them because they sound good or were taught by someone with samādhi. The commentary to the *Great Discourse on Causation* speaks of four types of people who hold the four wrong views above:

1. Those who construct and adopt a view as a result of gaining meditative attainments with a material kasiṇa, and so forth.
2. Their disciples, who learn those views from their teachers or from a lineage of teachings and accept and approve of those views.
3. Those who have not gained dhyāna by means of a kasiṇa and uphold one of these views as a result of confused reasoning.
4. Their disciples, who learn these wrong views from their teachers or lineage of teachings, and accept and approve of them.

In the case of the four wrong views, there are sixteen possibilities for error—there are four views and four types of people who hold each view. In looking at the various wrong views propagated today, we can see these same four types of people. All of them mean well, but they lack clear wisdom.

Fortunately, some people do not espouse any of these wrong views. Who are these people? Āryas who know reality with direct experience, those who have mastered the three baskets of the Buddha's teachings, those who have studied the Dharma well and understood any of the nikāyas (collections of sūtras), and those who have some accomplishment in insight meditation. These people can correctly identify the counterpart sign as a counterpart sign and know that the immaterial mental aggregates are immaterial mental aggregates. They do not confound the sign or the aggregates with a self because they know through analysis and wisdom that none of these can be a self. However, people who have accomplished samādhi but lack insight may fall prey to these views.

People hold to the four incorrect descriptions of the self as material, immaterial, finite, and infinite because they have not abandoned the view of a personal identity with its twenty ways of grasping the relationship between the self and the aggregates. In the *Great Discourse on Causation* the Buddha goes on to talk about the aggregate of feelings in particular, saying that someone may incorrectly grasp a self in relation to feelings in any of the following ways (DN 15:27): (1) feeling is my self; (2) feeling is not my self, my self is without experience of feeling; and (3) feeling is not my self, but my self is not without experience of feeling—my self feels, for my self is subject to feeling.

(1) *Feeling is my self.* This is the view of a personal identity based on the feeling aggregate, thinking feeling is the self. The Buddha advises this per-

son (DN 15:28): "Friend, there are these three kinds of feeling—pleasant feeling, painful feeling, and neutral feeling. Of these three kinds of feeling, which do you consider as self?" The Buddha then lays out the following points to consider:

- The three feelings arise at different times; when one is present, the others are not. Which feeling, then, is a constant self? Feeling as a whole cannot be the self because there are multiple feelings but there is just one self. Also, many feelings do not arise in one moment, which would have to happen if the entire feeling aggregate were a single self.
- If a certain feeling were the self, since that feeling is sometimes present and sometimes not, that would mean sometimes self would exist and sometimes not.
- Every feeling is impermanent, conditioned, dependent, and as such will disintegrate. It is impermanent because it doesn't exist after having been; it is conditioned in that it arises due to multiple causes that have come together; it is dependently arisen because it arises in dependence on specific other factors. As such, feeling has the nature of ceasing. Since each feeling is such a brief and dependent occurrence, how could feeling be a stable self?
- When experiencing a pleasant feeling, if we think, "This is my self," then when that feeling ceases, we would think, "My self has ceased. It has vanished and no longer exists." The same would happen regarding painful and neutral feelings.
- Since the thoughts of someone with wrong views is not rational, this person could think at different times, "This self of mine has pleasant feeling as its intrinsic nature; it has painful feeling as its intrinsic nature; it has neutral feeling as its intrinsic nature." It makes no sense at all to think that one thing (the self) can have three different intrinsic natures.
- Holding the view "feeling is my self" involves holding something that is transient, is a combination of pleasure and pain, and is subject to arising and ceasing as a real self. But it is not possible for such a thing to be a true self.

(2) *Feeling is not my self, my self is without the experience of feeling.* This is the view of a personal identity based on material form. This person rejects

the self as something that feels, and in doing so also rejects the other mental aggregates—consciousness, discrimination, and miscellaneous factors that arise associated with feeling—as related to the self. That leaves the unfeeling, inanimate material body, which they state is the self. The Buddha says we should ask this person, "Friend, where there is nothing at all that is felt, could the idea 'I am' occur there?"

Can the thought "I am" arise where no feeling exists? That is, can an inanimate object such as a table or window, which has no feeling whatsoever, have the thought "I am"? That is impossible. Thus holding the view "Feeling is not my self, my self is without experience of feeling" is unreasonable.

(3) *Feeling is not my self, but my self is not without experience of feeling—my self feels, for my self is subject to feeling.* This is the view of a personal identity based on the aggregates of discrimination, miscellaneous factors, and consciousness. While the feeling aggregate is not considered to be the self, the other three aggregates that are associated with feeling—especially the mental consciousness—are held to be the self. The self feels because these three aggregates feel. The person holding this view rejects the view that feeling is the self. But he accepts that the self has feelings and is subject to feeling. The other three mental aggregates perform the function of feeling because they are associated with it and arise concomitant with it. That is, feeling experiences the object, and the other aggregates feel because they are associated with feeling.

The Buddha says that a person with this view should be asked, "Friend, if feeling were to cease absolutely and utterly without remainder, then in the complete absence of feeling, with the cessation of feeling, could [the idea] 'I am this' occur there?" That is, if feeling ceased in the other three mental aggregates subject to feeling, would there be anything that could be considered "I am this"? Or alternatively, if those three aggregates ceased when feeling ceased, could the thought "I am" or "I am this" arise? "I am" refers to the view of a personal identity that takes the other three mental aggregates collectively to be the self, and "I am this" is the view of a personal identity that holds one of them individually to be the self. The Buddha dismisses both notions. The commentary compares them to the sharpness of a rabbit's horn. Since a rabbit's horn does not exist, what use is it to speak of its sharpness? That is, without the proper supporting base, we cannot talk about a quality of that thing. In this case, without the capacity to experience we cannot speak of a self that experiences.

The Buddha continues, saying that someone who does not hold any of the above three conceptions about feeling in relation to the self does not cling to anything in the world. How does someone arrive at the point of not holding any of these views? By dwelling in the four establishments of mindfulness. Such a person has explored each of the aggregates individually and all of them as a collection and with wisdom knows them as characterized by impermanence, duḥkha, and the absence of a self. Thus she does not cling to any of the aggregates as a self or as belonging to a self. Because she does not cling, she is not agitated by craving, views, or conceit. She attains nirvāṇa through the destruction of all defilements by the path. Then, with reviewing knowledge, she is able to look back and ascertain that the purpose of the holy life has been fulfilled and rebirth in saṃsāra has ceased forever.

REFLECTION

1. Do you ever have the sense that one feeling or the collection of feelings is the essence of who you are?
2. Observing your feelings, how long does a happy (pleasurable) feeling, unhappy (painful, suffering) feeling, or a neutral feeling last? Are these feelings stable enough to be considered an enduring person?
3. If any of your feelings were who you are, when that feeling ceased and a new one arose, one self would cease and a new self would arise. Does that make sense? Is that your experience?
4. Can your feelings function independent of your primary consciousnesses? Can they exist unrelated to your body or to your conceptual consciousness?
5. Conclude that feelings are transient, dependent on other factors, and are not suitable to be a stable self or the possession of such a self.

Is There a Self That Controls the Aggregates?

The Buddha refutes a self that is in control of the aggregates. When the non-Buddhist wanderer Saccaka (Aggivessana) approaches the Buddha and says that the five aggregates are the self, the Buddha challenges him (MN 35:12, 15–19):

> What do you think, Aggivessana? Would a head-anointed noble king—for example, King Pasenadi of Kosala or King Ajātasattu Vedehiputta of Magadha—exercise the power in his own realm to execute those who should be executed, to fine those who should be fined, and to banish those who should be banished? . . .
>
> [Aggivessana:] He would exercise it, Master Gotama, and he would be worthy to exercise it.
>
> [The Buddha:] What do you think, Aggivessana? When you say thus: "Material form is my self," do you exercise any power over that material form as to say: "Let my material form be thus; let my material form not be thus"? . . . When you say thus: "Feelings are my self," do you exercise any power over those feelings as to say: "Let my feelings be thus; let my feelings not be thus"? . . . When you say thus: "Discriminations are my self," do you exercise any power over those discriminations as to say: "Let my discriminations be thus; let my discriminations not be thus"? . . . When you say thus: "Miscellaneous factors are my self," do you exercise any power over those miscellaneous factors as to say: "Let my miscellaneous factors be thus; let my miscellaneous factors not be thus"? . . . When you say thus: "Consciousnesses are my self," do you exercise any power over those consciousnesses as to say: "Let my consciousnesses be thus; let my consciousnesses not be thus"?

At this point Aggivessana remained silent. It was clear to him that if the aggregates were the self and if there were a substantial self in control of the aggregates, the self should be able to control them. Since this is not the case, he understood that his beliefs were incorrect.

Contemplating this is helpful when our sense of self is inflated and seeks to control the people or the environment around us. Simply remembering that we have little control over our basic components—the aggregates—quickly quenches that arrogance. Although we may think "I am in control," we cannot prevent ourselves from falling ill, aging, and dying. When tasting something disagreeable, we cannot will ourselves to experience it as delicious. This lack of control is especially apparent in regard to the emotions that comprise the aggregate of miscellaneous factors. Our emotions arise when they wish under the influence of causes and conditions. As much as we may not want to fall into a rage and scream accusations that destroy relationships in the face of those we care about, without a strong basis in the antidotes to the afflictions, we have hardly any control once the afflictions take over our mind. As much as we might want to have affection for all beings, we cannot force ourselves to feel that without having created the causes by meditating on love.

If there were a solid self, one that is findable in the aggregates, then that self should be able to control the aggregates. Because the aggregates function under the control of their own causes and conditions, there is no solid self holding the reins. The Buddha makes this point in the *Characteristic of Selflessness* (SN 22:59):

> Monastics, form is not self. For if, monastics, form (the body) were self, this body would not lead to affliction, and it would be possible to determine the body: "Let my body be thus; let my body not be thus." But because the body is not self, the body leads to affliction, and it is not possible to determine the body: "Let my body be thus; let my body not be thus."

The Buddha continues speaking the same way about feelings, discriminations, miscellaneous factors, and consciousnesses. He presents two arguments why neither the body nor any of the other aggregates is the self. First, if one of the aggregates were the self, we should be able to control that aggregate and make it do or be whatever we want. But we cannot order a certain feeling to arise, for feelings arise dependent on their own conditions. Nor can we control our mind: doing a few minutes of breathing meditation shows us that as much as we wish to stay on the object of meditation, the mind wanders or becomes drowsy. A sense consciousness hearing a sound will arise when we want the mental consciousness to meditate. The mental factor of anger will arise when we want to experience love. There is no controlling self that governs the aggregates. Although we may feel like there is a self that is a commander and the aggregates are the troops that follow its orders, in fact no findable person at all is in charge, neither as one with the aggregates nor unrelated to them.

It is important to understand that although there is not an independent self that controls the aggregates, there is some intentional control over our mind, but not complete mastery. Having trained their minds through diligent practice, accomplished meditators can control and direct their minds. They do so dependent on causes and conditions; they have created the causes for virtuous states of mind to arise and for certain mental factors such as mindfulness, concentration, and wisdom to be strong. Therefore, it is possible to develop mental restraint and to steer our thoughts in a constructive direction.

Dharma practice is about subduing our mind and cultivating wholesome qualities. The way to approach this is by creating the causes. Although there is no controlling self that can will this to happen, nurturing constructive thoughts and emotions and applying antidotes to destructive ones will bring concordant results.

The second argument is that because the body and the other aggregates are impermanent, they are in the nature of duḥkha. Something that is in the nature of duḥkha is not suitable to be a permanent, eternal, blissful self that is in control.

REFLECTION

We often feel and assume that we are a real self that can control our body and mind. And sometimes we extend that and try to control other people, trying to make them become what we want them to be or to act the way we want them to act. Needless to say, this results in conflict and disappointment.

1. Contemplate: If a real self that controlled the body and mind existed, we should be able to pinpoint what it is. Search your aggregates and examine if the I is findable in or among them.

2. A sense of absence will ensue. Such a controller self cannot be found. Recognize through your experience, however, that decisions and choices can still be made and actions can be done despite the absence of such a controller.

3. Consider how your relationships would change if you gave up trying to control others. You could still try to advise or influence them purely with a motivation to benefit them and without any attachment to the outcome.

The Aggregates Are Not the Self

The Buddha employs many arguments to demonstrate why the aggregates are not the self. In the *Six Sets of Six Sutta* (*Chachakka Sutta*),[49] he refutes the claim that any of the aggregates or any part of the aggregates is the self (MN 148:10):

> If anyone says, "The eye is self," that is not tenable. The rise and fall of the eye are discerned, and since its rise and fall are discerned, it would follow, "My self rises and falls." That is why it is not tenable for anyone to say, "The eye is self." Thus the eye is not self.

The Buddha continues, repeating the same passage for forms, visual consciousness, contact dependent on the eye and forms, feeling arising from eye contact, and craving due to eye contact. He then negates these six factors—the sense faculty, object, consciousness, contact, feeling, and craving—in relation to the ear, nose, tongue, body, and mind as being the self.[50]

Both the mental sense faculty and mental phenomena arise and vanish in every split-second, as does the mental consciousness that perceives these objects. Thus none of them is suitable to be considered a permanent, substantial self. Similarly, contact arising due to mind, feelings arising due to mental contact, and craving arising from feelings dependent on mental contact—all of these are characterized by subtle impermanence. They arise and disintegrate in the very next moment. Therefore none of them can be an enduring person or a permanent personal identity that we can be assured exists.

The above is a condensed presentation; in meditation, contemplate the subtle impermanence of each of the thirty-six factors (sense faculty, object, consciousness, contact, feeling, and craving for each of the six senses), and investigate if it is suitable to be our self. When done in a thorough way, this meditation leads to the conclusion that everything from the eye sense faculty up to craving arising from mental contact—that is, all conditioned phenomena—are not self. Contemplating in this way is very powerful when we are stuck in the thought "I am my suffering" or "I am my anger."

A true self would have to be permanent, unchanging, and not affected by any other factors or conditions. However, each factor from the eye sense faculty up to the mental consciousness is impermanent and momentary. Therefore none of them is suitable to be such a self.

In the Pāli commentaries, this understanding is expressed by saying that the meditator now perceives the aggregates qualified by the characteristic of not-self—that is, of not being a self, of being selfless. (The noun "selflessness" appears infrequently in translations of Pāli writings; the adjective "not-self" or "selfless" is used instead.) With insight the meditator perceives the five aggregates qualified by the characteristic of not-self. This is perceived at deeper and deeper levels until insight reaches its peak and crosses over to the unconditioned, nirvāṇa.

In this way the Buddha negates all of the above—from the eye sense faculty up to the mental consciousness—as not being a self (MN 148:16–27):

> Now monastics, this is the way leading to the origination of [a personal] identity. One regards the eye thus: "This is mine, this I am, this is my self." One regards forms . . . visual consciousness, eye contact, feeling, craving thus: "This is mine, this I am, this is my self" (. . . and so on for each sense faculty, sense object, consciousness, sense contact, feeling, and craving).
>
> Now monastics, this is the way leading to the cessation of [a personal] identity. One regards the eye thus: "This is not mine, this I am not, this is not my self." One regards forms . . . visual consciousness, eye contact, feeling, craving thus: "This is not mine, this I am not, this is not my self" (. . . and so on through

each sense faculty, sense object, consciousness, sense contact, feeling, and craving).

The three distorted ways of viewing the aggregates—"This is mine, this I am, this is my self"—are produced respectively by craving, conceit, and wrong views. That is, craving sees the aggregates as mine,[51] conceit gives rise to grasping "I am," and wrong views hold the aggregates to be my self. Regarding the aggregates as I and mine leads to rebirth, and thus to a renewed existence of the five aggregates. Ending the notions of I and mine ends the process of rebirth, and thus no more regeneration of the five aggregates.

Nothing can be identified as self, either within the five aggregates or apart from them. The Buddha refutes the existence of an immutable self or soul that exists separate from the aggregates. He also refutes any of the aggregates individually or collectively being a self. With great compassion, he teaches us how to free ourselves from ignorance and the view of self and to attain the state beyond sorrow, nirvāṇa.

Labels, Concepts, and Conventions

In several sūtras, the Buddha explains that language can be used wisely by those who have eliminated grasping at a self. The realization of selflessness does not destroy conventional discourse or the ability to communicate with others through the use of language, and conventional discourse does not necessitate grasping a self. Words, labels, expressions, and concepts are used by arhats who have eliminated all self-grasping. In the *Sutta to Samiddhi*, the Buddha says (SN 1:20):

> Those who go by names, who go by concepts,
> making their abode in names and concepts,
> failing to discern the naming-process,
> these are subject to the reign of death.

The commentary explains that what goes by names and concepts is the aggregates. When ordinary people perceive the aggregates, their minds are influenced by believing them to be permanent, pleasurable, and to have or to be a self. These distorted conceptions stimulate the arising of afflictions and these people then "make their abode in names and concepts"—that is, they generate a multitude of afflictions in relation to the aggregates.

The *Itivuttaka* commentary explains the same verse, saying that beings who make their abode in names and concepts apprehend the aggregates as I or mine, or when the aggregates are not their own, they apprehend them as another person. Those who do this are subject to death and rebirth in saṃsāra. The *Sutta to Samiddhi* continues (SN 1:20):

> He who has discerned the naming-process
> does not suppose that one who names exists.
> No such case exists for him in truth,
> whereby one could say: "He is this or that."

Someone who understands the naming process understands the aggregates in terms of their individual characteristics; knows them as impermanent, unsatisfactory in nature, and selfless; and abandons craving for them by actualizing the supreme path. This arhat does not grasp what is designated as I, mine, or my self in dependence on the aggregates to be a real person. In fact, after leaving behind the aggregates and attaining nirvāṇa without remainder, this arhat cannot be said to be "this or that."

In the *Arahant Sutta*, the Buddha explains that an arhat uses words and concepts in accord with how things are done in the world, but without grasping them as self. Once a deva who resided in a forest heard some monks saying things such as "I eat," "I walk," "my bowl," and so forth. Thinking that they were arhats, the deva wondered how they could say "I" and "my," which, according to the deva's way of thinking, involves belief in a self—in I and mine. The Buddha answers the deva's query (SN 1:25):

> If a monastic is an arahant
> consummate, with pollutants destroyed,
> one who bears his final body,
> he might still say, "I speak,"
> and he might say, "They speak to me."
> Skillful, knowing the world's parlance,
> he uses such terms as mere expressions.

Someone who is an arhat and has his last saṃsāric body still uses conventional language that corresponds to how ordinary beings speak. He or she does so without grasping a real I, mine, or my self. The commentary says (SN 360n49):

> Although arahants have abandoned talk that implies belief in a self, they do not violate conventional discourse saying, "The aggregates eat, the aggregates sit, the aggregates' bowl, the aggregates' robe"; for no one would understand them.

Liberated beings still use ordinary words and worldly conventions to communicate with others. If they referred to their robe as "the aggregates' robe," people would think this to be very odd because no one speaks in that way.

The deva has a further doubt, wondering if arhats use words such as "I," "mine," and "my self" not because they hold the view of a personal identity but because they are subject to the conceit "I am." To this the Buddha replies (SN 1:25):

> No knots exist for one with conceit abandoned;
> for him all knots of conceit are consumed.
> Though the wise one has transcended the conceived,
> he still might say, "I speak,"
> he might say too, "They speak to me."
> Skillful, knowing the world's parlance,
> he uses such terms as mere expressions.

Arhats are free from the conceit "I am" and are beyond conceiving sparked by craving, views, and conceit. Nevertheless, they still speak in a way that others will understand. If they didn't, how could they teach the Dharma?

Along the same line, in the *States of Consciousness Sutta* (*Poṭṭhapāda Sutta*), when asked about the fabricated selves of beings in the desire realm, the form realm, and the formless realm, the Buddha said (DN 9:53):

> These are worldly expressions, worldly terms, worldly conventions, worldly concepts that the Tathāgata uses without grasping them.

Names and concepts can be used in two ways: someone who has ignorance and the view of a personal identity uses words and concepts believing that there is a true object to which they refer—there is a self that exists in these phenomena. On the other hand, people who are free from ignorance and the view of a personal identity do not grasp at true referents of words and concepts. They use them merely as conventions to convey a meaning, without grasping a self in the objects to which they refer.

If you are familiar with the Madhyamaka viewpoint, read the above verses again, this time from the perspective of the meaning of selflessness expressed in the Perfection of Wisdom sūtras.

The Self as a Convention

The topic of what carries karmic potentials from one life to the next has been a subject of concern for Buddhists from early on. The process of rebirth was not explained in detail in the Nikāyas—the collections of early sūtras—so each Abhidharma school took it up as a subject to explain. The Pāli Abhidharma explains it one way, the Sarvāstivāda—a prominent Abhidharma school that has strongly influenced Buddhism in Tibet—explains it in another. The Yogācāra school, which appeared around the fourth century, has yet another theory and introduces the idea of a foundation consciousness—a consciousness in addition to the six consciousnesses asserted by the early Abhidharma schools and the early Mahāyāna teachings. Karmic seeds and the latencies of afflictions and so forth are stored in the foundation consciousness, which carries them from one life to the next.

According to the Pāli tradition, it is not necessary to posit a findable self to explain how rebirth occurs and how karma continues to the next life. Rebirth is the natural result of the continuity of a consciousness with defilements. Even in this life, each moment of mind is connected to the moments before and after it because they are members of the same causal continuity. Each moment of consciousness receives all the stored up experiences that occurred previously—memories, habits, karmic potentials, and so forth. A person is nominally identified because there is a causal continuity of all these factors. At death the stream of consciousness continues on, assuming the support of a new physical body. A findable self is not needed for this impersonal process to occur.

There is no persisting individual consciousness that goes from one life to another as one and the same entity. Nevertheless, an ever-changing consciousness connects one life to another; consciousness is both conditioned by other factors and conditions other things. In the *Great Discourse on Causation*, the Buddha states that consciousness is the condition for name and form,[52] a process that begins with conception in the womb in the case of a human birth. If consciousness did not take place in the womb, name and form would not grow there. This rebirth consciousness has its own conditions and is dependent on other factors and thus lacks independent existence. Although consciousness goes from one life to the next, it continually changes, always arising and passing away, not remaining the same in the next moment. Although we say "This consciousness is reborn," there is nothing fixed to point to. Although the continuity of consciousness in the last moment of one life and the first moment of the next is the same continuity, consciousness itself has changed. In the *Serene Faith Sutta* (*Sampasādanīya Sutta*, DN 28:7), the Buddha speaks of the mindstream (*cittasaṃtāna,* P. *cittasaṃtāna*) as "the unbroken stream of consciousness that is established both in this world and in the next." The mindstream is present in worldings and in learners (those who have attained one of the first three paths), but it is not a self.

Pāli commentaries do not explain karma as leaving seeds that have a location and must be transmitted from one life to the next. Although Pāli sūtras and commentaries occasionally use the metaphor of seeds to illustrate karma, this metaphorical usage is not a philosophical position. The prevailing view is that when an action (karma) is done, the karma establishes a potential to bring forth its fruits when suitable conditions come together. However, the karma does not subsist somewhere. For example, the notes of a melody do not exist somewhere; they are not in a musical instrument such as a lute and are not brought forth when the musician plays the lute. Rather, depending on the lute, the breath or air, and the musician, the melody arises. Similarly, once performed, an action establishes a potential to bring forth results, but the action does not possess an enduring existence and is not located somewhere.

In *The Path of Purification*, Buddhaghosa says (Vism 17:170):

> When a fruit arises in a single continuity, it is neither another's nor from other (karma) because absolute identity and absolute otherness are excluded there.

"Absolute identity" means a single person—in whom each moment is identical to the previous and future moments—that persists from the time of creating the karma to the time of experiencing the result. There is no person who is both the agent of the action and the experiencer of the result. "Absolute otherness" means that one person does the action and a totally different, unrelated person experiences the result. This explanation mirrors the Prāsaṅgika explanation, which says that the person who creates the action is neither inherently one and the same as the person who experiences the result nor totally unrelated and different from the person who experiences the result. Instead, there is a continuity of experience—a continuity of the person—that is continuously changing. Earlier moments in this continuum create the karma and later moments experience the result. This continuity of the person spans one life to the next so that each karma brings its results.

The I is a convention. When we say "I am walking," or when the Buddha himself uses the word "I"—for example, saying "I was so-and-so in a previous life"—we are using conventional expressions. The I is imputed by conception. At the time of death, the form aggregate is left behind, but the continuum of mental aggregates—of momentary mental events—continues uninterruptedly from one life to the next. This is called the "mental continuum" (P. *citta-santāna*). When thinking of ourselves in a past or future life, we refer to earlier or later experiences within the same mental continuum. But there is not a real self that goes from one life to the next.

The fact that there is no identifiable self does not mean that we must divest ourselves of all conventional usage of words. Language and concepts about the self may be used in a skillful way without grasping them to be the same as the objects to which they refer. Doing so does not involve clinging to a view or to a self. The Buddha himself uses words in this conventional way. He said, "Self is the protector of self," meaning that we are responsible for the state of our mind, our actions, and thus the experiences they bring. The Buddha similarly encourages us, "You must purify yourself. You must train yourself," using the same Pāli word, *atta* or "self," that is used when he refutes an independent self. He speaks of "the acquiring of self" when referring to being reborn in another existence (see above quotation, DN 9:53).

There is no findable self, and the self is a convention. When challenged by Māra, who questions her about the origin of a being, Bhikṣuṇī Vajirā says (SN 5:10.553–54): "When the aggregates exist, there is the convention 'a being.'" The convention "self" refers to a conditioned, composite situation that lacks any lasting substance. There is no immutable basic substance that is a person. The physical and mental aggregates arise and cease in each moment, and this ever-changing process presents an illusion of self, an appearance of a person that in fact is nothing but the interdependent interplay of the aggregates.

Candrakīrti cites a corresponding passage from a Sanskrit sūtra in his *Autocommentary on the Supplement*. Tsongkhapa also quotes it in the insight section of his *Medium Exposition of the Stages of the Path* (FEW 63):

> [This mind grasping an inherently existent] self is a devilish mind.
> You are under the influence of Māra by viewing this.
> These compositional aggregates are empty.
> There is no sentient being [or self].
>
> Just as a chariot is spoken of
> in dependence on a collection of parts,
> so conventionally a sentient being
> [is spoken of] in dependence on the aggregates.

The mind apprehending and grasping an inherently existent self is a devilish mind that binds us in saṃsāra. Māra is the embodiment of self-grasping ignorance, the source of all afflictions that create the polluted karma that embroils us in duḥkha. The impermanent, conditioned aggregates are the basis of designation of the conventionally existent I. The view of a personal identity views the mere I and grasps it to exist autonomously, under its own power, independent of all other factors. Although the I is designated in dependence on the five aggregates, neither the aggregates individually nor the collection of aggregates is a sentient being, an I, self, or person. The I is merely a convention, a designation. A self that is able to set itself up does not exist either ultimately or conventionally.

Just as a chariot and a car are spoken about and designated in dependence on the collection of their parts—the wheels, axles, seats, and so forth—so too a person is designated and spoken of in dependence on the aggregates.

Aside from an important difference, the two verses have the same basic meaning in both Pāli and Sanskrit. The principal divergence is that the Sanskrit verses emphasize that a chariot and a sentient being are merely designated *in dependence on* their parts. They are neither one of their parts nor the collection of the parts. They cannot be found either in the parts or completely separate from them. They exist by mere name.

Similarly, according to the Prāsaṅgikas, the view of a personal identity does not grasp the aggregates as an inherently existent I. It observes the merely designated I and grasps it to be inherently existent. Self-grasping of phenomena observes the aggregates and grasps them as inherently existent. Those aspiring for liberation and full awakening must refute both the self of persons (an inherently existent I) and the self of phenomena (inherently existent aggregates) and realize the selflessness of persons and the selflessness of the phenomena, which includes the aggregates.

13 The Pāli Tradition: Eliminating Defilements

THE PĀLI SŪTRAS describe the gradual elimination of defilements from the mind and the attainment of realizations in multiple ways, but all of them come to the same point. A few of these will be discussed in this chapter.

The Buddha often talks about a person who is "an untaught ordinary person who has no regard for ariyas and is unskilled and undisciplined in their Dhamma, who has no regard for true people and is unskilled and undisciplined in their Dhamma." This is an ordinary person who knows nothing about the Buddhadharma, who has no idea of or regard for beings who are spiritually advanced, and who knows very little about how to work with their mind to subdue defilements.

The Buddha contrasts this person with "a well-taught ariya disciple who has regard for ariyas and is skilled and disciplined in their Dhamma, who has regard for true people and is skilled and disciplined in their Dhamma." How do we go from being an untaught ordinary person to being an ariya disciple?

The Four Foundations

The *Discourse on the Exposition of the Elements* builds on the meditation on the elements above and presents it within the context of four foundations: wisdom, truth, relinquishment, and peace. The sūtra sets this out (MN 140.7):

> . . . this person consists of six elements, six sources of contact, and eighteen topics of analysis by the mind, and he has four

> foundations. The tides of conceiving do not sweep over one who stands on these [foundations], and when the tides of conceiving no longer sweep over him, he is called a sage at peace. One should not neglect wisdom, should preserve truth, should cultivate relinquishment, and should train for peace. This is the summary of the exposition of the six elements.

A person is constituted by the *six elements*—earth, water, fire, air, space, and consciousness. As a group, these encompass the same field as the five aggregates, but with a different emphasis. The first five elements are included in the form aggregate.[53] The consciousness element goes with the aggregate of consciousness, although the consciousness element implies the presence of the other mental aggregates of feeling, discrimination, and miscellaneous factors. Whereas the schema of the six elements highlights the body as a composite phenomenon, the schema of the five aggregates emphasizes the mind as composed of many aspects.

The *six sources of contact* mentioned in the sūtra are the eye source and so on, up to the mental source, which is the mind as a source for contact.

Analysis by the mind (P. *manopavicāra*) involves investigation (*vitarka, vitakka*) and analysis (*vicāra*) of the object. The *eighteen topics of analysis by the mind* referred to in the sūtra derive from the six objects that are cognized by the six sources—form seen by the eye, sound heard by the ear, odor smelled by the nose, flavor tasted by the tongue, tactile sensation felt by the body, and mental phenomena cognized by the mind. Each of these six objects can produce three mental reactions—the feelings of happiness, displeasure, and equanimity—these are the eighteen topics of analysis of the mind.

The Buddha briefly speaks about the six sources of contact and the eighteen topics of analysis by the mind. By understanding these, as well as the six elements, a meditator will turn away from them and turn toward nirvāṇa with the aspiration to attain arhatship.

The four foundations are important elements for success on the path. These four are:

- From the outset, do not neglect the *wisdom* that arises from concentration and insight, cultivate it as you practice, and then employ it to penetrate nirvāṇa and gain the wisdom that is the arhats' knowledge of the destruction of all duḥkha.

- Initially, *truth* is preserved by speaking truthfully with the aim of realizing the ultimate truth, nirvāṇa.
- From the start, put energy into letting go of whatever affliction occurs in your mind. By cultivating *relinquishment* of the different levels of defilements on the path, at arhatship you will accomplish the relinquishment of all defilements.
- From the beginning, train the mind to become gradually more *peaceful*. This process culminates with an arhat's pacification of all defilements. At that time, the mind dwells in the peace of nirvāṇa.

Begin to familiarize yourselves with these four qualities from the start of your practice of serenity and insight and then continue to cultivate them on the path, bringing them to fulfillment with the attainment of arhatship. While the full-fledged or supreme foundations are possessed by arhats, to attain them you have to cultivate them now. By not neglecting wisdom and treasuring truth, you will preserve the realization of nirvāṇa in your mind. Due to that realization, all defilements will be relinquished from the root, and the ultimate peace of nirvāṇa will be attained.

In the *Discourse on the Exposition of the Elements*, the Buddha speaks to Pukkusāti, a meditator who, according to the commentary, has attained the fourth dhyāna. The mind of the fourth dhyāna is purified in that it is temporarily free from the five hindrances, which have been suppressed by the power of concentration. It is bright because, like a clean mirror, it reflects or knows its object clearly. The Buddha explains to Pukkusāti how to investigate and analyze feelings after emerging from the fourth dhyāna. Having been calmed and refreshed in the fourth dhyāna, the mind emerging from it is subtle and clear and is easily used for deep examination. That purified and bright mind now cognizes and then understands feeling (MN 140:19):

> What does one cognize with that consciousness? One cognizes, "[This is] pleasant," one cognizes, "[This is] painful," one cognizes, "[This is] neutral." In dependence on a contact to be felt as pleasant, there arises a pleasant feeling. When one feels a pleasant feeling, one understands, "I feel a pleasant feeling." One

> understands, "With the cessation of that same contact to be felt as pleasant, its corresponding feeling—the pleasant feeling that arose in dependence on that contact to be felt as pleasant—ceases and subsides."

The Buddha then continues speaking in the same way about painful and neutral feelings. Here he shows how the consciousness element is used to develop insight, with feeling as the object of that insight. The aim is to see the conditioned nature of feeling with insight. The Buddha begins by discussing cognizing the three feelings—pleasant, painful, and neutral. Here "cognize" means to experience that feeling and to know what feeling is being experienced.

Then, referring in particular to a pleasant feeling, he explains that it arises in dependence on a contact to be felt as pleasant. Contact is the coming together of the object and the consciousness by means of the sense source (sense faculty). Contact itself doesn't experience the object as pleasant. However, because that contact will give rise to a pleasant feeling, it is called "contact to be felt as pleasant." Due to this contact, a pleasant feeling arises. In this way, the pleasant feeling arises dependently. Practitioners then understand, "I feel a pleasant feeling." That is, practitioners don't simply cognize the pleasant feeling, they understand that it arose dependent on its corresponding contact. Then they understand that with the cessation of that contact to be felt as pleasant, the pleasant feeling also ceases. In this way, with wisdom practitioners go from knowing the feeling they are experiencing to understanding how it arises and ceases in dependence on its corresponding contact.

When mindfulness on feelings has been established, practitioners first train to know or cognize each feeling clearly and to be able to distinguish it from other feelings. Then they extend that mindfulness to see how that feeling arises; it is here that wisdom and insight are cultivated. They do not simply identify "This is a pleasant feeling" but investigate and analyze where that feeling came from and see that it arose due to a particular kind of contact. Because that feeling is dependent on causes and conditions, it is impermanent. Just as the contact to be felt as pleasant changes in every moment, the pleasant feeling, too, arises and passes away in every moment.

That feeling does not stand on its own; it exists simply because the causes and conditions for it exist.

The Buddha then says that unpleasant feelings arise due to contact to be felt as painful and cease when that contact ceases. Similarly, neutral feelings arise from contact to be felt as neutral and cease due to the cessation of that specific contact. It is like the relation between an electric current, an electric heater, and the heat that flows out to warm the room. When the switch is turned on and the electric current runs in the heater, heat radiates into the room. When the electric current ceases, the heat stops. In such a way, the arising of pleasant, painful, and neutral feelings is examined and understood.

Pukkusāti is strongly attached to the peace and equanimity of the fourth dhyāna. For this reason, after describing this insight meditation on the feelings, the Buddha also acknowledges that Pukkusāti could direct the equanimity of the fourth dhyāna to attaining the base of infinite consciousness, the base of infinite space, the base of nothingness, and the base of neither-discrimination-nor-nondiscrimination, which are meditative absorptions in the formless realm. According to which one of these he attains, after passing away from this life, he could dwell in that level of the formless realm for 20,000 eons, 40,000 eons, 60,000 eons, or 84,000 eons, respectively. If he chose to, Pukkusāti could leave aside the analytical insight meditation on the conditionality of feelings and actualize the four formless absorptions, where his equanimity "supported by that base, clinging to it, would remain for a very long time" in these marvelous meditative absorptions that are so much more peaceful than the fourth dhyāna he has already attained.

By explaining these four peaceful worldly absorptions that he could attain, the Buddha inspired Pukkusāti's confidence and interest. A skillful teacher, the Buddha also reminds him that these four meditative absorptions are conditioned and subject to clinging. Just as the pleasant, unpleasant, and neutral conditions are dependent, conditioned, arising after their corresponding condition arises and ceasing after their corresponding condition ceases, so too do these worldly meditative absorptions arise and cease depending on their conditions. Just as feelings are unreliable, unsatisfactory, and bound to saṃsāra, so too are these worldly meditative absorptions. Although such a meditator does not cling to existence in the desire realm or the form realm, he does cling to existence in the formless realm and is thus not free from the pollutants and fetters binding him to saṃsāra.

No matter how sublime these states of meditation are, danger lurks in them. From the perspective of a human being, 20,000 eons in sublime peaceful meditation seems almost like eternity, let alone the possibility of dwelling in an even higher state for 84,000 eons. The Buddha accomplished these levels of meditative absorption under the guidance of his first two teachers, after he renounced the householder's life and left the palace. But these states cannot be trusted because they are conditioned and transient. Once the karma for rebirth in one of the formless realms is exhausted, an ordinary person who lacks the wisdom realizing not-self passes away from that sublime state and may be born in one of the three unfortunate realms in the next life. Lofty as they are, these meditative absorptions are not a reliable refuge from duḥkha; in fact they are simply a temporary respite from the duḥkha of pain and the duḥkha of change—the meditator is still afflicted by the pervasive duḥkha of conditioning and will continue to cycle in saṃsāra.

Seeing the danger of directing his energy to attain the formless absorptions, a wise person will develop insight understanding that these meditative attainments are dependent, unsatisfactory, and not-self. Instead of delighting in the purified and bright equanimity of meditative attainments with subtle clinging, he will direct his wisdom to examine this state and ascertain that it is marked by impermanence, unsatisfactoriness, and not-self. This understanding will bring about the dismantling of the conditioning process that perpetuates saṃsāra from one life to the next. To avoid the danger of getting stuck in the formless realm, the Buddha instructs Pukkusāti (MN 140.22):

> . . . [not to] form any condition or generate any intention tending toward either existence or nonexistence. Since he does not form any condition or generate any intention tending toward either existence or nonexistence, he does not cling to anything in this world. When he does not cling, he is not agitated. When he is not agitated, he inwardly attains nibbāna. He understands thus: "Birth is destroyed, the holy life has been lived, what had

> to be done has been done, there is no more coming to any state of being."

Here "tending toward existence" means longing for the continued rebirth in saṃsāra of a self assumed to be real and everlasting. "Tending toward nonexistence" is longing for the total cessation of all existence whatsoever. The longing found in the wrong views of existence (absolutism) or nonexistence (nihilism) keeps us bound to saṃsāra. The absolutist view seeks the eternal existence of a real self, which does not exist; the nihilist view seeks total annihilation, which is impossible.

Most people tend toward clinging to existence. Frightened that the self will totally cease at death, they cling to the idea of a real self that will continue in the future. Meditators who have attained the formless absorptions and beings born in the formless realm are also impeded by this clinging for existence. Grasping to a real self, they are attached to existence in these meditative absorptions, and liberation eludes them.

By "not forming any condition," a person has no interest or intention for either future rebirths or for annihilation and thus does not create any further conditions that would keep him trapped in saṃsāra. Examining the process of arising and passing away, he understands that things arise through conditions and cease through the cessation of those conditions. Relinquishing such detrimental and fruitless longing for whatever is marked by the three characteristics, he does not cling to anything in this saṃsāric world. When this clinging ceases, so does agitation—the craving and restlessness that are involved in saṃsāra. Free from craving, he attains nirvāṇa, the cessation of all pollutants.

While an arhat is still alive, her nirvāṇa is said to be "nirvāṇa with remainder"—that is, her mind is free from defilements but she still has the remainder of her body, which is a true duḥkha because it was born from ignorance. She continues to experience pleasant, painful, and neutral feelings because previously created karma continues to ripen. However, she does not react with desire for pleasant feelings, aversion for painful ones, or ignorant apathy toward neutral feelings. Realizing that feelings are impermanent, she does not hold to them or delight in them.

Because of not having neglected wisdom—the first of the four foundations—she possesses the *supreme foundation of wisdom*, the knowledge of the destruction of all duḥkha. She also possesses the *supreme foundation of truth*. The Buddha says (MN 140.26):

> Her liberation, being founded on truth, is unshakable. For that is false which has a deceptive nature, and that is true which has a nondeceptive nature—nibbāna. . . . For this is the supreme ariya truth, namely, nibbāna, which has a nondeceptive nature.

Her liberation is unshakable because it is founded on truth—nirvāṇa, which is nondeceptive. Anything that gives rise to deception is false, but that which has a completely nondeceptive nature is nirvāṇa. Nirvāṇa is both the object of her realization and the cessation of duḥkha and its origins that this realization has brought about. Her liberation is not a temporary suppression of defilements due to entering samādhi. It is a firm liberation gained through realizing the truth, nirvāṇa.

When oppressed by ignorance, she had many attachments—many types of attachment and many things that she was attached to. Previously she had many acquisitions—the five aggregates mistakenly identified as mine, I, and my self, as well as defilements, formative actions or karma, and the five objects of sensual pleasure. Now that all craving has been laid down, she is free to relinquish all of these and to set down the load of the five aggregates that are the basis of birth, aging, and death. In this way, she is firmly placed on the *supreme foundation of relinquishment*.

Having pacified covetousness, greed, and attachment, malice, hatred, and anger, and ignorance and confusion, so that they can no longer arise in her mind, she has the *supreme foundation of peace*. This peace is also free from the "tides of conceiving," as the Buddha says (MN 140.30):

> The tides of conceiving do not sweep over one who stands upon these [foundations], and when the tides of conceiving no longer sweep over him, he is called a sage at peace.

The "tides of conceiving" (P. *maññussava*) is an evocative phrase—all of us know the feeling of being overwhelmed by the crashing waves of worries, fears, desires, and confusion. The mind churns out opinions and predictions; it proliferates with views and false imaginings. One such imagining is "I am this," which is based on the notion that there is a substantial I at the center of our being, something that is really I. Based on this, we seek an identity for that self, leading to imagining "I am this." "This" could be any of the aggregates that we take to be a real self, and on a coarser level, it is any of the innumerable identities we create for ourselves during our life—identities based on race, nationality, religion, profession, socioeconomic class, gender, and so forth.

Other tides of conceiving include "I shall be," which holds to an everlasting I that will continue to exist throughout all our rebirths, and "I shall not be," which is the view of annihilation, thinking the self will cease completely at death. "I shall possess form" and "I shall be formless" are more absolutist views, as are "I shall be percipient," "I shall be nonpercipient," and "I shall be neither-percipient-nor-nonpercipient." All these tides of conceiving originate in the three roots of conceiving: craving, conceit, and (wrong) views, which also lie behind grasping "This is mine, this I am, this is my self." This overabundance of distorted conceptions is like a disease, a tumor, a piece of shrapnel stuck deep inside that brings pain whichever way we move. An arhat has ceased all of these.

At some point in the aging process, an arhat "feels a feeling terminating with life" and understands "On the dissolution of the body, with the ending of life, all that is felt, not being delighted in, will become cool right here." That is, she knows that when this body dies, all feeling will also cease. Since feelings originating from ignorance are a disturbance, their cessation is seen as cooling and refreshing. Regarding what happens to an arhat at the time of death, the Buddha says (MN 140.24):

> ... just as an oil lamp burns in dependence on oil and a wick, and when the oil and wick are used up, if it does not get any more fuel, it is extinguished from lack of fuel.

The five aggregates subject to clinging are given up at death and the arhat attains nirvāṇa without remainder. There is no longer the residue of the aggregates born from ignorance and craving, and there is nothing present that could cause her to be born again. Without the craving for existence, rebirth in saṃsāra can no longer occur.

The sūtras are not clear on what specifically happens when an arhat dies.

After the death of a monk who had become an arhat just before he died, the Buddha commented (SN 22:87), "with consciousness unestablished, the clansman Vakkali has attained final nibbāna."

Freedom from Conceiving

Gaining a clear realization of nirvāṇa necessitates having path wisdom—supramundane wisdom that is strong enough to pierce through the obscurations of the fetters. The precursor of path wisdom is insight wisdom, a mundane wisdom that sees the three characteristics of impermanence, duḥkha, and selflessness.

In the *Discourse on the Root of All Things* (*Mūlapariyāya Sutta*, MN 1), the Buddha discusses the root cause of all phenomena included in the collection of five aggregates that makes up our individual identity. Here he pinpoints conceiving (P. *maññanā*)—the distorted imaginings we project on things—as the root of the continuous creation of rebirths in saṃsāra. While many conceptions and thoughts are valid and useful on the path, here "conceiving" or "conceptualization" refers to false notions, assumptions, and opinions created by our mind. These are so ingrained that we usually don't recognize them or, if we do, we simply assume them to be true and accurate, never stopping to question them. Conceptualization ascribes properties or relations to an object that the object does not have and misunderstands the object. This is not creative imagination that leads to inventions or artistic endeavors; it is distorted thinking that we believe to be true.

Conceptualization is very similar to proliferations or elaborations.[54] Proliferations and conceptualizations elaborate on the object, imputing false qualities or attributes to it. These false ideas do not come from the nature of the object but from our own subjective mental meanderings. Three defilements—craving, conceit, and afflictive views—are particularly involved with conceptualization, and through them everything we come into contact with is seen in terms of I, me, my, mine, and my self. Here is how these three defilements collude with conceptualization.

1. *Craving* gives rise to deluded conceptualizations of mine. Having contacted things that appear attractive to us, we want to possess them and make them mine. Things acquire significance for me because they are

potential possessions or things that I already own and do not want to part from. Conceptualizations due to craving proliferate when we think about things that are mine or could be mine, things that I want to be mine or no longer want to be mine.

2. *Conceit* gives rise to conceptualizations about I. The fundamental conceit is the thought "I am"—I am a self-existent person. Based on this, we compare ourselves to others and generate the proliferations "I am better than him. I am as good as her. I am worse than him." Conceit juxtaposes a "real" I with others and then generates conceptualizations of who we are in relation to them. Conceit then expands to compare our possessions, qualities, lives, opportunities, and even level of Dharma practice with those of others. These conceptualizations are all inventions of the afflictive mind; what those thoughts construct is not real.
3. *Afflictive views* are conceptualizations about our self. What is this self? Did the self have a beginning? How do I exist? What or who am I? Is the I the same as the body? Does it continue eternally after death or does it totally cease with the death of the body? Is it influenced by karma? Can it attain nirvāṇa? Reflecting on the identity of the I, we project some kind of substantial self, which leads to the conception "I am this and I am that." There are subtle views of what the I is that we are not even aware of and do not articulate to others, and there are coarser views of self through which we create contorted philosophies and psychological theories.

By using the process of conceiving as the basis, the sūtra explains the different ways in which four types of people relate to conceiving:

1. An untaught ordinary person is someone who lacks knowledge and practical experience of the Dharma and who has little or no regard for holy beings and their teachings. Such a person is often overwhelmed by distorted conceptualizations.
2. A trainee is a disciple in higher training who has had the initial clear realization of nirvāṇa but has not completed the path to arhatship.
3. An arhat is someone who has completed the training and is liberated from saṃsāra.

4. A tathāgata is a fully awakened buddha.

Interestingly, the Buddha did not include a specific category for people like most of us. Although we are not untaught people who lack faith and respect, we are not trainees who have had a direct realization of nirvāṇa either. We are somewhere in the middle, having studied the Buddha's teachings and put them into practice as best as we can. The Buddha did not make a category for people of our level because the advice he gave to trainees applies to us and because being immersed in distorted conceptualization also applies to us. However, in other contexts, the Buddhist texts spoke of "good-minded ordinary beings" (P. *kalyāṇa puthujjana*)—a monastic or lay follower who is of good character, has learned and practiced the Dharma, but has not yet had the profound meditative experiences of an ārya.

The Buddha speaks of how these four classes of people relate to twenty-four objects that are called the "bases of conceiving." The full explanation of conceptualization will be given with the first object—the earth element. We should apply this to the other objects that are briefly described as bases for conceiving. The Buddha begins with how an untaught ordinary person relates to the earth element (MN 1:3):

> ... [he] perceives[55] earth as earth. Having perceived earth as earth, he conceives [himself as] earth, he conceives [himself] in earth, he conceives [himself apart] from earth, he conceives earth to be mine, he delights in earth. Why is that? Because he has not fully understood it, I say.

This passage requires a lot of explanation in order to unpack its meaning, which fortunately the Pāli commentary and subcommentary supply. The earth element can be either internal—part of the five aggregates that constitute our own person—or external—the earth element in other living beings or in the environment. According to the commentary, it can also include the earth kasiṇa and things such as the gross body in which the earth element is dominant.

[An untaught ordinary person] perceives earth as earth. While the language "perceiving earth as earth" superficially gives the impression that the perception is accurate, that is not the case. The mind of a person who

does not know the Dharma and has no wish to practice or train his mind is imbued with ignorance and underlying tendencies toward all the other defilements. When an object—let's take the body as an example of the earth element—connects with his consciousness via a sense faculty, that is contact. Through contact a perception of the body arises. This is the initial perception of the body. Rather than the person proceeding to understand and correctly apprehend the nature of the body, due to ignorance he perceives the body in a distorted manner based on distorted conceptualization (inappropriate attention). That is, initially there is the simple act of perceiving that registers the body. Following this, due to distorted conceptualization, a subtle type of conceiving introduces some distortion. It grasps the body in a way opposite to how it actually is, seeing it as being a unitary whole, a self-existent substantial entity, when in fact the body is constituted of a multiplicity of conditioned, impermanent factors that are continuously arising and passing away. At this stage, the body is perceived as permanent, pleasurable, beautiful, and as a self, although the actual reality is that the body is impermanent, unsatisfactory in nature, foul, and lacks a self.

These initial perceptions occur very quickly. They are extremely brief mind-moments of cognition that arise and pass away and perceive an object that is also changing in each moment. Because our mind is obscured, we cannot attend to everything as it arises and passes away. Instead, all these events are fused together, and we perceive a world populated by solid, substantial people and things. In this way, the four distorted conceptions (*viparyāsa*, *vipallāsa*)—seeing what is impermanent as permanent, what is unsatisfactory as pleasurable, what is foul as attractive, and what is not a self as self—arise early on in the cognitive process. They are like assumptions that have never been questioned and on which we build the rest of our notions about ourselves, other people, and the world around us.

This process is what is meant by "he perceives the earth as earth." At this stage, perception accords with the distorted conceptualizations, but because perception of the body is stronger than conceptualization at this point, it is still called "perceiving the body."

Having perceived earth as earth indicates that based on this distorted perception, we are now primed to conceive the body through the proliferations of craving, conceit, and views.

He conceives [himself as] earth indicates conceiving the earth in relation to our own continuum and others' continuums. There is the conception of ourselves as a real entity who is a subject in relation to an independent object, in this case the earth. Everything is self-referenced, attaining importance dependent on how we conceive of it relating to ourselves—to I, me, my, mine, and my self. Due to craving, conceit, and views, we now conceptualize the relationship of the self and the body: "I am the body," "the body is mine," "another (thing or person) is the body," "the body belongs to another."

Conceiving "I am the body" or "another thing or person is the body" is conceptualization of views and conceptualization of conceit, because they are involved with identifying either our self or another's self in relation to the body. Thinking "I am my body," we could then conceive, "Death is terrifying because when the body ceases, I will cease," or "I can't bear to think of my loved one dying because he will cease to exist."

Conceiving "this body is mine" or "that body belongs to another" is conceptualization of craving, because craving is involved with possession—this is mine or it belongs to someone else. This is also conceptualization of conceit, because having made the body mine, we then proceed to compare it with others' bodies, thinking "mine is better than theirs," "mine is just as good as theirs," or "mine is inferior to theirs."

With conceptualizations of conceit we might think "I am this race, I am this gender, I am this age, I am from this socioeconomic class," and then, comparing ourselves to others, believe, "Therefore I am superior (or inferior) to people of other races. I am superior (or inferior) with respect to people in other socioeconomic classes. I am superior (or inferior) to people who are older (or younger)." Sentient beings have suffered immensely throughout history due to such conceptualizations.

Conceptualization of views is conceiving the body in a way that involves positing a real self. One view is that the self is a permanent, everlasting self that will always endure, no matter what happens to the body or mind. Another view is of a self that is temporary—it exists for a short time while the body is alive and then ceases totally, having no continuity whatsoever.

Conceptualizations of craving will arouse desire for other things that represent the earth element—for example, our hair. The mind proliferates with the thoughts "I like my hair," "I want to have hair like hers," "In my future life, I want to have the perfect kind of hair that everyone will admire," and on and on. Conceptualizations of conceit think "The color of my hair is nicer than his" and "Someone who criticizes my hair is criticizing me." Conceptualization of views gives rise to notions such as "My hair expresses my individuality" and "My hair expresses my true nature."

Such conceptualizations float through our mind most of the day. We may occasionally notice some of them but be oblivious to others, even though they influence our actions and moods. Here the example is the body as an illustration of the earth element, but as we will see when we look at the other twenty-three bases for conceiving, the mind continually proliferates with distorted notions about almost everything. These notions are problematic because they are not based on reality, and when we generate motivations and act based on them, problems in this and future lives ensue. Furthermore, distorted proliferations are not characteristics of arhats; in fact these holy beings have seen them as harmful and dismantled them.

Meditators who have attained dhyāna through meditating on the earth kasiṇa can also generate conceptualizations. They may adhere to the object perceived in their meditation as their self (conceptualization of views), they may take that object as a sign of their superiority (conceptualization of conceit), or they may think "this is mine" (conceptualization of craving).

He conceives [himself in] earth indicates seeing ourselves as existing in the body. For example, with conceptualization of views we think there is a self or soul that exists in the body—an independent spirit, self, or soul that is our essence abides in the material body. Then, with conceptualization of craving, we yearn for the immortality of that imagined self, and with conceptualization of conceit, we think "My essence is wonderful and great."

He conceives [himself apart] from earth means seeing ourselves as separate from the body. With conceptualization of views we could think "The self is an emergent property of the body," "The self is a different entity from the body," or "The body dies but the self is immortal and continues on after the body's demise."

He conceives earth to be mine is closely associated with the conceptualization of craving. Craving takes possession of the object: "This is my body, it is strong," "This is my body, isn't it beautiful?" or "Death is terrifying because I don't want to separate from my body." Under the sway of such conceptualizations, we believe others should relate to us in a way comparable to the type of body we have.

He delights in earth shows that craving has entered the picture in full force. Although the above phrases in the sūtra have to do with conceptualizations, craving is an emotional reaction that has been nourished by these proliferations. When explaining the second truth, the Buddha identified craving as the true origin of duḥkha and described it by saying that craving is what delights in this and that; craving is what delights here and there. Because the mind delights in external sensual objects or even in internal objects of meditation, craving perpetuates rebirth in saṃsāra. As long as we continue to seek delight, pleasure, and enjoyment in objects of craving, the round of rebirth will keep going. Delight in the form of craving comes here as the culmination of this series of conceptualizations because craving is the most fundamental root of all of these conceptualizations.

In this context "delight" means craving, not happiness or pleasure as such. This distinction is important, because otherwise the mind will proliferate with other conceptualizations, such as "Buddhism says happiness is the root of the suffering in saṃsāra, so it is bad to be happy," "I am evil because I want to be happy," or "Pleasure is bad, so I should avoid it and deliberately inflict suffering on myself to free myself from craving." Such distorted conceptualizations provoke more conceptualizations in the form of guilt and shame. All of these proliferations are painful impediments to true Dharma practice.

Why is that? Because he has not fully understood it, I say. Having described this variety of proliferations and given us a sense of how entangled we are in them—even if we are not an untaught person—the Buddha asks, "Why does an ordinary person conceive things in this deluded way? Why does he go on delighting in this way?" The reason is that he has not fully understood.

The Buddha spoke of an activity in relation to each of the four truths; in the case of true duḥkha, it is "The truth of duḥkha is to be fully understood." It is precisely the lack of understanding of the truth of duḥkha that acts as the gestation ground of conceptualizations. Due to ignorance and the lack of full understanding, when an untaught person contacts an object, that perception triggers the afflictive cognitive process of conceptualizations. Instead of moving from perception to a clear understanding of the object, perception instigates distorted perception: perceiving the body as the body, followed by conceiving himself as the body, conceiving himself in the body, conceiving himself as apart from the body, and conceiving the body as mine, followed by the emotional response of delighting in the body, becoming attached to it, craving and seeking enjoyment in it, and then acting on that craving.

What is it that the uninstructed ordinary person has not understood? The three characteristics. He has not fully understood that the basis of all these conceptualizations—in this case the body or earth element—is impermanent, unsatisfactory, and not-self. He has not understood that the conceptualizations themselves are impermanent, unsatisfactory, and not-self. The lack of full understanding is ignorance, which is the underlying condition for all these deluded conceptualizations. Ignorance is the breeding ground for craving, conceit, and views, which blossom as these diverse conceptualizations. Understanding the three characteristics with correct wisdom as they apply to the earth element and all other things is an essential step to dismantle the proliferations.

This process begins with mindfulness applied to the stream of experience, moment after moment. Through fine tuning mindfulness by means of consistent and repeated practice, we will be able to discern the distinct brief occasions of perception. Observing them arise and pass away so quickly, we will also be able to observe how the mind fuses them together to form gross perceptions of seemingly solid substantial objects. The wisdom observing how the mind makes up these seemingly substantial objects will cut through the conceptualizations of permanence, pleasure, beauty, and self.

The commentary describes the resultant full understanding as being of three kinds: (1) *Full understanding of the known* is insight wisdom that knows "This is the internal earth element, this the external earth element. This is its characteristic, this is its function, this its manifestation, and this its proximate cause." (2) *Full understanding by scrutiny* is insight wisdom that scrutinizes the earth element in forty-two ways, seeing it as impermanent, duḥkha, not-self, a sickness, and so forth. (3) *Full understanding by abandoning* involves abandoning desire and attachment for the earth element through generating the supramundane path.

The Bases of Conceiving

After discussing the earth element, the Buddha continued with twenty-three other objects that act as the bases of conceiving. The manner of conceiving in each one is the same: the uninstructed ordinary being (1) perceives A as A, (2) conceives A, (3) conceives himself in A, (4) conceives himself apart from A, (5) conceives A to be mine, and (6) delights in A. Even though a brief description of each basis is given below, take some time to reflect on how each one could be conceived by craving, conceit, and views in these six occasions. Make examples from your life and from what you have seen around you.

1–4. Earth, water, fire, and wind. These are the four elements that constitute our bodies.

5. Beings (P. *bhūta*). Sometimes bhūta means anything that exists, including inanimate objects. Other times it refers to the four primary elements or to all sentient beings. Since the four elements have already been mentioned, and other types of sentient beings are mentioned below, the commentary says that here "beings" refers to sentient beings below the level of the devas—human beings, animals, hungry ghosts, and hell beings. Conceptualizations regarding beings could be: "Beings are so lovely. I want to be born among them." "I am superior to those beings." "I want to possess this being and be with him or her always." "All beings have a soul." "The lives of beings are predestined and controlled by the creator." "These are my parents, children, and loved ones."

6. Devas. Since higher levels of devas are mentioned separately, here devas refers to the celestial beings in the six heavenly worlds in the desire realm. Conceptualizations of craving are common here: someone craves to be born with these devas and to have their belongings and radiance.

7. Pajāpati is a god similar to Śakra (P. Sakka), the ruler of the Deva Realm of the Thirty-three (*Tāvatiṃsa*). An uninstructed ordinary person could conceive, "I want to be born in the company of Pajāpati and the gods," "Pajāpati is permanent and indestructible." Or having been born as Pajāpati, he could conceive, "I am the ruler of all beings."

8. Brahmā is the supreme deity worshipped by the Brahmins. Mahābrahmā was the first deity to be born at the beginning of the present eon and he will live until its end. Other levels of Brahmā gods, all of whom have attained the first dhyāna and dwell in the first form realm, are included here.

9. Gods of Total Radiance are the highest level of gods dwelling in the second form realm, which corresponds to the second dhyāna. Although

just the name of the highest gods in the second form realm is mentioned, it includes the lower gods in that realm.

10. Gods of Refulgent Glory are the highest level of gods in the third form realm. Mentioning them includes the lower gods in the third form realm.

11. Gods of Great Fruit are the gods of the fourth form realm, which corresponds to the fourth dhyāna. Thus 8–11 are gods in the form realm. Ordinary beings who have attained these meditative states or who are born in the form realm may fall prey to a number of conceptualizations. For example, thinking "This meditative attainment is mine," they could become arrogant. Conceiving "I am bliss, I am liberated, thus I no longer need to abide by ethical conduct," they could engage in many destructive actions.

12. Overlord (Abhibhū). The commentary says that this refers to beings in the nonpercipient realm of unconscious beings without discrimination, which is located within the fourth form realm. Someone might conceive of the Overlord as being permanent and having a self. Or someone could yearn to be born with the Overlord or to possess what he possesses.

13–16. Base of infinite space, base of infinite consciousness, base of nothingness, base of neither-discrimination-nor-nondiscrimination are the four formless realms. Ordinary beings can be proficient in meditation and attain these deep states of samādhi of the formless realm. They may then misunderstand these experiences and conceive of them to be a Universal Self or an Infinite Self. Likewise, they may mistake these states for liberation and then feel betrayed when the karma for rebirth there has exhausted and they find themselves about to be reborn in an unfortunate realm. Uninstructed ordinary beings may also crave these states, considering themselves superior to others because of having attained them, and thus falling to conceptualizations due to views, craving, and conceit.

17–20. "The seen" refers to objects that are seen by the eye. "The heard" is sounds heard by the ear. The sensed includes odors, tastes, and tactile sensations. The cognized is known through the mind source. These include all objects perceived by the six sense faculties. In the desire realm, many conceptualizations proliferate based on these objects, especially seeing them as attractive, as the source of happiness, permanent, and having a self.

21–22. Unity and diversity. These are two ways to approach all phenomena included in the five aggregates. Unity refers to attaining deep samādhi where the mind is totally unified. An untaught being could crave the bliss or peace of this samādhi, or conceptualize about the experience of unity, thinking "I am everything," "I am one and everything is apart from me," or "Everything is mine and I pervade it." Diversity is the meditative experience of pluralism, which leads to conceptualizations that what is ultimately real is the diversity of elements that temporarily come together. Someone could conceive "Each thing is different and unrelated to others" or "I want to know the individual characteristics of the diverse objects in order to control them."

23. "All" refers to an experience of all. Conceptualizations such as "Everything is my self," "I am one with everything," "I have emerged from the All," "All was created by God," or "All lacks cause and condition" could arise in reference to this.

24. Nirvāṇa is not directly perceived by ordinary beings, so here "nirvāṇa" does not refer to the nirvāṇa realized by the arhats. According to the commentarial explanation, it refers to the understanding of nirvāṇa held by non-Buddhists, for example thinking that indulgence in sense pleasure without any restraint is nirvāṇa here and now, that one of the dhyānas is nirvāṇa, or that one of the formless realms is nirvāṇa. Through conceptualization of craving untaught ordinary beings think of nirvāṇa as wondrous sense pleasure or as the bliss or peace of deep states of samādhi. With conceptualizations of conceit they think, "I have attained nirvāṇa." With conceptualizations of views they think, "I am nirvāṇa." They may also conceive of themselves as being a permanent self that exists in nirvāṇa or as the self being one thing and the absolute reality of nirvāṇa as being another.

Untaught ordinary beings flounder in a myriad of conceptualizations about how a real self is related to any of these twenty-four bases. Considering the extent to which these proliferations overrun our mind in almost every moment of our saṃsāric existence gives rise to the aspiration to be free from them. Contemplating that the minds of sentient beings are similarly tormented by these conceptualizations gives rise to deep compassion.

It is important to remember that not all conceptions are harmful; correct conceptions aid us on the path. We learn and reflect on the meaning of this sūtra with our conceptual mind, and this aids us in gaining correct views. It is proliferations and erroneous conceptualizations that must be reined in and their distorted thoughts dismantled. Discriminating wisdom, which may be conceptual, is essential to discern a correct understanding from distorted conceptualization. One guideline is that if our sense of I is fortified, erroneous conceptualization is at work. On the other hand, when we are not reactive to criticism and our mind is free from anxiety, worry, and fear, erroneous conceptualizations have lessened.

By dismantling these multiple, intertwined, and afflictive layers of conceptualization regarding phenomena in saṃsāra as well as nirvāṇa itself, meditators come to see them as they really are: impermanent, in the nature of duḥkha, and not-self. With additional practice, these meditators will break through and directly perceive nirvāṇa.

REFLECTION

Contemplate how conceptualization colludes with craving, conceit, and afflictive views.

1. Make examples in your life of how craving gives rise to deluded conceptualization of mine. How does labeling things "mine" change how you relate to other people and possessions?
2. Make examples of how conceit gives rise to conceptualizations of I. Do you grasp a real I that you compare to others and then consider it superior to others? Do you hold to a real I that you consider more important than others? What effect does this have on your experience of happiness and pain?
3. Make examples of how afflictive views are conceptualizations about the self. Do you get lost in philosophical speculations about the origin of the world that go nowhere? Do you learn and investigate the Buddha's teachings and try to resolve your confusion?

Stages of Development

Usually the stages of development of understanding and realization are said to be stream-enterer, once-returner, nonreturner, and arhat. To mesh this with the structure of four types of persons—the untaught ordinary person, trainee, arhat, and tathāgata—from the *Discourse on the Root of All Things* mentioned above, stream-enterers, once-returners, and nonreturners are subsumed under trainees.

The situation of the first type of person, the untaught ordinary person, was discussed at length above. A trainee—a disciple in higher training—is someone who has entered the stream leading to liberation, the irreversible course to liberation. A trainee is not just any disciple who is practicing the three higher trainings, but someone who has a clear realization that directly perceives nirvāṇa, which ensures that she will never fall back to the level of an ordinary being. Her right view is immovable, and she now has the ability to perfect the āryas' eightfold path and gain full liberation. The Buddha says this person (MN 1:27):

> . . . directly knows earth as earth. Having directly known earth as earth, she should not conceive [herself as] earth, she should not conceive [herself] in earth, she should not conceive [herself apart] from earth, she should not conceive earth to be mine, she should not delight in earth. Why is that? So that she may fully understand it, I say.

After the simple perception of earth, the trainee directly knows earth as earth. She does not perceive earth as earth as the untaught ordinary person does, but has developed insight into the nature of earth. Her direct knowledge (P. *abhiññā*) knows earth (or any other object) in terms of its specific characteristics. This direct knowledge was cultivated through mindful attention to earth. When mindfulness is continuously sustained on an object, the object's specific characteristics become more readily apparent and are now observed directly. Instead of knowing earth only through the veil of conceptualization, a trainee experiences its distinguishing characteristic, which in the case of earth is its degree of hardness. Similarly, when she directly knows water, she knows, not just conceptually but through mindful attention, its specific characteristic of flowing and cohesion.

Direct knowledge cognizes not only an object's specific, distinguishing, or individual characteristics, but also the general or common characteristics that it shares with other phenomena. As mindfulness deepens, the meditator sees that earth arises due to conditions and ceases when its conditions have ceased. She knows earth is impermanent, unsatisfactory by nature, and not-self. She knows that thus earth is unable to bring lasting peace and that attachment to it leads only to duḥkha. These three characteristics are earth's general or common characteristics that it shares with all other conditioned phenomena in saṃsāra.

Insight meditation aims to see things as they really are, which means to see them as impermanent, unsatisfactory, and not-self. None of the five aggregates are I, mine, or my self. As insight into the three characteristics increases, full understanding of the four truths dawns, and the meditator knows the aggregates themselves, their arising, their cessation, and the eightfold path as the way to their cessation. At this time, she realizes nirvāṇa, attains the fruit of a stream-enterer, and also becomes a trainee.

A trainee has completely eliminated views because she has arrived at the right view of the Dharma and has gained the eye of Dharma that sees the truth of the teachings. Having eliminated the view of a personal identity, a trainee can no longer hold other wrong views, and thus does not conceive due to views. But he still has tendencies for the other two types of conceiving—craving and conceit. Thoughts of sensual desire may arise in the mind of a stream-enterer or once-returner, and thoughts of craving for existence in the form or formless realms may arise in the mind of a nonreturner. To encourage these trainees to continue their practice and attain liberation, the Buddha speaks to them, saying, "Do not conceive earth, do not conceive your self in earth, do not conceive your self apart from earth, do not conceive earth to be mine. Do not delight in earth." Not satisfied with direct knowledge of earth, a trainee follows these instructions in order to fully understand earth and release all deluded conceptualizations about it. The same instructions apply to conceiving the rest of the twenty-four bases of conceptualization so that he may fully understand them and fulfill his deepest aspiration to attain liberation.

Like trainees, arhats directly know earth as earth, but unlike trainees, arhats have completed the training and possess full understanding. They do not conceive earth, conceive their self in earth, conceive their self apart from earth, conceive earth is mine, or delight in earth. Having fully understood earth, they are free from any inclination to conceive of things in terms of I, me, my, mine, my self, you, yours, or your self. They have extinguished all views, craving, and conceit and have abandoned all pollutants—the pollutants of sensuality, existence, ignorance, and views—and have no remaining tendencies toward conceptualizations.

Arhats do not see earth or anything else as a permanent object that substantially exists. Nevertheless, they accept terms and concepts as tools for conventional communication and use them to express themselves and understand others. In doing so, they do not fall prey to thinking there is a substantial reality that corresponds to the objects of conversation or that exists in them.

Emphasizing the qualities of arhats' liberation, the Buddha mentioned four reasons arhats do not conceive. The first was mentioned above—because they have fully understood earth (and the twenty-three other bases), their origin, their cessation, and the eightfold path as the path to that cessation. In addition, they do not conceive because they are free from desire—both sensual desire and desire for renewed existence in saṃsāra—having eradicated it from the root. Arhats' relief from the affliction of desire is not temporary; there are no dormant seeds of desire lurking under the surface, ready to explode into manifest desire when the suitable conditions are encountered. Furthermore, arhats do not conceive because they are free from hate, aversion, and all forms of anger. Again, this is not due to temporarily suppressing these afflictions, but through eradicating them at their root. The final reason arhats do not conceive is that all ignorance and confusion have been conquered and can no longer afflict the mind. There are no deluded thoughts of I, me, my, and mine or of any permanent, substantial entity anywhere.

Descriptions of the awakened beings in the sūtras usually culminate with arhats, but in this sūtra, the Buddha concludes with the Tathāgata as the ultimate person. The Buddha is an arhat, so whatever was said regarding arhats' lack of conceptualizations holds true for the Buddha as well. The Tathāgata directly knows earth, and because he has fully understood earth, he does not conceive it in any way or delight in it. He does not conceive earth because he has fully understood it to the end—by means of his perfect knowledge he has understood everything about earth; nothing remains hidden or obscure to him. While arhats have full understanding of some phenomena, the Tathāgata has full understanding of all phenomena.

Furthermore, the Tathāgata does not conceive of or delight in earth because he has understood that craving is the root of duḥkha and that craving leads to birth, aging, and death. Because the Buddha has penetrated dependent origination, he wants nothing further to do with saṃsāra and has eliminated all of its causes and results. He discovered and actualized the full wisdom that uproots saṃsāra, and with the cessation and complete destruction of all defilements, he has awakened to supreme perfect awakening.

14 | The Pāli Sūtras and the Prāsaṅgika View

WE MAY BE CURIOUS to what extent the view of emptiness and selflessness presented in the Pāli sūtras differs or is the same as the view presented in the Prāsaṅgika tenet system. Earlier in this volume some similarities between the Pāli sūtras and the Prāsaṅgika view were pointed out. These include the sections "Similar Refutations in the Pāli Tradition," where we examine if the I and the aggregates are the same or different; "Pāli Tradition: The Six Elements Are Not the Self," which refutes the five material elements of earth, water, fire, wind, and space and the mental element of consciousness being the person; "Four Possibilities of Arising as Presented in the Pāli Canon," which examines arising to determine if phenomena arise from self, other, both, or causelessly; and the previous two chapters that explain more of the Pāli tradition's approach to self, where we see similarities to Prāsaṅgika thought as well as new presentations.

This is not the time to tackle in depth the question of the similarities and differences between the Pāli sūtras and the Prāsaṅgika view, and I (Chodron) lack the knowledge to do this. However, I would like to share some of what I've learned through my study of both the Pāli sūtras and the Prāsaṅgika view. In doing so, we may see ways in which the meanings coincide and complement each other. Within each Buddhist tradition and within Buddhism as a whole, there are common views that are generally accepted as well as views that have been discussed and debated for centuries. This is not a fault but a benefit, for it spurs us to contemplate these teachings more deeply. In addition, diverse explanations enable students with various dispositions and interests to find an explanation that fits their present temperament.

Emptiness and Selflessness

In chapter 10 of *Searching for the Self* we discussed the realization of emptiness and selflessness by śrāvakas and solitary realizers, who aspire to attain individual liberation by realizing selflessness. Prāsaṅgikas assert that śrāvakas and solitary realizers realize the same emptiness as bodhisattvas, even though the view of selflessness espoused in the Fundamental Vehicle tenet systems differs from that explained in sūtras the Prāsaṅgikas say are definitive. Here the division into tenet systems and the grouping of some as Fundamental Vehicle and others as Universal Vehicle (Mahāyāna) is according to the Sanskrit tradition, in particular in the Buddhism of Tibet.

Although we don't know if the scholar-adepts in North India had access to the Pāli scriptures, since those were found predominantly in Sri Lanka, they certainly were familiar with parallel scriptures in other Fundamental Vehicle schools present in India. Since the scriptures of those schools are no longer available, the corresponding Pāli verses are cited below. The first section discusses some of the passages in Pāli scriptures that Prāsaṅgikas point to when stating that Fundamental Vehicle āryas realize the same emptiness and selflessness as the Prāsaṅgikas. The second section consists of some additional passages in the Pāli canon that I (Chodron) found that support this.

Meanings That Coincide

A Ball of Foam Sutta

In chapter 10 of *Searching for the Self*, we noted that Prāsaṅgikas speak of passages that are also found in the Pāli sūtras and commentaries where the Buddha taught the Prāsaṅgika view of emptiness. Let's look at how these sūtra passages are explained by Pāli commentators. The first is from *A Ball of Foam Sutta* (*Pheṇa Sutta*, SN 22:95):

> Form is like a ball of foam,
> feeling is like a water bubble,
> discrimination is like a mirage,
> miscellaneous factors are like a plantain trunk,
> and consciousness is like an illusion;
> so explained the Kinsman of the Sun [the Buddha].

Before expounding this, the Buddha describes each aggregate as void (P. *rittaka*), hollow (P. *tucchaka*), and insubstantial (P. *asāraka*). Regarding the form aggregate, for example, he says (SN 22:95):

> Monastics, suppose that this river Ganges was carrying along a great ball of foam. A person with good sight would inspect it, ponder it, and carefully investigate it, and it would appear to him to be void, hollow, insubstantial. For what substance could there be in a ball of foam? So too, monastics, whatever kind of form there is, whether past, future, or present, internal or external, gross or subtle, inferior or superior, far or near: a monastic inspects it, ponders it, and carefully investigates it, and it would appear to him to be void, hollow, insubstantial. For what substance could there be in form?

The Buddha then proceeds to say the same thing about each of the other aggregates, changing only the simile. The terms "void, hollow, and insubstantial" are found in other early sūtras as well where they refer to things being false, deceptive, and illusory.

The commentary on the Saṃyutta Nikāya unpacks the meaning of these analogies. Just as foam lacks any substance, form lacks a permanent, stable substance, a self. Both foam and forms such as the body have holes that are home to many creatures. Just as foam expands and breaks up, the body grows and then dies and decomposes.

Just as a bubble is fragile and cannot be held because it bursts as soon as it is touched, so too feelings are fragile, vanish, and cannot be grasped as permanent or stable. Bubbles arise and cease quickly; likewise our happy, miserable, and neutral feelings do not last long. Bubbles arise depending on conditions; our feelings arise dependent on an object, a sense faculty, contact, and defilements.

We may see a mirage, but there is no way to drink that "water." Discriminations are equally deceptive and insubstantial. Mirages deceive thirsty people, who anticipate relief from their thirst although no water is there. Similarly, discriminations mislead and captivate people with the idea that an object is permanent, pleasurable, and pure.

Miscellaneous factors are like a plantain trunk in that the trunk of a plantain tree appears strong and solid but is hollow; there is nothing to be found in it. It is merely a collection of different sheaths without any essence. Similarly, miscellaneous factors are a collection that has no essence, they lack a permanent core that makes intentional decisions.

A magical illusion is insubstantial and cannot be grasped. Similarly, consciousness makes us think that a person does various activities with the same mind, whereas the mind changes from one moment to the next and cannot be grasped.

After synthesizing the above by teaching the six-line verse "Form is like a ball of foam . . . ," the Buddha says (SN 22:95):

> However one may ponder them
> and carefully inspect them,
> they appear but hollow and empty
> when one views them carefully.

The Sanskrit tradition's explanation of the five similes below is similar, although it emphasizes the aggregates' false and deceptive appearance. In the Sanskrit tradition presentation, the five similes illustrate the deceptive appearance of the aggregates as well as their dependence on other factors.[56]

Just as a ball of foam appears hard and sturdy but is actually delicate and can't withstand the slightest touch without bursting, so too the body appears truly existent but cannot withstand ultimate analysis, and its seeming true existence is easily destroyed. The body is deceptive not only because it appears firm but also because it appears to truly exist although it does not.

Water bubbles arise depending on causes and conditions and quickly vanish. So too our pleasant, unpleasant, and neutral feelings appear real and permanent when in fact they are dependent and transient. Our pleasant feelings do not last forever and are inevitably followed by painful feelings. If feelings existed truly, they would not change and would not be followed by suffering.

A mirage appears to be water, but no water is present. Similarly, things discerned by discriminations as well as the discriminations themselves appear to truly exist, whereas they do not exist that way at all. If we try to find truly existent discrimination within its basis of designation, we can't find it.

A plantain tree appears to have a hard core, but when the broad leaves around it are removed, no core is found. Likewise, the emotions and views that form the aggregate of miscellaneous factors seem to exist from their own side when in fact they are essenceless—false appearances to a mistaken mind. Though appearing powerful and solid, miscellaneous factors are fabrications created by the mind and have no essence.

Magical illusions, such as ghosts sitting next to you on a ride at a theme park, appear to exist objectively, although they are fabricated and no ghosts whatsoever are there. Similarly, the six consciousnesses appear to exist truly; they appear to be independent of their objects when in fact they arise dependent on their objects and sense faculties. Being dependent, they cannot exist truly.

Pāli commentators do not use terms such as "selflessness of persons" and "selflessness of phenomena"—those terms developed later in the Sanskrit tradition in northern India. However, the meaning is there in the Pāli texts. Although the explanation in the Pāli commentary of the six-line verse does not match Nāgārjuna's explanation exactly, each practitioner will understand the passage according to their dispositions and the maturity of their faculties. In this way, through such passages in the Pāli canon, Fundamental Vehicle practitioners can learn, meditate on, and realize the Middle Way view of the emptiness of inherent existence. In post-meditation time they practice seeing things as like illusions, arising as insubstantial appearances. Thus śrāvaka, solitary realizer, and bodhisattva āryas realize the same emptiness: the lack of inherent existence of the five aggregates as well as of the person who is merely designated in dependence on them. Although they may follow different vehicles, their view of the ultimate truth is the same.

REFLECTION

1. Review the five similes that illustrate the emptiness of the five aggregates: form is like foam, feelings are like water bubbles, discriminations are like a mirage, miscellaneous factors are like the trunk of a plantain tree, and consciousnesses are like illusions.

2. Contemplate the meaning of the similes and practice viewing the five

aggregates in this way, first according to the Pāli explanation, then according to the Prāsaṅgika explanation.

3. How does this influence the way you relate to your body, feelings, and so forth?

Nāgārjuna in Precious Garland

In his *Commentary on the Sixty Stanzas*, Candrakīrti speaks of another passage indicating that the Prāsaṅgika view is found in the Pāli scriptures. This passage from a Fundamental Vehicle sūtra was explained by Nāgārjuna in *Precious Garland* (RA 386):

> In the Great Vehicle nonarising is taught,
> and in the other (the Fundamental Vehicle) extinction—namely, emptiness.
> Since cessation and nonarising are the same,
> accept [that Mahayana scriptures are authentic].

Nāgārjuna indicates that nonarising—that is, the absence of inherently existent arising or production of the aggregates as taught in the Mahāyāna—and cessation—the extinction of inherently existent products, in particular the aggregates, as taught in the Fundamental Vehicle—come to the same point. Both refer to the emptiness of inherent existence. Here "cessation" doesn't mean the cessation of the aggregates through practicing the path (nirvāṇa without remainder), because when an arhat is alive, they haven't yet attained nirvāṇa without remainder, and when they have actualized nirvāṇa without remainder, the arhat is not present because they have passed away and their polluted aggregates have ceased.

In the Mahāyāna, nonarising means that phenomena do not arise inherently from their own nature. Specifically, afflictions, karma, and duḥkha do not arise under their own power; they are naturally empty of inherent existence from the "beginning."

In the Fundamental Vehicle, *extinction* refers to the primordial lack of inherent existence of the aggregates. That is, the aggregates by their very nature are empty. Inherent existence has never existed; phenomena have always lacked inherent existence and emptiness is their ultimate nature.

Candrakīrti's Commentary

Candrakīrti's *Commentary on (Nāgārjuna's) Sixty Stanzas of Reasoning* quotes a passage from a Fundamental Vehicle sūtra that illustrates that extinction in the Fundamental Vehicle and nonarising in the Mahāyāna have the same meaning—the emptiness of inherent existence. This passage was spoken by Śāriputra after he attained arhatship (GR 96):

> That which is the total elimination of *this* suffering, a definite elimination, purification, extinction, freedom from craving, cessation, well pacified, dissolution, where no additional suffering is led to, this nonorigination, and nonarising, this is peace, this is excellence. It is thus. For *this* is the definite elimination of all the aggregates, it is the extinction of saṃsāra, it is freedom from craving, it is cessation, and nirvāṇa.

I (Chodron) asked Bhikkhu Bodhi[57] to locate this passage in the Pāli canon and he responded: "I don't recognize this as a particular citation by Ven. Sāriputta. The first part of this is unfamiliar as a sequence, although the individual terms have Pāli counterparts. The second part clearly corresponds to a familiar stock 'definition' of Nibbāna found in many places in the Nikāyas. The Buddha is shown using it as a characterization of Nibbāna after his awakening in MN 26, with parallels in SN 6:1 and in *Vinaya Mahāvagga I*. I usually translate it: 'This is the peaceful, this is the sublime, that is, the stilling of all formations, the relinquishment of all acquisitions, the destruction of craving, dispassion, cessation, Nibbāna.' In the *Mālunkyāputta Sutta* (MN 64:9) it is a theme for meditation that leads to nonreturning or arhatship. It is mentioned, too, in *The Numerical Discourses of the Buddha*, in 'The Meditative Experience of Nibbāna-I.'"

Candrakīrti probably quoted this passage from a Sarvāstivādin sūtra written in Sanskrit, as those were available in northern India, where he usually lived. Gyaltsab Darma Rinchen says that these terms indicate emptiness.[58]

From the viewpoint of the Fundamental Vehicle, "extinction" (S. *kṣaya*) usually refers to the extinguishment of afflictions brought about by the application of the antidote, meditation on selflessness, the true path. However, Candrakīrti does not think this is the extinction spoken of in the sūtra citation. He says "that which is the total elimination of *this* suffering, a definite elimination, purification, extinction, freedom from craving, cessation, well pacified, dissolution" refers to our present polluted aggregates, whereas "where no additional suffering is led to . . . it is cessation, and nirvāṇa" refers to not taking polluted aggregates in future rebirths. Since the present aggregates exist, those attributes describing them also exist. Thus this passage is not talking about abandoning the present polluted aggregates due to practicing the path. This passage must therefore refer to the natural extinction or absence of true existence that is the nature of all phenomena and is realized in meditative equipoise on emptiness.

From the Mādhyamikas' perspective as explained in Maitreya's *Sublime Continuum*, "extinction" means that the aggregates are primordially extinct—that is, they are primordially and naturally empty of truly existent arising. This is the absence of inherent existence that has always been the ultimate nature of the aggregates and person. It is also the emptiness that is realized in meditative equipoise on emptiness. From this viewpoint, the essentialists' position is problematic, because when an arhat attains nirvāṇa with remainder, he or she is still alive, so the arhat would exist and their polluted aggregates would not have ceased, and when the arhat passes away and attains nirvāṇa without remainder, the polluted aggregates would have ceased but there would not be a person who has attained nirvāṇa.

Therefore Mādhyamikas speak of nirvāṇa as the emptiness of true existence and the "remainder" as the false appearance of true existence. Therefore an arhat first attains nirvāṇa without remainder. This occurs during meditative equipoise directly perceiving emptiness, at which time there is no appearance of truly existent phenomena at all. When the arhat emerges from this equipoise, in post-meditation time they experience nirvāṇa with remainder of the appearance of truly existent things. They recognize these appearances as false, like an illusion. In short, the "extinction" mentioned in the sūtra citation above is the natural, primordial extinction of true existence. Nirvāṇa in the sense of primordial extinction as taught in Pāli sūtras is the same as nonarising taught in the Mahāyāna sūtras. Both refer to the natural absence of true existence of persons and phenomena.

The Advice to Kātyāyana Sūtra

Another passage in Pāli sūtras that Prāsaṅgikas say speaks of the emptiness of inherent existence is referred to in Nāgārjuna's *Treatise on the Middle Way* (MMK 15:7):

> The Transcendental Lord, through understanding
> "it exists" and "it does not exist,"
> refuted both existence and nonexistence
> in the *Kātyāyana Sūtra* [*Kaccānagotta Sutta*].

Here the Buddha refutes the two extremes of inherent existence and total nonexistence, which are also negated in the *Kaccānagotta Sutta* in the Pāli canon.[59] This sūtra begins (SN 12:15):

> Then the Venerable Kaccānagotta approached the Blessed One, paid homage to him, sat down to one side, and said: "Venerable Sir, it is said, 'right view, right view.' In what way, Venerable Sir is there right view?"
>
> [The Buddha replied,] "This world, Kaccāna, for the most part depends on a duality—on [the notion of] existence and [the notion of] nonexistence. But for one who sees the origin of the world as it really is with correct wisdom, there is no [notion of] nonexistence in regards to the world. And for one who sees the cessation of the world as it really is with correct wisdom, there is no [notion of] existence in regard to the world."

As explained in the Pāli commentary and subcommentary on the Saṃyutta Nikāya, the notion of existence (P. *atthitā-diṭṭhi*) refers to absolutism (eternalism, P. *sassata*), holding that the world and the self exist eternally and permanently. The notion of nonexistence corresponds to nihilism (annihilation, P. *uccheda-diṭṭhi*), holding that the continuity of the world completely ceases and that the continuity of the person is severed and does not exist after the death of the body. Most people in this world—with the exception of the āryas—hold one or the other of these views.

By saying that there is no notion of either existence or nonexistence, the Buddha is not deliberately being ambiguous. He is not shying away from saying that things either exist or do not exist, because in other instances he makes clear statements about this. For example, in the *Discourse on Flowers* in the Pāli canon, the Buddha says (SN 22:94):

> Monastics, I do not dispute with the world; rather, it is the world that disputes with me. A proponent of the Dhamma does not dispute with anyone in the world. Of that which the wise in the world agree upon as not existing, I too say that it does not exist. And of that which the wise in the world agree upon as existing, I too say that it exists.

When the Buddha does not respond with what we consider a clear answer, it is due to incorrect metaphysical assumptions in the mind of the questioner. In the case above, people believe that if the world exists, it exists forever, permanently. Their belief arises because they see some continuation of identity between a cause and its effect and then believe a permanent entity exists that bridges the cause to the result. Describing the absolutist view, the commentary says (SN 735n30):

> The absolutist view might arise in regard to the world of formations, taking it to exist at all times, owing to the apprehension of identity [or essence] in the uninterrupted continuum occurring in a cause-effect relationship.

This view does not arise in a person who has right view, because she knows that each moment in a continuum of cause and effect arises from causes, ceases, and gives way to a new moment in the continuum. Thinking the carrot we see one moment is the same as the carrot we see five minutes later is adherence to absolutism; we are holding the carrot to be one unchanging entity, not a series of changing moments. However, knowing that each moment of the carrot arises from causes and conditions, passes away, and produces another moment of the carrot is a realistic view that does not involve holding an absolutist view. When we substitute "person" for "carrot," it becomes evident that holding the person to exist without change throughout time is a wrong view. An everlasting immutable person does not exist. Someone who holds an absolutist view thinks there is a soul or personal entity that is separate from the body and continues in the same form eternally. He believes that at death, the body ceases, but the permanent soul continues independent of the physical and mental aggregates. As the quotation from the commentary above shows, the absolutist view pertains to seeing an identity in all conditioned things of the world, not just the person.

A person who holds a nihilistic view sees a person or thing cease and then concludes it has no continuation whatsoever. This person thinks that when a person ceases at death, no being is reborn. If someone thinks that the self and body are the same, then when the body ceases at death she will believe the person also totally ceases: there is no rebirth, no experience of karmic results, and no liberation from saṃsāra because the continuity of the person has terminated.

With right view, a person who sees the cessation of the world as it really is with correct wisdom does not hold to absolutism, and a person who sees the origin or coming into being of the world as it really is with correct wisdom does not hold to nihilism. That is, correctly understanding passing away removes the view of permanence because we realize that things cease due to the cessation of their causes and conditions and do not endure without change over time. Correctly understanding how things arise counteracts nihilism, because arising indicates that something comes into existence in dependence on previous causes and conditions. It does not arise causelessly, from a permanent cause, or from a discordant cause. In other words, what existed before does not just disappear into nothingness; it serves as the cause for what comes into being after it. This process of continuous, dependently arisen change—arising and passing away—occurs without an enduring entity that goes from past to present or from present to future.

The sūtra continues with the Buddha saying (SN 12:15):

> This world, Kaccāna, is for the most part shackled by engagement, clinging, and adherence. But this one [with right view] does not become engaged and cling through that engagement and clinging, mental standpoint, adherence, underlying tendency; he does not take a stand about "my self." He has no perplexity or doubt that what arises is only dukkha arising, what ceases is only dukkha ceasing. His knowledge about this is independent of others. It is in this way, Kaccāna, that there is right view.

> "All exists" (P. *sabbaṃ atthi*): Kaccāna, this is one extreme. "All does not exist" (P. *sabbaṃ natthi*): this is the other extreme. Without veering towards either of these extremes, the Tathāgatha teaches the Dhamma by the middle: With ignorance as condition, formative actions [come to be]; with formative actions as condition, consciousness [comes to be] . . . Such is the origin of this whole mass of dukkha. But with the remainderless fading away and cessation of ignorance comes cessation of formative actions; with the cessation of formative actions, cessation of consciousness . . . Such is the cessation of this whole mass of dukkha.

The second paragraph of the above citation resembles Nāgārjuna's verse in the *Treatise on the Middle Way* (MMK 15:10):

> To say "it exists" is to reify.
> To say "it does not exist" is to adopt the view of nihilism.
> Therefore a wise person
> does not subscribe to "it exists" or "it does not exist."

In short, the Buddha teaches the Middle Way free from both extreme views, as the Pāli citation above affirms.

By means of craving and views, ordinary beings "engage in, cling to, and adhere" to the phenomena of the three realms—desire, form, and formless—as I and mine. Craving and views are seen as "mental standpoints" because they are the basis for nonvirtuous minds. They are seen as "adherences and underlying tendencies" because they adhere to the mind and lie dormant in it.

Āryas do not see the aggregates subject to clinging as I or mine, as a soul, or as a substantially existent person. Instead, looking at their personal experience, they see merely a collection of conditioned phenomena—the five aggregates—arising and passing away dependent on causes and conditions. Right view knows there is no findable being or substantially existent person in this process. Being a "teaching of the middle," the Buddha's teaching is free from the absolutist view that is the source of saṃsāra and its duḥkha. It is also free from the nihilistic view that if a real person does not continue after death, then our actions do not bring results. Such a view leads to ethical chaos, with people indulging their afflictions because they believe that their actions do not bear results.

Āryas' knowledge is said to be "independent of others" in that it is personal, direct knowledge. By seeing the actual nature or truth of the Dharma, āryas have made Dharma their own. Because they have experienced the meaning of the Dharma themselves, their understandings no longer rely on external factors for validation, although they may seek guidance from the Buddha or his experienced disciples. The Buddha teaches the view of the Middle Way, free from the extremes of absolutism and nihilism; this Middle Way is the teaching of dependent origination that explains the evolution and cessation of saṃsāra. The antidote to this whole mass of duḥkha known as saṃsāra is direct, personal knowledge of the deathless, nirvāṇa.

To understand the importance of the *Kaccānagotta Sutta* we look to the *Sutta to Channa* (SN 22:90), where, according to the commentary on the sūtra, the monk Channa had not done the "discernment of conditions" in which the conditions for the five aggregates are contemplated prior to insight meditation on the three characteristics. As a result of this omission, when Channa began to cultivate insight and saw that the aggregates were empty of self, he was seized by the fear "I will be destroyed, and because there is no self, my karma will not bring results." Seeking a way out of his terror, he approached Ānanda and asked for instructions. In response Ānanda recited the *Kaccānagotta Sutta* to Channa, who then abandoned the two extremes of existence and nonexistence and became a stream-enterer.

Having understood the meaning of permanence and nihilism in the Pāli canon, let's look again at Nāgārjuna's verse cited above that shows the Madhyamaka perspective (MMK 15.7):

> The Transcendental Lord, through understanding
> "it exists" and "it does not exist,"
> refuted both existence and nonexistence
> in the *Kātyāyana Sūtra* [*Kaccānagotta Sutta*].

This verse refers to a reasoning negating inherent existence called "refutation of the four extremes" that negates: (1) existence (inherent existence), (2) nonexistence (total nonexistence), (3) both (inherent existence and total nonexistence), and (4) neither (some other inherently existent option).

Affixing the word "inherent" is important in this refutation. The inherent existence of phenomena, not their conventional existence, is refuted. Phenomena's total nonexistence, not their passing away, is refuted. This argument says that the I, for example, (1) is not inherently existent, (2) is not totally nonexistent, (3) is not a unity of inherent existence and total nonexistence, and (4) is not some other inherently existent alternative that is neither inherently existent nor inherently nonexistent. Someone could reach the erroneous conclusion that things are neither existent nor nonexistent by searching for an object, such as a table, with reasoning analyzing the ultimate. Not finding it among its parts, he concludes there is no object. Then he thinks, "My mind searching for the object also cannot be found among its parts, so it, too, is nonexistent. But how could that be, because the mind doing this analysis must exist?" Embroiled in confusion, he says that things are neither existent nor nonexistent.

Nāgārjuna says that in the *Kaccānagotta Sutta*, the Buddha refutes the two extremes of inherent existence (superimposition, eternalism, absolutism) and total nonexistence (deprecation, nihilism, annihilation). Since the only way to do this is through realizing the emptiness of inherent existence of persons and phenomena, teachings on this view of selflessness are found in Fundamental Vehicle sūtras, and the emptiness of inherent existence of all phenomena is realized by śrāvakas and solitary realizers who practice according to these sūtras.

Additional Passages from the Pāli Tradition

Scriptures in the Pāli canon as well as later commentaries are filled with passages that can be read from a Prāsaṅgika viewpoint. Some of these are quoted below.

Buddhaghosa, who lived in the fifth century (about three hundred years after Nāgārjuna), quotes the ancients as saying (Vism 16:90):

> For there is suffering, but none who suffers;
> doing exists although there is no doer;
> extinction [nibbāna] is ultimate truth, but no extinguished person;
> although there is a path, there is no goer.

The theme of this verse harkens to chapter 2, "Examination of Motion," in Nāgārjuna's *Treatise on the Middle Way* where he examines how the goer, going, and area gone over exist. It also resembles the point of chapter 8, "Examination of the Agent and Action," where Nāgārjuna states:

> That which is an agent
> does not perform an existent action.
> Nor does that which is not an agent
> perform some nonexistent action.

In *Treatise on the Middle Way* (11.1), Nāgārjuna refers to a recurring statement in the Pāli sūtras when he said:

> When asked if the beginning is known,
> the great sage said "no."
> Cyclic existence is without origin or end
> because there is no beginning or end.

A similar statement in the Pāli sūtras is found in each of the sūtras in the *Connected Discourses without Discoverable Beginning* (*Anamataggasaṃyutta*, SN 15):

> This saṃsāra is without discoverable beginning. A first point is not discerned of beings roaming and wandering on hindered by ignorance and fettered by craving.

By making such a statement, the Buddha directly refutes the notion of an independent creator and an intrinsic beginning that itself has no cause. Nāgārjuna says that in addition to this, the Buddha refutes an inherently existent beginning of saṃsāra to show that saṃsāra does not ultimately exist; it has no findable essence. Although each sentient being's saṃsāra has an end, this end is not a findable event with its own essence. Can we locate the exact moment someone attains liberation? Something that has no discernible—that is, no inherently existent—beginning or end cannot have a findable middle either. Where or when can we locate saṃsāra?

Emptiness from the View of the Pāli Sūtras and Prāsaṅgika Tenets

The word "not-self" or "selfless" (P. *anattā*) appears more frequently in the Pāli sūtras than the word empty (P. *suñña*). Interestingly, in the Pāli canon, both words are used more often as adjectives than as nouns. For example, the texts speak of phenomena as being selfless or empty more often than they use the nouns "selflessness" or "emptiness."

While "empty" and "emptiness" are used less frequently than "selfless" in Pāli scriptures, they are significant words in Buddhism. For example, the fourth defeat for monastics is lying about one's attainments—claiming to have spiritual realization that one does not have. Among those are the attainments of emptiness liberation (P. *suññatā-vimokkha*), emptiness concentration (P. *suññatā-samādhi*), and emptiness attainment (P. *suññatā-samāpatti*).

The Buddha considered emptiness an important topic and encouraged the monastics to pay attention to it. In the *Drum Peg Sutta*, he expressed concern about the long-term survival of the profound teachings and advises (SN 20:7):

> Therefore, monastics, you should train yourselves thus: "When those sūtras spoken by the Tathāgata that are deep, deep in meaning, supramundane, dealing with emptiness[60] are being recited, we will be eager to listen to them, will lend an ear to them, will apply our minds to understand them; and we will think those teachings should be studied and mastered." Thus should you train yourselves.

We'll now look at some instances in which the Buddha mentions empty and emptiness through the perspective of the Pāli commentaries. Afterward, you may want to read these same passages from the perspective of Nāgārjuna's teachings.

In the *Simile of the Vipers Sutta*, the Buddha speaks of the six sense sources as being like an empty village. Using the simile of a man fleeing from danger, the Buddha says (SN 35:238):

> He would see an empty village. Whatever house he enters is void, deserted, empty. Whatever pot he takes hold of is void, hollow, empty.

And in the *Virtuous Sutta*, he speaks of the five aggregates subject to clinging as (SN 22.122):

> . . . impermanent, suffering, as a disease, as a tumor, as a dart, as misery, as an affliction, as alien, as disintegrating, as empty, and not-self.

The commentary consolidates these eleven attributes into the three characteristics, with empty and not-self being the characteristic of not-self.[61]

The Buddha delivered two sūtras, the *Shorter Discourse on Emptiness* (MN 121) and the *Greater Discourse on Emptiness* (MN 122). The *Greater Discourse* encourages monastics to practice in solitude in order to understand emptiness. The Buddha says (MN 122:6):

> Ānanda, there is this abiding discovered by the Tathāgata: to enter and abide in emptiness internally by giving no attention to all signs.

According to the commentary, "signs" refers to any sign of conditioned things, which include the five aggregates. The commentary also says "abiding in emptiness by giving no attention to all signs" means to abide in the fruition attainment of emptiness (*suññataphala samāpatti*), which is the fruition attainment of arhatship. Here "emptiness" is another word for nirvāṇa, and this fruition attainment is entered into by focusing on the empty aspect of nirvāṇa.

The commentary explains that each day in the afternoon, the Buddha entered and abided in the fruition attainment of arhatship by meditating on nirvāṇa as emptiness. Dwelling in emptiness in this way is peaceful and sublime. If someone wants to enter and abide in emptiness internally, the Buddha recommends that he attain the fourth dhyāna, which "steadies his mind internally, quiets it, brings it to single-pointedness, and concentrates it." The Buddha continues (MN 122:10):

> Then he gives attention to emptiness internally. While he is giving attention to emptiness internally, his mind enters into emptiness internally and acquires confidence, steadiness, and decision.

The Buddha then instructs meditators to give attention to emptiness externally and to give attention to emptiness both internally and externally. The commentary explains that giving attention to emptiness internally is seeing the emptiness of our own aggregates; seeing emptiness externally is seeing the emptiness of others' aggregates; seeing emptiness internally and externally is alternating between the two. In this way, practitioners know their own aggregates and the aggregates of others as empty of self and empty of being the property of a self (empty of pertaining to self).

This is called the liberation of mind by emptiness (P. *suññatā cetovimutti*). It is not a supramundane path because it is concerned with conditioned aggregates, albeit their selflessness. The commentary on the *Sutta on the Greater Series of Questions and Answers* (MN 43) agrees that the liberation of mind by emptiness is insight into the emptiness of self in both persons and phenomena and is mundane in that it focuses on the lack of self in worldly things.[62] However, by meditating on it repeatedly, one will reach the arhat's fruition attainment of emptiness that the Buddha dwells in, as he mentioned above.

In the *Shorter Discourse on Emptiness* (MN 121), Ānanda asks the Buddha if he correctly heard the Buddha say, "I often abide in emptiness." The Buddha replies affirmatively and reports that even now he often abides in emptiness. He then proceeds to talk about more and more subtle objects of meditation. Here "emptiness" has the connotation of the mind being empty of coarser objects and grosser levels of experience. Each time the Buddha instructs Ānanda to attend to a more subtle object, the Buddha says, "Thus he regards it as empty of what is not there, but as to what remains there he understands that which is present thus: 'This is present.' Ānanda, this too is his genuine, undistorted descent into emptiness." Here the Buddha encourages the meditator to focus on the negation of what is not there—the previous object in the sequence. He sharpens the distinction between a negation and an affirmative phenomenon by then encouraging the meditator to be aware of what is there—an affirmative phenomenon that is more unitary, with fewer distracting attributes than the previous object.

The meditator's experience of what is empty and what is present follows this sequence:

1. Be aware that the area is empty of animals, wealth, and laypeople, but the monastic community is present.
2. Then focus on the emptiness of monastics, but the forest is present.
3. There is the emptiness or absence of forest, but earth is present. According to the commentary, "earth" refers to the earth kasiṇa, through which the meditator attains the four dhyānas.
4. The meditator now leaves behind perception of earth as the quality of solidity, but infinite space is present. Here coarse objects associated with the desire realm and objects of meditation of the dhyānas, such as kasiṇas, are no longer perceived, but phenomena associated with the formless absorptions are. This doesn't necessarily entail that the meditator has attained these absorptions, only that their objects are perceived.
5. The meditator's field of awareness is empty of infinite space, but infinite consciousness is present.
6. It is empty of infinite consciousness, but nothingness is present.
7. It is empty of nothingness, but signlessness is present.

At this point, the meditator enters the signless concentration of mind. She then reflects on and applies insight to this concentration itself and sees it is conditioned and impermanent. She knows that even the sublime signless concentration of mind possesses the three characteristics, and with this insight she is able to break through to realize nirvāṇa. By repeatedly cognizing nirvāṇa, her mind is liberated from the three pollutants of sensual desire, existence, and ignorance, and she gains the knowledge that birth and death in saṃsāra have been ceased. Having attained nirvāṇa with remainder, the only disturbance that remains is that bound up with her present physical body with its six sense faculties. She understands that her field of perception is empty of these three pollutants and of any disturbance by them. As the Buddha then tells Ānanda, "This is the genuine undistorted, pure descent into emptiness, supreme and unsurpassed."

Here we see that the meditator understands emptiness in a gradual manner: it is not realized in a flash with little effort but comes about by preparing the mind step by step. At first emptiness is understood in a very coarse manner as the lack of animals, wealth, people, and so on. Then the meditator knows emptiness in terms of the absence of the earth kasiṇa, the object of dhyāna meditation. This is followed by knowing emptiness as the absence of the objects of three of the four formless absorptions. It is only by applying insight to the meditating mind and discovering its deeper nature that the meditator now sees emptiness as the lack of the three characteristics. Feeling no delight in anything associated with ignorance and saṃsāra, she experiences the breakthrough and realizes nirvāṇa, the supreme emptiness.

In a short sūtra entitled *Empty Is the World*, Ānanda asks the Buddha, "It is said, 'Empty is the world, empty is the world.' In what way, Venerable Sir, is it said, 'Empty is the world'?" In response, the Buddha explains (SN 35:85):

> It is, Ānanda, because it is empty of self and of what belongs to self that it is said, "Empty is the world." And what is empty of the self and what belongs to the self? The eye, Ānanda, is empty of self and of what belongs to self. Forms are empty of self and of what belongs to self. Visual consciousness is empty of self and of what belongs to self. Eye contact is empty of self and of what belongs to self. . . . Feeling arising from eye contact is empty of self and of what belongs to self.

The Buddha continues with the ear and its object, consciousness, contact, and feeling, and says the same about the nose, tongue, body, and mind and their objects, consciousnesses, contacts, and feelings. Here emptiness is a quality of all phenomena, both those associated with the person, such as the body, as well as those not, such as external forms.

We find more references to emptiness in the Saṃyutta Nikāya. In the *Kāmabhū Sutta* (SN 41:6), Bhikkhu Kāmabhū refers to emptiness-contact (P. *suññataphassa*). The commentary says this is the contact in the attainment of fruition, which is experienced after a meditator has arisen from the attainment of the cessation of discrimination and feeling. Here the attainment of fruition (P. *phalasamāpatti*) is focused on emptiness. This is an exceptional meditative state in which the bliss of nirvāṇa is directly experienced.

Nirvāṇa is also called "emptiness" because it is empty of the afflictions. By equating emptiness with nirvāṇa, emptiness refers to the absence of the afflictions as well as to nirvāṇa as the unconditioned, which is the object of the supramundane paths and fruits.

In the *Godatta Sutta* (SN 41:7), a lay follower asks Bhikkhu Godatta what is the liberation of mind by emptiness. He responds that a meditator reflects, "Empty is this of self or of what belongs to self." This indicates a concentration based on insight into the selfless nature of phenomena. Later in the sūtra, Godatta explains several supramundane liberations that are "empty of attachment, empty of anger, and empty of confusion." These are the supramundane paths and fruits that see nirvāṇa directly. The commentary explains that although the liberation of mind by emptiness is not mentioned separately, it is included because all supramundane liberations are empty of attachment, anger, and confusion (SN 1445n317). In this context, emptiness refers to nirvāṇa.

The *Dhammapada* also speaks of emptiness as meaning nirvāṇa, the object of arhats' meditation (Dhp 92–93):

> Those who do not accumulate and are wise regarding food,
> whose object is emptiness, the unconditioned freedom—
> their track cannot be traced,
> like the path of birds in the sky.
>
> Those whose pollutants are destroyed and who are unattached to food,
> whose object is emptiness, the unconditioned freedom—
> their path cannot be traced,
> like the path of birds in the sky.

In the *Nibbāna Sutta: Unbinding,* emptiness is the object of the supramundane realization (Ud 8.2):

> It is hard to see the unaffected,
> for the truth is not easily seen.
> Craving is pierced in one who knows;
> for one who sees, there is nothing.

In conclusion, in the Pāli tradition "empty" has two principal meanings: (1) "empty of self or what pertains to self" is realized by insight that is considered mundane because it analyzes worldly, conditioned objects, and (2) "empty of attachment, anger, and confusion" refers to nirvāṇa and is realized by supramundane wisdom. What, then, is the relationship between emptiness and nirvāṇa in the Pāli tradition? Some passages seem to equate them; for example, the *Path of Discrimination* (*Paṭisambhidāmagga*) says:

> What is the supreme emptiness (P. *agga suñña*)? The quieting of all formative actions, the relinquishing of all clinging to rebirth, detachment, cessation, nibbāna—this is the supreme emptiness.

The supreme emptiness is nirvāṇa. By realizing it, the grasping of a self together with the craving and duḥkha that arise from it are eradicated. The practice of the four establishments of mindfulness leads to this realization by enabling practitioners to penetrate the single nature (*ekasabhāva*) of supreme emptiness nirvāṇa, which is saturated with the one taste (*ekarasa*) of liberation (*vimutti*).

Here emptiness is equated with nirvāṇa, which is the absence or cessation of clinging and all other causes of saṃsāra. But emptiness is also the absence of self, and according to the early sūtras, this pertains to all phenomena, not just to the person.[63] In the Nālandā tradition, nirvāṇa is spoken of as the cessation of duḥkha and its origins and as the ultimate nature of the purified mind—the purified emptiness of inherent existence of a mind that is forever free from obscurations. Similarly, in the Pāli tradition, nirvāṇa may be spoken of as the goal of practice—the abandonment of greed, hatred, and ignorance—as well as the object of meditation of a path consciousness.

Selfless and Deceptive

Dependent origination and selflessness are hallmarks of the Buddha's teachings. Referring to these two principles, with clear reasons the Buddha refuted many misconceptions prominent in non-Buddhist circles, such as an external creator who created the world and the beings in it; a permanent, unified, and independent self; a substantially or inherently existent person findable among the aggregates; and an underlying substance out of which all phenomena manifest. To refute such wrong views, the Buddha taught selflessness and the deceptive nature of phenomena, teachings that are preserved in both the Pāli and Sanskrit traditions.

In the *Dhammapada*, the Buddha says (Dhp 279): "All dhammas [phenomena] are not self." The particular phenomena referred to here are the five aggregates, twelve sense sources, and eighteen constituents. In some contexts these three categories refer only to elements related to the person; in other contexts the five aggregates include all impermanent phenomena, and the twelve sources and eighteen constituents include all phenomena.

Early Buddhism—which relied on the sūtras and preceded the writings of the Abhidharmikas—did not distinguish between the selflessness of the person and the selflessness of phenomena. It seems the early Mahāyānists posited the two selflessnesses in response to the substantialist and reductionist tendencies of the Abhidharmikas, especially the Sarvāstivādins in northern India. Like the sūtras, the Sarvāstivādins asserted that the person is selfless because it is composed of many impersonal components. However, they went a step further than the sūtras and said that the irreducible components of both mind and matter were ultimate realities. A famous example of this is the simile in *Questions of King Menander* in which it is said that a chariot does not possess ultimate reality but its components do. This was then compared to the person, saying the person does not exist ultimately and is imputed, but its parts—the aggregates, sense sources, consciousnesses, and so forth—are ultimately existent.

Early Mādhyamikas, such as Nāgārjuna, would have found such assertions as contradicting the Buddha's final intent in teaching selflessness. They said the Sarvāstivādins and other Abhidharmikas were giving phenomena an ontological existence that they in fact do not have. In refuting this reification, they made a distinction between the selflessness of persons asserted by the Sarvāstivādins and the selflessness of phenomena that was accepted by the Mādhyamikas.

The *Path of Purification*, which was written many centuries after the early sūtras and was influenced by the Abhidharmikas, explains "selfless" as meaning "coreless" (Vism 20:16):

> . . . so too all that [form] is not self in the sense of having no core. In the sense of having no core because of the absence of any core

> of self grasped as self, an abider, a doer, an experiencer, one who is his own master.... The same method applies to feeling, and so on.

Buddhaghosa elaborates on the meaning of corelessness (Vism 21:56):

> Form has no core, is coreless, without core, as far as concerns (1) any core of permanence, or (2) core of lastingness, or (3) core of pleasure, or (4) core of self, or as far as concerns (5) what is permanent, or (6) what is lasting, or (7) what is eternal, or (8) what is not subject to change. Feeling (a lengthy list follows of aggregates, senses sources, constituents, links, dhyānas, and so forth) has no core, is coreless, without a core (with the eight points above).... Just as a reed has no core, is coreless, without core, just as . . . a lump of foam, a water bubble, a mirage, a plantain trunk, an illusion has no core, is coreless, without core, so too form [and so forth] has no core, is coreless, without core . . .

Here, selflessness and corelessness appear to refer to there being no permanent person or substantially existent person who is not in the nature of duḥkha. However, "coreless" is a powerful word and the list of phenomena it applies to is lengthy. In addition, the analogies Buddhaghosa gives of a mirage, illusion, and so forth are of deceptive objects, things that do not exist the way they appear. We can't help but wonder if "coreless" could have a deeper meaning than the nonexistence of a substantial self.

The *Uraga Sutta* echoes this message of corelessness where it says (Sn 1:1):

> He who does not find core or substance
> in any of the realms of being,
> like flowers which are vainly sought
> in fig trees that bear none,
> such a monastic gives up the here and the beyond,
> just as a serpent sheds its worn-out skin.

And the *Attadaṇḍa Sutta* says (Sn 4:15):

This world completely lacks essence;
it trembles in all directions.

The implication of some early Pāli teachings is that grasping any phenomenon as having any kind of essential nature in itself is an impediment. This is expressed in the *Sutta of the Simile of Foam*, which was discussed above and is quoted by Mādhyamikas to show that the emptiness of phenomena is taught in scriptures in northern India that were parallel to the Pāli scriptures. It is also expressed in *Mogharāja's Question* (*Mogharājamāṇavapucchā*, Sn 5:15) where the Buddha says:

Contemplate the world as empty,
Mogharāja, always mindful!
Root out the underlying view of self;
in this way you will transcend death.
[When] contemplating the world like this,
the lord of death does not catch sight of you.

Looked at from one perspective, it appears that in the sūtras the Buddha assumes that phenomena in the world are insubstantial and therefore does not specifically speak of their mode of existence. He did not teach the dharmas as ultimates (*paramārtha, paramattha*). Abhidharma commentators first began using the term "ultimate"; they considered the four elements and so forth as ultimate because they are the irreducible components of existence—they are the final items of analysis out of which all other things are composed. As noted in the "Coda: The Pāli Abhidharma" in *Searching for the Self*, the dharmas being ultimate and having own-nature (*svabhāva, sabhāva*) initially did not mean that they ultimately existed, existed by their own nature, or inherently existed—as *svabhāva* later came to mean. Nāgasena in the *Questions of King Menander* says the person is posited in dependence on the aggregates and is not found in the ultimate sense. Pāli Abhidharmikas did not say the dharmas were partless particles, as asserted by Sarvāstivādins. Still, the minute dharmas and minute moments of consciousness began to be seen as more real than things that were designations (*prajñapti, paññatti*).

The Sarvāstivāda school was popular in northern India, and some of its views later spread to Tibet and were known as Vaibhāṣika tenets. Sarvāstivādins were substantialist, attributing to phenomena and persons an ontological existence they did not have. In addition to saying the smallest particles of material and the smallest moments of consciousness were ultimates, they claimed that past and future phenomena were substantially existent. Nāgārjuna must have come into contact with these views, and seeing them as contrary to the Buddha's intent, he refuted *svabhāva*—own-nature—on phenomena as well as on persons. In doing so, he explicitly expanded the meaning of "self," claiming all phenomena are selfless. Nāgārjuna and later Mādhyamikas took *svabhāva* to mean inherent existence.

The Abhidharmikas' and Sarvāstivādins' views can be contrasted with sūtras in which the Buddha clearly says that all dharmas are unreal, deceptive, and false. These sūtras are much more in line with the Prāsaṅgika view. For example, the *Sutta on the Exposition of the Elements* (*Dhātuvibhanga Sutta*) says (MN 140:26):

> That is false which has a deceptive nature, and that is true which has a nondeceptive nature—nibbāna. Therefore a bhikkhu possessing [this truth] possesses the supreme foundation of truth. For this, monastics, is the supreme ariya truth, namely, nibbāna, which has a nondeceptive nature.

In the *Contemplation of Dualities*, the Buddha is even more explicit, pointing out that name and form—mental and material phenomena—are seen as deceptive, untrue, and unreal (Sn 3:12.15):

> In this world . . . that which is regarded as "This is true," the ariyas have seen it well with correct wisdom thus: "This is false." . . . In this world . . . that which is regarded as "This is false," the ariyas have seen it well with correct wisdom thus: "This is true." . . . The Teacher further said this:
>
> Behold the world together with its devas
> conceiving a self in what is not-self.
> Settled on name-and-form,
> they conceive "This is true."

In whatever way they conceive it,
it turns out otherwise.
That indeed is its falsity,
for the transient is of a false nature.

Nibbāna is of a non-false nature:
that the ariyas know as truth.
Through the breakthrough to truth,
hungerless, they are fully quenched.

Here, the Buddha explains that the veiled truths, such as our body and mind, that the world takes to be real and true are in fact unreal, deceptive, and have a false nature. The world takes what is not-self to have a self. Nirvāṇa, on the other hand, is true, and by seeing it as true āryas attain liberation.

This returns us to the statement quoted above where the Buddha succinctly stated in the *Dhammapada*:

> All dhammas [phenomena] are not-self.

This may also be translated as "all phenomena are without a self" or "all phenomena are selfless." Regardless, it is striking that here the Buddha applied the quality of lacking a self to all phenomena.

What is intriguing here is that so many of the passages found in both Pāli and Sanskrit sūtras can be read from multiple perspectives with the words expressing multiple meanings. Needless to say, we value the explanations expressed by centuries of wise sages and scholars of both traditions, who have unpacked the meaning of these passages. However, when we look beyond the perspectives of one Buddhist tradition or tenet system, we may discover unexpected richness and similarities in the perspectives of other Buddhist traditions.

The Buddha's teachings on selflessness are precious and profound. Understanding them and realizing them in meditation will free our minds from all wrong views, fetters, and afflictions. Exploring the various ways in which the Buddha expresses the liberating message of the lack of a true, findable self and the insubstantiality of phenomena will expand our minds and transform our relationship with ourselves as well as with the beings and the world around us.

Notes

1. Roger Jackson, *Is Enlightenment Possible?* (Ithaca, NY: Snow Lion Publications, 1993), 348.
2. See chapter 6 of *Searching for the Self* for more about the various objects of consciousness.
3. These are coarse misconceptions in the context of the Judeo-Christian concept of a soul or the Hindu concept of an ātman. In other contexts grasping things as permanent refers to an innate grasping.
4. See chapter 3 of *The Foundation of Buddhist Practice* for more on the five aggregates.
5. The Tibetan terms for these five arguments are, respectively, *rdo rje gzegs ma'i gtan tshigs*, *yod med skye 'gog gi gtan tshigs*, *mu bzhi skye 'gog gi gtan tshigs*, *rten 'brel gyi gtan tshigs*, and *gcig du bral gyi gtan tshigs*.
6. Tibetan texts often cite these verses, referencing a Fundamental Vehicle sūtra as their source. These same verses are also found in an āgama in the Chinese canon thought to be from the Mūlasarvāstivāda sect. Regarding verse 1, line 3, the word *śuddha* appears in the Pāli and probably in the Sanskrit. Although usually translated as "pure," Bhikkhu Bodhi explains that in this case it has an idiomatic sense as "sheer," "bare," "mere." That is, there are only the conditioned aggregates with nothing additional like a self or substance. In Tibetan, *śuddha* means pure and often refers to the natural purity of phenomena—their emptiness of inherent existence. In that case, the line reads "these conditioned aggregates are empty" or "there is only a heap of empty aggregates."
7. The author of the *Milindapañha* is unknown. Some people say Nāgasena and the king are fictional characters. Others say Menander was a king in Bactria and Nāgasena was born in Kashmir in the second century BCE and belonged to the Sarvāstivāda school.
8. An alligator and a grapefruit may exist at the same time for a short while, but that doesn't mean they are one nature. The alligator can exist without the grapefruit and vice versa.
9. For more on negations, see SRR, 57–58.
10. These verses are 147cd–151ab in the Tibetan text. They were translated by Tenzin Tsepag with assistance from Bhikṣu Nicky Vreeland and Jeremy Russell. Also see a commentary on this text by Choden Rinpoche and Yongdzin Losang Jinpa, in Panchen Losang Chokyi Gyaltsen, *A Discussion between Self-Grasp-*

ing and the Wisdom Realizing Selflessness, at https://happymonkspublication.org/product/a-discussion-between-self-grasping-and-the-wisdom-realizing-selflessness/.

11. The word translated as "fuel" is *upādāna*, which may also be translated as "clinging," so there is wordplay in the above passage that is difficult to reproduce in translation. Rebirth is for one with clinging, not for one free of clinging.
12. Robert A. F. Thurman, *The Central Philosophy of Tibet: A Study and Translation of Jey Tsong Khapa's Essence of True Eloquence* (Princeton, NJ: Princeton University Press, 1991).
13. For more on the twelve links of dependent origination, see chapters 7–9 in *Saṃsāra, Nirvāṇa, and Buddha Nature.*
14. Here "found" means existent. "Reducibly" and "irreducibly" were added to distinguish between the mode of existence of the elements and the mode of existence of the person according to the commentarial method of analysis based on the Pāli Abhidharma. The elements are said to be real, whereas the person is imputedly existent. For more about this topic, see the appendix in *Searching for the Self.*
15. "Conditionality" indicates a result arising dependent on its cause.
16. See chapter 7 of *Saṃsāra, Nirvāṇa, and Buddha Nature* for more on the sense faculties (sense sources).
17. The Pāli sūtras do not indicate exactly what is meant by the mental faculty. In the Abhidharma commentarial tradition, however, the mental faculty includes all six consciousnesses as well as the bhavaṅga, a subliminal consciousness.
18. This argument is set up according to the counterpervasion in the syllogism: "Consider the I, it does not inherently exist, because it does not exist as inherently one or as inherently separate and unrelated." The counterpervasion is: "If it is not the opposite of the thesis, it necessarily is not the opposite of the reason." In this syllogism, the counterpervasion is: "If it inherently exists, it is necessarily inherently one with or inherently different from (the aggregates)." The third and fourth points in the meditation explore the pervasion of the syllogism: "If it is not inherently one with the aggregates or inherently separate from them, it does not inherently exist."
19. For more on substantial existence and imputed existence, see the "Sautrāntika" subheading in chapter 4 of *Searching for the Self.*
20. This topic comes in the broader context of diamond slivers—the reasoning that refutes inherently existent arising—and will be explained in chapter 6 below.
21. See chapter 8 of that book.
22. Non-mentation (T. *sems med pa*) means that to a third party, a person appears to be without the normal mental functions of the waking state. Vaibhāṣikas explain eight states of non-mentation in which they say no consciousness is present. However, this view is not shared by the other tenet systems, which say that a subtle state of mind still exists at these times. An example is the mind in meditative equipoise on selflessness, which is very alert and precise.
23. "Appropriate" (*upādāna*, T. *len pa*) may also be translated as "cling."

24. The Saṃmitīya Vaibhāṣikas say all five aggregates are the person. It's unclear if they mean each aggregate or all five aggregates together is an illustration of the I.
25. This and the preceding quotation were translated by Shenghai Li in his PhD dissertation, "Candrakīrti's Agama: A Study of the Concept and Uses of Scripture in Classical Indian Buddhism," University of Wisconsin-Madison, 2012, 242.
26. Candrakīrti makes this argument in MMA 6.9.
27. We may counter this by saying that the time of the seed and the time of the sprout border each other, just like two countries. But in those cases, there is still space between the two because the border occupies space. If there weren't a small space, the seed and the sprout could not be distinguished as two separate things.
28. See chapters 7 and 8 in *Saṃsāra, Nirvāṇa, and Buddha Nature* to learn about the twelve links of dependent origination.
29. Although Svātantrika Mādhyamikas and Prāsaṅgika Mādhyamikas agree that an ultimately existent object cannot be found with ultimate analysis, Svātantrikas accept inherent existence conventionally. Their reason is that there must be something inherent in an object so that it can be correctly posited by the force of appearing to a nondefective awareness. If things lacked inherent existence conventionally, they say, there would be no way to establish conventionalities, and anything could be called anything. For this reason, they apply "ultimately," saying that things do not ultimately arise from another. In fact, they apply "ultimately" to all four subsyllogisms: the sprout is not ultimately self-arisen because its arising has purpose; the sprout does not ultimately arise from another because it is a dependent arising, and so forth.
30. Nāgārjuna used the word *utpanna*, which means arise or born, whereas in this sūtra it is *kṛta* (P. *kata*), create.
31. See chapter 3 of *The Foundation of Buddhist Practice.*
32. An analytical cessation (*pratisaṃkhyānirodha*) is a final cessation of a portion of obscurations or all obscurations based on analyzing the ultimate nature (emptiness), such that those obscurations can never arise again. These are true cessations, the third of the four truths. Nirvāṇa is an analytical cessation that comes into existence when all afflictive obscurations have been eradicated. A nonanalytical cessation (*apratisaṃkhyānirodha*) is the temporary absence of afflictions due to the necessary conditions for their arising being incomplete. A nonanalytical cessation is like throwing a thief out of your house but not locking the door. An analytical cessation comes into being when the door is locked.
33. The Tibetan terms for these are, respectively, *ngo bos grub pa, rang bzhin gyis grub pa, rang dbang gis grub pa.*
34. This way of speaking of the meeting of the two is only possible for the Prāsaṅgikas because they assert that everything exists dependently and lacks true existence.
35. These later scholars include Tsongkhapa and Changkya Rolpai Dorje. This is explained in depth in EMW 266–92 and 298–301.
36. See chapter 4 of *In Praise of Great Compassion* to learn about this meditation.
37. In some scriptures, it is said that emptiness is not dependent. In that context, the

meaning is that emptiness does not depend on any other factors to make it the ultimate nature of phenomena.

38. Thanks to Francis Paone for sharing this anecdote.
39. These reasonings are subdivisions of a type of sign or reason known as "correct non-observation signs," which are explained in the textbook *Signs and Reasons*. For more information see Katherine Rogers, *Tibetan Logic* (Boulder, CO: Snow Lion Publications, 2009).
40. Khedrup Norsang Gyatso (1423–1513) advocated a syncretic approach to the teaching and practices of Mahāmudrā in the Kagyu and Gelug traditions. He is the author of *Ornament of Stainless Light*, a commentary on the *Kālachakra Tantra*.
41. Konchog Jigme Wangpo (1728–91) was the second Jamyang Shepa.
42. The term "Middle Way" may give us the idea that this view is halfway between the two extremes of absolutism and total nonexistence. In fact, the Middle Way view has nothing to do with the two extremes; it is completely outside them and is not the "average" or midpoint between the two.
43. In tantric sādhanas, after dissolving the offering objects or our ordinary body into emptiness, the sādhana says, "Within emptiness, the offerings (or deity) arise. . . ." That is, within the lack of inherent existence, the dependently arising offerings, deity, and mandala appear. A tantric practitioner aims to remain within the awareness of emptiness when meditating on offerings, mandala, deity, and so forth as mere dependently designated appearances.
44. The colophon contains this interesting statement: "This extremely profound way of meditating on the Middle Way view by ordinary individuals who have not developed serenity is the intent of Je Rinpoche [Tsongkhapa] and his disciples as noted by [Khedrup] Gelek Palsang." Tsongkhapa, *Guiding Instructions on the Profound Middle Way View according to Prāsaṅgika Madhyamaka*, in vol. 18 of the Je Yabse Sungbum Project (Mundgod, India: Drepung Loseling Pethub Khangtsen Education Society, 2019), 525. www jeyabsesungbum.org.
45. A type of banana plant, plantains are actually large herbs, not trees. Although they appear to have a trunk, the "trunk" is actually a hollow cylinder formed by leaf sheaths.
46. Gandharvas are born in the demigod realm. They live by eating scents and are known for their skill as musicians.
47. University scholars and professors have made some interesting comments about this. David Kalupahana argued in *Mūlamadhyamakakārikā of Nāgārjuna* that Nāgārjuna was not a Mahāyāna Buddhist because his sources were whatever version of the early sūtras he had access to; A. K. Warder made a similar argument. Joseph Walser in *Nāgārjuna in Context* argued that Nāgārjuna was an early Mahāyāna Buddhist living in a mostly non-Mahāyāna monastery, and he intentionally used the sources that everyone at his monastery would accept—early sūtras that are parallel to those in the Nikāyas of the Pāli canon and the Āgamas of the Chinese canon. By doing so, he improved the chances that the *Treatise on the Middle Way* would be preserved and reproduced by his monastery after he

died. These are interesting ideas, and more research needs to be done regarding this topic. David J. Kalupahana, *Mūlamadhyamakakārikā of Nāgārjuna: The Philosophy of the Middle Way* (Delhi: Motilal Banarsidass, 1991); A. K. Warder, *Indian Buddhism* (Delhi: Motilal Banarsidass, 2008); Joseph Walser, *Nāgārjuna in Context: Mahāyāna, Buddhism, and Early Indian Culture* (New York: Columbia University Press, 2005).

48. See chapter 9 in *Following in the Buddha's Footsteps* for more about kaṣinas, the dhyānas, and how to cultivate serenity and concentration.
49. The six sets of six factors are the six internal sources (sense faculties), six external sources (objects), six classes of consciousness, six types of contact, six classes of feeling, and six kinds of craving.
50. The mental sense faculty includes all six consciousnesses, which can connect a mental phenomenon to the mental consciousness. The mental sense faculty also includes the bhavaṅga, dhyānas, and formless absorptions. The objects of the mental sense faculty are mental phenomena—anything that can be known by the mental consciousness. In addition to the phenomena source, which is a set of objects uniquely cognizable by the mental consciousness (P. *mano-viññāṇa*), objects of the other five senses can also be mental objects. This is true in the case of the super-knowledges such as the divine eye (clairvoyance) that can see physical objects that are far away. Another example is remembering the red color of a pen. Initially the eye consciousness perceives the red. The eye consciousness serves as the mental faculty to convey that data to the mental consciousness, which then identifies the object as a red pen. Later, when we remember the red pen, it becomes a mental object unique to the mental consciousness. Mental factors, subtle forms, concepts, visualizations, and so forth are also considered mental phenomena.
51. In some situations the expression "This I am" is associated with the view of a personal identity, not conceit. But in the series of three, "This I am" represents conceit, and "This is my self" is the view of a personal identity.
52. "Name" refers to the mind and mental factors, and "form" indicates the body of the next life. This is the fourth of the twelve links of dependent origination.
53. Strictly speaking, the standard definition of the aggregate of form speaks of the four elements of earth, water, fire, and air, as well as matter derived from the four elements. The space element is an aspect of derived matter.
54. *Prapañca, papañca*, T. *spros pa*. This term is translated as "elaboration" elsewhere in this book. Pāli translators use "proliferation," which implies thoughts that multiply uncontrollably. Conceiving or conceptualization is also related to the Tibetan word *rnam rtog* (S. *vikalpa*), which sometimes refers to any thoughts, including accurate ones, but most often it refers to distorted conceptions.
55. The Pāli word that is translated as "perceives" is *sañjānāti*, the verbal basis for the noun *saññā*, which in this book has been translated as "discrimination" when it appears as the third of the five aggregates.
56. This verse is quoted in Nāgārjuna's *Commentary on Bodhicitta* (*Bodhicittavivarana* 11–13) and in Tsongkhapa's *Illuminating the Intent*. Some of these similes and others like them are found in the *Diamond Cutter Sūtra*.

57. Bhikkhu Bodhi is an American Theravāda Buddhist monk and scholar.
58. See Daniel Cozort, *Unique Tenets of the Middle Way Consequence School* (Ithaca, NY: Snow Lion Publications, 1998), 256–58.
59. For more on this sūtra, which is found in early Mahāyāna sources and in early Chinese translations, see Shenghai Li, "Candrakīrti's Āgama: A Study of the Concept and Uses of Scripture in Classical Indian Buddhism," PhD dissertation, University of Wisconsin-Madison, 2012, 174–79.
60. Here "emptiness" means what is realized by āryas and refers to nirvāṇa.
61. There are more references to emptiness in the *Path of Discrimination* (*Paṭisambhidāmagga*), a text attributed to Śāriputra, which is the twelfth book of the Khuddaka Nikāya. See *The Path of Discrimination (Paṭisambhidāmagga)*, translated from the Pāli by Bhikkhu Ñāṇamoli (London: Pali Text Society, 1997), 7. However, I haven't had the opportunity to explore them.
62. MN 1238nn451, 458. In other contexts it seems that the liberation of mind by emptiness is supramundane; for example, in the *Godatta Sutta* (SN 41:7).
63. Private correspondence from Bhikkhu Anālayo, Dec. 29, 2011. Supported by private correspondence from Bhikkhu Bodhi, Jan. 15, 2012.

Glossary

absolutism (eternalism, permanence, *śāśvatānta, sassata*). The belief that phenomena inherently exist and have an essence that goes from one moment to the next.

abstract composites (*viprayukta-saṃskāra*). Impermanent phenomena that are neither forms nor consciousnesses.

acquired afflictions (*parikalpita*, T. *kun btags*). Afflictions learned in this life through learning and adopting flawed reasoning of mistaken philosophies and ideologies.

acquisition (*prāpti*, T. *'thob pa*). Asserted by Vaibhāṣikas, it is like a rope that ensures karma will go from one life to the next.

affirming negative (*paryudāsapratiṣedha*, T. *ma yin dgag*). A negative that is realized upon explicitly eliminating an object of negation and that projects another phenomenon in the wake of that negation.

afflictions (*kleśa*). Mental factors that disturb the tranquility of the mind. These include disturbing emotions and attitudes, and wrong views.

afflictive obscurations (*kleśāvaraṇa*, T. *nyon sgrib*). Obscurations that mainly prevent liberation; afflictions and their seeds.

aging (*sthityanyathatva, thitassa annathatta*). Alteration of that which exists.

aggregates (*skandha, khandha*). The four or five components that make up a living being: form (except for beings born in the formless realm), feelings, discriminations, miscellaneous factors, and consciousnesses.

analysis (*vicāra*, T. *dpyod pa*). A mental factor that examines an object in detail.

analytical meditation (*vicārabhāvanā*, T. *dpyad sgom*). Meditation done to understand an object.

appear (T. *snang*). The object merely appears to the mind. It is not necessarily apprehended, ascertained, or realized.

appearing object (*pratibhāsa-viṣaya*, T. *snang yul*). The object that actually appears to a consciousness. The appearing object of a conceptual consciousness is a conceptual appearance of something.

apprehend (T. *'dzin*). The consciousness engages the object. It may apprehend the object correctly or incorrectly.

apprehended object (engaged object, *muṣṭibandhaviṣaya*, T. *'dzin stangs kyi yul*). The main object with which the mind is concerned—that is, the object that the mind is getting at or understands.

arhat (P. *arahant,* T. *dgra bcom pa*). Someone who has eliminated all afflictive obscurations and attained liberation.

arising/production (*utpāda, uppāda*, T. *skye ba*). The coming into being of something that wasn't present before.

ārya (P. *ariya*). Someone who has directly and nonconceptually realized the emptiness of inherent existence.

ascertain (T. *nges*). In general, an ascertaining consciousness is a conceptual consciousness that correctly knows its object. It is able to induce a recollection of the object appearing to it.

attain its identity. Come into existence.

autonomous syllogism (*svatantra-prayoga*, T. *rang rgyud kyi sbyor ba*). A syllogism where the parties involved agree that all parts of the syllogism inherently exist; Svātantrikas' preferred form of reasoning.

base of emptiness. The object whose mode of existence is being analyzed.

base and the based (the support and the supported, T. *rten brten pa*). One thing (the base or support) supports another (the based, the supported), which depends on it.

basis of designation (basis of imputation, T. *btags gzhi*). The collection of parts or factors in dependence on which an object is designated or imputed.

bhavaṅga. A passive stream of subliminal consciousness that exists during all occasions when a clearly cognizing consciousness is not present and from which active consciousnesses arise. It is described in the Pāli commentaries and Abhidharma but not in the sūtras.

bodhicitta. A main mental consciousness induced by an aspiration to bring about the welfare of others and accompanied by an aspiration to attain full awakening oneself.

bodhisattva. Someone who has spontaneous bodhicitta and is training to become a buddha.

characteristics (*svalakṣaṇa*, T. *rang gi mtshan nyid*). Attributes of an object. Things have characteristics, but they do not exist by their own characteristics.

coarse afflictions. Afflictions stemming from grasping a self-sufficient substantially existent person, as contrasted with subtle afflictions.

cognitive obscurations (*jñeyāvaraṇa*, T. *shes sgrib*). Obscurations that mainly prevent full awakening; the latencies of ignorance and the subtle dualistic view that they give rise to.

comprehended object (*prameya*, T. *gzhal bya*). That which is the object known or cognized by a reliable cognizer.

conceived object (*adhyavasāya-viṣaya*, T. *zhen yul*). The object conceived by a conceptual consciousness; it is the apprehended or engaged object of a conceptual consciousness.

concentration (*samādhi*). A mental factor that dwells single-pointedly for a sustained period of time on one object; a state of deep meditative absorption; single-pointed concentration that is free from discursive thought.

conceptual appearance (*artha-sāmānya*, T. *don spyi*). A mental image of an object that appears to a conceptual consciousness.

conceptual consciousness (*kalpanā*, T. *rtog pa'i shes pa*). A consciousness that knows its object by means of a conceptual appearance.

conceptual fabrications. False modes of existence and false ideas imputed by a conceptual consciousness.

conceptuality (*kalpanā*, T. *rtog pa*). Thought; a mind that knows its object via a conceptual appearance.

conceptualizations (*vikalpa viparyāsa*, T. *rnam rtog*). Distorted thoughts that range from exaggerating the desirability or beauty of an object to grasping impermanent things as permanent, and so forth.

concomitant (T. *mtshungs ldan*). Accompanying or occurring together in the same mental state.

conditionality (causal dependence). Dependence on causes and conditions.

confusion (*moha*, T. *gti mug*). Ignorance.

consciousness (*vijñāna, viññāṇa*, T. *rnam shes*). That which is clear and cognizant.

consequence (*prasaṅga*, T. *thal 'gyur*). A form of reasoning that shows the other party the inconsistencies in their assertions; the form of reasoning widely used by the Prāsaṅgikas.

conventional existence (*saṃvṛtisat*). Existence.

conventional truth. *See* veiled truth.

correct assumption. A conceptual consciousness that correctly apprehends its object but does not realize it, so it is not incontrovertible.

counterpart sign (P. *paṭbhāga-nimitta*). The meditation object of a dhyāna consciousness; a conceptual object that arises on the basis of a visible object.

cyclic existence (*saṃsāra*). The cycle of rebirth that occurs under the control of afflictions and karma.

death (*maraṇabhava*). The last moment of a lifetime when the subtlest clear-light mind manifests.

defilement (*mala*, T. *dri ma*). Either an afflictive obscuration or a cognitive obscuration.

definitive (*nītārtha, nitattha*, T. *nges don*). Prāsaṅgikas: a sūtra or statement that mainly and explicitly teaches ultimate truths.

dependent arising (*pratītyasamutpāda*, T. *rten nas 'byung ba, rten 'brel*). This is of three types: (1) causal dependence—things arising due to causes and conditions; (2) mutual dependence—phenomena existing in relation to other phenomena, such as their parts; and (3) dependent designation—phenomena existing by being merely designated by terms and concepts.

dependent existence (*pratītyasamutpāda*, T. *rten grub*). The third level of dependent arising. All phenomena exist as mere imputations designated by conceptuality in dependence on their basis of designation.

designated object (*arthaprajñapti*, *atthapaññatti*, T. *btags don*). The object designated by term and concept in dependence on its basis of designation.

desire realm (*kāmadhātu*). One of the three realms of cyclic existence; the realm where sentient beings are overwhelmed by attraction to and desire for sense objects.

deva. A person born as a heavenly being in the desire realm or in one of the meditative absorptions of the form or formless realms.

dhyāna (P. *jhāna*). A meditative stabilization of the form realm.

different (*nānātva*, T. *tha dad*). Phenomena that are diverse; phenomena that are not identical.

different nature. Two things that exist at different times and/or in different places and can be perceived separately.

direct cause. A cause that immediately precedes its result. Parents are the direct cause of a child.

direct perceiver (*pratyakṣa*, T. *mngon sum*). A nonmistaken awareness that is free from conceptuality. Prāsaṅgikas: an awareness that is free from conceptuality.

direct reliable cognizer (*pratyakṣa-pramāṇa*). A new nondeceptive nonmistaken awareness that is free from conceptuality. According to Prāsaṅgikas, it is a nondeceptive awareness that knows its object without depending on a reason.

distorted conception (inappropriate attention, *ayoniśo-manaskāra*, T. *tshul bzhin ma yin pa'i yid la byed pa*). Distorted thoughts that project exaggerations and erroneous qualities on objects, leading to the arising of afflictions.

dualistic appearance (T. *gnyis snang*). The appearance of subject and object as separate or the appearance of inherent existence.

duḥkha (P. *dukkha*). The unsatisfactory experiences of cyclic existence.

Dzogchen. A tantric practice emphasizing meditation on the nature of mind, practiced primarily in the Nyingma tradition.

eight worldly concerns (*aṣṭalokadharma*). Attachment and aversion regarding material gain and loss, disrepute and fame, blame and praise, pleasure and pain.

eighteen constituents (*dhātu,* T. *khams*). These are the six objects, six sense faculties, and six consciousnesses.

elaborations (proliferations, *prapañca, papañca,* T. *spros pa*). Ignorance and other mental fabrications that obscure the ultimate nature of phenomena, their emptiness.

emptiness (*śūnyatā*, T. *stong pa nyid*). The lack of inherent existence and true existence.

engaged object (apprehended object, *pravṛtti-viṣaya*, T. *'jug yul*). The main object with which the mind is concerned.

enjoyment body (*saṃbhogakāya*). The buddha body that appears in the pure lands to teach ārya bodhisattvas.

erroneous (*viparyāsa*, T. *phyin ci log pa*). Wrong, incorrect, perverted.

erroneous consciousness (T. *log shes*). A consciousness that errs with respect to its apprehended object because what this consciousness apprehends does not exist.

essentialists (proponents of true existence, T. *dngos por smra ba*). Buddhist and non-Buddhist philosophers following a non-Madhyamaka tenet system who assert that the person and aggregates truly exist—that is, Yogācārins and below.

eternalism. See absolutism.

exalted knower (*jñāna*, T. *mkhyen pa*). A realization in the continuum of someone who has entered a path. It exists from the path of accumulation to the buddha ground. Exalted knower, path, ground, pristine wisdom, and clear realization are mutually inclusive.

existence by its own characteristics (*svalakṣaṇa,* T. *rang gi mtshan nyid kyis grub pa*). Existence from its own side.

existent (*sat*). That which is perceivable by mind.

extreme of absolutism (*śāśvatānta*). The extreme of eternalism; believing that phenomena inherently exist.

extreme of nihilism (*ucchedānta*). The extreme of nonexistence; believing that our actions have no ethical dimension or that nothing exists.

fetters (*saṃyojana*). Factors that keep us bound to cyclic existence and impede the attainment of liberation. The five lower fetters—view of a personal identity, deluded doubt, view of rules and practices, sensual desire, and malice—bind us to rebirth in the desire realm. The five higher fetters—desire for existence in the form realm, desire for existence in the formless realm, arrogance, restlessness, and ignorance—prevent a nonreturner from becoming an arhat.

focal object (*viṣaya*, T. *dmigs pa*). The main object the mind refers to or focuses on. Syn. observed object.

form body (*rūpakāya*). The buddha body in which a buddha appears to sentient beings; it includes the emanation and enjoyment bodies.

form realm (*rūpadhātu*). The saṃsāric realm in which beings have bodies made of subtle material; they are born there due to having attained various states of concentration.

formless realm (*ārūpyadhātu*). The saṃsāric realm in which sentient beings do not have a material body; they are born there due to having attained high states of meditative absorption.

foundation consciousness (*ālayavijñāna*, T. *kun gzhi rnam shes*). A storehouse consciousness where all latencies and karmic seeds are placed. It carries these from one life to the next and, according to Yogācāra Scripture Proponents, it is the self.

four distorted conceptions (*viparyāsa*, *vipallāsa*, T. *phyin ci log rtog*). Seeing what is impermanent as permanent, what is unsatisfactory as pleasurable, what is foul as attractive, and what is not a self as self.

four truths of the āryas (four noble truths, *catvāry āryasatyāni*). The truths of duḥkha, its origin, its cessation, and the path to that cessation.

free from conceptuality (*kalpanā-apoḍha*, T. *rtog bral*). Without the appearance of a conceptual appearance.

full awakening (*samyaksaṃbodhi*). Buddhahood; the state in which all obscurations have been abandoned and all good qualities developed limitlessly.

Fundamental Vehicle. The vehicle of śrāvakas and solitary realizers; the path that leads to liberation.

grasping inherent existence (*svabhāvagraha*). Grasping persons and phenomena to exist truly or inherently. Synonymous with grasping true existence (Prāsaṅgika).

grasping true existence (true grasping, *satyagrāha*). Grasping persons and phenomena to exist truly or inherently with an intrinsic essence.

highest yoga tantra (*anuttarayogatantra*). The most advanced of the four classes of tantra.

ignorance (*avidyā*). A mental factor that is obscured and grasps the opposite of what exists. There are two types: ignorance regarding ultimate truth and ignorance regarding karma and its effects.

illusion-like emptiness (T. *sgyu ma lta bu'i stong nyid*). In times subsequent to meditative equipoise on emptiness, things once again appear truly existent, although one knows they aren't.

impermanence (*anitya, anicca*). Momentariness; not remaining in the next moment. Coarse impermanence is the ending of a continuum; subtle impermanence is something not remaining the same in the very next moment.

imputedly existent (*prajñaptisat*, T. *btags yod*). (1) Vaibhāṣikas: Something that when it is broken into smaller pieces or moments of time can no longer be ascertained. (2) Sautrāntikas up to Svatantrikas: Something that can be identified only by identifying something else. (3) Prāsaṅgikas: Something that exists by being merely designated by term and concept.

indirect cause. A cause that does not immediately precede its result. Grandparents are the indirect cause of a child.

inference (*anumāna*, T. *rjes su dpag pa*). (1) A cognizer that knows its object through reasoning, (2) a conclusion reached through a syllogism on the basis of evidence and reasoning.

inferential reliable cognizer (*anumāna-pramāṇa*). An awareness that knows its object—a slightly obscure phenomenon—nondeceptively, purely in dependence on a reason.

inherent existence (*svabhāvasiddhi*, *sabhāvasiddha*, T. *rang bzhin gyis grub pa*). Existence without depending on any other factors; independent existence. Prāsaṅgikas negate it both ultimately and conventionally. This term does not have the same meaning in Pāli texts as in Madhyamaka.

innate (*sahaja*, T. *lhan skyes*). Existing with the mind from beginningless time; something not acquired anew in this life.

insight (*vipaśyanā*, *vipassanā*, T. *lhag mthong*). A wisdom of thorough discrimination of phenomena conjoined with special pliancy induced by the power of analysis.

insight knowledge (P. *vipassanā-ñāṇa*). Mundane (*lokiya*) knowledge of the three characteristics gained through insight. It leads to supramundane (*lokuttara*) path knowledge that realizes the four truths and nirvāṇa.

insight wisdom (P. *vipassanā-paññā*). A mundane wisdom that sees the three characteristics of impermanence, duḥkha, and selflessness. It is gained through insight and leads to stream-entry.

interpretable (provisional, *neyārtha*, *neyyattha*, T. *drang don*). A scripture or statement that speaks about the variety of phenomena and/or cannot be taken literally.

investigation (*vitarka*, *vitakka*, T. *rtog pa*). A mental factor that seeks a rough idea about an object.

karma. Intentional actions of body, speech, or mind.

karmic seeds. The potencies from previously created actions that will bring their results.

kasiṇa (S. *kṛtsna*). Colored disks or elements used as meditation objects to cultivate serenity.

knowable object (*jñeya*, T. *shes bya*). That which is suitable to serve as an object of an awareness; an existent.

latencies (*vāsanā*). Predispositions, imprints, or tendencies.

liberation (*mokṣa*, T. *thar pa*). A true cessation that is the abandonment of afflictive obscurations; nirvāṇa, the state of freedom from cyclic existence.

liberation (*vimukti, vimutti*, T. *rnam grol*). Sanskrit tradition: Complete freedom from saṃsāra; Pāli tradition: a conditioned event that brings nirvāṇa.

Madhyamaka. A Mahāyāna tenet system that refutes true existence.

Mahāmudrā. A type of meditation that focuses on the conventional and ultimate natures of the mind.

manifest afflictions. Afflictions active in the mind at the present moment (contrasted with seeds of afflictions).

meditative equipoise on emptiness. An ārya's mind focused single-pointedly on the emptiness of inherent existence.

mental consciousness (*mano-vijñāna*). A primary consciousness that knows mental phenomena in contradistinction to sense primary consciousnesses that know physical objects.

mental direct reliable cognizers. Nondeceptive mental awarenesses that know their objects by depending on another consciousness that induces them.

mental factor (*caitta*). An aspect of mind that accompanies a primary consciousness and fills out the cognition, apprehending particular attributes of the object or performing a specific function.

mere conditionality (*idaṃ pratyayatā*, T. *rkyen 'di pa tsam nyid*). Arising by causes and conditions, mutual dependence, and dependent designation.

Things exist through mere conditionality without ultimate analysis or investigation.

mind (*citta*). The part of living beings that cognizes, experiences, thinks, feels, and so on. In some contexts it is equivalent to primary consciousness.

mindfulness (*smṛti*, *sati*). A mental factor that brings to mind a phenomenon of previous acquaintance without forgetting it and prevents distraction to other objects.

mindstream (*cittasaṃtāna*). The continuity of mind.

mistaken awareness. An awareness that is mistaken in terms of its appearing object.

momentary (*kṣaṇika*). Not enduring in the next moment without changing.

monastic. Someone who has received monastic ordination; a monk or nun.

mutually exclusive contradictory (T. *dngos 'gal*). The situation of one item contradicting the other when all phenomena are included or exhausted in the two.

nature truth body (*svabhāvika dharmakāya*). The buddha body that is either the emptiness of a buddha's mind or the true cessations in that buddha's continuum.

negative (*pratiṣedha*, T. *dgag pa*). An object (1) whose name eliminates an object of negation, or (2) that explicitly appears in a way that an object of negation has been negated. Equivalent with exclusion (*apoha*, T. *sel ba*), other exclusion (*anyāpoha*, T. *gzhan* sel), and isolate (*vyatireka*, *ldog pa*).

nihilism (*ucchedānta*, *vibhavadiṭṭhi*). The belief that our actions have no ethical dimension; the belief that nothing exists.

Nirgranthas. Jains; followers of Mahāvira, a contemporary of the Buddha.

nirvāṇa. The state of liberation of an arhat; the emptiness of a mind that has been totally cleansed of afflictive obscurations.

nominalities (*vyavahāra*, T. *tha snyad*). Things that exist by being merely designated in dependence on a basis of designation.

nominally different. Two phenomena are nominally different when they are not the same thing and can be distinguished by conception.

nonabiding nirvāṇa (*apratiṣṭha-nirvāṇa*). A buddha's nirvāṇa that does not abide in either the extreme of cyclic existence or in the extreme of personal liberation.

nonaffirming negative (*prasajyapratiṣedha*, T. *med dgag*). A negative phenomenon in which, upon the explicit elimination of the object of negation by an awareness, another phenomenon is not suggested or established. A phenomenon that is the mere absence of an object of negation.

nonconceptual consciousness (*nirvikalpaka*, T. *rtog med shes pa*). A consciousness that knows its object directly, not by means of a conceptual appearance.

nondeceptive (*avisaṃvādi*, T. *mi slu ba*). Incontrovertible, correct; the way it appears to a reliable cognizer directly realizing it is in accord with the way it exists.

nonduality. The nonappearance of subject and object, of inherent existence, of veiled truths, and/or of conceptual appearances in an ārya's meditative equipoise on emptiness.

nonerroneous (*aviparīta*, T. *phyin ci ma log pa*). Correct, right.

nonexistent (*asat*). That which is not perceivable by mind.

non-mentation (T. *sems med pa*). A state in which to a third party, a person appears to be without the normal mental functions of the waking state.

nonmistaken (*abhrānta*, T. *ma 'khrul ba*). (1) Sautrāntikas: not mistaken with respect to a consciousness's appearing object. (2) Prāsaṅgikas: a consciousness without the appearance of inherent existence.

non-wastage (*avipraṇāśa*, T. *chud mi za ba*). Asserted by Vaibhāṣikas, it is likened to an IOU, voucher, or seal that ensures karma will go from one life to the next.

object (*viṣaya*, T. *yul*). That which is known by an awareness.

object of negation (*pratiṣedhya* or *niṣedhya*, T. *dgag bya*). What is negated or refuted.

objective existence (*viṣaya siddhi*, T. *yul steng nas grub pa*). Existence unrelated to other factors. Syn. inherent existence.

observed object (*ālambana*, *ārammaṇa*, T. *dmigs yul*). The basic object that the mind refers to or focuses on while apprehending certain aspects of that object.

one (*ekatva*, T. *gcig*). A singular phenomenon; a phenomenon that is not diverse; identical.

one nature. Two phenomena are one nature when they arise, abide, and cease simultaneously and do not appear separate to direct perception.

ordinary being (*pṛthagjana*, *puthujjana*, T. *so so skye bo*). Someone who is not an ārya.

passing away (*vyaya*, *vaya*, T. *'jig pa*). Ceasing, disintegrating.

path (*mārga*, *magga*, T. *lam*). An exalted knower that is conjoined with uncontrived renunciation.

path knowledge (P. *magga-ñāṇa*). A supramundane path that knows the four truths and nirvāṇa.

path of meditation (*bhāvanāmārga*, T. *sgom lam*). The fourth of the five paths. This begins when a meditator begins to eradicate innate afflictions from the root.

path of preparation (*prayogamārga*, T. *sbyor lam*). The second of the five paths. It begins when a meditator attains the union of serenity and insight on emptiness.

path of seeing (*darśanamārga*, T. *mthong lam*). Third of the five paths. It begins when a meditator first has direct, nonconceptual realization of the emptiness of inherent existence.

path wisdom (P. *magga ñāna*). Supramundane wisdom that is strong enough to pierce through the obscurations of the fetters.

permanent (*nitya*, *nicca*, T. *rtag pa*). Unchanging, static. It does not mean eternal.

permanent, unitary, independent self. A soul or self (ātman) asserted by non-Buddhists.

person (*pudgala*). A living being designated in dependence on the four or five aggregates.

pollutant (*āsrava, āsava*). A set of three or four deeply rooted defilements: sensual desire, existence (craving to exist in a saṃsāric form), and ignorance. Some lists add view.

polluted (*āsrava, āsava*). Under the influence of ignorance or its latencies.

posit (*vyavasthāna*, T. *bzhag pa*). To establish, determine, or postulate an object; to designate an object through its appearing to a consciousness.

positive (affirmative, *vidhi*, T. *sgrub pa*). A phenomenon that is not realized by the conceptual consciousness apprehending it by explicitly eliminating an object of negation.

Prāsaṅgika Madhyamaka. A Mahāyāna tenet system that asserts that all phenomena lack inherent existence both conventionally and ultimately.

primal substance (fundamental nature, *prakṛti, pakati*, T. *rang bzhin*). A truly existent substance out of which everything is created, as asserted by the non-Buddhist Sāṃkhya school.

primary consciousness (*vijñāna*). A consciousness that apprehends the presence or basic entity of an object. They are of six types: visual, auditory, olfactory, gustatory, tactile, and mental.

pristine wisdom (*jñāna*, T. *ye shes*). A realization in the continuum of someone who has entered a path.

probing awareness (reasoning consciousness, *yuktijñāna*, T. *rigs shes*). A consciousness using or having used reasoning to analyze the ultimate or conventional nature of an object. It can be either conceptual or nonconceptual.

pure-ground bodhisattvas. Bodhisattvas of the eighth, ninth, and tenth grounds who have eliminated afflictive obscurations. When they eradicate cognitive obscurations, they will become buddhas.

realization (*adhigama*, T. *rtogs pa*). An awareness that eliminates superimpositions on an object and is able to induce ascertainment of a phenomenon. It may be either inferential or direct.

realize (*adhigam*, T. *rtogs*). To cognize an object correctly such that the mind is able to induce a correct ascertainment of the object and eliminate misconceptions about it.

reliable cognizer (*pramāṇa*). A nondeceptive awareness that is incontrovertible with respect to its apprehended object and enables us to accomplish our purpose.

reviewing knowledge (*paccavekkhaṇañāṇa*). In stream-enterers, once-returners, and nonreturners it is a knowledge in post-meditation time that reviews the path, its fruition, the defilements abandoned, the defilements that remain, and nirvāṇa. Arhats have no reviewing knowledge of defilements remaining.

samādhi. *See* concentration.

Sāṃkhya. A school of Hindu philosophy that asserts a primal substance and that effects exist in a nonmanifest state in their causes.

saṃsāra. The cycle of rebirth that occurs under the control of afflictions and karma.

Sautrāntika. A Fundamental Vehicle tenet system that asserts that functional things are ultimate truths and phenomena that exist by being imputed by thought are veiled truths.

Sautrāntika-Svātantrika Madhyamaka. A Mahāyāna tenet system that accepts external objects and refutes inherent existence ultimately but not conventionally.

self (*ātman*, *attan*, T. *bdag*). (1) a person, (2) inherent existence, (3) a permanent, unitary, independent soul or self.

self-empty (T. *rang stong*). An object's being empty of its own inherent nature.

self-grasping (*ātmagrāha*). Grasping inherent existence.

selflessness of persons (*pudgalanairātmya*, T. *gang zag gi bdag med*). The nonexistence of a self-sufficient substantially existent person or an inherently existent person.

selflessness of phenomena (*dharmanairātmya*, T. *chos kyi bdag med pa*). The emptiness of all phenomena other than persons.

self-sufficient (T. *rang rkya ba*). Being a different nature from its parts.

self-sufficient substantially existent person (T. *gang zag rang rkya thub pa'i rdzas yod*). A person that can be identified without identifying its aggregates; a self that is the controller of the body and mind. Such a self does not exist.

sense direct reliable cognizers. Incontrovertible awarenesses that know their objects—sights, sounds, smells, tastes, and tangible objects—directly by depending on a physical cognitive faculty.

sense faculty / cognitive faculty (*indriya*). The subtle material in the gross sense organ that enables perception of sense objects. For the mental consciousness, it is previous moments of any of the six consciousnesses.

sentient being (*sattva*). Any being with a mind, except for a buddha.

serenity (*śamatha, samatha*). Sanskrit tradition: concentration arisen from meditation that is accompanied by the bliss of mental and physical pliancy, and in which the mind abides effortlessly without fluctuation for as long as we wish on whatever virtuous object it has been placed. Pāli tradition: one-pointedness of mind; the eight attainments (meditative absorptions) that are the basis for insight.

sign (*nimitta*). A mental image that arises in stabilizing meditation and is used to attain single-pointed concentration.

signlessness (*ānimitta*, T. *mtshan ma med pa*). The emptiness that is the absence of inherent existence of the cause of any phenomenon.

solitary realizer (*pratyekabuddha*). A person following the Fundamental Vehicle who seeks liberation and emphasizes understanding the twelve links of dependent arising.

śrāvaka (hearer, P. *sāvaka*). A Fundamental Vehicle practitioner who follows the path leading to arhatship and who emphasizes meditation on the four truths.

substantial cause (*upādāna-kāraṇa*). The cause that becomes the result, as opposed to cooperative causes that aid the substantial cause in becoming the result.

substantially existent (*dravyasat*, T. *rdzas yod*). (1) Vaibhāṣikas: an object that can be identified even when broken into smaller pieces or moments of time. (2) Sautrāntikas up to Svātantrikas: an object that can be known directly without another object being identified. (3) Prāsaṅgikas: inherently existent.

suchness (*tattva*, T. *de kho na nyid*). Emptiness, the ultimate mode of existence.

superimposition (*samāropa*, T. *sgro btags*, *sgro 'dogs*). A quality or mode of existence that does not exist and is imputed or projected onto an object or person; for example, a self of persons.

supramundane (transcendental, *lokottara*, *lokuttara*). Pertaining to the elimination of fetters and afflictions; pertaining to āryas.

Svātantrika Madhyamaka. A Mahāyāna tenet system that asserts that phenomena do not exist inherently on the ultimate level, but do exist inherently on the conventional level.

syllogism (*prayoga*). A proof statement consisting of a subject, predicate, and reason, and in many cases, an example.

tathāgata. A buddha.

tenet (*siddhānta, T. grub mtha'*). A philosophical assertion or belief.

tenet system/school. A set of philosophical assertions regarding the basis, path, and result that is shared by a group of people.

thesis (*pratijñā*). What is to be proven—the combination of the subject and the predicate—in a syllogism.

thing (*bhāva*, T. *dngos po*). (1) Something that can perform a function; syn. product; (2) inherent existence.

thought (*kalpanā*). Conceptual consciousness.

three characteristics. Three qualities of conditioned phenomena: impermanence, duḥkha, and not-self (selfless).

three criteria to establish existent phenomena. It is known to a conventional consciousness; its existence is not invalidated by another conventional reliable cognizer; it is not invalidated by a mind analyzing emptiness.

three criteria of a correct syllogism. Presence of the reason in the subject, pervasion or entailment, and counterpervasion.

three realms (*tridhātuka, tedhātuka*). Desire, form, and formless realms.

true cessation (*nirodhasatya*). (1) A freedom induced by an uninterrupted path in which a corresponding portion of obscurations has been abandoned; (2) an emptiness of the mind induced by an uninterrupted path in which a corresponding portion of obscurations has been abandoned.

true existence (*satyasat*). Existence having its own mode of being; existence having its own reality.

true-grasping. See grasping true existence.

truth body (*dharmakāya*). The buddha body that includes the nature truth body and the wisdom truth body.

twelve links of dependent origination (*dvādaśāṅga-pratītyasamutpāda*). A system of twelve factors that explains how we take rebirth in saṃsāra and how we can be liberated from it.

twelve sources (*āyatana*, T. *skye mched*). That which opens or increases the arising of consciousness. They consist of six external sense sources (forms, sounds, odors, tastes, tangible objects, and other phenomena) and six internal sense sources (eye, ear, nose, tongue, body, and mental sense faculties).

two truths (*satyadvaya*). Ultimate truths and veiled (conventional) truths.

ultimate analysis (T. *don dam pa'i dpyod pa*). Analysis that examines what an object really is and its deeper mode of existence.

ultimate truth (*paramārthasatya*, *paramattha-sacca*, T. *don dam bden pa*). The ultimate mode of existence of all persons and phenomena; emptiness; objects that are true and appear true to their main cognizer, a wisdom nonconceptually and directly realizing emptiness.

underlying tendencies (*anuśaya*, *anusaya*). Latent dispositions on the mind that enable manifest afflictions to arise when the appropriate causes and conditions are present. These are attachment to sensuality, anger, views, deluded doubt, arrogance, existence (in the three realms), and ignorance.

uninterrupted path (*ānantāryamārga*, T. *bar ched med lam*). In the context of the supramundane path, a wisdom directly realizing emptiness that is in the process of eliminating its corresponding portion of defilements. In the context of cultivating dhyāna, a path that is in the process of temporarily suppressing some portion of manifest afflictions.

union of serenity and insight. A path that consists of both serenity and insight and in which the bliss of mental and physical pliancy has been induced by analysis.

unmistaken (*abhrānta*, T. *'khrul pa med pa*). Not mistaken with respect to its appearing object.

unpolluted (*anāsrava*). Not under the influence of ignorance.

unreliable awareness. An awareness that is not incontrovertible because it does not realize its object and cannot help us accomplish our purpose. These include correct assumers, inattentive perceivers, doubt, and wrong awarenesses.

Vaibhāṣika. A Fundamental Vehicle tenet system that accepts directionally partless particles and temporally partless moments of consciousness as ultimate truths and asserts truly established external objects.

veiled truth (*saṃvṛtisatya*, *sammuti-sacca*, T. *kun rdzob bden pa*). That which is true only from the perspective of ignorance. This includes all phenomena except ultimate truths. Syn. conventional truth.

veilings (*saṃvṛti*, T. *kun rdzob*). Objects of perceivers of falsities. All phenomena that are not ultimate truths are veilings. Syn. conventionalities.

view of a personal identity (view of the transitory collection, *satkāyadṛṣṭi*, *sakkāyadiṭṭhi*). An afflictive view grasping the I or mine as inherently existent (according to the Prāsaṅgika system).

view of a personal identity grasping I (*ahaṃkāra*, T. *ngar 'dzin gyi 'jig lta*). According to the Prāsaṅgikas: an afflictive view that holds the I to be inherently existent.

view of a personal identity grasping mine (*mamakāra*, T. *nga yi bar 'dzin pa'i 'jig lta*). An afflictive view holding what makes things mine as inherently existent (according to the Prāsaṅgika system).

Vinaya. Monastic discipline.

wind (*prāṇa*, T. *rlung*). One of the four elements; energy in the body that influences bodily functions; subtle energy on which levels of consciousness ride.

wisdom truth body (*jñāna dharmakāya*). The buddha body that is a buddha's omniscient mind.

worldly convention (*lokavyavahāra*, T. *'jig rten gyi tha snyad*). The common perspective and norms through which people can communicate and work together. It is the standpoint from which veiled truths are known, in contrast to the perspective of āryas, which knows ultimate truths.

wrong or erroneous awareness (*viparyāsa jñāna*). A mind that is erroneous with respect to its apprehended object, and in the case of conceptual cognizers with respect to its conceived object.

Yogācāra (*Cittamātra*). A Mahāyāna tenet system that accepts eight consciousnesses, including a foundation consciousness and an afflictive consciousness, and asserts the true existence of other-powered (dependent) phenomena but does not assert external objects.

Yogācāra-Svātantrika Madhyamaka. A Mahāyāna tenet system that does not assert external objects, asserts six consciousnesses, and refutes inherent existence ultimately but not conventionally.

yogi/yoginī. A meditator on suchness.

yogic direct perceiver. Nondeceptive and nonconceptual mental consciousness that knows its object by depending on a union of serenity and insight.

Recommended Reading

Anālayo, Bhikkhu. *Compassion and Emptiness in Early Buddhist Meditation*. Cambridge, UK: Windhorse Publications, 2015.

Blumenthal, James. *The Ornament of the Middle Way: A Study of the Madhyamaka Thought of Śāntarakṣita*. Ithaca, NY: Snow Lion Publications, 2004.

Cabezón, José Ignacio. *A Dose of Emptiness*. Delhi: Indian Book Centre, 1993.

———. "Buddhist Narratives of the Great Debates." In *Argumentation* 22 (March 2008): 71–92. https://doi.org/10.1007/s10503-007-9077-4.

Diamond Cutter Sūtra. http://emahofoundation.org/images/documents/DiamondSūtraText.pdf.

Hopkins, Jeffrey. *Kön-chog-jig-me-wang-po's Commentary on (Jang-kya Röl-pay-dor-je's) "Song of the View, Identifying Mama": Lamp for the Words*. UMA Institute for Tibetan Studies, 2021 (www.uma-tibet.org).

———. *Meditation on Emptiness*. Boston: Wisdom Publications, 1996.

———. *Tsong-kha-pa's Final Exposition of Wisdom*. Ithaca, NY: Snow Lion Publications, 2008.

H. H. the Dalai Lama. *Indian Buddhist Classics, Volume 2: The Mind*. Boston: Wisdom Publications, 2020.

Jinpa, Thupten. *Self, Reality, and Reason in Tibetan Philosophy*. New York: RoutledgeCurzon, 2002.

Karunadasa, Yakupitiyage. *The Buddhist Analysis of Matter*. Somerville, MA: Wisdom Publications, 2020.

———. *Early Buddhist Teachings*. Somerville, MA: Wisdom Publications, 2018.

———. *The Theravāda Abhidhamma: Inquiry into the Nature of Conditioned Existence*. Boston: Wisdom Publications, 2019.

Klein, Anne Caroline. *Path to the Middle: Oral Mādhyamika Philosophy in Tibet*. Albany: State University of New York Press, 1994.

La Vallée Poussin, Louis de (French trans.), and Leo M. Pruden (English trans). *Abhidharmakośabhāṣyam of Vasubandhu*. 4 vols. Fremont, CA: Asian Humanities Press, 1991.

Lindtner, Christian. *Master of Wisdom: Writings of the Buddhist Master Nāgārjuna*. Berkeley, CA: Dharma Publishing, 1997.

Ñāṇamoli, Bhikkhu, trans. *The Path of Discrimination*. Onalaska, WA: Pariyatti, 1997.

Newland, Guy. *Appearance and Reality: The Two Truths in the Four Buddhist Tenet Systems*. Ithaca, NY: Snow Lion Publications, 1999.

Ngawang Samten, Geshe, and Jay L. Garfield, trans. *Ocean of Reasoning: A Great Commentary on Nāgārjuna's "Mūlamadhyamakakārikā," by rJe Tsong Khapa*. New York: Oxford University Press, 2006.

Perdue, Daniel. *Debate in Tibetan Buddhism*. Ithaca, NY: Snow Lion Publications, 1992.

Rhys Davids, T. W., trans. *The Questions of King Milinda*. Delhi: Motilal Banarsidass, 1992.

Sopa, Geshe Lhundup, and Jeffrey Hopkins. *Cutting through Appearances: Practice and Theory of Tibetan Buddhism*. Ithaca, NY: Snow Lion Publications, 1989.

Tegchok, Khensur Jampa. *Insight into Emptiness*. Edited by Thubten Chodron. Boston: Wisdom Publications, 2012.

———. *Practical Ethics and Profound Emptiness: A Commentary on Nagarjuna's Precious Garland*. Translated by Bhikshu Steve Carlier. Edited by Thubten Chodron. Somerville, MA: Wisdom Publications, 2017.

Thabkhe, Geshe Yeshe. *The Rice Seedling Sūtra*. Somerville, MA: Wisdom Publications, 2020.

Yi, Jongbok. "The Meaning of *rigs shes* in the Geluk Tradition." *Critical Review for Buddhist Studies* 20 (2016): 95–136. https://www.academia.edu/31227337/The_meaning_of_rigs_shes_in_the_Geluk_tradition.

Index

O

P

T

About the Authors

The Dalai Lama is the spiritual leader of the Tibetan people, a Nobel Peace Prize recipient, and an advocate for compassion and peace throughout the world. He promotes harmony among the world's religions and engages in dialogue with leading scientists. Ordained as a Buddhist monk when he was a child, he completed the traditional monastic studies and earned his geshe degree (equivalent to a PhD). Renowned for his erudite and open-minded scholarship, his meditative attainments, and his humility, Bhikṣu Tenzin Gyatso says, "I am a simple Buddhist monk."

Peter Aronson

Bhikṣuṇī Thubten Chodron has been a Buddhist nun since 1977. Growing up in Los Angeles, she graduated with honors in history from the University of California at Los Angeles and did graduate work in education at the University of Southern California. After years studying and teaching Buddhism in Asia, Europe, and the United States, she became the founder and abbess of Sravasti Abbey in Washington State. A popular speaker for her practical explanations of how to apply Buddhist teachings in daily life, she is the author of several books on Buddhism, including *Buddhism for Beginners*. She is the editor of Khensur Jampa Tegchok's *Insight into Emptiness*. For more information, visit sravastiabbey.org and thubtenchodron.org.

Also Available from the Dalai Lama and Wisdom Publications

Buddhism
One Teacher, Many Traditions

The Compassionate Life

Ecology, Ethics, and Interdependence
The Dalai Lama in Conversation with Leading Thinkers on Climate Change

Essence of the Heart Sūtra
The Dalai Lama's Heart of Wisdom Teachings

The Essence of Tsongkhapa's Teachings
The Dalai Lama on the Three Principal Aspects of the Path

The Fourteenth Dalai Lama's Stages of the Path, vol. 1
Guidance for the Modern Practitioner

The Good Heart
A Buddhist Perspective on the Teachings of Jesus

Imagine All the People
A Conversation with the Dalai Lama on Money, Politics, and Life as It Could Be

Kalachakra Tantra
Rite of Initiation

The Life of My Teacher
A Biography of Kyabjé Ling Rinpoché

Meditation on the Nature of Mind

The Middle Way
Faith Grounded in Reason

Mind in Comfort and Ease
The Vision of Enlightenment in the Great Perfection

MindScience
An East-West Dialogue

Opening the Eye of New Awareness

Practicing Wisdom
The Perfection of Shantideva's Bodhisattva Way

Science and Philosophy in the Indian Buddhist Classics, vol. 1
The Physical World

Science and Philosophy in the Indian Buddhist Classics, vol. 2
The Mind

Science and Philosophy in the Indian Buddhist Classics, vol. 3
Philosophical Schools

Sleeping, Dreaming, and Dying
An Exploration of Consciousness

The Wheel of Life
Buddhist Perspectives on Cause and Effect

The World of Tibetan Buddhism
An Overview of Its Philosophy and Practice

Also Available from Thubten Chodron

Insight into Emptiness
Khensur Jampa Tegchok
Edited and introduced by Thubten Chodron

"One of the best introductions to the philosophy of emptiness I have ever read."—José Ignacio Cabezón

Practical Ethics and Profound Emptiness

A Commentary on Nagarjuna's Precious Garland
Khensur Jampa Tegchok
Edited by Thubten Chodron

"A beautifully clear translation and systematic explanation of Nagarjuna's most accessible and wide-ranging work. Dharma students everywhere will benefit from careful attention to its pages."—Guy Newland, author of *Introduction to Emptiness*

Awakening Every Day

365 Buddhist Reflections to Invite Mindfulness and Joy

Buddhism for Beginners

The Compassionate Kitchen

Cultivating a Compassionate Heart
The Yoga Method of Chenrezig

Don't Believe Everything You Think
Living with Wisdom and Compassion

Guided Meditations on the Stages of the Path

How to Free Your Mind
Tara the Liberator

Living with an Open Heart
How to Cultivate Compassion in Daily Life

Open Heart, Clear Mind

Taming the Mind

Working with Anger

About Wisdom Publications

Wisdom Publications is the leading publisher of classic and contemporary Buddhist books and practical works on mindfulness. To learn more about us or to explore our other books, please visit our website at wisdomexperience.org or contact us at the address below.

Wisdom Publications
199 Elm Street
Somerville, MA 02144 USA

We are a 501(c)(3) organization, and donations in support of our mission are tax deductible.

Wisdom Publications is affiliated with the Foundation for the Preservation of the Mahayana Tradition (FPMT).